P9-DMC-312

THE NON-ALIGNED THE UN AND THE SUPERPOWERS

Council on Foreign Relations Books

The Council on Foreign Relations, Inc., is a non-profit and nonpartisan organization devoted to promoting improved understanding of international affairs through the free exchange of ideas. The Council does not take any position on questions of foreign policy and has no affiliation with, and receives no funding from, the United States government.

From time to time, books and monographs written by members of the Council's research staff or visiting fellows, or commissioned by the Council, or (like this book) written by an independent author with critical review contributed by a Council study or working group are published with the designation "Council on Foreign Relations Book." Any book or monograph bearing that designation is, in the judgment of the Committee on Studies of the Council's board of directors, a responsible treatment of a significant international topic worthy of presentation to the public. All statements of fact and expressions of opinion contained in Council books are, however, the sole responsibility of the author.

THE NON-ALIGNED THE UN AND THE SUPERPOWERS

Richard L. Jackson

Foreword by
Ambassador David D. Newsom

PRAEGER

PRAEGER SPECIAL STUDIES • PRAEGER SCIENTIFIC

New York • Philadelphia • Eastbourne, UK
Toronto • Hong Kong • Tokyo • Sydney

Library of Congress Cataloging in Publication Data

Jackson, Richard L., 1939–
The Non-aligned, the UN, and the Superpowers.

Bibliography: p. 267–274
Includes index.
1. Developing countries—Foreign relations.
2. United Nations. 3. United States—Foreign relations—Developing countries. 4. Developing countries—Foreign relations—United States.
5. Soviet Union—Foreign relations—Developing countries. 6. Developing countries—Foreign relations—Soviet Union. I. Title. II. Title:
The Non-aligned, the U.N., and the Superpowers.
JX1395.J314 1983 327'.091716 83-13836
ISBN 0-03-062561-0 (alk. paper)

Published in 1983 by Praeger Publishers
CBS Educational and Professional Publishing
a division of CBS Inc.
521 Fifth Avenue, New York, NY 10175 USA

56789 052 9876543

Printed in the United States of America
on acid-free paper

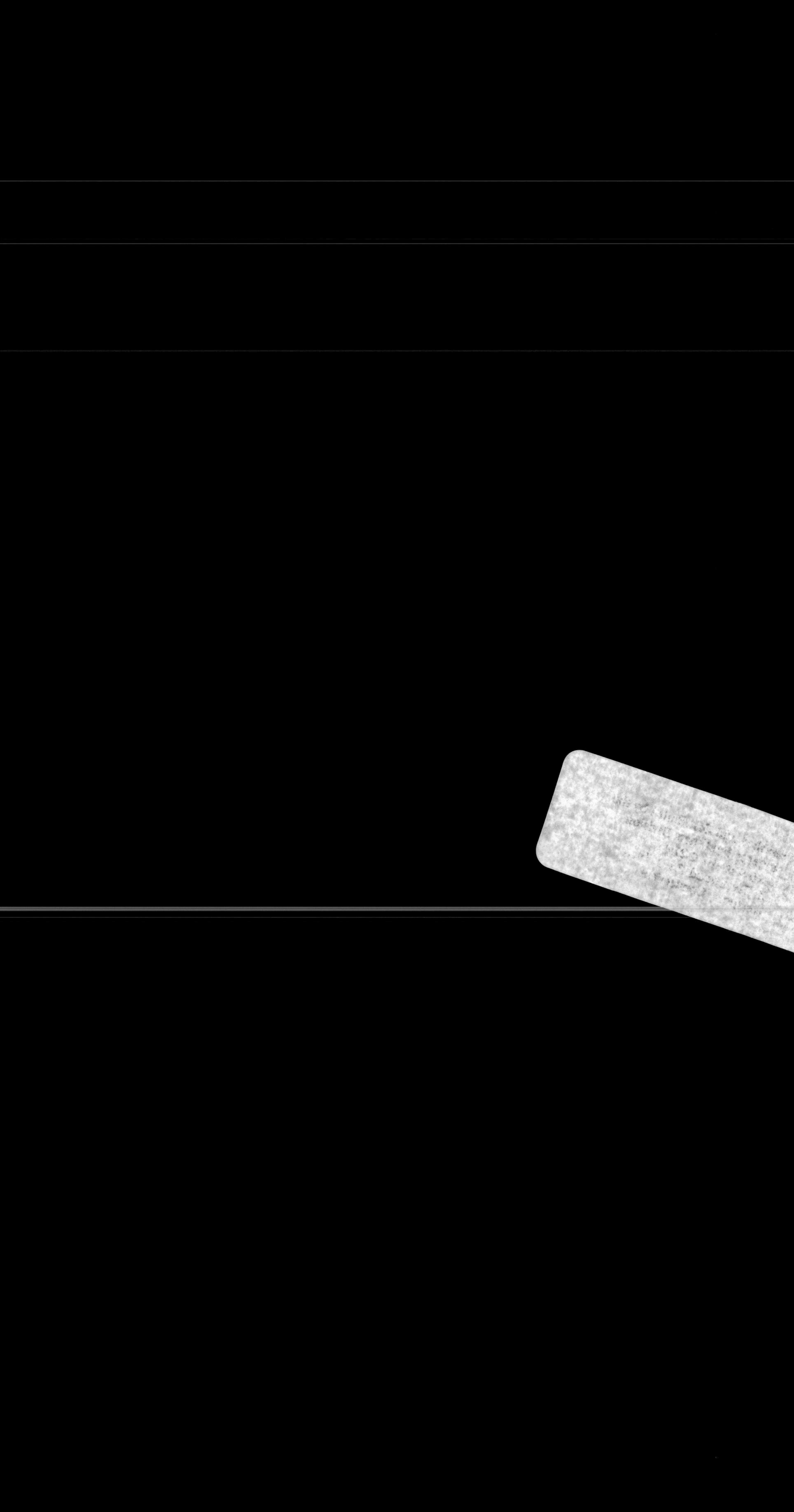

Published and Distributed by the
Praeger Publishers Division
(ISBN Prefix 0-275)
of Greenwood Press, Inc.,
Westport, Connecticut

To
Una Chapman Cox

Whose imagination, vision, and generosity
made this book possible

Foreword

by Ambassador David D. Newson

Richard Jackson has, in this book, documented from his own unique experience the story of the Non-Aligned Movement and the United Nations.

Basic to a comprehension of this study, particularly for Americans, is an understanding of the special difficulties the United States has faced in responding to attitudes of the newly independent nations. It is one of the ironies of the post-World War II period that the United States, believed by so many to have inspired the colonial world to seek independence, should, of all nations, have the greatest problem in relating effectively to the collective movement created by these new nations.

The problem has been one of perception. The new nations were born in environments of real or perceived struggle. There were often severe contests for power within independence movements. In some cases, such as Algeria, independence came only after a bitter war. In other cases, independence came more easily but was still marked by the rhetoric of struggle.

The leaders of the new nations were frequently charismatic personalities and spellbinding orators who helped create an environment of confrontation. They pictured their problems as lying in the previous policies of colonialism and their salvation as coming through revolution. The only allies of interest were those who would pledge unequivocal allegiance to this anti-colonial struggle. Communist parties with their supportive rhetoric and organizational capacity were frequently among such allies; in the early days of independence, new country leaders did not want to look too closely at long-range objectives. Zhou Enlai was seen as a special hero at the initial gathering of the "non-aligned" at Bandung in 1955.

The meeting at Bandung symbolized still another aspect of the community of new nations: solidarity. Leaders of independence movements had known each other in world capitals, sometimes in exile. Together they had built visions of their own independence and of their common goals in a world of new nations. Even in the earliest days of these movements, they resented efforts by outsiders to divide them or to differentiate among them.

The new nations, often weak and insecure in their untried sovereignty, did not want the complications of involvement in the struggle between the superpowers. The concept of non-alignment had a strong appeal; after the break between Yugoslavia and the Soviet Union, the concept found a powerful champion in Marshal Tito.

The U.S. expectation of the orientation of the new nations was quite different. These were nations that were born out of the tutelage, in large measure, of democratic nations in Europe. Many, at the time of independence, had parliaments, elections, courts, the apparent institutions of a democratic society. Most Americans expected that these nations would be natural allies in any choosing of sides in the global East–West struggle.

The impression gained even greater momentum because many of the new leaders quoted the founding fathers of the United States: Washington, Jefferson, and Madison. Many likened their struggle to that of the United States against Great Britain. Americans believed, also, that Tito's experience with the Soviet Union would be a salutary lesson for the new nations.

It was therefore a cause of frustration and concern in the United States when, in fact, many of these nations chose a path of "non-alignment." The path appeared to equate the international ambitions and conduct of the United States with those of the Soviet Union. The United States was not prepared for the "plague on both your houses" attitude. The U.S. resentment toward this approach deepened as the new nations, in the United Nations and in other multilateral forums, seemed to be more bitter toward the United States than they were toward the Soviet Union. "Non-alignment" seemed to become "non-alignment" only against the United States. John Foster Dulles called it "immoral."

The post-war experience of the United States paralleled that of the period of decolonization. While the new countries focused on their struggle with the Europeans, the U.S. approach to world problems centered on the conduct of the Soviet Union and its Communist allies around the world. The American people, hoping for a return to peace in the world, had the illusion shattered by Soviet conduct in Eastern Europe, Greece, Berlin, and Korea. They had difficulty in understanding why the rest of the world—and, in particular, the fragile new nations—could not see that threat.

To the new nations, these quarrels were those of others. Their concentration was on achieving independence and helping other countries to the same goal. In this objective, the United States was found wanting.

American rhetoric and actions in the postwar world had created great expectations among many of those looking for independence. The writings of the early political philosophers in the United States were taken at face value, even if not always correctly interpreted. The problem was compounded by repetitive rhetoric from the United States speaking of "freedom" and "the rights of men." These words, to many in the colonial world, meant freedom from foreign rule, not necessarily freedom for the individual.

The overwhelming power and influence of the United States in the postwar world were known. Time and again, in crises over demands for independence, the United States seemed to these countries, in contradiction to its declared principles, to be siding with the colonial power rather than with those seeking "freedom."

Those in the new nations or in colonies seeking independence knew also of the Marshall Plan. Their view of it may have been skewed, but they saw it—and the levels of aid—as a measure of the capacity of the United States to help others. In their own difficult days after independence, however, there were no Marshall plans. There were, instead, what many regarded as the excessively fastidious and limiting conditions on unexpectedly modest amounts of U.S. assistance.

Fundamental differences arose between the United States and the new nations because American policies did not meet their expectations. There was also much that the United States, in the creation of its policies and the drafting of its rhetoric, did not understand about the movement toward independence in the middle decades of the twentieth century. The struggle for independence in 1776 had been by Europeans in America against Europeans across the Atlantic. There had been no issue of race. The United States already had strongly established democratic institutions. The economic prospects of the new continent were bright. Against the background of these traditions, most American leaders, looking at the newly independent world for the first time, were not prepared for the emphasis on race, on humiliation, on economic privation, and for the policies and demands that went with those concerns.

At the same time, Americans asked the new nations whether the Soviet Union did not represent an even greater threat to the full expression of man's freedom and a far less capable source for economic answers. Many of the new nations' leaders would acknowledge this, but return to their expectations of the United States and to their disappointment with its support for the objectives of their own struggle.

The early years of these new nations and of the "non-aligned" concept was also a time when the United States was seeking, as a cardinal point of its foreign policy, to create anti-Soviet alliances around the world. The objective was to duplicate NATO in the Middle East and in East Asia. Pressures were brought to bear in the 1950s on many of the new leaders to "stand up and be counted." Aid, and particularly military aid, was made contingent upon some form of alliance relationship. Such policies awakened the fear of the involvement that lay at the heart of demands for "non-alignment."

Two other circumstances complicated the "non-aligned" perception of the United States: the U.S. position on three critical issues and the U.S. attitude toward revolution.

Throughout the history of "non-alignment" three issues have dominated the "non-aligned" agenda: the Middle East, southern Africa, and the conduct of the global economy. On each of these issues, the United States, because of its power, was central to any solution. To many of the new and developing nations, the United States was on the wrong side.

The European allies of the United States, despite the colonial history, were closer to many of these countries, and better understood the attitudes and the interests involved. Because they had less of a central responsibility, they could afford to take what appeared to be a position more sympathetic to the new nations. The United States, thus, frequently became the isolated target of the "non-aligned" nations.

The Soviet Union, also, had little direct responsibility in the ultimate solution of any of these three problems. Moscow could, therefore, stand on the sidelines and exploit the differences with the United States. What appeared so frequently to be a tilt by the non-aligned nations toward the Soviet Union was occasioned by the calculated exploitation of the deep dilemmas faced by the United States.

Much of the history and mythology of the new nations appeared to express rhetorical and political sympathy with revolution. That also put them at odds with the United States. Movements seen as seeking "liberation" from domination almost automatically gained the sympathy and support of the "non-aligned." In the forefront of such "revolutionary" and "liberation" movements was the Palestine Liberation Organization. The prominent place of this movement among the non-aligned meant that the attitude of the organized Palestinians would determine in large measure the attitude of the entire movement toward the Middle East question. The position of the United States, dictated by international responsibilities for the issue and its own domestic environment, was inescapably opposed to resolutions of the "non-aligned" on this issue.

In southern Africa, the movement's views were determined by those groups seeking to undermine apartheid and to isolate South Africa from the world community. Again, the United States, with its more balanced views, seemed to be at odds with the broad consensus of the new nations. Its isolation was exploited by the more radical states of the movement and by the Soviets.

In the latter days of the movement, as economic issues came to dominate the agenda, the United States also found itself isolated. The creation of the move toward a "new international economic order" became one of the objectives of the Non-Aligned Movement. While other nations, including many of the Europeans, equivocated about "global negotiations" and the other demands, the United States took firm positions against what it considered unrealistic demands on resource transfer, debt, commodity prices, technology transfer, and the reorganization of the world's primary financial institutions. Again, the Soviet Union, with a minuscule capacity to influence these major issues, could appear to be less opposed.

If, despite these basic differences, the possibility did exist for a more reasonable U.S. attitude toward the movement, it was almost certainly reduced by actions and policies of the Non-Aligned Movement itself.

The membership of two states clearly seen in the United States as allies of the Soviet Union—Vietnam and Cuba—badly damaged any claim to true "non-alignment." The rationale given by others in the group, that these countries did not have formal defense treaties with the Soviet Union, was seen as the height of sophistry.

Nations close to the United States, such as Pakistan and the Philippines, sought entry into the Non-Aligned Movement, but were blocked on the grounds that they had formal ties with the United States. The military relationships were certainly no stronger than those between the Soviet Union and Vietnam and Cuba.

Pakistan saw in the Non-Aligned Movement an important forum for its continuing quarrel with India. With the fall of the shah in Iran and the collapse of the Central Treaty Organization, Pakistan, unfettered now by that obligation, successfully sought and obtained membership. The Philippines has been granted only observer status.

The irony of this aspect of the Non-Aligned Movement was particularly apparent in the fall of 1979, when the conference of these nations was held in Havana under the chairmanship of Fidel Castro. Efforts to provide a more balanced agenda were made by the United States through intermediaries, but the frail health of Marshal Tito and the timing of the revelation of a Soviet combat brigade in Cuba served to blunt these efforts.

Enthusiasm in the United States for the movement has also been diminished, as Richard Jackson points out in this work, by the pressure on U.N. delegations of the non-aligned states to follow the resolutions of the conference in the U.N. General Assembly.

In the non-aligned conferences, decisions are made by consensus—or so it is made to appear. In the minds of many in the United States, this process permits the more radical and better-organized states to dominate the preparatory work of drafting the resolutions and the passage of the resolutions by the full body. The voices of the more moderate states seem to carry little weight.

The result is that the United States faces annually in the U.N. General Assembly a series of positions often inimical to it, but positions to which the majority of the member states feel obligated. Delegations from many countries are given no restrictions on these issues other than to follow the lead of the non-aligned positions. Intercession by U.S. representatives in capitals often prove fruitless. This aspect of the activities of the Non-Aligned Movement has done much to undermine support in the United States for the United Nations.

The generally negative attitude that has developed toward the movement is also fed in the United States by what seems to be a reluctance of the member states to face up to serious problems that involve them. Despite an embryonic effort at Havana, there was never any genuine protest within the movement to the rapid increase in the oil price by OPEC, even though this had a serious impact on a number of the member nations. Similarly, the movement appears to many Americans to pay little attention to human rights abuses in member states while severely criticizing South Africa and non-member friends of the United States. In the eyes of many in the United States, also, the movement treated the Soviet invasion of Afghanistan far too uncritically.

Differences between the United States and the Non-Aligned Movement were, perhaps, inevitable. Few Americans, at the beginning or now, are prepared to accept what appears to be a basic premise of many nations in the movement: that there is little to choose between the two superpowers. This premise runs totally counter to the general feeling in the United States that it represents the symbol of freedom for all nations.

The period since World War II has seen in the decolonization of European empires one of the greatest upheavals in the political circumstances of peoples in history. The United States was, in a sense, only on the periphery of that upheaval. It is not surprising, thus, that it understood so little of the impulses of the independence movements and had such difficulty in relating to the results of decolonization.

Similarly, the United States was not well known to most of the new nations' leaders. Its literature and its declared principles were known but not always fully understood. Both created expectations that the nation could not fulfill in terms sought by the new nations. The contradictions were exploited by the Soviets.

Even the existence of democracies within the movement did not mitigate the problems with the United States. In some ways, the United States had greater problems in finding common ground with the movement's largest democracy, India, than it did with some of the non-democratic members.

Some predict that, with the growing attention of nations to internal problems, the force of "non-alignment" may wane. Perhaps this is so. The versions of history, the traditions and the frustrations of development, however, will probably continue to provide the glue of common experience and some degree of solidarity among those nations new to independence in the twentieth century. If so, the continuing adjustment of perspectives between those nations and the United States will remain a feature of international politics. For that reason, Richard Jackson's study is a valuable contribution to a greater understanding of a significant fact of the current relations between the United States and a substantial number of the world's sovereign states.

Contents

Author's Note

This book was written in 1981–83 under the Una Chapman Cox Sabbatical Program of the Department of State. The late Mrs.Chapman Cox of Texas pioneered and made possible a program under which up to three career Foreign Service Officers are freed from normal responsibilities to undertake an in-depth, one-year project related to professional interests. In my case, her generosity provided expenses related to this book, including travel as an unofficial observer to the Seventh Non-Aligned Summit Conference in New Delhi.

The idea for this book evolved from assignments to U.S. embassies in two non-aligned countries, Somalia and Libya, followed by later work as a political adviser in the U.S. Mission to the U.N. In the latter post, I gained a new perspective on the Non-Aligned Movement (NAM) and was assigned to cover the February, 1981 NAM Ministerial Conference in New Delhi.

The book, like all Gaul, is divided into three parts covering the history and evolution of the NAM, the interaction of the movement with the United Nations, and the attitudes and strategies of the superpowers toward the non-aligned. I was neither at Bandung nor at meetings of the NAM prior to 1981, and Part I of necessity draws heavily on interviews, NAM documentation, and excellent work by U.S. Bajpai, Eugene Berg, K.P. Misra, Lazar Mojsov, M.S. Rajan, Peter Willetts, and other historians of the movement. While the antecedents and history of non-alignment have been covered elsewhere, an understanding of the movement's gradual evolution into one of the major international lobbies is essential to what follows.

As an observer of the United Nations during the period from 1980–83, I became convinced that the Non-Aligned Movement and the U.N. have interacted at the most basic level with lasting impact on both institutions. In the process, the U.N. has in my view become the primary raison d'être of the NAM. Part II deals with the interaction of these institutions and the apparent collision course of the United States with both. My observations are based largely on the years from 1979–83, and non-aligned history is, of course, continuing to unfold with both the United Nations and the NAM evolving in directions that can be predicted only in broad outline.

Representing about two-thirds of the total U.N. membership, the NAM has had an undeniable impact on the world body, including the functioning of both the General Assembly and the Security Council. The non-aligned today largely control the machinery of the U.N. deliberative organs and set the agenda and structure of the organization. As a result, the United Nations is used less and less for purposes of problem solving and conflict resolution and increasingly for rhetorical and declarative exercises that have little or no relevance to realities of the world. To be sure, rhetoric marked the world organization well before the NAM was formed in 1961; yet by the mid-eighties posturing and irresponsible verbiage, particularly along bloc lines, have substantially diminished the capability of the United Nations to fulfill the purposes set out in its charter.

In a book dealing primarily with the Non-Aligned Movement there is, or course, danger that the NAM will appear uniquely responsible for the problems and disappointments of the United Nations today. In fact, the non-aligned majority in New York has flowed into a power vacuum created by U.S.-Soviet division and lack, over the years, of consistent Western leadership. Nor should the analysis here of non-aligned influence in the United Nations provide ammunition for opponents of U.S. participation in that body. Withdrawal from the United Nations, despite its failings, would—at least in this author's view—lead to an even less stable, less manageable world.

The final section attempts to consider the difficult interaction in the final decades of the twentieth century between the United States and an international order shaped by a non-aligned majority. Progress on the many present points of difference will depend, in my view, on the degree of substantive flexibility shown by both sides on problems of the Middle East, southern Africa, and economic reform, and on a growing world economy with promise of improvement in global standards of living. Both may be lacking well into the 1980s.

Economic inequality does not per se preclude constructive dialogue and maintenance of an international order serving the interests of strong and weak, rich and poor alike. Yet for the United States and other Western donors, communication is clouded by growing resentment of taxation without adequate representation for an international system beyond their control. For many Third World leaders, the frailty of political and economic structures makes it politically imperative to blame outsiders rather than attacking underlying local problems and entrenched elites directly. The result is often a familiar litany of colonial guilt for all world problems. Prospects for dialogue, to which there is no acceptable alternative, thus continue to rest—as in individual societies—

not on equality, but on an almost equally elusive diplomatic goal, a shared concept of fairness.

Extraneous to these global concerns, yet in today's world inextricably linked, is the reality of East–West competition. Part III, therefore, deals with divergent U.S. and Soviet policies toward the NAM, non-aligned perceptions of the superpowers, and the correlation of NAM and Soviet positions in the U.N. I believe it would be a mistake, however, to view the NAM as an extension of Soviet influence or to attribute, as some do, its radicalization and growing anti-Westernism since the 1970s to a grand strategy developed in Moscow. With the exception of a radical fringe, like Cuba and Vietnam, which clearly belong within the Soviet orbit, the movement is essentially an interest group and lobby for the Third World. Its positions, however contradictory, evolve from perceptions of its interests, and cannot long be co-opted by either superpower. In fact, efforts to draw the movement into purely East–West issues have usually backfired, resulting in hostility and negativism. Non-aligned suspicion of the United States stems, thus, from differences of policy on the Middle East, southern Africa, and economic reform, and, to a lesser extent, from the anti-Western residue of colonialism.

Moscow has been the obvious beneficiary, yet it has been a free ride, not the result of long-term calculation or diplomatic initiative. Soviet and non-aligned interests have, in fact, coincided in challenging a postwar international order established by the United States and the rest of the West. The United States, in contrast with Russia, tends to be cast as the major obstacle to change, uncaring if not hostile to non-aligned aspirations. Soviet success in promoting an image of shared interests with the Third World, notwithstanding evidence to the contrary, such as military occupation of non-aligned Afghanistan, has been through the politics of posturing. Moscow remains largely irrelevant to solutions in the Middle East, Namibia, or economic reform. In development, it has little to offer, and its trade with the Third World is a small fraction of the U.S. share. Seen in this light, survival of the Non-Aligned Movement in its present rhetorical and anti-Western guise can only represent a serious failure of American diplomacy since the 1960s.

The NAM is a deliberately loose association of 101 members, many of which disagree on its role and most fundamental objectives. While labels are misleading, for purposes of shorthand I have referred throughout to Cuba and the dozen non-aligned states that annually vote at the U.N. for the Soviet invasion of Afghanistan and, for the most part who are tied by treaty to Moscow as "radicals," and to the countervailing force of about 20 countries, like Singapore and Egypt, as "moderates." Few of either persuasion would, however, share the interpretation presented here. It is inevitably written with the perspective of an outsider from a country by definition excluded from the movement. On the other hand, my intent is not to denigrate the non-aligned, and selection of the topic itself reflects a conviction that the NAM has evolved into a factor in international relations that outsiders can no longer afford to ignore. Despite predictions to the contrary, the movement has repeatedly survived periods of internal disarray, and India's presidency from 1983–86 promises to renew flagging Third World faith in non-alignment. Further, the linkages between the NAM and United Nations now require a carefully coordinated U.S. policy toward both institutions.

Many in the U.N. Secretariat and the U.S. government, and among the non-aligned themselves, have been most generous with interviews. Since the final product cannot reflect their divergent views, I will not embarrass them by name. In fact, these pages reflect purely my own views and are not necessarily those of the Department of State.

Special thanks, however, are due to Bruce Jackson, John Donovan, John Graham, Robert Rosenstock, Kenneth Adelman, David Newsom, Helen Freeman, Susan Johnson, Sally Morphet, Carl Gershman, and Bob Shaplen, who read all or parts of the manuscript and made many useful comments. Particularly useful in the final stage of revision was a review group at the Council on Foreign Relations including Paul Kreisberg, Grace Darling, Peter Grose, Arthur Lall, John MacDonald, William Maynes, Richard Petree, George Sherry, James Sutterlin and Jennifer Whitaker. While they, of course, bear no responsibility for the contents and conclusions of this book, each contributed insights and perspectives which added much to the final version. Thanks are also due to Carol Huffman Finks and Dolores Wright, who shared the burden of typing. Finally, my publisher, Patrick Bernuth of Praeger, has been a constant source of encouragement and a marvel to work with.

March 31, 1983

I

The Non-Aligned Movement as an Institution

1

Definitions of Non-Alignment

I would not say what is pure,
purer or impure non-alignment.
Indira Gandhi, 1983

Non-alignment is a word that, through overuse and misuse, has for many people lost specific meaning. Much was made of it in the 1950s and early 1960s when, in the first flush of independence, new countries of Africa and Asia claimed to find in non-alignment an identity and strength in numbers permitting a middle ground, although not necessarily equidistance, between superpowers. In the intervening years, however, both the concept and the organization have been surrounded with misconception.

The concept of an independent foreign policy course between East and West was belied by the selection as chairman for 1979–83 of Cuba, a member of the Council for Mutual Economic Assistance (COMECON) tied closely to the Soviets and committed to communism. Nor do most declarations of the non-aligned reflect this theoretical balance, tending to single out the United States by name for criticism while referring to the Soviet Union in indirect terms and then only rarely. The most recent example, the Political Declaration adopted by the Seventh Summit at New Delhi on March 12, 1983, castigated the United States 23 times by name while avoiding critical reference to the Soviet Union, then occupying non-aligned Afghanistan with 105,000 troops and backing Vietnamese military intervention in non-aligned Kampuchea.

For many, the non-aligned are inseparable from the more amorphous concept of the Third World, the so-called Group of 77 (G-77) in North–South economic negotiations, and, in general, the majority of developing and recently independent states that form an often automatic and anti-Western consensus at the United Nations. Distinctions between these groupings are further blurred by rivalries among them and different perceptions of each by their members.

Non-alignment has thus been difficult for outsiders to understand, and Westerners, faced with its contradictions, have tended to downplay the non-aligned and to underestimate their impact both in the United States and outside. Western press coverage has been episodic and focused on specific aspects, such as Fidel Castro's hosting of the 1979 Non-Aligned Summit in Havana. In a period of diminished U.S. idealism about the United Nations, critics regard the non-aligned as merely part of an uninterrupted, often unintelligible, flow of rhetoric in the world body. The latter, in turn, they discount as without relevance or direct effect on the world.

The Institution

As an organization, the Non-Aligned Movement (NAM) is easy to define in a narrow sense. It began at a summit conference of 25 states convoked by Marshal Tito at Belgrade in September 1961. Membership depended on criteria worked out in advance, but interpreted with varying degrees of flexibility over the years. The common bond was to be a foreign policy independent of the superpowers or associated blocs, then polarized by the Cold War. The new grouping was seen as an alternative to these divisions, not as a third bloc in its own right. Hence, no charter, no headquarters, and no permanent secretariat were envisaged. By the New Delhi Summit in March 1983, 99 states and two liberation movements were full members of the NAM.

Continuity is provided by the compilation of declarations and resolutions from the various non-aligned meetings, held approximately every three years at the summit level (except in 1967). NAM positions are reached by consensus, not actual voting, although members may later enter reservations for the record. The consensus procedure of debate until a majority opinion emerges maximizes the appearance of unity, but weakens the positions taken, which are not binding and are often repudiated by members in other contexts. It puts the responsibility for interpreting the sense of long-winded NAM debates on the chairman, who is selected by consensus to host a summit and remain in office for three years, until the next meeting. In the interim, NAM foreign ministers convene annually in New York during the fall General Assembly session and elsewhere as fixed by the preceding summit. The Non-Aligned Coordinating Bureau (NACB), established in 1973 and now numbering 74 members, meets more regularly in New York, and occasionally elsewhere, to implement summit decisions and coordinate positions among the larger membership.

The NAM should not be equated with the G-77, although the two groupings share economic goals and reinforce each other. The larger G-77, now expanded to 125 members, of whom 80 percent belong to the NAM, was formed to represent the developing countries during the 1964 U.N. Conference on Trade and Development (UNCTAD) at Geneva, and has continued to do so at subsequent UNCTAD meetings, special General Assembly sessions on economic issues, and other specialized conferences. Its focus is entirely economic, and its status as a negotiating body in the North-South dialogue is recognized by the developed countries. As such, the G-77 benefits from the permanent secretariat and backing of UNCTAD. While the NAM and G-77 memberships overlap, some leaders of the G-77, such as Brazil, Mexico, and Venezuela, are not full members of the NAM, whose orientation tends to be more radical. More important, the NAM, while involved in economic issues, is broader in focus, acting as coordinator and lobby for its membership on a range of political, social, and economic issues. The "catalytic and pivotal" role that the NAM claims to exert over the G-77 has tended to fluctuate with the leadership and issues involved. While the NAM has often taken the lead, as in elaborating demands of the New International Economic Order (NIEO) at Algiers in 1973, there is no direct correlation between the two groups.

The Third World, by contrast, is a loose concept, not an institution or an organized lobby. Coined as a term in France during the early 1950s, it refers to the underdeveloped, and for the most part Southern Hemisphere, states that comprise the majority of the United Nations, NAM, and G-77. Elaborate economic criteria have been devised to define and categorize the Third World, but these relate more to development than to group dynamics. In practical terms, the role of the NAM has been to articulate and advance the interests and demands of the Third World. Yet its original focus on worldwide issues of promoting peace, resolution of disputes, and coexistence was considerably broader. NAM theoreticians like Yugoslavia—depending on the criteria, itself in a gray area between the Third World and the developed world—therefore insist on the movement's global rather than Third World mission.

The Concept

The idea of non-alignment, as distinct from the institution, is more difficult to come to terms with. The posture of non-involvement or neutralism toward larger, threatening powers goes back at least to the

Greek city-states. The term "non-alignment" appears to have been coined by Prime Minister Jawaharlal Nehru in a speech of April 28, 1954, in Colombo. To Western ears, the word implies a sense of balance or equidistance between the "aligned" nations or superpowers. Yet for Nehru its content, articulated before the actual term in speeches dating from 1946, embodies a separate identity and role for developing states rather than fixed positions defined in relation to outside blocs. In its modern variant, the concept is also an effective strategy for maximizing economic aid from rival blocs eager to extend their influence or limit that of others.

The difficulty of dealing with non-alignment as a philosophy or set of values common to the NAM is the diversity of its membership. Like the Holy Roman Empire being neither holy, Roman, nor an empire, it has become a truism to say that the non-aligned are not, in fact, non-aligned. To be sure, no nation can speak authoritatively for the others, and each of the 101 members has slightly different perceptions of the movement. Like rival guardians of "true" Marxism-Leninism, several NAM members have staked out their own versions of "genuine" non-alignment. Indian and Yugoslav emphasis on "original principles" is, for example, bitterly attacked as revisionism by Cuba and Vietnam.[1] For some, non-alignment has also assumed idiosyncratic dimensions related to national interests and psychology. In India, the concept is inextricable from complex relations with the superpowers and China, and from India's emergence as an independent state under Mahatma Gandhi. For Yugoslavia, it evolved as an alternative socialist model following the break with Moscow. The solution, adopted by some analysts of the NAM, is therefore to define the content of non-alignment as the sum of positions taken at each of the seven summits held to date and reflected in voluminous conference documentation. Yet NAM positions have changed greatly over the years, and conference records are as important for their omissions as for the usual agreed communiqués.

The question of a common NAM ideology—a contradiction of sorts in a movement spanning the capitalist economies of Singapore and Kuwait, the conservatism of Saudi Arabia and Morocco, and the hard-core communism of Cuba, Vietnam, and North Korea—has, nevertheless, over the years occupied much of the movement's time. This is, in part, because of the need to negotiate every word among states of different political persuasions, in the process investing otherwise innocuous phrases with meanings lost to the outsider. The focus on ideology and general principles—which occupy much of the standard NAM declarations—also reflects input and unique concerns of individual members. Yugoslavia, for example, has been at pains to synthesize the idea of non-alignment with a Marxist view of international relations and, through ideology, to maintain influence over a movement in which it enjoys little regional backing. Contributions of India and Sri Lanka, particularly in the movement's early years, derived from Asian traditions of non-violence and pacificism. Cuba, despite setbacks, has fought an intermittent battle to ally the movement ideologically with the socialist bloc, which it endorses as the "natural ally of the non-aligned."

The function of ideology in the NAM arguably has been less as a framework of common values than as a tool for key members seeking center stage and as a vehicle for presenting a semblance of unity in an increasingly diverse membership. The majority of members show little interest in philosophical principles, and become active only on specific political or economic issues. The nexus or glue of the Movement is, therefore, not coherent theory but a shared and inchoate identity. Gamal Abdel Nasser stated in 1961 that non-alignment "means that we ought to decide what we believe in and not according to what might satisfy any particular country. It means that our policy is not attached to the policy of any other country or the big powers."[2] His loose definition remains valid for most members today, and suggests that psychological rather than political or economic dimensions best explain the movement's survival and its still growing membership. As Deputy Prime Minister J.S. Regenvanu of Vanuatu, the 101st NAM member, put it in March 1983: "For us being a non-aligned country means being able to say what you believe without fearing that it could result in undesirable relations with one or the other bloc."

In the wave of independence during the 1960s, new states with twin legacies of colonialism and underdevelopment sought an identity in numbers. Their high initial expectations often gave way in later years to frustration, if not cynicism, before intractable economic problems and fragile political structures. Yet the residue of shared experience has continued to shape the NAM, explaining its emphasis on decolonization when few colonies remain and its strident economic demands upon the West.

The continued relevance of the NAM is evident in its survival and growth since the 1960s that have tested its rationale during alternating periods of cold war and détente. Its strength, however, lies not in philosophical consistency, but in the patchwork of compromises through which members have placed the institution's survival above national ideologies or positions on specific issues. In the process, only one country, Burma—perhaps the most genuinely non-aligned in a philosophical sense—has withdrawn from the movement. Cuba, for example, could have split the movement during the Havana Summit by insistence on the "natural ally" thesis, but chose not to. The equally explosive differences between oil-importing and oil-exporting members have also been glossed over for the sake of unity.

The justification for these compromises—even by ideological intransigents—lies, for small states, in enhanced strength and influence through membership and, for larger members, in the power base implicit in a movement of 101 states. As Colombian President Belisario Betancur put it in early 1983, prior to his country's admission to the NAM:

> Our proposal to join the non-aligned group is an affirmation of sovereignty and a search for new forums, for new partnerships with those who have problems similar to Colombia's. It's a question of not being a satellite of any one power center and of maintaining our own power of decision.[3]

Outside Perspectives

Non-member states tend to view the NAM through the prism of specific issues in which differences loom larger than common identity. The failure of numerous NAM mediation missions to end the Iran-Iraq war, the continued occupation of Afghanistan by the Soviets and of Kampuchea by Vietnam all contribute to an image of impotence. Nor are these cases novel. The NAM has typically responded in disarray to internecine war, whether between Somalia and Ethiopia, Yemen and Egypt, or Libya and Chad. As in the United Nations, the cumulative result of resolutions and declarations year after year, on essentially the same agenda, has been to devalue the currency. Further, in the case of the NAM, its positions clearly are not binding, or necessarily even predictive of voting patterns in the United Nations.

U.S. and Soviet reactions and strategy toward the non-aligned have tended toward short-term judgments on the basis of litmus issues like Afghanistan, Kampuchea, Puerto Rico, and Israel. This focus has in both cases overlooked the movement's impact on the United Nations, where its common goals as well as internal divisions have shaped the overall U.N. agenda and affected the workings of its principal organs, the General Assembly and the Security Council. Because of this, the NAM poses both dilemmas and options for the superpowers, and its internal dynamics warrant closer study than they have yet received.

The issues before the NAM have for the most part remained unresolved, with nearly identical problems on the agendas of each summit meeting. The movement has thus been largely unsuccessful in shaping world events, either those involving the major powers or disputes between the non-aligned themselves. The more significant contribution of the NAM has been the irrevocable altering of the international agenda and the context in which world problems are considered, in particular the role and functioning of the United Nations. Certainly the tripling of its membership and complex economic interrelationships would have broadened the focus of the United Nations with or without the Non-Aligned Movement. Yet the movement has shaped the process, ensuring that positions of its members become those of the larger organization. A large body of non-aligned doctrine, derived from summit and ministerial meetings outside New York, has thus been translated, with little change and often over Western objections, into resolutions of the General Assembly. These resolutions, in turn, are regularly invoked as terms of reference, whether on issues of decolonization or of economic reform, to structure the thinking and approach of the United Nations to world problems. The cumulative result has been an identification of the United Nations with Third World interests, which the non-aligned accept as a natural result of parallel objectives. The reaction of Western states, particularly the United States, has been, by contrast, largely negative as they exercise less and less control over U.N. positions determined outside New York by a majority from which they are excluded.

A paradox of the Non-Aligned Movement today is that its influence over the agenda and structure of the United Nations has continued to increase while its internal cohesion and sense of mission have grown steadily weaker. Put differently, the enlarged membership that has led to non-aligned control of key U.N. committees, an absolute majority in the General Assembly, and a dominant subgroup on the Security Council, has also resulted in disarray within the movement on divisive political and economic issues. No longer does the NAM command the solidarity and shared purpose that marked the mid-1970s, when, under Algerian leadership, it presented a nearly united bargaining front against the West. By the early 1980s, rivalry for leadership and divergent national interests had caused many, both within and outside the movement, to question what its members share in common.

As the movement became more amorphous from the mid-1970s on, members' realization of its influence over the U.N. system probably contributed as much as anything to its survival and ability to attract new recruits. U.N. parlimentary practice reinforces and rewards the non-aligned as the largest voting bloc, and individual states without appreciable influence in their own right derive added status from NAM membership. While members still dispute the term "bloc" and the inference of an automatic non-aligned majority, the movement has evolved, from quite different beginnings, into precisely that. In the process, non-alignment has been redefined to mean nearly the opposite of the "non-bloc" envisioned by Marshal Tito and Prime Minister Nehru at Belgrade in 1961.

The interaction of the NAM and United Nations inevitably raises larger issues of the continuing viability of the world body and the appropriate role of the United States and other Western states within it. As U.N. priorities have been redirected toward the concerns of a new majority and away from the postwar focus on peacekeeping and political issues, unfulfilled and probably excessive American expectations have led to widespread disillusionment about the value and continued relevance of the world body. Faced with a succession of wars and crises resistant to U.N. mediation, Secretary-General Javier Pérez de Cuellar stated frankly in his annual report of September 7, 1982, that "The United Nations itself has been unable to play as effective and decisive a role as the Charter certainly envisaged for it." From an American point of view, however, the United Nations has continued to provide more modest benefits of behind-the-scenes diplomacy; a starting point for negotiations, whether on the Middle East or southern Africa; and tangible progress in the specialized agencies. Viewed as an ongoing political process of largely symbolic rather than literal significance, the United Nations is still a unique source of information on and contact with virtually every nation of the world. As developed in Part III, a more flexible U.S. approach to the United Nations must begin with a consistent policy toward the non-aligned as the largest bloc within it.

2

Origins of Non-Alignment

When elephants fight, it is
the grass that suffers.
Tanzanian Proverb

Much has been written on the origins of the Non-Aligned Movement, and it is not necessary to retrace its beginnings in detail. Yet an assessment of the NAM today and of its impact on the United Nations requires at least a general examination of how the movement started and what it originally set out to be.

Lack of communication during the colonial period between territories that today form the Third World was profound. All channels led to the metropolis—whether Paris, London, Lisbon, Brussels, or elsewhere—and lateral contacts or flows of information were discouraged and nearly non-existent. An early exception was the furtive 1927 Congress of Oppressed Nationalities in Brussels, which brought together representatives from the colonial world, many then students in Europe. These included Jawaharlal Nehru, Leópold Senghor, and Ho Chi Minh.

Regular contact between the few already independent countries and vast emerging areas of the Third World did not begin until after World War II. Wartime service by colonial troops played a part, but the immediate catalyst was a new spirit of internationalism evident in 1945 with the founding of the United Nations. At San Francisco, Asian, African, and Latin delegations met for the first time on the margins of deliberations to set up the United Nations, and these preliminary contacts gave rise to a series of exploratory meetings throughout the late 1940s and the 1950s. The idea, for example, of a separate meeting of Asian states that materialized in 1947 at New Delhi as the Asian Relations Conference was first floated in San Francisco.[4]

These early meetings were an indispensable gestation period for the NAM, which was born in 1961. They formed a series of widening concentric circles corresponding to the transition of new states from regional to global consciousness. The Asians, further along the road to independence after the war, took the lead in organizing regional conferences, which, by the mid-1950s, had become Afro-Asian in outlook. The addition, by the time of the Belgrade Summit in 1961, of

Europeans (Yugoslavia and Cyprus) and Latin Americans (Cuba and observers from Bolivia, Brazil, and Ecuador) further broadened the focus.

The Regional Phase

While Asians, led by India, held a series of conferences in the 1940s and 1950s, the diversity of Asia, combined with geographical proximity to China and the USSR, stood in the way of an overall regional organization. The early Asian conferences were attended, therefore, by a shifting cast of characters and, to this day, no unified regional organization has emerged. By contrast, the Arab League was established in 1945 and followed in 1951 by the Organization of American States (OAS). Merger of the rival Casablanca and Brazzaville groups into the umbrella Organization of African Unity (OAU) took somewhat longer, and was completed in 1963.

The New Delhi Asian Relations Conference of 1947 was intended to promote better understanding among states of the region and to discuss a broad agenda of economic, social and agricultural issues. Its genesis at San Francisco probably reflected a fear among Asians that the United Nations would prove no more permanent or responsive to their continent's interests than the League of Nations. In retrospect, attendance at New Delhi was more interesting than the actual proceedings. Among the 28 delegations were those from the Soviet Republics of Armenia, Azerbaijan, Georgia, Kazakhstan, Mongolia, Tadzhikistan, Turkmenistan, and Uzbekistan. All of these subsequently disappeared from the conference circuit, and discussion of communism and its implications at later Afro-Asian or non-aligned meetings overlooked Asia, focusing on European manifestations only. Delegations from Tibet and Jewish Palestine also made first and last appearances at the New Delhi meeting.

Had a common identity evolved from this diverse grouping, Asian and non-aligned history might have followed different paths. Inclusion of Soviet Asian republics would certainly have imposed other issues and options. In the event, the group never met again, and the Asian Relations Organization that it created was dissolved in 1955 at Bandung with remaining assets of six chairs (one broken), two tables, one typewriter, and two cabinets.[5] A second conference, held at New Delhi in early 1949, brought together different participants and was largely confined to coordinating reactions to Dutch police action against Indonesia.

Bandung: Origins, Reality, and Myth

Bandung widened the circle, allowing Asian and African delegations to take the measure of each other for the first time on home ground. Its origins, however, were Asian, and of its 29 delegations, only six came from Africa: Egypt, Ethiopia, Gold Coast (now Ghana), Liberia, and Sudan. Much has been written of the legendary "spirit of Bandung," credited with, among other things, creation of the NAM. In fact, the meeting was a necessary step along the way. Yet non-alignment was not a criterion for participants at Bandung. SEATO and Baghdad Pact members like Turkey, Pakistan, Iran, Iraq, Thailand, and the Philippines took part alongside China (then a close Soviet ally) and Japan. In the end, Bandung, like earlier conferences, was undermined by Asian divisions and complexity. The myth of its "spirit" survived, however, providing reassurance and continuity to emerging states.

The organizational impetus for Bandung came from a five-nation meeting in 1954 at Colombo. Ceylon (now Sri Lanka), with an ambitious new prime minister, John Kotelawala, seized the initiative to gain stature with its larger neighbors.[6] The resulting meeting of Burma, Ceylon, India, Indonesia, and Pakistan, known as the Colombo Powers or Colombo Five and coinciding with the Geneva Conference on Indochina, focused on Indochinese issues and the general question of communism. The Five also endorsed Indonesia's proposal for a larger gathering of Afro-Asian states and planned a preparatory meeting at the end of the year in Bogor, Indonesia. The latter, which included most countries present four months later at Bandung, covered a wide-ranging agenda, but is generally remembered as a prelude to Bandung.

Philosophically, Bandung was strongly influenced by five principles (Panchsheel) contained in an agreement on trade in Tibet signed by India and China during April 1954. These principles, derived from Indian traditions of nonviolence, were promoted by Prime Minister Nehru as a new basis for international relations. They were respect for territorial integrity and sovereignty, mutual non-aggression, mutual non-interference in internal affairs, equality and mutual benefit, and peaceful co-existence. While discredited by later friction between India and China that ended in the war of 1962, the Panchsheel were elaborated, after prolonged debate, into ten principles at Bandung, and provided a framework for the evolution of non-alignment.

Bandung foreshadowed the NAM in its agenda devoted to problems of colonialism, economic development, and maintenance of peace. Acerbic exchanges between Pakistan, seeking to highlight dangers of communism, and China, then deeply in the Soviet orbit, also pointed most delegates toward the middle ground of non-alignment. By the time of Belgrade in 1961, China, SEATO members, and Baghdad Pact members were all omitted from the guest list.

The importance of Bandung, on which its myth is based, really lay in contacts made there and in the sense of community among emerging states. Gamal Abdel Nasser, for example—outside the Arab world for the first time—found acceptance at Bandung that can only have reinforced his decision the following year on Suez. For the Afro-Asian states, Bandung marked a first entry onto the world stage. Léopold Senghor describes it as the most important event since the Renaissance that spelled "death to the inferiority complex of colonial peoples."[7] In terms of the NAM, it was a further step toward an evolving consensus and a chance to take the measure of new states, winnowing out those beyond the mainstream. In any case, the Bandung group never met again. The Soviet and Chinese-sponsored Afro-Asian Peoples Solidarity Organization (AAPSO) attempted to co-opt its spirit, and functioned as a Communist propaganda outlet in the Third World.

The Founding Trio

While half a dozen states have played leadership roles in the NAM at different stages of its history, Yugoslavia, India, and Egypt banded together to get the movement off the ground. While their early contacts were not always easy, reflecting both rivalry between strong leaders and differences of ideology, the Cold War and events in the late 1950s brought about a remarkable identity in their national goals and approaches to international relations. Each was, to some degree, isolated in its region, and found strength in a collective resistance to the great powers. Each also saw in the NAM an opportunity to project national power and influence onto a larger stage. For Tito, seeking a middle ground after the break with Moscow in 1948, non-alignment offered just such an alternative. Nehru, the Panchsheel notwithstanding, was clearly worried by his then monolithic neighbors to the north and by U.S. regional military alliances. Nasser, an army colonel new to national leadership, had much to gain from non-aligned support in his high-risk flirtation with East and West.

A working partnership among the three countries evolved first in the Security Council, of which they were all members in 1950 and where they developed common approaches to a number of issues during the Korean War. President Tito consolidated these contacts with visits to Nehru in late 1954 and to Nasser the following year.

Wide-ranging, three-way discussions on non-alignment and the division of the world into competing blocs were held in July 1956 at Brioni, an island offered to the NAM in 1983 by Yugoslavia as a "place of continuous fostering of non-aligned ideas and aims." The informal consensus that emerged led to a series of continuing bilateral contacts among the three leaders throughout the 1950s and early 1960s and coordination of respective positions in time of crisis. Yugoslavia, for example, took the lead in the United Nations in using the "uniting for peace" procedure to back Egypt during the Suez crisis. As this working relationship developed, other Third World countries joined the discussions. By the mid-1950s, Indian delegates estimated that a group of 18–20 countries could be relied on to support a common point of view on most U.N. issues. These early meetings were the genesis of the Afro-Asian coalition that by the decade's end had begun to reshape the United Nations. Most of the same states also formed the nucleus that was institutionalized in 1961 as the Non-Aligned Movement.

Launching of the NAM

The heightened consciousness among new states, traceable to Bandung, and the evolving partnership of Tito, Nasser, and Nehru were essential elements leading to the Belgrade Summit of 1961. Yet the beginning was by no means smooth. Nehru's sponsorship was uncertain until the last minute; even Nasser was unconvinced of the timing. Pressures from Russia and China also continued for a second Bandung with Chinese and, if possible, Soviet participation. The driving force behind the summit was clearly Tito. To consolidate support, he dispatched a high-level mission to 12 Latin American countries in 1959 and himself visited Ghana, Togo, Liberia, Guinea, Mali, Morocco, Tunisia, Sudan, and Egypt in early 1961. Tito also met at the Yugoslav Mission in New York during the 1960 General Assembly with Nasser, Nehru, Kwame Nkrumah, and Sukarno.[8] Following a preparatory conference in Cairo during June, the Belgrade Summit opened on September 1 with Indian backing secured early in August.

Belgrade is usually identified as the starting point of the NAM, not because the 25 states assembled there consciously created a new institution, but because they later proved to be the nucleus of what evolved as an organized movement. It is doubtful, however, that, with the exception of Tito, those present fully grasped their role as founding fathers of the NAM or, for that matter, even gave thought to whether to meet again. Belgrade, like later NAM summit meetings, was preoccupied with the internal dynamic of drafting a final declaration, hammering out consensus on its controversial points, and finishing the agenda with a minimum of delay.

Nor were the aims of its key participants identical. Nehru, on the verge of outright war with China and preoccupied with Cold War tensions, struggled to focus the conference on the larger issues of war and peace. Nkrumah, by contrast, and with support from the Africans, insisted on the priority of decolonization. Nasser and the Arabs were already focused mainly on the question of Israel and Palestinian rights, while Sukarno had not given up the idea of a second Bandung and was evolving an amorphous theory of New Emergent Forces (NEFOs) to rally the radicals. Tito, as host, played a conciliatory role, developing consensus where possible.

Limited attendance at Belgrade (see Appendix A), worked out in advance at the Cairo preparatory meeting, included radical Africans of the Casablanca group, but not those of the more moderate Brazzaville faction. As a result, participants were evenly divided between Asians and Africans (11 each), 2 Europeans (Yugoslavia and Cyprus), and 1 Latin American (Cuba). African issues thus did not occupy the central role at Belgrade that they assumed in later years. Nehru, supported by V.K. Krishna Menon, was able to outmaneuver the Africans in setting priorities. At his insistence, a separate "Statement on the Danger of War and an Appeal for Peace" was issued, and global issues ranked ahead of decolonization in the final declaration. Yet he made few converts and, in the words of Indian historian G.H. Jansen, speeches by his colleagues were "little more than the usual shrillings on the anti-colonial penny-whistle."[9] Other priorities, however, such as the need for economic cooperation between Third World countries, were more widely shared, and led to the Cairo Economic Conference of 1962—and, indirectly, to establishment of the U.N. Conference on Trade and Development (UNCTAD) in 1964. Belgrade also agreed on a letter from the non-aligned to U.S. President John Kennedy and Soviet Premier Nikita Khrushchev urging renewed contacts to avoid conflict and reduce tensions.

In many ways the Belgrade Summit—although smaller in numbers and perhaps more manageable—foreshadowed the pattern of later conferences. It addressed the issues of the day, but failed to agree on the most controversial points. After much debate, only a bland call for restraint was made regarding the German crisis, inflamed by the Berlin Wall. Nor, despite references to the nuclear menace, was there any mention of the Soviet Union, which had resumed testing on the eve of the conference. Regional divisions that frequently separated Nehru and most of the Asians from the African group at Belgrade have persisted to the present. Finally, the ability of larger and better-prepared delegations, such as India and Yugoslavia, to manage the outcome and influence smaller colleagues was particularly evident at Belgrade. Their disproportionate influence has remained an anomaly in a movement otherwise described as democratic, making it vulnerable over the years to aggressive leadership.

Many of the concerns and themes voiced at Belgrade have continued to echo at all later NAM conferences. Condemnation of apartheid and discussions of Palestinian rights, disarmament, self-determination for colonial peoples, unequal terms of trade, and commodity fluctuations between North and South have permeated every meeting of the NAM. Their continued presence on the agenda is both a unifying element in a movement divided on many other issues and a source of frustration and impotence that, despite so many years of declarations, all of these problems remain intractable and beyond the power of 101 NAM members to remedy.

The Cold War Influence

Belgrade and the exploratory meetings that preceded it occurred in a period of acute East-West tension and colonial strife. The pivotal meetings coincided with particular stress points in the Cold War. Bandung met as Chinese shelling of Quemoy and Matsu, islands off Taiwan, threatened confrontation with the United States. The Belgrade Summit convened less than a month after construction of the Berlin Wall and one day after Moscow resumed nuclear testing in violation of a 1958 understanding with the United States and United Kingdom. These crises were episodes in a decade of confrontation that relegated smaller states to the sidelines. In these fluid conditions, some Third World states took refuge in protection by one or the other superpower. The majority, however, sought the security in numbers provided by the nascent NAM.

Forty years of peace may today offer dubious reassurance, but in the 1950s the threat of nuclear weapons was immediate, and evidence of testing, including Third World sites in North Africa and the Pacific, abundant. Some Western critics of the NAM have argued that, from the outset, its bias has been toward Moscow. Yet for those on the sidelines, the conflicts of the 1950s and early 1960s offered, on balance, little reassurance about either side. Reaction to North Korean aggression and Chinese intervention in Korea was diluted by conflict elsewhere pitting

Western states against colonial populations. Lessons of the Soviet invasion of Hungary in 1956 were offset for many emerging states by the simultaneous British, French and Israeli attack on Egypt and, later, by the Bay of Pigs in 1961.

Shared colonial experience tended to focus the non-aligned on wars for independence and post-colonial convulsions. In this prism, French involvement in Indochina, culminating at Dien Bien Phu in 1954; a bloody war of liberation in Algeria; Portuguese repression in Angola; and events following Belgium's precipitate withdrawal from the Congo in 1960 all loomed large. The cumulative impact of Cold War and colonial struggles was a climate of insecurity, even fear, among states riven with internal problems and independent for the first time. The Indo-Chinese War of 1962 showed that even the largest and most populous were not immune.

Momentum of Independence

Finally, the fact of independence itself, particularly that of African states that burst on the world scene in the early 1960s, was a major factor in the evolution of non-alignment as a movement and set of ideas. As newcomers joined well-established states like Egypt, Yugoslavia, India, and Ethiopia, they brought new concerns to the movement. In practical terms, the sheer number of new states—16 from Africa in 1960 alone—altered the geographic balance of the United Nations and made possible a major coordinating role for the NAM. After Belgrade, Africa's impact was also felt in the shift away from global issues of war and peace to a primary focus on decolonization.

These new states, whether independent by the sword, as in Algeria, or by the pen, as in most of the French colonies in West Africa, shared both a sense of vulnerability as latecomers to the world stage and high expectations. To most, shelter in NAM and OAU numbers seemed preferable to isolation in an uncertain environment dominated by former colonial powers. At the same time, new flags were run up in the expectation that economic stagnation, illiteracy, tribalism, and other ills were legacies of colonialism and would disappear with independence. These hopes were often abetted by early Western aid programs that also underestimated the problems of development. In the NAM and United Nations, they were reflected in resolutions calling for abolition of colonialism, disarmament, and redistribution of wealth that, like independence, could come at once, with the stroke of a pen.

Just as the euphoria of independence shaped the NAM, its ebbing in later years led to a more realistic and tactical approach to the movement by second-generation NAM leaders. Bleak economic prospects for most members, fragile political structures, and intractable domestic problems, many the results of arbitrary colonial boundaries, both widened the gulf between North and South and altered perceptions of the NAM as a lobby for the Third World.[10] Also, during this period, the hopes of Third World moderates were often discredited by opponents as new countries chose not to adopt or follow the democratic model. The limitations of independence thus have led in recent years to a more trade unionist approach to the NAM, focused on economic issues, benefits in specialized U.N. bodies, and measurable power in the United Nations itself.

3

Evolution of the NAM

A new force, not a bloc, has been created here and it can play an enormous role both now and in the future. Because this is not just a question of 25 countries. I am certain that in the future there will be another 25 and more. We have not created a third bloc, but rather a collective force which will act through the UN.

Marshal Tito, 1961

Since its inception in 1961, the NAM has passed through three stages of development. The first lasted from Belgrade in 1961 to the Lusaka Summit in 1970, and was a transitional period during which the movement's continued existence was not yet certain. Lusaka took the first steps to set up institutional mechanisms and regularize previously random NAM procedures. It was followed by a period of consolidation and radicalization of the movement that lasted until the Havana Summit in 1979. In this interval, the movement focused increasingly on economic demands, and the Arab and African blocs within it made common cause on decolonization, defining apartheid and Palestinian rights in anti-colonial terms. Starting at Havana, the NAM entered a new period of rivalry for leadership, polarization between radical and moderate members, and questioning of the basic premises of non-alignment. The catalyst was a concerted power bid by Cuba, which marked the transition to a new and untested generation of NAM leaders.

Survival: 1961–1970

The NAM had not jelled at Belgrade in an institutional sense. The atmosphere there of world crisis had fostered a sense of common identity, but left little time for procedural issues. In the absence of further scheduled meetings, continuation of the NAM depended on personal initiative or interest by one of its founders. During the turbulent 1960s, which altered many of the assumptions at Belgrade and tested the movement's very survival, only Tito consistently provided this leadership. As recommended at Belgrade, a specialized economic conference was held in 1962 at Cairo, but, although under NAM auspices, the invitation list of 47 countries was much broader. The meeting was, nevertheless, important in contributing to the formation of UNCTAD in 1964 and was further evidence of early NAM involvement in the economic sphere.

As much as anything, fear of a new and rival Afro-Asian meeting marking the tenth anniversary of Bandung galvanized the non-aligned into a second summit in 1964 at Cairo. A second Bandung would exclude Yugoslavia and include China, and the underlying issue was, therefore, China's relationship to the Third World. The Indochinese War of 1962 gave small states pause, although few of the non-aligned dared to criticize China's invasion and a small mediation meeting at Colombo came to little. India, in any case, was adamantly opposed to any conference involving China, although the humiliation of the war and the discrediting of the Panchsheel had reduced India's impact in the NAM. Nehru's death before the Cairo Summit further undercut Indian influence.

There was also the divisive question of the ambitions of the USSR, by then opposed by China, to join the Bandung group. Strong Chinese pressure and Sukarno's ambition to recapture Indonesia's former role led to scheduling a second Afro-Asian meeting for Algiers in 1965. Against this background, Tito moved expeditiously to promote a second NAM summit, touring Latin America, meeting with Nasser again at Brioni in 1963 and visiting Algiers to gain agreement. A preparatory meeting in Colombo was called to work out the agenda and attendance. The Cairo Summit thus preempted the Afro-Asian conference momentum, and Algerian President Ahmed Ben Bella's ouster in June 1965, and that of Sukarno the following year, ended hopes for a new Bandung.

Unlike Belgrade, both the Cairo Summit and the subsequent Lusaka Summit in 1970 met at moments of relative calm, with few issues of war and peace in the balance. Nasser, a legend in the Third World for his stand on Suez, was at the height of power, dominating the first summit meeting of the Arab League and the second of the OAU at Cairo earlier in 1964. His influence was reflected in the decision to enlarge the second NAM Summit, extending blanket membership to the Arab League and OAU. This nearly doubled attendance to 47 participants and 10 observers. While some African moderates declined to attend, the growth was largely African, with 28 OAU members—60 percent of the Cairo participants, compared to 44 percent at Belgrade.

Following the first UNCTAD meeting at Geneva in 1964, and establishment there of the G-77, the Cairo Summit came at a moment of unusual solidarity in the Third World. Its final declaration refers for the first time to the need for a "new international economics policy," foreshadowing later NAM demands for the NIEO, and calls for NAM solidarity with the G-77. The African majority also pushed hard on decolonization issues, and the Cairo Declaration is considerably harsher toward the West than that of Belgrade. It asserts that "colonized peoples may legitimately resort to arms" and contains multiple references to imperialist and colonialist exploitation. Unlike the Belgrade Declaration, the United States is cited by name, and Cuba succeeded in inserting reference to the alleged colonial status of Puerto Rico.

Yet the 1964 Summit was not without conflict. Tito's opposition to international blocs, and emphasis on use of the United Nations and on peaceful resolution of disputes, were not shared by radicals, led by Sukarno. They continued to promote a new grouping, Afro-Asian in focus and committed to revolutionary tactics outside the United Nations. Tito prevailed on most issues, and the Cairo Declaration, while more radical and twice the length, followed the Belgrade model, further elaborating non-aligned principles of co-existence and settlement of disputes. The Cairo Declaration also shrank from taking positions on sensitive issues affecting NAM members, such as the war in Indochina, the strife between Indonesia and Malaysia, and the fighting in the Horn of Africa.

With less intense pressures than at Belgrade, the delegates once again adjourned without addressing the movement's future beyond an injunction in the declaration to consult together at the United Nations. There seems still to have been only limited perception of the NAM as a permanent body. The summit did pre-empt a new Bandung, but the latter, riven by Sino-Soviet tensions, would probably have collapsed of its own weight. One of its mainstays, Sukarno, perhaps foreseeing his overthrow, kept the lid on at home by including in his 200-man delegation to Cairo every major Indonesian opposition leader.[11] At Cairo, the NAM seemed still to be a movement in search of a role, and the final declaration is largely that of a bystander deploring, for example, failure to completely implement the 1960 General Assembly "Declaration on Granting Independence to Colonial Countries and Peoples" and exhorting Moscow and Washington to disarm.

Cairo was followed by a period of drift and, for many NAM members, frustration with the course of events. While more states and potential recruits to the NAM gained independence, they brought new problems as well. Military coups, particularly in Africa, became commonplace, underscoring the vulnerability of political structures. By the end of the decade, only Tito and Nasser survived among the movement's central figures. Territorial conflicts erupted between NAM members in the Sahara, Southeast Asia, West Africa, and the Horn of Africa. Nigeria was torn by civil war. Colonial unrest continued without prospect of solution in southern Africa, and a white Rhodesian regime unilaterally declared independence in 1965. In the Arab world, crushing defeat by Israel in 1967 compounded existing divisions and bitterness.

Nor were improved East–West relations cause for relief. Coexistence seemed to some of the non-aligned actually to increase prospects for great power entanglement in the Third World.[12] U.S. military action in the Dominican Republic in 1965, continuing great power involvement in the Congo crisis, and, most of all, intensification of the Vietnam War all stood out. Outside the Third World, the Soviet invasion of Czechoslovakia in 1968 received less attention from the non- aligned. As some Indians point out, the Czech people adopted the classic Gandhian tactics of non-violence and passive resistance, yet were brutally put down by the Soviet army without protest from the NAM or India.

During these years, there was little enthusiasm for reactivating the NAM. Tito and Nasser met at New Delhi in 1966 with the new Indian prime minister, Indira Gandhi, but the session was exploratory and lacked the decisiveness of earlier meetings among the three countries. Tito, perhaps with most at stake in the movement's existence, continued to canvass the Middle East, Africa, and Asia during 1968. Hopes to organize NAM mediation efforts on Vietnam and the Middle East were unsuccessful, however, and even Nasser evinced little interest. Soviet pressure to forestall a conference that might condemn the invasion of Czechoslovakia may also have played a role. As before, Tito persisted, however, and eventually secured agreement for a new summit after a consultative meeting at Belgrade in 1969 and ministerial discussions during the General Assembly that year. A preparatory meeting in Dar es Salaam during April 1970 roughed out an agenda and, significantly, provided for a standing committee to handle preparations.

The Lusaka Summit of September 1970 established the NAM on a permanent basis, but was in some respects a non-event. Following six years of relative dormancy within the movement, it commanded an unimpressive turnout. Of 70 countries invited, 54 came, with only 16 at the summit level. Nasser did not attend; Nehru, Nkrumah, and Sukarno were dead or overthrown. In this vacuum Tito and Zambian

President Kenneth Kaunda channeled the meeting toward institutional issues and rededication to principles of non-alignment. The summit occurred with a cease-fire finally in place in the Middle East, troop reductions under way in Vietnam, and no major crisis to confront. The result was a milder, more conservative declaration than any subsequent non-aligned document that the Nicaraguan Foreign Ministry described as "a backward step in relation to the Cairo Summit."[13]

Lusaka also underlined economic concerns with a separate "Declaration on Non-alignment and Economic Progress," and called for "urgent structural changes in the world economy." The summit's major accomplishment, however, was procedural; in his opening speech President Kaunda decried the lack of adequate NAM machinery and called for steps to "ensure continuity in the development of the Non-Aligned Movement and the implementation of our decisions."[14] The result was a two-part resolution calling on Kaunda as chairman to take "necessary steps" to maintain contact among NAM members, ensure continuity, and carry out decisions, and, second, requesting member states to coordinate positions in the United Nations and specialized agencies.

Radicalization

The early 1970s saw an acceleration of Third World diplomatic activity with a series of closely linked NAM and G-77 meetings devoted to economic issues. The developed countries paid only intermittent attention to these deliberations until the OPEC states quadrupled oil prices in late 1973. Yet these early meetings developed the economic package, later known as the NIEO, which the Third World has aggressively promoted ever since.

Algeria, emerging from a period of consolidation and introspection following the 1965 takeover by Colonel Hoari Boumedienne, played a lead role in both the NAM and G-77. A ministerial meeting of the G-77 at Algiers in 1967, attended by UNCTAD Secretary-General Raul Prebisch, roughed out positions on raw materials, manufactured goods, finance, transport, and other elements vital to the Third World. The resulting Algiers Charter gave coherence to the G-77 and a basis for action at the 1968 UNCTAD meeting in New Delhi.[15] Economic demands were further refined at meetings of the G-77 at Lima in 1971, of UNCTAD at Santiago, Chile, in 1972, and of NAM foreign ministers at Georgetown, Guyana, later in 1972. The last of these set up working groups on key economic issues within the movement.

Concentration on economics reflected a gradual radicalization of the Third World in the early 1970s, pushed by economic deterioration and events in southern Africa and the Middle East. Underscoring demands in UNCTAD and the United Nations were acute shortages and spiraling prices throughout the Third World at a time when aid from the developed countries was beginning to taper off. Inflation doubled and tripled food prices while drought cut local production and recession in the developed world choked off markets.

Lack of progress toward independence in Portuguese Africa, Rhodesia, and Namibia, and persistence of apartheid in South Africa coincided with growing tension in the Middle East and renewed war in 1973. The African and Arab blocs soon realized that by making common cause, they could use their superior numbers to influence NAM and U.N. positions. Countries like Algeria and Egypt, belonging to both groups, were instrumental in forging this identity, which placed the NAM as a whole on a more anti-Western course. African states began to cut ties with Israel, and following the 1973 war most severed diplomatic relations.

On the ideological level, Third World reaction to political and economic developments of the 1960s and early 1970s coincided with the rise of the New Left. Rejecting the postwar consensus and complacency of Western ideology, American and European intellectuals of the New Left turned increasingly to the Third World as a model and ideal. Writers like Frantz Fanon, rooted in the experience of the Algerian revolution, had profound influence on leftist political thought in both the Third World and the West. Fanon was joined by Jean Paul Sartre and others in urging a "collective catharis" for colonial peoples through violence against their oppressors. The simultaneous emergence of the New Left in the West and of a sense of group identity, symbolized by the NAM, in the Third World, was mutually reinforcing. European intellectuals turned away from traditional allies in favor of radical elements in the developing world. Even within the Socialist International, the warnings of Senegalese President Léopold Senghor against "those who claim kinship with Marxism-Leninism" were disregarded in the rush to recognize groups like the Polisario or the Popular Movement for the Liberation of Angola (MPLA).

As host for the 1973 Summit, Algeria benefited considerably from these trends and exercised a more aggressive style of leadership than its predecessor. Deeply anti-colonial, endowed with natural resources, and well along the road to a managed state economy, it served as a new model for radical and socialist NAM members. An intensive diplomatic campaign by Algeria resulted in record attendance by 75 countries, with 54 heads of state or government. These were buttressed by attendance of U.N. Secretary-General Kurt Waldheim and observers from "liberation groups" of three continents, including the fledgling Puerto Rican Socialist party.

Houari Boumedienne argued forcefully to shift the focus of non-alignment from peaceful coexistence and traditional principles to militant anti-colonialism and anti-imperialism. For him the basic tension was between rich and poor rather than East and West, and emphasis on the "injustices" of "imperialist and neo-colonialist" economic policy was an integral part of the anti-colonial orientation. Boumedienne further argued that détente among superpowers brought little gain to the Third World. Outnumbered, Tito and others, moderate by NAM standards, chose not to dispute the issue directly. Challenge, however, came from another quarter.

Fidel Castro, attending his first meeting of the NAM, argued that the central division was still between East and West, and for "the closest alliance among all the world's progressive forces." He was reinforced by a supportive message from Soviet Communist party Chairman Leonid Brezhnev, describing the socialist bloc as "natural allies" of the NAM. Castro, in turn, was challenged by a rival revolutionary, Colonel Muammar el-Qaddafi of Libya, who proclaimed his independence of both Moscow and Washington. Reconciliation between the two came only with Castro's sudden announcement of diplomatic rupture with Israel.

Nevertheless, the final declaration eschewed Castro's formulation and made critical reference to "hegemony," a shorthand for the USSR. It was thus a clear-cut victory for Boumedienne, upholding the primacy of decolonization over traditional NAM principles and identifying the existing economic order as a legacy of colonialism. World financial institutions were seen as a vehicle for recolonization of the Third World by industrialized countries. The process of zeroing in on economic demands begun at Lusaka was made explicit in a separate economic declaration, an action program, and six economic resolutions. Each reflected virtual unanimity among NAM members and foreshadowed a new role for the movement in articulating demands of the poor against the rich.

The corollary of this orientation was a more strident anti-Westernism, reinforced by Arab and African grievances. The Algiers Declaration and resolutions specifically condemned U.S. policies in South Africa, the Middle East, Angola, Vietnam, Cambodia, Cuba, Panama, and Puerto Rico, labeling the latter "one of the main enclaves of colonialism in Latin America."[16] In a rhetorical declaration of war, the final document asserted:

> ...faced with the obstinacy of the colonial powers and the complicity of their protectors, in particular some states members of NATO, namely the US, France, the UK and Germany, the oppressed people have no alternative but legitimate recourse to armed struggle....

Boumedienne emerged from the September 1973 Summit with a mandate to lead the NAM for three years, until the next summit. The meeting had increased the chairman's power by endorsing and broadening the role of the earlier preparatory committee, which now functioned as the 17-member Non-Aligned Coordinating Bureau (NACB). It also called for a continuing coalition with the G-77, describing the NAM as a "catalytic force in the G-77." As an influential member of both groups, it was inevitable that Algeria would use the NAM chairmanship to reinforce their common focus. Collaboration between the two thus became extremely close in these years, and responsibility for Third World economic policy was blurred. Boumedienne, for example, proposed the controversial 1974 sixth special session of the General Assembly in his capacity as "current president of the group of non-aligned countries."

Dialogue on economic reform, until then met with resistant and desultory Western participation, took on a new dynamic in late 1973. The fourth Arab-Israeli war in October was followed by an oil embargo against developed countries considered supporters of Israel, and in December by an OPEC decision to quadruple oil prices. For the first time, vital interests of the developed countries, geared to low-cost imported oil, were at stake. Diplomatic activity was intense, and catapulted the NAM and G-77 into new prominence. The NACB met in March 1974 to coordinate non-aligned strategy for the special session that opened in April, chaired by General Assembly President Bouteflika of Algeria. The special session adopted without a vote, but with reservations by the United States and other developed countries, a "program of action for establishment of a New International Economic Order" based directly on the economic platform of the Algiers Summit. The subsequent regular session of the General Assembly pushed through, by a lopsided vote of 120–6 (including the United States and five European allies), the controversial Charter of Economic Rights and Duties of States (CERDS), described by critics as conferring rights on developing countries and duties on the developed world.

Under Algerian direction, coordination of non-aligned economic strategy became the rule during 1975 at a special session on raw materials in Dakar and at further meetings of the NACB in Havana and of the NAM foreign ministers in Lima. Bloc positions increasingly characterized Third World bargaining at a seventh General Assembly special session in 1975, UNCTAD in 1976, and, in 1976–77, the Paris Conference on International Economic Cooperation (CIEC), where a representative group of 19 spoke for the G-77 and NAM.

The Algiers Summit thus marked the beginning of the NAM as a voting bloc within the United Nations and international agencies, subject to growing pressure on its members to conform to non-aligned positions in their voting patterns. U.S. diplomats, lobbying among Third World delegations for support on key votes during the 1973 General Assembly session, were for the first time rebuffed with the explanation that states could not vote against consensus positions reached at Algiers. A radical history of the movement, issued by Nicaragua in 1983, also pinpoints the Algiers Summit as the beginning of "an anti-Western and anti-imperialist majority in the UN."[17]

While some strains were evident, the tandem approach of the NAM and G-77 to economic issues crystallized during Algeria's chairmanship. The larger G-77, which met less frequently than the NAM and at lower levels, became an implementing and negotiating body, recognized within the United Nations and assisted by international civil servants at UNCTAD headquarters in Geneva. The NAM, by contrast, met every three years at the summit level, taking decisions on policy issues beyond the purview of G-77 experts. The Algiers Summit, for example, provided the NIEO framework within which the G-77 conducted specific negotiations. Strains were caused by G-77 members like Pakistan and the Latin American group, not then party to the NAM, who saw it as a rival organization. Pakistani Prime Minister Zulfikar Ali Bhutto charged in 1976 that the NAM was an "exclusive club" tending to "splinter the collective strength of the Third World."[18] Yet calls for a broader conference of developing countries were rejected by the NAM majority. Similarly, the contrast between apparent G-77 harmony and NAM disarray was deceptive, given uniform Third World positions on most economic matters and broader NAM responsibility for more contentious political issues.

Use of the oil weapon was initially applauded by the NAM and seen as new leverage in bargaining with the industrialized North. Algeria, as an oil producer and host of the 1975 OPEC Summit, reinforced this view. Yet it was clearly a two-edged sword. The least-developed majority of the NAM suffered most from the new prices, and subsidies from oil-producing members proved uneven and inadequate. Non-aligned rhetoric, however, continued to blame the colonial legacy and "neocolonialism" of industrialized countries and transnational corporations for economic deterioration largely due to oil prices. Yet in private there were doubts, muted in hopes of Arab oil subsidies and in order to present an appearance of Third World unity in negotiations with the North. The cleavage between oil-rich and other NAM members remained a latent and potentially explosive element in an already heterogeneous movement.

Chairmanship of the NAM passed to Sri Lanka at the 1976 Colombo Summit. Coming after a period of intense activity, Colombo was not a major summit and broke little new ground, reiterating positions taken at Algiers and continuing the trend toward radicalism and the priority of economic reform and decolonization. Eighty-five countries attended, but only 41 with heads of state or government. The meeting avoided questions of oil, and no major crises dominated its proceedings. Localized issues, such as an acrimonious dispute between Algeria and Morocco, were divisive, but the final declaration preserved a facade of unity by papering over or striking from the record issues on which consensus could not be reached.

Corridor disputes at Colombo pitted radicals like Iraq, Cuba, North Korea, and Libya, seeking to blame the United States on most issues, against India, Indonesia, Yugoslavia, and Sri Lanka, which feared that intemperate declarations could damage Third World bargaining positions in negotiations then in progress. The result was a standoff in which the radical consensus prevailed, but many members later expressed reservations. The final declaration, for example, equated Zionism and racism and, in the aftermath of the Israeli commando raid at Entebbe, Uganda, condemned "racist and hostile collusion between South Africa and Israel."

Following his controversial appearance at Algiers, Castro did not attend Colombo, instructing his foreign minister to lobby quietly for the next summit to be held in Havana. Approval of this (and consequent Cuban chairmanship of the movement) was, in retrospect, the major decision of Colombo. The summit also expanded the NACB to 25 members, balanced roughly between pro-Cuban radicals and moderates, thus ensuring further acrimony during preparations for Havana.

The Challenge of Havana

Cuba's impending leadership caused a period of intense jockeying between radicals eager to reorient the movement and more moderate members seeking to blunt Castro's influence and reassert traditional NAM principles. The ideological battle over definitions of non-alignment, carried on between Cuba and Yugoslavia at a series of preparatory meetings before the Havana Summit, was in reality a power struggle for control of the movement. Cuban intentions, while muted because of efforts by adversaries to postpone or cancel the summit, were evident at an NACB meeting at Havana in May 1978. In its aftermath Yugoslavia intensified its campaign, and speeches by Tito and Foreign Secretary Vrhovec decried efforts to "reorient" the NAM as a "natural ally" of the socialist bloc. Castro countered by blasting "theoreticians" who questioned Cuba's non-aligned credentials and advocated "passive neutrality."

Debate sharpened at a July 1978 meeting of NAM foreign ministers in Belgrade that Tito had contrived to host in an effort to use his considerable prestige to limit Castro's room to maneuver. His opening speech argued that the NAM should be "anti-bloc" and confront "hegemony" as well as imperialism and neocolonialism. It also contained a thinly veiled attack on Soviet and Cuban involvement in Africa. The latter sparked heated debate. Cuba's military presence in Angola since 1975 had been overlooked by the NAM, and even praised during the Colombo Summit as a response to repeated South African attacks across the border. Deployment of combat troops to Ethiopia, in obvious coordination with Moscow, was a different matter, involving conflict between two NAM members. At Belgrade, Egypt, Somalia, and others therefore challenged Cuba's forthcoming presidency, and even its membership in the NAM, but were outnumbered and unable to prevail. In the end, Somalia, Saudi Arabia, Kampuchea, and Zaire entered reservations on holding the Sixth Summit in Havana.

After much wrangling, Havana was confirmed as the 1979 summit site, but moderates prevailed in cataloging previous NAM principles in the final Belgrade Declaration. The latter also criticized for the first time "developed socialist" (that is, Communist) countries for providing less than .1 percent of their GNP for development assistance. As it turned out, most of these gestures toward balance between East and West were abandoned at Havana, but at the time moderates hoped thereby to limit Cuba's latitude in drafting the next summit declaration.

A final pre-summit meeting of the NACB was held at Colombo in June 1979, but by then most members were reconciled to Cuba's new role, and threats to boycott Havana were transparent. Cuba and Yugoslavia appeared to have reached a tacit modus vivendi whereby Havana would downplay the "natural ally" thesis in return for Yugoslav acceptance of its leadership. Rancorous issues of Egyptian membership in the NAM following Camp David and which, if any, Kampuchean delegation to seat were bucked to the summit. Colombo did, however, stake out tough, anti-Western positions that played into Cuba's hands in preparing for the summit.

Much has been written of the Havana Summit, and critics maintain that the NAM has since been in a period of relative obscurity. Yet world attention to Havana was heightened by factors outside the movement itself: by Castro's zeal to publicize his installation as chairman through invitations to 1,000 foreign journalists and by the fascination of U.S. media with Havana and bilateral U.S.-Cuban relations. The fact of Cuba's presidency also forced Washington to take stock of the movement's recent history. Leadership of the major Third World political grouping by an avowed Communist cast doubt on dictionary definitions of non-alignment, as well as the Carter administration's commitment to improved relations with developing countries. Cuba could ill afford the estimated $140 million conference costs, and many pointed to Soviet sponsorship in the form of massive sugar subsidies and other aid. Castro's vitriolic anti-Americanism and military campaigns in Africa further riveted attention on Havana.

The crossroads of the NAM at Havana was evident from the opening speeches. Castro, dressed in fatigues and jabbing the air for emphasis, ran through a litany of anti-imperialist and anti-colonial themes. Tito, aged 87 and seated, followed with a restrained speech emphasizing "authentic principles and objectives" of non-alignment. The generation gap was evident to all, and fostered an impression of Cuban activism and control. Yet, in the elaborate bargaining that followed, Castro's home-court advantage was by no means decisive, and the final declaration and annexes, running to several hundred pages, reflect many trade-offs. Tito and others left Havana convinced they had blunted Cuba's takeover and preserved the NAM, while Castro and his allies saw it as a successful first step toward realigning the movement. Like so many conferences of the NAM, there was ample room for both sides to claim victory.

By September 3–9, 1979, NAM membership stood at 95, with an additional 15 countries present as observers or guests. Cuba exploited this amorphous grouping by tightly controlling the conference proceedings. Iraq and Mozambique were installed as chairmen of the key Political and Economic committees, adding to the radical orientation of the drafting process. Speeches by leaders opposed to Castro were scheduled for evening hours when halls were empty, galleries were packed to applaud pro-Cuban speeches and deride others, and key conference documents were distributed to Cuban allies only. The draft declaration circulated by Cuba in July was Marxist and doctrinaire, surprising moderates lulled by Cuban flexibility at the Colombo meeting. Nor were other delegations' objections incorporated in a second draft issued at the meeting's start.

These heavy-handed tactics caught moderates off guard, with limited time to negotiate amendments to a massive and radical draft. In subsequent bargaining, Cuba yielded gradually on issues of non-aligned theory, taking full credit for its "flexibility" and spirit of compromise. References to alliance with the Soviet bloc were deleted, and the final document warned of dangers in "hegemony and domination." The retreat was pragmatic, since only Afghanistan, North Korea, Benin, Mozambique, Vietnam, Laos, Congo, Madagascar, Grenada, Seychelles, and Ethiopia appeared to endorse the "natural ally" thesis. It was also tactical, since preoccupation with ideology by countries like Yugoslavia and India allowed Cuba to push through tough, anti-Western criticism on almost all Third World political and economic issues.

Two political issues divided the summit: continued Egyptian membership, in light of Camp David, and recognition of a Kampuchean delegation. Pressed by Arab radicals, Cuba engineered a dubious late-night consensus placing Egypt on 18 months' probation and harshly condemning the peace treaty. President Anwar Sadat's absence from Havana and concurrent talks with Prime Minister Menachem Begin in Israel, as well as the intimidating atmosphere of Havana, probably cut into strong African support for Egypt. Vietnamese occupation, with Soviet backing, of Kampuchea posed the issue of NAM distance from the Soviet bloc. Castro gave royal treatment to Communist-backed Heng Samrin on an official visit to Cuba, while billeting representatives of Pol Pot 20 miles from Havana. Using the power of the chair, Cuba ultimately pushed through a decision to leave the Kampuchean seat empty, over strong objections from the Asian delegations.

The Havana Summit, whose debates ran an extra two days (including all-night sessions), left a residue of resentment. Both Castro and NAM moderates stopped short of splitting the movement by either insistence on alliance with the Soviet bloc or introduction of a rival draft. Potential division between OPEC and impoverished members was also headed off by blaming oil price increases on inflation in developed countries and relegating energy to the North–South dialogue. Yet many delegates felt the results were not representative and entered reservations, which Havana delayed publishing until long afterward. John Graham, a U.S. Foreign Service officer covering the summit, wrote that on major issues the "Cubans used their power of the chair to engineer results which did not represent a true consensus." He concluded that "If in the end the East was not explicitly defined as an ally in the NAM Havana Declaration, the West was certainly defined more clearly than ever before as the adversary."[19] Castro underscored the point in his subsequent address to the General Assembly: "The non-aligned countries know full well who our historic enemies are, where the threats come from and how we should combat them."

Havana was a high-water mark for non-aligned condemnation of U.S. policies, excoriating American policy in the Middle East and southern Africa, repeatedly equating Zionism and racism, and calling for Puerto Rican independence. To secure this outcome, however, Castro had to accept a number of setbacks, including failure to seat the Heng Samrin delegation, repudiation of the "natural ally" thesis, total revision by Algeria of the Economic Declaration, enlargement of the NACB to reduce the chairman's power, and insertion of non-aligned principles and a charter on NAM procedures.

Once away from Havana, consensus reached under Cuban pressure began to crumble. Burma, which declared during the summit that NAM principles are "not recognizable anymore" and "are dying," made good its threat to resign.[20] Within a month of the summit, most NAM members voted at the United Nations to accept the credentials of the Pol Pot delegation, reversing the Havana formula. A summit endorsement of Havana as site for the next UNCTAD meeting was quietly ignored. A Cuban draft declaration for the NAM ministerial meeting in New York was emasculated from 26 to 6 non-controversial paragraphs. While Castro's speech to the General Assembly was well applauded, he focused on economics, skirting divisive political issues and calling for a fund of $300 billion for development. Most damaging, Cuba's campaign, based on NAM leadership, to gain the Latin American vacancy on the Security Council stalled against Colombia. After an unprecedented 157 ballots, Mexico emerged as a compromise choice.

Resentment of Cuba's muscular presidency would probably have subsided but for the Soviet invasion of Afghanistan in December 1979. The latter exposed Cuba's dependence on Moscow, temporarily paralyzed the movement and ended Cuba's chances for a Security Council seat. At issue for the first time was the occupation of a NAM member state by one of the superpowers. Unwilling to break with Moscow, Cuba blocked calls for a special NAM meeting on the invasion, and Castro eventually endorsed the Soviet move before the Communist party Congress in Havana. The majority of the NAM, however, condemned the occupation and supported General Assembly calls for withdrawal of foreign troops by margins of 104–18 in 1979, 111–22 in 1980, 116–23 in 1981, and 114–21 in 1982. Only the Soviet bloc and a dozen NAM radicals, led by Cuba, voted against these resolutions. In the longer run, Afghanistan vitiated a Cuban leadership role comparable to that of Algeria in 1973–76 and eroded the movement's ability to deal with other subjects. Iranian pressure for condemnation of the abortive U.S. raid to rescue the hostages was, for example, resisted on grounds that such debate would resurrect the Afghan issue. Even the NACB waived its monthly meetings in New York during early 1980 because of paralysis over Afghanistan.

The next ministerial meeting, moved up to February 1981 in New Delhi to avoid a second meeting in Havana, aired the movement's continuing divisions on more neutral ground. Havana was still a fresh memory for most delegates, and moderates were determined not to be caught off balance again. A group of about 20 "like-minded" delegations banded together to offset Cuban leadership and Nicaragua's chairmanship of the Political Committee. The result was a more balanced declaration that ended Egypt's probation and called for troop withdrawals from both Afghanistan and Kampuchea. It nevertheless contained harsh criticism of the United States on the Middle East and Puerto Rico. Meeting in the aftermath of Tito's death on May 4, 1980, and of adverse reactions to Cuba's leadership, India, Yugoslavia, Sri Lanka, and others sought to reassert the relevance and even the continued existence of the NAM. Cuba was clearly forced to take a lower profile, focusing primarily on Latin American issues.

The 1981 meeting in New Delhi both neutralized Cuba's leadership and reaffirmed most members' commitment to the movement's survival. Yet in the two years that followed, the NAM remained in a period of transition and apparent drift. In addition to Afghanistan, the spectacle of prolonged and costly warfare between two members, Iran and Iraq, added to the malaise. Repeated NAM mediation missions to Baghdad and Teheran lacked the authority and leadership to succeed, and the movement was paralyzed by the impending presidency of Iraq, decided during the Havana Summit (before the Iraqi invasion of Iran in September 1980).

Corridor discussions intensified as the invasion turned to military stalemate and the summit, scheduled for Baghdad in early September 1982, approached. Few members wished to antagonize Iraq by openly calling for a change of venue or to extend Cuba's unpopular presidency by default. Decisive action was therefore postponed, in hopes that the military situation would improve, and meetings of the NACB held in Kuwait, Havana, and Nicosia, Cyprus, between April and July 1982 failed to resolve the issue. In the interim, Iraq proceeded with elaborate summit preparations, including construction estimated at over $1 billion and three versions of a draft declaration for the summit.

Iran's counter-invasion of Iraq on July 13, 1982, put new pressure on the summit, however, and was followed by an air strike on Baghdad and a serious bombing at the Iraqi Ministry of Planning. With the planned September 6–10 Summit reaching a point of no return, Castro on August 3 took advantage of members' concern with security to call for a ministerial meeting at Havana in order to set another time and place for the Seventh Summit. By then, there was an emerging consensus that the summit could not be held in Baghdad without danger to participants and damage to NAM prestige from a poorly attended meeting dominated by security concerns. Iran, with backing from Cuba, Libya, and (indirectly) the Soviets, had always vehemently opposed Baghdad as a venue. NAM moderates like Yugoslavia and Bangladesh also became convinced that a summit there would irreparably harm the movement. Furthermore, the unexplained shooting down over Iran of the plane carrying Algerian Foreign Minister Muhammad Ben-yahia on May 3, 1982 remained a warning to others.

Cuba's bid to host a new ministerial meeting was not accepted, but Castro's intervention effectively foreclosed the Baghdad Summit. Rather than sacrifice further prestige by insistence on going through with it, Iraq's beleagered President Saddam Hussein relinquished the chairmanship to India in hopes of salvaging the Eighth Summit for Baghdad in 1986. He also proposed a ministerial meeting in Baghdad to formalize the arrangement, but through a compromise formula of Zambian President Kenneth Kaunda, India's selection was routinely endorsed at the annual pre-General Assembly meeting of non-aligned foreign ministers in New York on October 4–9. Significantly, the New York meeting left open the issue of the 1986 presidency, and Libya, North Korea, and Syria reaffirmed their rival candidacies. In the process, Castro obtained by default a six-month extension of Cuba's term, albeit at the cost of damaged relations with Iraq and a rebuff to his proposal for a ministerial meeting.

India, already one of several candidates for the presidency following Iraq, thus obtained the office three years earlier by virtue of the Iran-Iraq war. While its selection, essentially through a private deal with Iraq, was irregular even by NAM standards, most members were relieved by its willingness to step in on short notice and by the prospect of a founding member and major NAM power as president. Temporary extension of Cuba's tenure, already neutralized by widespread general resentment and the active opposition of moderate activists, seemed to many a small price to pay for a return under India to more traditional leadership by the movement's centrist faction. To be sure, the added six months of Cuban control extended the period of doubt and indecision that had beset the movement since 1980. Yet in the period prior to the March 1983 Summit in New Delhi, most members seemed confident that strong leadership by India could restore the prestige and credibility of the movement, badly eroded during the Cuban years.

4
Internal Dynamics

The bloc's unity—particularly the unity of the big blocs, and to a certain extent the smaller blocs, too—is bought, in many cases, at the price of the groups' acquiescence in the most extreme demands of the most extreme members.

Ambassador Jeane J. Kirkpatrick

Triennial summit meetings with elaborate conference documentation form the official record of the NAM. Final declarations offer a static picture every three years of the movement's position on a range of world issues that can be compared with those of previous summits. Yet these are often more significant for their omissions than for agreed positions and are affected by internal pressures inevitable in a movement of 101 diverse members. In the context of rivalries for leadership of the movement and competing regional interests, individual phrases and ideological principles, as at the United Nations, are invested with peculiar significance. Repetition, for example, of NAM dedication to peaceful coexistence or resolution of disputes often masks inability to agree upon more specific issues. Even decisions on operational matters such as the functions of the NACB or the unresolved issue of a permanent secretariat tend to be influenced as much by power rivalries as by substantive considerations.

Nor is the frenetic atmosphere of a NAM summit meeting conducive to reflection or balanced judgment. As the movement's membership has quadrupled between Belgrade and New Delhi, so have the range and complexity of issues facing the NAM. At Belgrade, 25 relatively homogeneous delegations were barely able to reach common positions on a limited, but weighty, list of issues. Today, the varied interests of over 100 members require that virtually all international issues, from parochial to global, be considered. Malta's dispute with Libya over the continental shelf, Madagascar's claims to the Isles Glorieuses, and those of the Comoros to Mayotte share space with Kampuchea and Afghanistan. In the process, summit documentation has proliferated from nine pages at Belgrade to well over 100 at recent summits. The absence of voting procedures in the NAM further requires that all delegations be heard, leading to endless speeches to establish consensus on controversial issues.

Given these pressures, it is inevitable that decision-making during a one-week summit is affected both by the conference momentum and by the movement's internal dynamics. Consider, for example, the probable chaos if the U.S. Congress were required, within one week, to formulate and endorse written positions on all international issues. In the NAM, the problem is further compounded by differences of language, national interest, and political outlook. Nor is non-aligned business the only focus of a summit, which offers an unparalleled opportunity for heads of state to consult privately on bilateral or regional concerns. As at the United Nations, much of the business is handled in corridors and on the margins of the formal proceedings. The latter, under pressure of proliferating agendas, are conducted at non-stop plenary and committee meetings striving for agreement on a final declaration within the conference deadline. Far from standing back to gain perspective on world events, meetings have become "more a drafting exercise than a deliberative process."[21] In recent years, all-night sessions and even carry-overs of several days have become commonplace, and NAM wags suggest the dove be replaced by the owl as symbol of the movement. An extract from *The Hindustan Times* of March 11, 1983, captures the frenetic atmosphere in the closing days of a summit meeting:

> The political committee, which was racing against time, could not reach a consensus on steps to end the Iran-Iraq conflict till after midnight. The committee will continue the debate on the Iran-Iraq question through out [*sic*] the night to be able to present the final draft to the plenary tomorrow.

On the surface, the movement's lack of modern conference procedures and the tumult of summit meetings would seem to result in arbitrary decision-making. Certainly the pressure of other issues and the timing of consideration of a question often determine the scrutiny it receives. At the same time, the movement's unwieldy size and the volume of conference work have forced regional groups within the NAM, as well as the NACB, to take the initiative. A position endorsed by a regional group, such as the dominant African bloc, will usually be accepted without challenge and with a minimum of debate, thus reducing the conference work load.

Conversely, issues involving areas without an effective regional group, such as Asia, and inter-regional disputes require extensive debate. Issues in the latter category, such as Egypt's NAM membership following Camp David, often upstage others of more global significance. The workings of the regional groups and the NACB, neither envisaged by the movement's founders, have thus become central to it.

Consensus and Reservations

The idea of consensus, rather than actual voting, is at once vital to the movement's identity and at the root of its organizational problems. It both provides a facade of Third World unity and prevents precise agreement on non-aligned positions. It originated in the earlier club-like conception of the NAM as a loose grouping of 25 like-minded states meeting to talk through problems of mutual interest. Voting was neither necessary nor consistent with the Belgrade group's stated intent to avoid becoming a new bloc. As the movement grew in later years to encompass new members of diametrically opposed political persuasion, retention of the consensus procedure became necessary to maintain a semblance of unity and ensure the movement's survival. Voting on an increasing number of issues ranging from Afghanistan to Puerto Rico would starkly divide the NAM, undercutting the tacit assumption of common values and interests. Votes in other cases would isolate individual members, calling into question their continued participation. Although proposed by Iraq at Colombo and by some Association of South East Asian Nations (ASEAN) states at Havana, voting has, therefore, never been adopted as a procedure in the NAM.

Acceptance of a consensus, however, is less binding and allows members to compromise in the interests of NAM unity without being accountable, through a recorded vote, either to domestic constituencies or to third parties. Efforts by the United States and others to hold individual members responsible for collective NAM positions thus have usually been unsuccessful. In fact, refuge in consensus often allows militarily or economically weak members to resist pressures from outside states. On the negative side, non-binding positions, sometimes repudiated at the United Nations, as in the aftermath of Havana, detract from the seriousness with which the movement is regarded by outsiders and many of its own members.

To be sure, a political body of 100 states is almost by definition burdened with rhetoric. The United Nations, with carefully established voting procedures, is itself a prisoner of interminable speeches and explanations of vote, for the most part rhetorical and repetitious. In both the United Nations and NAM, domestic audiences influence the length and content of plenary speeches, which often hold scant interest for other delegations. Particularly among smaller NAM states, for which membership confers prestige and international stature, the temptation to be heard on equal terms with fellow heads of state is almost irresistible. Yet the requirements imposed by the consensus rule that the chairman interpret members' positions on all issues by means of open debate multiplies the time devoted to speeches. A divisive issue, one of 100 on the agenda, may require 30 or more separate speeches before relative alignments are clear.

Nor is there total agreement on what constitutes consensus. Cuba, Vietnam, and other radical members support the view taken at a preparatory meeting in Kabul, Afghanistan, during 1973 that it is merely a convergence of views. This, of course, gives maximum leverage to a strong chairman like Cuba, supported by a small, but disciplined, cadre. Other Latin Americans have tended to favor unanimity as a basis for consensus. Similarly, some Asian members advocate unlimited debate until all members with reservations agree not to openly oppose the consensus.

The question of reservations is equally troubling and the reverse of consensus. As issues and membership have multiplied, a significant number of states, beginning at the Colombo Summit, have disassociated from specific sections of summit declarations. Morocco, for example, may have reservations on Algerian-backed language on the Sahara, or Egypt on condemnations of Camp David. Some members have even entered general reservations on summit declarations or on unspecified elements "not consistent with national foreign policies." The impact of reservations remains in dispute, however. During its presidency, Cuba maintained that they had no effect on consensus and could be disregarded, inserting in an annex to the Havana Declaration a statement that "It is also generally agreed that reservations cannot block or veto a consensus." Yugoslovia, committed as ever to unity of the movement, argued that decisions taken with many reservations were discredited and without weight.

Conference hosts, whose prestige rests to some degree on successful mediation, tend to delay publication of reservations until their impact is lessened. Thus, 38 reservations on the Puerto Rican and Middle Eastern sections of the February 1981 New Delhi Declaration were withheld for six months. In practical terms, the existence of reservations is little more than a reminder that NAM consensus is non-binding and unenforceable. The procedure allows members to smooth relations with non-member states by claiming to disassociate from specific positions. In overall terms, however, the sharp increase of members entering reservations is an indication of the complex issues facing the movement today. While only a few did so at earlier meetings, 38 states recorded reservations at the Colombo Summit, 40 at Havana, 36 at New Delhi in 1981, 30 at Managua in 1983 and 43 at the 1983 Summit.

Membership

In the absence of a charter or written rules of procedure, the criteria for membership and their interpretation over the years have helped to shape the movement's identity and self-image. These criteria, while relatively specific, have been interpreted flexibly in the interest of enhanced prestige and an expanded membership. The result has been an uneven and somewhat random geographic distribution. In the Arab world and Africa, all but Israel and South Africa belong. Asia also is well represented, with the exception of Japan, China, South Korea, Taiwan, the Philippines, Thailand, Burma, the ANZUS (Australia, New Zealand, United States) members, and a half-dozen Pacific mini-states. In Latin America, however, only 17 of 32 states belong, and there are only 3 European members. The quadrupling of membership and selective application of the original criteria explain in large part the movement's transformation into the amorphous grouping that it is today.

Criteria for NAM membership were drawn up at Cairo in June 1961, at a meeting of ambassadors from 19 countries to prepare for the Belgrade Summit. From the outset, opinion was divided between countries like India, which favored an open-ended, broad membership, and others, like Yugoslavia, that supported a closely knit, restrictive group. To a large degree, presence at the Cairo gathering pre-empted the invitation list for Belgrade and, of many states considered, only an additional six were eventually seated at Belgrade. Jansen writes of the selection that "since eliminations were out of the question, and only additions could be considered, the process gave an unfortunate impression of first-class neutralists picking fastidiously from among second-class neutralists."[22]

The five criteria devised at Cairo have, nevertheless, remained the only guidelines for membership in the movement, and were reaffirmed by both the Havana and New Delhi summits. They require the following:

1. An independent policy based on peaceful co-existence and non-alignment, or disposition toward such a policy

2. Support for national liberation movements

3. Non-membership in multilateral military alliances related to great power conflicts

4. Non-membership in bilateral or regional defense pacts related to great power conflicts

5. Non-acceptance of foreign military bases in the context of great power conflicts.

Rigid application of these criteria would exclude even some of the NAM founders; M.S. Rajan estimates that one-sixth of the Belgrade participants and one-third of those at the Cairo and Lusaka summits had military links with a great power.[23] Yet, strict construction has not been the rule, and the criteria themselves are deliberately ambiguous. Rajan questions, for example, whether economically and militarily dependent new states can be expected to follow an independent and non-aligned policy.[24] On the other hand, what state could not in some form be said to have a "disposition" toward such a policy? Support for liberation movements, whether material or merely moral, also became blurred as competing groups proliferated in the 1960s. Nor were members prepared to recognize all liberation movements such as the National Union for the Total Independence of Angola (UNITA) and the Revolutionary Front for the Independence of East Timor (FRETILIN) in Indonesia. Ultimately, the NAM was forced to accept the recommendations of regional organizations on which to support. To date, only the Palestine Liberation Organization, (PLO), the South-West Africa People's Organization (SWAPO), and, for a brief period before the independence of Zimbabwe, the Patriotic Front have been accorded full membership. In the military sphere, multilateral pacts have been generally interpreted to mean the North Atlantic Treaty Organization (NATO), the Central Treaty Organization (CENTO), the South East Asia Treaty Organization (SEATO), ANZUS, and the Warsaw Pact, but others, such as the 1947 Rio Pact, have been selectively invoked. Even less clear has been the distinction between bilateral pacts and military assistance or mutual defense agreements. Finally, foreign bases can be dismissed as mere facilities or port and landing rights, or as contrary to the policies of subsequent governments not signatory to base agreements.

In practice, membership procedures resemble those of an expanding club. The five criteria remain on the books, and may be selectively invoked against applicants deemed politically unacceptable, but are in most cases interpreted loosely to ensure growth. While attendance at Belgrade reflected a compromise between advocates of inclusive and exclusive groupings, the former clearly triumphed three years later at Cairo, with blanket invitations to Organization of African Unity (OAU) and Arab League members. In the process, growth per se became a goal, and the success of summits came to depend on the number and level of delegations attending. The five criteria, while still defining the ideal member, gradually assumed a largely negative function despite periodic calls from various factions for ideological purity.

India, by citing Pakistan's participation in CENTO and SEATO, was able to postpone its admission until 1979, when, with both pacts defunct, no grounds for refusal existed. At Colombo in 1976, applications of both Pakistan and Romania were considered. Both were denied for practical political considerations of Indian opposition to Pakistan and unwillingness to antagonize Moscow by admission of Romania. Similarly, Cuba, as the only Latin American founding member, became an arbiter for regional candidates and blocked Bolivia until 1979. Havana's role as "keeper of the gate" probably discouraged applications throughout the 1970s from Brazil, Mexico, and Venezuela, although these states monitored NAM proceedings closely as observers.

North Korea, by virtue of its seat on the NACB, which recommends on membership, has in effect had a veto over South Korea. Both Koreas applied for membership at the 1975 Lima ministerial meeting, but only North Korea was accepted. Recalling South Korean support for the United States in Vietnam, Hanoi's foreign minister, Madame Binh, stated flatly that Vietnam would withdraw if Seoul were admitted. U.S. bases in South Korea and the Philippines would, in any case, be cited as obstacles were these countries to apply, despite the fact of comparable Soviet bases in NAM states such as Vietnam, South Yemen, and Ethiopia, and Soviet occupation of Afghanistan. Opposition by individual members cannot, however, exclude applicants with organized support, and a walkout by Indonesia, Malaysia, and Laos during a 1972 ministerial meeting in Guyana could not block admission of Vietnam and Cambodia.

Only NATO and Warsaw Pact members have not been admitted, and here, too, the distinction is shaded by acceptance of Portugal and Romania as "official guests," a category in theory subject to looser application of the criteria. Foreign bases or facilities at one time or another in countries such as Cyprus (United Kingdom), Malta (United

Kingdom), Libya (United States), Vietnam (United States and USSR), Cuba (United States and USSR), Somalia (USSR and United States), and Ethiopia (United States and USSR) have been no drawback to membership in good standing. In the last two cases, the superpowers even reversed position, with Somalia offering the United States use of former Soviet naval facilities at Berbera and Ethiopia replacing an American communications site at Asmara with a Soviet naval base in the Dahlak Islands. Similarly, "treaties of friendship and cooperation" involving provision for military coordination with Moscow did not affect the status of NAM founders India and Egypt. Parallel Soviet treaties, some later abrogated, were signed with Somalia, Angola, Mozambique, South Yemen, Iraq, Syria, North Korea, Afghanistan, Libya, Ethiopia, São Tomé and Príncipe, Vietnam, and Cuba. The latter two are in addition full members of the Council for Mutual Economic Assistance (COMECON), and the Kabul regime is, of course, dependent on 105,000 resident Soviet troops.

The end result of sacrificing membership standards for an enlarged body has been twofold. The obvious contradictions in its composition have undercut the movement's sense of purpose and claimed moral authority. Commenting on "dilution of the membership criteria in favor of partial objectives of non-alignment," Sushil Kumar and others have noted that "the need to cover up the contradictions has given non-alignment a greater outward orientation and this to an extent has led to a more intensified anti-imperialist exegesis...."[25] Determination to influence superpower behavior by example and persuasion, perhaps never realistic, has given way to more conventional lobbying tactics. Defensiveness over internal divisions has skewed the group's agenda, within the NAM and United Nations, away from controversy and toward issues where there is demonstrable unity. The second effect has been procedural. Quadrupling the organization's size has shattered the club-like structure set up by Tito, Nasser, and Nehru, and hastened reliance on regional groupings and the NACB.

Regional and Other Subgroups

Cleavages within the NAM, like any large political institution, go in several directions. Subgroups tend to be formed around ideology, specific interests, and region. All function as lobbies to maximize their strength in the overall body and to offset competing factions, but the regional groups have the additional, and more important, role of carrying much of the non-aligned work load. By contrast, ideological and interest-oriented factions exist on a more ad hoc basis. The regional groups are well entrenched in the movement, and their relative strength, degree of unanimity, and relations with each other fundamentally affect the larger body and the outcome of summit meetings. Their importance is evident in a proposal by Sri Lankan Foreign Minister Shahul Hameed that the NAM chairman be backstopped by four regional chairmen who hold regular, separate meetings.[26]

Ideological differences have always existed between issue-oriented "pragmatists" and "traditionalists" committed to NAM principles. Cuba's chairmanship and the emergence of a small, but organized, pro-Soviet minority altered this equation. Havana's move to realign the movement with Moscow forced moderates to organize in self-defense, and this cleavage will beset NAM conferences well into India's presidency and beyond, until the movement turns to other issues. While few in number, hard-core radicals led by Cuba coordinate closely before NAM meetings and arrive with a strategy to seize control of key conference committees and divide responsibility for specific issues. Thus, at New Delhi in February 1981, Angola, for example, castigated France over remote Mayotte Island, and Cape Verde blasted Indonesia on East Timor, leaving Cuba, Ethiopia, Nicaragua, and Vietnam free to lead the attack on the United States over Puerto Rico. Faced with such tactics, a loose group of some 20 moderates spanning countries such as Singapore, Bangladesh, Pakistan, Nigeria, Tunisia, and Argentina met regularly to blunt the Cuban challenge. An important objective of such a group, cutting across regions, was to ensure balance in the handling of related issues, such as Afghanistan and Kampuchea.

Both ideological factions mounted vigorous campaigns in the year before the Seventh Summit to influence contents of the summit declaration and, before the venue was changed, Iraq's prospective approach to the presidency. Singapore took the initial lead among moderates months before the summit, meeting with Argentina, Jamaica, Oman, Pakistan, and Peru to develop strategy for key preparatory meetings. As planning intensified for the abortive Baghdad Summit, others such as Indonesia, Malaysia, Bangladesh, Nepal, Somalia, Sudan, Egypt, Bahrain, Saudi Arabia, Tunisia, Kenya, Nigeria, Senegal, Zaire, and Ecuador joined the effort to offset Cuban influence and strike a more balanced position on East-West issues. Still others, like Yugoslavia, were sympathetic but preferred to play a mediating role between factions.

By the June 5–6, 1982, NACB meeting in Havana to prepare for Baghdad, the group of nearly 20 moderates was well organized to play a central role. While the final communiqué from Havana reflected strong NAM reactions to Israel's invasion of Lebanon and the conflict in the

Falklands, moderates toned down several radical initiatives, including an explicit call for Israel's expulsion from the United Nations. In New York the following October, a deadlock developed between Cuba and an expanded group of moderates that prolonged the annual two-day ministerial from October 4 to October 9, throwing other U.N. schedules into disarray. Galvanized by Cuban abuse of the chair, the moderates accused the chairman of misinterpreting consensus and failing to publish reservations. They further called for more evenhanded references to the United States and Soviet Union. While ultimately not successful, their initiative signaled an intention to participate more actively in non-aligned decision-making and tended to discredit Cuba as its chairmanship came to an end.

Interest groups among the non-aligned tend to have a shorter life in relation to specific issues. Oil-producing members, for example, acted in concert at Havana to diffuse the blame for price increases, and groups of the least developed or landlocked states have organized at different times for their specific interests. A more lasting example is the grouping of Indian Ocean states that rallied around the concept of an Indian Ocean Zone of Peace (IOZP) beginning in the early 1970s. Led by India, for which the zone would represent an extension of regional influence, and Sri Lanka, eager to host the first IOZP conference, the group achieved non-aligned endorsement and formed a recognized negotiating committee within the United Nations.

Of regional groups within the NAM, by far the largest and most important is the African bloc comprising all 51 OAU members (including SWAPO) and more than half the movement. While the OAU was badly strained during 1982 when disagreement over admission of the Sahara Democractic Arab Republic (SDAR) and which Chadian government to recognize prevented a quorum during two attempts to hold the annual meeting in Tripoli, it has over the years been the most cohesive group within the NAM. Despite divisions, the African group played a unified role at the New Delhi Summit, and OAU solidarity was reaffirmed after initial difficulties at a summit meeting in Addis Ababa during June 1983. The OAU Charter specifies that all members shall follow a policy of non-alignment, and its large secretariat in Addis Ababa and office in New York are well positioned to backstop African initiatives in the movement. Typically, the OAU foreign ministers meet in advance of major non-aligned conferences to decide which issues to consider in the larger body and to draft an African section for the NAM declaration. Also typically, there is no consensus on inter-African disputes—for example, between Somalia and Ethiopia, Chad and Libya, or Nigeria and Cameroon—that, if referred to the NAM or United Nations would, in their view, reflect badly on OAU mediation abilities. Such matters are, therefore, omitted from draft declarations, which instead focus on consensus issues of southern Africa such as Namibian independence, excoriation of apartheid, and condemnation of periodic South African raids into Angola.

Once the African group has agreed, its position will be accepted nearly verbatim by the NAM, either through incorporation into an advance draft circulated by the conference host or as an addition once a meeting is under way. Other regional or interest groups, eager to secure African support on their own, less clear-cut, issues, will not oppose language on which the Africans agree. The pressures of limited time and other, more divisive issues also act to limit debate beyond obligatory support in plenary speeches. Thus the Africans, more than others, have latitude to orchestrate the NAM, and through it the United Nations, for their own ends. The case in 1981 of proposed sanctions against South Africa over Namibia illustrates the relationship. Following the collapse of cease-fire negotiations at Geneva, the OAU ministers met at Addis Ababa in January and agreed to seek U.N. sanctions. Their strategy was endorsed verbatim by the NAM at New Delhi the next month, and an extraordinary ministerial meeting of the NACB was held at Algiers in early April to rally support for Security Council debate later that month. While the latter initiative occurred before the policies of new U.S. and French administrations were formulated, and was stalemated by Western vetoes, momentum for it had become irreversible through successive conference endorsements.

The Arab bloc, centered on the 21-member Arab League, is the next most vocal group, but far less unified than the Africans. Bitter inter-Arab splits between moderates such as Saudi Arabia, Oman, Tunisia, and Morocco, and "rejectionists" such as Syria, Libya, and the PLO ensure heated debate. Further friction was caused by Egypt's suspension from the Arab League following Camp David and the overlapping membership of one-third of its members in the OAU, which, on certain issues, divides loyalties. Finally, the Arab League is encompassed within the more amorphous 42-member Islamic Conference, founded in 1969, which coordinates policy on Muslim-related issues stretching beyond the Middle East. The latter selects a working-level chairman each year to coordinate policy in New York; and Pakistan, Iraq, and Niger have served in that capacity in 1980, 1981, and 1982, respectively. Bangladesh is expected to assume that role in late 1983.

Despite divisions, the Arab group is clearly an important bloc within the NAM. Unlike the Africans, its positions are usually not formulated in advance, and tend to evolve from protracted, informal wrangling among its members during NAM meetings. The radical contingent, led by the PLO and Syria, and bolstered by the movement's long-standing view of Israel as a colonial issue, has generally had the upper hand. Typically, agreed language on the Middle East will be among the final sections to emerge at a summit, and will derive from late-night trade-offs and extreme pressures among the Arabs. The bitterness of these debates and demands by busy heads of state to wind up the proceedings usually restrain non-Arab members from reopening the issue in plenary, although many later take reservations. NAM positions on the Middle East, as a rule, thus tend to be more inflammatory than on other areas.

The Latin American group within the NAM is an anomaly that does not correspond to the larger Organization of American States (OAS). Among its 17 members, relative moderates outnumber radicals such as Cuba, Nicaragua, and Grenada; yet the latter generally prevail. Differences of policy and political orientation within the group are so pronounced that one would expect consensus to break down, and Latin American issues to be decided by plenary. This does not happen, however, for several reasons. First, Cuba was the only Latin American NAM member until the 1970s, and 10 of the 17 Latin American nations did not join until the Havana or New Delhi Summit. This, combined with Castro's presidency, gave Havana considerable leeway on Latin American issues. Second, the issues put forward by Havana, such as the Panama Canal, the U.S. base at Guantánamo, and independence for Puerto Rico, have colonial overtones within the NAM that make more moderate Latin Americans reluctant to espouse the U.S. side. Third, Afro-Asian delegations, which since Belgrade have formed over 80 percent of the movement, tend to view Latin American issues as remote, and look to the Latin Americans themselves for guidance. Finally, Latin American pride and unwillingness to seem divided by comparison with Africans or Arabs works in favor of consensus.

An exception to the movement's customary non-involvement in Latin American issues was the 1982 conflict between Britain and Argentina over the Falkland (Malvinas) Islands, which commanded close attention among the non-aligned and at least temporarily "Latinized" the movement. In its aftermath, Cuba moved to exploit this opening to draw additional Latin American states into the NAM. While most Latin American moderates had in the past limited participation to observer status or remained outside the non-aligned orbit, resentment of the British invasion and U.S. support offered an opportunity for Cuba to forge new ties on its own terms. By late 1982, for example, Cuba appeared to support Venezuela's membership application, possibly in return for backing by Caracas of Nicaragua's candidacy for the Security Council. Viewed by many as a ploy to advance Venezuelan territorial claims gainst Guyana, the application was finally withdrawn under pressure.

Nor was non-aligned support for Argentina's irredentist claims lost on a continent where boundary disputes are legion. Bolivia thus took care to include language in the New York and New Delhi declarations supporting its claim against Chile for an outlet to the sea. For the first time in NAM history, at the October 1982 ministerial meeting in New York, Latin American rather than Arab or Asian issues dominated the proceedings, with the Falkland/Malvinas conflict and the Guyanese-Venezuelan dispute over the Essequibo region in the forefront. The movement was further "Latinized" during an "extraordinary" meeting of the NACB, held in Managua on January 10–14, 1983, and devoted exclusively to Latin American and Caribbean issues. (See Chapter 6.)

Typically, during meetings of the Latin American group, Cuba, backed by radical allies, will take the lead in formulating positions. Moderates within the group, such as Argentina, Peru, and Jamaica, will then negotiate over the most egregious excesses, but will be unable to alter the section's overall anti-Western and anti-U.S. tone. The draft will then be presented to the plenary as an agreed Latin American text and accepted without debate. While states like Egypt or Bhutan or Zaire might then note reservations—for example, on unbalanced treatment of Puerto Rico—Latin Americans would usually be the last to do so, in order not to undermine their group's solidarity. The willingness and ability of Latin moderates to stand against Cuban pressures varies, however, by issue and by location of the meeting. A Cuban effort in New York during December 1981 to push through a NAM condemnation of alleged U.S. threats against Nicaragua was effectively blunted. In that case, Argentina, Panama, and others watered down a Cuban-Nicaraguan draft to refer only to non-intervention in all Central American states.

The input of Latin American moderates within the movement has thus, in general, been limited by the unbalanced, and from a U.S. point of view egregious, draft resolutions put forward as starting points for discussion by Cuba and Nicaragua. Both the 1979 Havana and the 1983 Managua communiqués conformed to this pattern and, while less strident in their final form than earlier drafts, remained uniformly hostile toward the United States. Preoccupation with individual disputes or claims, whether the Falklands, Bolivia's outlet to the sea, Belize, the Essequibo, or the Peruvian-Ecuadorian border, also encourages silence by many Latin Americans on broader NAM issues. Other

Latin American moderates hesitate to antagonize leftists at home by challenging Cuba in a public forum, particularly on issues secondary to them. The end result is that mavericks like Grenada, population 108,000, with little to lose, often play a disproportionate role. During the January 1983 Managua meeting, Grenada intervened most frequently and dominated the proceedings on a number of issues.

Asia and Europe lack regional caucuses within the NAM. In the former, historical and political divisions have prevented consensus or overall political groupings. This absence has allowed subgroups, notably the movement's three ASEAN members (Singapore, Malaysia, and Indonesia) to play a leading role—for example, in lobbying for withdrawal of Vietnamese troops from Kampuchea and non-acceptance of the Heng Samrin regime. Formed in 1967 for economic and cultural cooperation, ASEAN has evolved into a closely knit political grouping with influence in the NAM disproportionate to its numbers. Typically, the five ASEAN states gather in advance of major non-aligned meetings to coordinate strategy, and Thailand and the Philippines, while not party to the NAM, are actively involved in the lobbying effort. The long-time ambassador of Singapore to the United Nations, Tommy Koh, is particularly well versed in NAM and U.N. practice, and usually leads the ASEAN effort at the working level. Ultimately, however, the lack of a regional caucus requires that Asian issues, whether Kampuchea or the status of East Timor, be debated in plenary to establish consensus. Europe, by contrast, is an exception outside the movement's Third World purview. Yugoslavia, Malta, and Cyprus have little on which to caucus, and Belgrade tends to follow non-aligned issues on a global basis, while the others focus on more localized issues.

The imbalance of regional blocs within the NAM and fluctuating relations among them influence which issues preoccupy the movement. Despite the Bandung myth of Afro-Asian solidarity, differing histories and traditions have kept the two distinct. In the early years, tension was evident in debate over the relative priorities of decolonization and global peace. Similarly, the common cause between Africans and Arabs, forged in the early 1970s over Israel and southern Africa, is subject to periodic strain. In the aftermath of Havana, where the Africans were divided and moderates like Senegal were rebuffed by Castro, the group has been more assertive in challenging others.

Egypt's 18-month probation from the NAM, forced through at Havana by Iraq and others as "punishment" for Camp David, was a case in point. Reacting to this slight against an OAU member, Africans overwhelmingly faced down during the next meeting in New Delhi an Arab campaign, backed by 19 states, to expel Egypt. The time and manuevering devoted to the issue, however, far outweighed its importance, and were purely functions of the organization's peculiar regional balance. Resentment of Castro by moderate Africans surfaced again during the October 1982 ministerial meeting in New York, when Foreign Minister Mogwe of Botswana, backed by Lesotho, Liberia, Somalia, Morocco, Senegal, Zaire, Gabon, and Tunisia, challenged Cuba to be more evenhanded.

THE NACB

The NAM has always consisted of a small core of active participants and a majority who become involved only on specific issues. Although the movement is in theory democratic, the influence of individual members within it varies considerably. In practical terms, during the Havana Summit, delegations of 40 or more from Yugoslavia, Vietnam, Cuba, Indonesia, and Ethiopia exercised a more dominant role than those of three or less fielded by Sudan, Swaziland, Chad, Malawi, and Mauritius. The smallest delegations were barely able to keep abreast of proliferating paperwork and committee sessions.

Different levels of participation and the burden of coordinating a large and unwieldy movement made creation of an executive committee inevitable. The issue was, however, caught up in the overall leadership struggle, and Yugoslavia's campaign during the late 1970s to circumscribe the role of the NACB and "democratize" the movement was at bottom designed to curb Cuban power. First organized prior to Lusaka to handle summit preparations, the committee was expanded at Algiers into the 17-member NACB, increased to 25 members at Colombo, 36 at Havana, and finally enlarged at New Delhi to its present 74 seats. The latter reflects insistence on a careful regional balance, with 36 seats designated for Africa, 23 for Asia, 12 for Latin America, and 3 for Europe. In fact, intense regional rivalries and lack of voting procedures kept three seats vacant from 1979 to 1983. Competition for more regional seats may also have prompted Cuba to encourage new Latin American members of the NAM, such as Belize, Ecuador, Saint Lucia, Bahamas, Barbados, and Colombia, all of which attended the 1983 New Delhi Summit for the first time as full members.

Divided until the New Delhi Summit about equally between moderate and radical members, the NACB has in the past tended to be more radical and outspoken than the general NAM membership, particularly during Cuba's presidency. Some conservative members have never sought a seat, fearing isolation by a radical majority or even condemnation of national policies such as ties with Israel or South Africa. While its members are nominally selected for three years at each summit, in practice the same countries are usually kept on and form a nucleus of activist or "first class" NAM members. (See Appendix A.) An exception was the removal of Egypt in 1976, under pressure from hard-line Arab members. Suspicion among the NAM rank and file that the NACB might evolve as an elite decision-making body led to its four successive expansions. As described by Sri Lankan Foreign Minister Shahul Hameed, outsiders feared that it would become an exclusive "cabinet—an inner circle—a cabal of decision-makers."[27] There were also pressures, at first resisted by Havana, that NACB meetings be open to all members. In fact, these sessions, in sheer numbers, are often indistinguishable from NAM plenary meetings, and outsiders can now participate in NACB decisions if they are directly involved in the issue.

The New Delhi decision to double NACB membership is likely to have far-reaching implications for its operation. It, too, was taken in the context of factional jockeying for power. Moderate members, concerned by radical manipulation of NACB procedures under Cuba, pushed to make membership open to all, with a quorum required for decisions, thus effectively abolishing the bureau. Cuba and its supporters, to maintain their own leverage, argued for a membership of 36 in addition to the 7 NAM chairmen as ex officio members. The resulting expansion to 74 was interpreted as a victory for moderates, and should make future NACB deliberations more representative of the general membership. As in the overall movement, however, decision-making will be more cumbersome and probably dependent on smaller ad hoc groups.

The functions of the NACB have been subject to close scrutiny and numerous working papers but, in the absence of permanent staffing, have gradually evolved into those of an executive committee. Yugoslavia, in a report at the Colombo Summit on the bureau's composition and mandate, argued against strong executive powers that would take decision-making away from the common members. Iraq, in a 1977 working paper, argued the opposite case for a permanent, centralized secretariat. The latter, first proposed at the Algiers Summit and sporadically pushed by Libya, Tanzania, and Iraq, has always been defeated on the grounds of cost and possible domination of the NAM by the host country. While some Indian officials were tempted prior to the Seventh Summit by visions of New Delhi as a Third World Geneva or New York, India has always opposed a permanent secretariat, and chose instead, in March 1983, to establish a division for NAM affairs in its Foreign Ministry. In the meantime, the range of issues considered at monthly ambassadorial-level meetings of the NACB in New York and special ministerial sessions elsewhere has continued to expand well beyond the original role of conference preparation.

Coordination of NAM activities and positions in the United Nations, always part of the bureau's mandate, has become more time-consuming. The Havana Summit also specifically charged the bureau to convene as a group within the G-77 to ensure the movement's "catalytic" role in that body.[28] In addition, the NACB supervises the work of "coordinator countries" responsible for 21 economic subjects, such as fisheries and telecommunications, which were set up in 1972 and expanded at Havana in March 1982, and of nine political working groups for issues such as Cyprus, Korea, and Palestine. Beyond these functions, it serves at the direction of the NAM president—which, under an activist like Castro, can involve considerable paperwork. Press releases and communiqués from the bureau, although curtailed by the Havana Summit to cover only previously agreed NAM positions, remain an important NACB prerogative.

Three additional factors have increased NACB influence on the movement's composition and orientation. First, it has assumed primary responsibility for membership matters. NACB recommendations are routinely endorsed without challenge, and informal indications of disapproval by one or more bureau members are sufficient to discourage new applicants. By 1983, India, as incoming chairman, was even referring to the bureau questions relating to official guests at the New Delhi Summit. Second, increasing use of "extraordinary" NACB ministerial meetings has allowed the bureau to anticipate and shape NAM strategy in key areas. Meetings of this type were held on southern Africa at Maputo, Mozambique, in 1979 and Algiers in 1981, and served to galvanize non-aligned support for strategies of the African group. Sessions on Palestine were held in Kuwait during April, and Cyprus during July, 1982 to build a more radical consensus on the Middle East prior to the canceled Baghdad Summit. An extraordinary meeting was also held on Latin American issues at Managua in January 1983. In each case, a small cadre of radicals was able to use control of the bureau to schedule meetings that shaped the NAM position on key issues.

Finally, relegation of disputed issues to the NACB for recommendations has consolidated its central policy-making role. Heads of state, unable to agree under pressure of a summit on Egypt's membership or which Kampuchean delegation to seat, save face by calling for a bureau report. The New Delhi Summit, for example, was able to conclude nearly on time and with a semblance of unity only by referring hot potatoes like Kampuchea and the venue of a 1986 summit to working groups of the bureau. Whatever it recommends is likely to be accepted in order to avoid further acrimony at the higher level. The NACB, in most cases paralyzed by the same divisions that prevent agreement at a summit, thus becomes the arbiter of last resort.

The movement's adaptation, through the NACB and regional groups, to political and internal limitations, has been gradual and defies easy classification. The Belgrade Summit stated categorically that "the non-aligned countries represented at this conference do not wish to form a new bloc and cannot be a bloc."[29] This attitude remains entrenched, and periodic descriptions of the NAM as a Third World bloc elicit vehement denial. The Yugoslav writer Edvard Kardelj maintains, for example, that the movement "lacks requisite political or military power to impose its interests on others as a bloc."[30] To an outsider, the debate appears semantic, revolving around military and superpower connotations of the word "bloc" current during the Cold War. As M.S. Rajan points out, the distinction between "movement" and "bloc" is a subtle one, and "the Non-aligned Movement may eventually yield place to a third bloc, the non-aligned bloc, without planning to do so or without even being conscious of its own transformation."[31] In a more general sense, the NAM, although divided on many issues, has already evolved into an important lobby, considered by outsiders to be the largest U.N. voting bloc.

In the process, contradictions of ideology and composition, inherent in its present size, have turned members from idealism to the more pragmatic, issue-oriented approach of a lobby or powerful interest group. Dr. A.W. Singham noted at the 1977 Howard University Symposium on Non-Alignment that the NAM has "essentially advanced a trade union bargaining process onto a global level."[32] Division into regional groups, although unequal, and growing executive powers of the NACB facilitate the movement's adaptation to this new role.

5

Chairmanship of the NAM

We are firmly anti-imperialist, anti-colonial, anti-neocolonial, anti-racist, anti-Zionist and anti-Fascist because these principles are a part of our thinking; they constitute the essence and origins of the Movement of Non-Aligned Countries and have formed its life and history ever since its founding.

Fidel Castro, 1979

Starting with Algeria in 1973, the chairmanship, or presidency, as it is sometimes known, has become increasingly important in setting the tone and broad direction of the movement. The proliferation of issues, growth in membership, and activism of the NACB, headed by the NAM chairman, have all served to consolidate power in that office. Differences between individual nations in an increasingly polarized membership require that the chairman undertake exhaustive bilateral consultations in advance of plenary meetings, constructing in the process a pre-cooked scenario for their outcome. As at the United Nations, considerations of prestige affect public positions in plenary, and most compromises are struck in advance or on the margins of the meeting itself. Senior Indian officials, for instance, met at length with at least 40 NAM members before the New Delhi Summit.

The chairman's prerogative of preparing the first draft of summit declarations is particularly important in structuring the final outcome. Thus, having tabled a relatively balanced first draft for the New Delhi Summit, India was able to play the role of referee, claiming that the final declaration was a consensus document not necessarily reflecting Indian positions for which it could be held to account. The starting draft was, in effect, a "Christmas tree" that other members could adorn with pet issues or phobias. By contrast, the earlier Cuban approach was to begin meetings on the basis of an extremely radical draft, only gradually giving ground to modifications by moderates. Such different tactics, of course, reflect divergent interpretations of the chairman's role as lobbyist for national positions or as mediator between the conflicting interests of 101 members. Reflecting on Sri Lanka's chairmanship,

Foreign Minister Shahul Hameed noted the need for presidents to distinguish between "national and non-aligned objectives."[33]

While the overall membership tends to resist heavy-handed abuse of the chair, as under Cuba, for national purposes, there are few remaining checks and balances on a president's power. The early collegial relationship of Tito, Nehru, and Nasser limited the scope of whoever happened to hold the office. Equally, the active participation of a smaller membership has given way to apathy among the larger group. Finally, there is no permanent secretariat in place from one presidency to the next to advise incumbents and serve as a restraint on excess. Each chairman of the NAM depends on a national foreign affairs bureaucracy for staff support, and swings in orientation and approach are thus not uncommon.

Management of consensus within the NAM, articulation of non-aligned interests, and deployment of a diplomatic strategy to advance them also demand resources and a level of sophistication possessed by few members. Most NAM states lack the worldwide diplomatic network and across-the-board international interests to make the system work in the absence of a secretariat. While there have been some obvious exceptions to the rule, the presidency is increasingly hostage to the most powerful members with sufficient diplomatic and financial resources. The large foreign affairs establishments and far-flung diplomatic networks of Algeria, Yugoslavia, Egypt and India clearly permit a more complete mobilization of the non-aligned lobby than would be possible under its smaller members. Even Cuba, despite its aggressive tactics, won grudging respect from most members for advance preparation and diplomatic activism. The limited number of viable candidates further strengthens the presidency in relation to the general membership.

Over the years, the NAM has been dominated by a few dynamic and highly ambitious members willing to devote unlimited time and energy to the movement. In each case, their activism has stemmed from a combination of commitment to non-alignment and purely national objectives. Yet the mixture has varied in recent years from Sri Lanka, a small state with traditional non-alignment as a cornerstone of its foreign policy, to Cuba, which clearly perceived the movement as a vehicle to advance specific, and not necessarily compatible, national, and ideological objectives. This inherent tension between the movement's agenda and the hidden or national agenda of its chairman has accounted for widespread resistance to reforms that could further centralize the NAM and bolster the chairman's power.

The interplay among the half-dozen dominant partners in the NAM, ranging from cooperation to outright hostility, also affects the organization's morale and the alternation of dynamism and inertia that has characterized its summits. The most profound impact on politics of the Third World was made at the 1961 Belgrade and 1973 Algiers summits. Both occurred under chairmen strong enough to insist on their particular vision, but with solid backing from the movement's other principal architects. The Havana Summit, by contrast, and despite the unprecedented publicity it received, pitted the leading members against each other, neutralizing their various initiatives and ensuring that only the least common denominator emerged. The collaboration of leaders at the movement's core has also been affected by the death of key figures, sudden shifts in national leadership, and periods when attention turns inward to domestic needs. These, occurring without warning, have on occasion left the movement adrift and vulnerable to new struggles for the lead roles.

The motives that impel members to seek the burden and costs of a three-year presidency differ in specifics, but often include domestic political factors, ambition for international acceptability or influence, and dedication to particular issues within the NAM. To a surprising degree, domestic factors predominate, and the prestige and pageantry of a NAM summit is often used to offset and divert attention from civil unrest, economic deterioration, lackluster political performance, or unpopular military adventures. The influx of 100 delegations, and the attendant motorcades and press conferences, commonplace if not an irritant in New York or Geneva, can still elicit strong national pride and support elsewhere.

Internationally, the NAM presidency allows an ambitious member to break out of diplomatic isolation, shore up bilateral ties with selected states, and exercise influence disproportionate to its size. Small and relatively poor island states like Cuba and Sri Lanka can thus transcend national and regional limitations to assume a global role, or military regimes in Havana, Baghdad, or Tripoli can seek the office to allay accumulated suspicion of past aggressive policies. Judicious use of the chair and compromise at key junctures can also augment aid flows and access to oil or nuclear technology. Finally, the chairman's power can be used to position the NAM, and through it the United Nations, on particular issues, such as IOZP for Sri Lanka and Puerto Rican independence for Cuba.

The movement's ambiguity toward leadership applies even to the choice of "president" or "chairman" as a title. Yugoslavia and India have long favored "chairman" because of its connotation of collegial control and responsibility to the overall body. Cuba, by contrast, insisted for much of its term on "president" because of the greater executive authority and mandate implied. In practice, the terms have been used almost interchangeably. The movement's loose procedures have, in any case, offered considerable scope for ambitious leaders. The consensus rule, for example, encourages vigorous lobbying and steam-roller tactics by an aggressive chairman like Cuba. Control over rules of order at summit meetings also makes it easy to sidetrack attempted amendments, and the president has the advantage of formulating draft agendas and declarations. These controls, together with membership growth and reliance on the NACB, have since the early 1970s sharply increased the role and powers of the president.

The movement's growth has also narrowed the field of eligible NAM chairmen. A small hill village, like Bogor or Bandung, cramped for meetings in the 1950s, would today be impossible. Thousands of delegates, press, security, and conference staff now require either the most modern of world capitals or new facilities constructed, as in Iraq, at an estimated cost of over $1 billion. International air connections, first-class lodging, and sophisticated communications are among the requirements that simply exclude most member states. Thus, while the movement puts a premium on democratic process, in practice its presidency is becoming a monopoly of the largest, richest, or foreign-financed members. NAM efforts to reverse this trend by a cost-sharing formula, based on member contributions to the United Nations, have not worked. First, reimbursable expenses cover conference services and staffing rather than prior investment in infrastructure, and, second, even these are rarely paid. Sri Lanka, the last small state without means to host a summit, has, since 1976, received only a fraction of its costs and almost nothing from Arab members.

In these circumstances, it is not surprising that the honor is not widely sought. Security Council membership, involving global prestige and responsibilities with little added cost, is, by contrast, the object of strong competition. Within the NAM, the field was further limited in 1973, following adverse reaction to three successive summits in Africa, by an informal system requiring rotation of the presidency among regions. Since then, few candidates have emerged every three years, virtually ensuring the presidency to those willing and able to pay. Further, less developed members have understandably been reluctant to jeopardize oil supplies or aid by opposing richer candidates. The necessity to hold regular meetings and preserve the organization thus muted objections to Cuba's Soviet ties or, until the actual conference site was threatened, Iraq's prolonged war against Iran.

In the first decade, the close coordination and general supervision of the movement, provided by Tito, Nehru, and Nasser, made the presidency less important. When one of the three was not actually in the chair, their overall guidelines were followed by others. Zambia's presidency, while important for procedural innovations, thus made little imprint. As the triumvirate broke down and only Tito remained through the 1970s, chairmen assumed more latitude. Algeria and, to a lesser extent, Sri Lanka exercised a more aggressive style of leadership, but remained within the accepted mainstream of non-aligned principles. The subsequent accession of Cuba to the presidency marked a transition to leadership less committed to founding principles and eager for political influence beyond a specific region. While India assumed the presidency by last-minute compromise in 1983, others eager for the office and typical of the next generation of would-be leaders included Iraq, Libya, Syria, and North Korea. Although moderates opposed Cuban efforts to redirect the movement, Castro's activism was at the outset compared favorably with earlier periods of inertia. Small states, while committed to the original principles, appeared to welcome the image of Third World dynamism and power inherent in the new-style leaders.

Decision by Triumvirate

Shared interests evolving during the 1950s, and the combined prestige of Yugoslavia, Egypt, and India left a strong imprint on the movement's first decade. Regular consultation among Tito, Nasser, and Nehru from the 1956 Brioni meeting on shaped the framework in which the larger group met. The three formed a body of elders that, while not always in agreement on particular issues, still exerted a restraining influence on radicals and not-always-well-thought-out proposals of members like Sukarno or Nkrumah. While their informal entente had vanished by the 1970s, the principles and general approach they fostered did not come under direct challenge until the end of that decade. The three states, in any case, continued to attach great significance to the movement and often cooperated, but no longer in such close concert.

Since the 1960s, Yugoslavia has been the most committed booster of non-alignment. Isolated from the East after its 1948 break with the Soviets and withdrawal from the Information Bureau of Communist Parties and Workers (COMINFORM), it had not sought or found acceptance in the West, which backed rival Italian claims to Trieste. Identity with the Third World, through the vehicle of non-alignment, was thus a brilliant political ploy. Belgrade's ability as a European, white, and moderately developed state to overcome inevitable Third World suspicions is testimony to its success, although many in the movement regard the Yugoslav interpretation of national liberation and other NAM articles of faith as "Eurocentric."

In the recollection of George Kennan, U.S. ambassador in Belgrade from 1961–63, Tito's indefatigable commitment to the NAM was at bottom a means to justify the 1948 break with Moscow. Speaking in East Germany in 1958, Soviet Communist party Secretary Nikita Khrushchev said that the way to deal with Tito was to ignore him. The extent of Khrushchev's continuing hostility was evident in a private message to Tito boasting that Moscow would resume nuclear testing one day before the Belgrade Summit, and "then we'll see who is relevant." Tito, whose real aim was to force the Communist bloc to recognize the legitimacy and propriety of his break with Moscow, was stung by these rebuffs, and set out, through the NAM, to meet Khrushchev's challenge. By hosting its first summit and taking the lead among Third World countries whose attitudes were important to the USSR, Tito was eventually invited to Moscow and, to the chagrin of Soviet hard-liners, given a standing ovation by the Supreme Soviet. In Kennan's view, "he had shown them in other words how isolated he was. It must have been the high point of his life. And none of this could he have achieved without the NAM."[34]

Tito's death in 1980 reduced Yugoslavia's leverage in the NAM, but his successors have continued to give the movement high priority. Non-alignment still dominates Yugoslav political writing, and Belgrade's unchanged geopolitical landscape offers few other options. Despite reservations about the movement's evolving course, Yugoslavia will probably redouble its efforts during India's 1983–86 presidency to reassert a more centrist leadership closer to the founders' vision. Dependence on Iraqi oil and growing Yugoslav exports to NAM markets such as India will reinforce this orientation.

For India, commitment to the NAM flowed from traditional fears of encirclement sharpened by proximity to China and Russia, Western collective security pacts, and superpower naval activity in the Indian Ocean. Emphasis on shared principles was also compatible with the moral tone of the Gandhi-Nehru era. Preoccupation with domestic and Asian issues, as well as doubts about the movement's growing African and anti-colonial focus, left India a somewhat reluctant founder, dragged along in the early years by Tito and Nasser. Nehru's forceful performance at Belgrade carried the day, but also raised private doubts about the role in a movement composed of small, weak states, of a nation with more people than the combined populations of all other members at that time.

In addition, events of the next two decades undercut Indian influence and moral authority. The takeovers of Goa in 1961 and Sikkim in 1973 aroused suspicion among small states, as did war with China in 1962 and with Pakistan in 1965 and 1971. In the non-aligned context, war with China, undermining the Panchsheel principles and forcing India to seek military assistance from both Washington and Moscow, was particularly damaging. So was formalization of the latter relationship in a 1971 Treaty of Peace and Friendship. India, in any case, played a diminished role in the NAM during these years as a result of Nehru's death in 1964 and the preoccupation of succeeding prime ministers with domestic and Asian crises. Its re-emergence in the 1980s was capped by the New Delhi Summit (described in Chapter 6).

In the 1960s and 1970s, India continued, however, to pay close attention to NAM positions relating to Pakistan, North–South economic ties, U.S. naval facilities at Diego Garcia, and the IOZP. The 1981 NAM ministerial meeting offered New Delhi a chance to enhance its image as a world leader and to obscure its growing isolation from NAM moderates over failure to condemn the Soviet invasion of Afghanistan and recognition of the Moscow-backed Heng Samrin regime in Kampuchea. NAM credentials, reburnished by a well-run conference reaffirming the movement's unity at a moment of obvious disarray, further tempted Prime Minister Gandhi in February 1982 to express interest in the 1985 presidency.

As events unfolded, India's opportunity for the presidency came sooner, in 1983, as a result of continued warfare between Iran and Iraq and collapse of the Baghdad Summit. While India's candidacy for 1985 would have been contested by Libya and others, and required an exception to the informal practice of geographic rotation, in 1983 members saw in India's offer a means of extrication from an embarrassing commitment to Baghdad. Although Nehru was one of the founding trio, his daughter, Indira Gandhi, was the first Indian to hold the presidency 20 years later. The transfer of leadership from Cuba to India under unprecedented circumstances was engineered by a few activist members and ratified only after the fact by the NAM majority. Nevertheless, it again demonstrated the movement's resiliency in surmounting internal disarray and surviving by strategic compromise.

Both the timing and the method of assuming the presidency were probably welcome to India. To have gained office in 1985 through a vigorous campaign, whose success was by no means assured, would have raised high political and financial expectations for a presidency by the largest NAM state. The gesture, by contrast, of assuming office on short notice enhanced India's stature and coincided with Prime Minister Gandhi's decision, following her reelection in 1980, that India should play a more active leadership role in the movement. At odds with most non-aligned moderates over Afghanistan and Kampuchea, India perceived more active participation in the NAM as a way to rebuild its traditional ties and enhance its world role after a period of preoccupation with domestic and Asian crises.

In contrast with Cuba, India has considerably greater weight within the movement by virtue of its size. General resentment of Castro's leadership further offered an opportunity to highlight India's long experience with non-aligned issues and its skill in parliamentary procedures and tactics. Mrs. Gandhi's effort to avoid the intrusion of East-West political issues into non-aligned meetings promised a change from Castro's campaign to forge an "alliance" between the NAM and the USSR. With the world's tenth-largest industrial base, India also had a clear interest in practical economic measures for access to technology, markets, and capital rather than Cuban-style rhetoric based on an assured balance-of-payments subsidy from Moscow. Refocusing the movement on economic rather than political issues in the period before the New Delhi Summit additionally helped to play down New Delhi's political differences with others in the NAM.

The role in the movement of the third partner, Egypt, has fluctuated with the vicissitudes of the Middle East. An emergent Nasser, then at the center of radical Arab politics, both shared non-aligned distrust of the great powers and saw in the movement the potential for wider Egyptian influence. NAM membership was also good domestic politics. Faced with age-old problems of the Nile Valley—poverty, overpopulation, and sectarian division—Nasser used the NAM, as well as the Arab League, OAU, and the Afro-Asian People's Solidarity Organization (AAPSO), to dazzle an unsophisticated public and keep opponents off balance. Egypt's role as a bridge between African and Arab states and the strongest member of either group made it a pivotal state in any Third World organization.

Defeat by Israel in 1967 and Nasser's death in 1970 diminished Egypt's role. Anwar Sadat, while continuing to give public support to non-alignment, was much less committed to the movement than his predecessor. Despite Egypt's strong showing in the 1973 war with Israel, leadership of the divided Arab world was already beginning to shift toward radicals like Syria, the PLO, and Algeria. Within the NAM, the latter group engineered Egypt's exclusion in 1976 from the enlarged NACB. Sadat's dramatic visit to Jerusalem in 1977 and the Camp David Agreements of the following year, making peace after four wars with Israel, isolated Egypt overnight from other Arab nations. The latter, encouraged by the Soviet Union, expelled Egypt from the Arab League and relocated its headquarters from Cairo to Tunis. Within the NAM, Cairo was placed on the defensive to thwart Arab pressures for its suspension and to moderate, to the extent possible, condemnation of its role at Camp David. A price of peace, willingly paid but perhaps underestimated by Sadat, was prolonged isolation of Egyptian delegations to both the NAM and the United Nations.

While Cairo, drawing on political capital with colleagues in the OAU, was successful in withstanding non-aligned pressure, the challenge altered the scope of its activities. Previously engaged in all non-aligned business, Cairo sent large "one-issue" delegations to NAM meetings at Havana and the 1981 New Delhi ministerial meeting. Their mandates were to preserve Egypt's membership in good standing and limit damage from radical Arab colleagues. African support and unwillingness to expel a founding member averted expulsion, although full restoration of its former influence may still depend on a Palestinian settlement and withdrawal of foreign troops from Lebanon.

Since assuming office following the Sadat assassination in October 1981, the Mubarak government has made considerable efforts to strengthen its position in the NAM. Egypt played a prominent role during the April 5–8, 1982, NACB meeting in Kuwait as a first step back to acceptance. In late 1982, President Hosni Mubarak visited both Belgrade and New Delhi to cement ties and remind member states of Egypt's founding role. Non-aligned ties probably also served to offset an impression of dependence on the United States in a period of particularly close relations. At the New Delhi Summit in March 1983, a large delegation, headed by Mubarak, worked hard to complete Egypt's reintegration into the NAM. They were partially successful, and easily deflected Libya's renewed call for expulsion. Yet Egypt's bid to again take part in deliberations of the Arab regional group was rebuffed, although Mubarak held bilateral meetings at New Delhi with several other Arab heads of state.

Algeria and Sri Lanka

During the second decade of the NAM, Algeria and Sri Lanka remained within the movement's mainstream and were able to moderate between conservatives like Singapore and Senegal and hard-core radicals like Cuba and Vietnam. While the movement became increasingly radical and anti-Western under Algeria, that nation was opposed to the radical fringe. As chairman, it resisted Cuban pressure to ally the movement with Moscow and insisted on Third World independence from the "two imperialisms" of East and West. Algeria's doctrinaire socialism and commitment to wars of national liberation translated into deep hostility toward the West and determination to use the movement as a lever to end colonialism and to restructure an economic order shaped by the developed world. Single-minded pursuit of these twin goals earned Algiers a reputation as the new ideologue of non-alignment, not unlike that of Belgrade on East–West issues. In pursuing common goals during the 1970s, both Algeria and Sri Lanka benefited from the leadership vacuum to assert a more aggressive and free-wheeling mandate for the chairman.

Unlike later claimants, Algeria did not wage a protracted campaign for NAM leadership. At the 1970 Lusaka Summit, no provision was made for the next presidency, although by informal agreement of Tito, Kenneth Kaunda, and Mrs. Bandaranaike, it was expected to pass to Sri Lanka. Subsequently, however, the African group rallied around Algeria, and their majority ensured a formal endorsement at the Georgetown, Guyana, ministerial meeting in 1972. Algeria's parallel roles in the G-77, Arab League, and OPEC dovetailed with non-aligned initiatives and made it a natural leader for the NAM in 1973. Unlike his predecessors, Colonel Boumedienne, backed by Foreign Minister Bouteflika and a large staff, lobbied aggressively for specific action programs both as summit host and as chairman in the ensuing years. The Algerians, for the first time, used tight control of conference procedures to manage the summit's outcome and to sidetrack extraneous issues or amendments. The result was a more coherent and anti-Western package than the generalizations and sometimes conflicting positions of earlier summits.

Following a period of dynamic activity from 1973 to 1975, possibly the high point of NAM unity, Algeria appeared to turn inward in the final year of its presidency and away from a catalytic international role. Domestic imperatives, escalation of warfare in the Sahara between Moroccan troops and the Algerian-backed Polisario Liberation Front, and protracted natural gas negotiations with the United States all played a part in this shift. Third World economic demands, tailored in large part by Algeria, also had by 1975 received little satisfaction from the West despite pressures of oil pricing. (Even well into the 1980s, agreement was still pending on the form and terms of "global negotiations" to take up the programs first enunciated at Algiers.) Under the circumstances, Boumedienne turned increasingly to domestic concerns, and the transition to Sri Lanka's term was uneventful.

In later years, Algeria's thrust in the movement concentrated on economic issues and lobbying for non-aligned support of its side in the Sahara dispute with Morocco. Boumedienne's prolonged illness and death in Moscow in 1979 also precipitated a new period of internal consolidation and diminished international activity. His successor, Chadli Benjedid, consistent with this lowered profile, was one of the few heads of state at the Havana Summit who declined to address the plenary. Algeria, nevertheless, worked behind the scenes to revise the draft Havana Economic Declaration, which was little more than a rehash of earlier NAM positions, and collaborated with Yugoslavia to further enlarge the NACB as a possible counterweight to Cuban power. At the New Delhi Summit, as well, Algeria played a relatively restrained role, focusing its attention on the movement's economic priorities. Once a leading radical in non-aligned terms, Algeria appears to have moved toward the center as countries like Cuba, Nicaragua, and Vietnam have inherited the radical mantle. Its growing conservatism will probably project well into the 1980s, although Algeria will continue to be active on the twin issues of a Palestinian settlement and Lebanon. If Colonel Qaddafi were ever to realize his ambition for the NAM chairmanship, Algeria would be on guard against his rival pan-Arab and Maghrebian ambitions.

Sri Lanka's standing bid for the presidency was endorsed at Algiers when a rotational system was initiated, allotting the next summit to Asia. Having shared in the evolution of non-alignment and the earlier planning for Bandung, Colombo was overshadowed in the first decade by Egypt, India, and Yugoslavia. The opportunity to be the first Asian chairman offered at least temporary parity with the major non-aligned states and was consistent with its own imperatives of maintaining independence in a region of colossal neighbors and seeking international standing to deal with them on a more equal footing. An elaborate, Chinese-funded conference center, already constructed at Colombo, was suitable for a summit and required little further capital investment.

Sri Lanka's pursuit of the presidency appeared to stem more from these international concerns than as a foil to domestic problems à la Nasser. The 1971 Sinhalese-Tamil disturbances had been followed by a period of calm, and appeared not to be a factor in seeking the presidency. In fact, the summit was, if anything, a political liability to Mrs. Sirimavo Bandaranaike's Freedom party, which lost at the polls in 1977. Although it was not a major campaign issue, J.R. Jayewardene and the United National party were able to exploit the summit's exorbitant costs to a country with per capita income then under $200. Sri Lanka thus became the only country to date whose presidency spanned two governments. While the transition led to a wait-and-see approach by some members, possibly reducing Colombo's room to maneuver, there was little difference between the two parties on non-aligned policy. In practice, responsibility for foreign affairs, previously Mrs. Bandaranaike's preserve, devolved to the Foreign Ministry, and non-aligned matters were routinely handled by a small staff in New York. The shift was less dramatic than might have been the departure, for example, of a Castro at mid-term.

The absence of burning issues among the non-aligned during 1976–79, other than drawing the battle lines for Cuba's presidency, made Sri Lanka's term somewhat uneventful. Colombo was able, however, to effectively promote its special interests in the IOZP, disarmament (including plans for a special General Assembly session), and more detailed criteria governing "non-intervention in the internal affairs of states." Concern for democratic and orderly procedures during the Colombo Summit may, according to Sri Lankan sources, have marginally restrained Cuban excesses three years later. The rules of conference procedure, as employed by Sri Lanka, were in any case later codified and included as an appendix to the Havana Declaration, where they remained rarely cited and little observed during the next three years. In addition to activism on the Indian Ocean, Sri Lanka has evolved into an important player on economic issues of the NAM, and President Jayewardene was much sought out as a mediator during the New Delhi Summit.

Cuba

Castro was the first of a new breed of NAM chairman: able to pay his way (albeit through Soviet subsidies), committed to specific national and ideological goals, and on the radical fringe of the movement. The latter ensured a period of confrontation, with the chairman acting as advocate and chief lobbyist rather than, as in the past, reconciler and preserver of unity. From the outset, it was inevitable that Havana would push for maximum realignment of the movement with Moscow and harsh criticism of the West on specific issues, that the effort would galvanize resistance from moderate members, and that the confrontation would stop somewhere short of splitting the NAM. The exact point of compromise remained unclear, although with time Cuba's heavy-handed tactics and inaction on Afghanistan limited its ability to reorient the NAM.

From the early years, Cuba's role in the movement has been a function of its relations with Washington and Moscow. Admission as the only founding Latin American member in 1961 was a direct result of the Bay of Pigs invasion earlier in the year. The image of a small island fending off invasion by a superpower ensured NAM acceptance of a regime otherwise suspect for extremism and remote from the Afro-Asian majority. In later years, fear and hostility toward the United States shaped Cuban initiatives within the movement, which focused particularly on issues close to home: Puerto Rico, Panama, Guantánamo, and the economic boycott.

Growing dependence on Moscow was also a catalyst for deeper Cuban involvement in non-aligned affairs. Castro's first personal appearance at the 1973 Summit followed a significant expansion, during the previous year, of Soviet influence on the island. While he was at pains to take the Soviet line in Algiers, vigorously touting the "natural ally" thesis, closer identification with the Third World gave credibility to his claimed independence from Moscow. As an active member of the non-aligned, Cuba was also able to more effectively promote initiatives favored by Moscow that, if put forward by a Warsaw Pact state, would be discounted by the Third World. The growing role of Cuba in the movement, seconded by states like Vietnam, North Korea, and Ethiopia, had much to do with Moscow's gradual re-evaluation of non-alignment.

The presidency in 1979 gave substance to Cuban ambitions for an independent, global role well beyond the normal horizons of a small, impoverished, and problem-ridden Caribbean island. It conferred, at least until the December 1979 invasion of Afghanistan, a symbolic independence from Moscow, as well as the opportunity to enhance Cuba's and Castro's prestige in the Third World and to restructure the NAM as a "truly revolutionary" institution. The timing of its presidency coincided with an intensification of Cuban activity in the Third World, particularly Africa, after years of less than successful concentration on revolution in Latin America. In late 1975, Castro, with Soviet backing, had dispatched an estimated 20,000 combat troops to help the radical Neto faction become the official government in Angola. In 1978, again with Russian help, he sent about 17,000 troops to bolster a Communist regime in Ethiopia. By that year, about one in five Cuban military personnel were stationed abroad. Cuba also relied on assistance programs to offset its military image, dispersing 11,000 civilian technicians throughout the Third World.

Yet by 1983, the balance sheet, from Havana's point of view, was at best mixed. The presidency had enhanced awareness of Cuba's international role and its influence on non-aligned positions. Yet Castro was only partially successful in forging a broad Third World alliance to oppose the United States and Western Europe. The Havana Summit was unquestionably the high-water mark of non-aligned hostility to the West, but many of the decisions taken there did not reflect the consensus and were later reversed. In a negative sense, Castro was probably able, as president, to limit damage to Cuban and Soviet interests from the Afghan and Kampuchean invasions by blocking concerted action in the NAM. The effort was costly, however, and Afghanistan, in particular, brought Cuba's commitment to the NAM into direct conflict with its economic and military dependence on Moscow. The latter clearly took precedence, and, speaking to the Cuban Communist party Congress on December 17, 1980, Castro specifically endorsed both the Soviet invasion of Afghanistan and application of the Brezhnev Doctrine to Poland.

Havana's failure to condemn the invasion and occupation of a member state by a superpower sacrificed much of its remaining credibility. Efforts as president to mediate various non-aligned disputes, such as Malta's conflict with Libya and the Iran-Iraq war, backfired partly for this reason. Malta rebuffed the Cuban role, and both Iran and Iraq appeared to see Castro as a less-than-honest broker. Even as the Baghdad Summit approached, Cuba, as president of the NACB, was unable to implement its repeated calls for effective mediation. When Foreign Minister Malmierca visited Baghdad on August 26, 1982, to gain Iraqi agreement for new summit arrangements, his threat to withhold further Cuban mediation was thus seen as empty. Havana's campaign for a seat on the Security Council also failed despite its claims to have non-aligned endorsement. Overall, Afghanistan and resentment of Cuba's aggressive style appear to have blunted efforts to realign the movement or significantly bolster Cuba's national role.

The degree of resentment over Cuban leadership was dramatically clear during a General Assembly vote of September 24, 1982, when the non-aligned overwhelmingly repudiated a Cuban effort to inscribe Puerto Rico on the General Assembly agenda. Following it, Cuban Foreign Minister Malmierca was barely able to maintain control of the annual non-aligned ministerial meeting in New York during early October, and was forced to abruptly adjourn the proceedings on several occasions when support for Cuba was not forthcoming from the floor. These setbacks are unlikely, however, to dampen future Cuban activity in the NAM or determination to use it as a sounding board to castigate the United States. As a final act of his presidency, Castro for this reason insisted on holding an extraordinary meeting of the NACB at Managua in January 1983, where an all-out propaganda attack on the United States could be more easily orchestrated.

Iraq's Non-Presidency

Iraq's spectacular bid for the presidency, while unsuccessful because of miscalculation in Iran, is an obvious case of aggressive pursuit of NAM leadership to advance national interests abroad and to offset domestic pressures. At the time of its selection as seventh chairman during the Havana Summit, Iraq was isolated diplomatically, yet determined to play a larger role in regional and international affairs. Saddam Hussein had replaced the ailing Ahmed Hassan al-Bakr in July 1979, and was in the process of enlarging his popular support and assuming control of the Baath party. Within the Middle East, that party's radical ideology and commitment to a uniform political order in all Arab states had led to suspicion of Iraq, and the NAM presidency was a means to greater respectability. Iraq's role in the NAM was also enhanced by the misfortunes of its traditional rivals: ostracism of Egypt after Camp David, disintegration in Iran under Ayatollah Ruhollah Khomeini, and internal strife in Syria. Burgeoning oil wealth in the late 1970s permitted Iraq to exploit the resulting vacuum and develop into a dominant military power of the Persian Gulf. While by no means as closely tied as Cuba to the Soviet orbit, Baghdad probably also perceived the presidency as useful to demonstrate independence from Moscow.

In the period leading up to the abortive Baghdad Summit, Iraq mounted a concerted effort to expand its international involvement, receiving visits from numerous heads of state, establishing new embassies abroad, and dramatically increasing foreign aid to Arab and NAM countries. By the late 1970s, Baghdad was providing about $1 billion a year in foreign assistance and offering interest-free loans to compensate developing countries for increased oil prices. The basis for this largess was oil, which by 1979 had reached 3.5 million barrels a day and conferred new influence among buyers, including Yugoslavia, Brazil, Japan, and Western Europe.

Baghdad's new internationalism and activism in the NAM were also intended to rally political support at home and to disarm a range of domestic critics. The Baathist regime's base remained Sunni Muslims, who formed 20 percent of the population, outnumbered by the 60 percent Shiite majority and roughly equal to the Kurdish population. The Kurds represented a separatist threat that periodically flared into violence. A more serious danger was potential Shiite unrest, fanned by the Khomeini revolution that threatened to transcend borders and radicalize Shiite Muslims in Iraq. This threat eventually prompted Baghdad, in September 1980, to invade Iran, seeking to damage or topple the Khomeini regime and advance Iraqi claims to sovereignty over the disputed Shatt-al-Arab waterway. A swift, surgical stroke into Khuzistan, planned to capitalize on Iran's military disarray, degenerated into prolonged warfare with heavy losses on both sides. In the first year, Iraq sustained over 10,000 killed, and total casualties were estimated as high as 50,000. While the fighting had relatively little effect on property and life in Baghdad, its prolongation inevitably shook confidence in Saddam Hussein and led to a mood of frustration and fatigue. A war of attrition, fought by Iraq's primarily Shiite troops against Iranian Shiites, could only be a political liability.

In these circumstances, the Seventh NAM Summit became increasingly important as an expedient to divert the attention of a war-weary public. Headed by veteran diplomat and 1981–82 General Assembly President Ismat Kittani, a large Iraqi staff lobbied at all NAM meetings to counter sentiment to change the venue and, in contrast with Cuba, to project an image of statesmanship and conciliation. During a December 1981 NAM ministerial labor conference in Baghdad, Saddam Hussein called pointedly for the movement to "be more truly non-aligned." As Iran's "Operation Ramadan" brought fighting into Iraq for the first time during July 1982, Baghdad reaffirmed its commitment to the September summit. Highest priority was assigned to completion of the conference complex, including artillery protection and air-raid tunnels between hotels and the conference center. Flags of expected participants were displayed throughout Baghdad by early summer.

Only when forced by President Castro's unilateral announcement of August 3 did Saddam Hussein reluctantly agree to India's alternative presidency. With no guarantee of succeeding India in 1986, the decision represented for Iraq a considerable loss of time and money, as well as prestige within the NAM. While the summit very nearly took place on schedule, Iran's capability to strike Baghdad and its clear intent to disrupt the meeting ultimately proved decisive. The spectacle of a non-aligned summit in the midst of war between members would, in any case, have severely undercut traditional non-aligned claims to mediation and peaceful resolution of disputes. The episode further underscored the discrepancy between Iraq's national agenda as prospective chairman and that of the overall movement. Unlike Cuba prior to the Havana Summit, Baghdad could not disguise its real objectives in face of a highly visible war of its own making. As president, Iraq would also probably have been tempted to put national and narrow Arab interests above those of the overall movement by forcing the issue of Israel's expulsion from the General Assembly.

Beyond India

The precedent of India's irregular accession to the chairmanship could pose problems for the future. Although the circumstances were unique, other states may be tempted to oppose or seek to reverse decisions made at the summit level. Lurches every three years from chairmen of such different political orientation and systems as Cuba and India, in any case, detract from the continuity of the movement. As a result, summits marking such transitions tend to be dominated by ideology and debate over the movement's orientation, with frequent use of catchwords such as "natural alliance," "equidistance," "genuine" or "authentic" non-alignment, return to "original principles," and "non-alignment plus." Obsessive concern at such summits with shaping the incoming chairman's approach to the presidency and influencing the choice of a successor tend to limit innovative approaches to the substantive agenda. Debate over issues like Kampuchea and the Indian Ocean becomes a test of strength among rival factions in the movement, unrelated to "real world" solutions.

The selection process itself limits to some extent an incoming chairman's ability to control the outcome of a summit. The declarations of the New Delhi Summit, for example, were more strident on the Middle East, Central America, and southern Africa than anticipated by those who expected a shift away from rhetoric of the Cuban years. They reflected a vigorous campaign by Cuba and its allies to maximize their continuing leverage, particularly on Latin American issues, and to limit the countertrend toward more centrist positions. On the other hand, non-aligned chairmen, or "chairpersons," in Mrs. Gandhi's phrase, have usually tended, with the exception of Cuba, to downplay their influence over summit declarations in order not to be held accountable, particularly by the superpowers, for specific, hostile positions of the NAM.

Summit meetings, occurring at the outset of a president's term, are intensively covered by the media and, for the general public, represent from the tip of the NAM iceberg, glimpsed every three years. Great attention is given to their final declarations, which are often important as points of reference for the Third World majority at the United

Nations. Yet summits are only the visible part of a chairman's responsibility, and probably less important than mobilization of non-aligned opinion and resources over a three-year term. The behind-the-scenes role, largely focused in New York, involves coordination of ongoing, day-to-day activities on many levels. (See Appendix H.) Vital to this process is the chairman's ability to set non-aligned priorities in the period between summits, to enforce linkages between positions in various international bodies, and to deploy its diplomatic resources to sustain the movement's activism. Given the tendency of more passive members to minimize involvement from one summit to the next, the degree of support commanded by the chairman directly affects the movement's discipline and effectiveness as a Third World lobby. Cuba, by overplaying its hand at Havana and going against the majority on Afghanistan and Kampuchea, presided over a fractured body by the end of its term. India, by adopting a less belligerent and more impartial stance toward the 1983 Summit, is better positioned to play an organizational role, but inherited a badly polarized movement.

In the longer run, much will depend on selection of a broadly acceptable chairman to follow India. The question overhung the New Delhi Summit, but despite Fidel Castro's demand that a decision "be made at this august meeting" and the fear of many delegates that failure to do so would reflect continuing division, no agreement was reached. Warfare that blocked the Baghdad Summit raged unabated, and Iraq's candidacy was inextricably linked to continuing, but ineffectual, NAM mediation between Baghdad and Teheran. A new and ill-fated Iranian military offensive, launched just before the summit, was probably in part planned to discredit the Iraqi candidacy and keep the war issue alive. Most delegates favored a compromise solution, and trial balloons by Nigeria and Guinea offered temporary hope. Yet Iraq still commanded the support of about 40 members, including many bound by ties of oil and aid, as well as of India, beholden by its earlier deal to exchange presidencies with Iraq. Ultimately, the need for consensus prevented agreement as these states proved unwilling to risk rupture with Baghdad.

As debate intensified at New Delhi, other claimants, impelled by varying national interests, pressed their own cases. Although Muammar Qaddafi did not attend, Libya was vociferous in promoting its ambitions for an international and pan-Arab role, largely frustrated during Qaddafi's nearly 15-year rule. Its bid to be chairman was part of a concerted campaign including the OAU presidency in 1982 and even that of the General Assembly in 1984. Such plans foundered, however, over Libya's stubborn insistence on seating the SDAR and the Chadian rebel government of Goukouni Oueddei during two abortive attempts to hold the 1982 OAU Summit in Tripoli. Otherwise, Libya, as head of a unified OAU, might have been a serious, however improbable, contender for the NAM chairmanship. For similar reasons of international legitimacy and prestige, North Korea remains an unlikely candidate for the presidency in 1986, in part to offset South Korea's bid to host the 1986 Asian Games and 1988 Olympics. Finally, Syria also has lobbied for the office, probably as a spoiler to the candidacy of Iraq.

These, and possibly other candidacies for 1986, will be decided at a ministerial plenary to be held in Angola during August 1985. While taking note that an "overwhelming majority" of members favored Iraq, the heads of state made no recommendation at New Delhi. The environment of the ministerial meeting in Luanda, Angola, will, however, favor radical candidates, and Iraq, although less extreme than in past years, could still emerge as chairman in 1986 if its war with Iran is ended or reduced to a low level. In the longer term, effective leadership of the non-aligned will depend on more active involvement by larger members with resources and influence, such as Nigeria and Indonesia, which have tended to stay on the sidelines. The field of candidates, narrowed to members with wealth and larger ambitions, could also be expanded if the movement's increasing emphasis on Latin America eventually attracts potential leaders like Brazil or Mexico.

Reprinted with permission of S.G. Ravishankar.

6
The New Delhi Summit

Real success lies not in what is happening here at the conference, but what will happen in the Movement in the future.

Indira Gandhi, March 1983

A movement as large and procedure-bound as the NAM, like an ocean liner, changes course only by slow degrees. The Seventh Summit was clearly shaped by the three and a half years of Cuban leadership that preceded it. Some members speculated in advance that adverse reaction to Cuba's style of leadership could bring about a positive swing of the pendulum toward balance and moderation. This appears not to have been the case at the Seventh Summit itself, but may still prove accurate in the longer run. Others foresaw that reaction to Cuba would lead to a period of renewed factional differences and jockeying for power under India, limiting the prospect for innovation on issues of substance. Some, like Deputy Prime Minister Rajaratnan of Singapore, went so far as to predict darkly that "The people of the world will view this summit as merely a foregathering of leaders whose pronouncements and rhetoric will not put one extra grain of rice into their near empty rice bowls or a roof over their heads or provide jobs to prop up their fading sense of dignity as human beings."

While it is difficult for an outsider barred from the proceedings to fit the jigsaw puzzle together, the outcome of the Seventh Summit was probably influenced as much by the movement's internal dynamics, outlined in earlier chapters, as by any grand design. The African, Arab, and Latin American regional groups once again proved to be the strongest components of the NAM. Their decisions, reached in closed caucus, were passed along for routine approval by the heads of state, defying efforts by intermediate committees to give harmony or balance to the overall package of summit documents. Only Asian questions like Kampuchea, not subject to a regional group, and larger issues of the Indian Ocean, the next summit, and economics engaged the full plenary and finally resulted in broadly based agreement to disagree.

While some delegates, even Mrs. Gandhi, referred to the end of the colonial era and the need to find a new, more relevant ethos for the movement, the anti-colonial dynamic also remained a powerful force in shaping the summit's outcome. Ironically, Jawaharlal Nehru had said at the Belgrade Summit some 20 years earlier that talk of imperialism was "like flogging a dead horse."[35] Yet the Political Declaration continued to define non-alignment in the negative and anti-imperialist terms of Fidel Castro:

> The quintessence of the policy of non-alignment has always consisted of the struggle against imperialism, colonialism, neo-colonialism, *apartheid,* racism including Zionism, and all forms of foreign aggression, occupation, domination, interference or hegemony as well as against great power and bloc policies tending to perpetuate the division of the world into blocs. It rejects all forms of subjugation, dependence, interference or intervention, direct or indirect, overt or covert and all pressures—political, diplomatic, economic, military and cultural—in international relations.

With few colonies left to rally around, the heads of state were forced further afield, endorsing, for example, Argentina's claim to the uninhabited South Sandwich Islands, several thousand miles from the South American mainland, and making claim to Antarctica "for the benefit of all mankind." A penultimate version of the Economic Declaration went so far as to describe the antarctic region as a "hotbed of international tension."

The specific results of the New Delhi Summit were political and economic declarations, totaling 138 pages, and a miscellany of related appeals, messages, and action programs. As an overall package, the summit documents bear the imprint of decision-making by regional and interest groups within the NAM and show little attempt at even-handedness toward non-member states. The key Political Declaration, for example, castigates the United States 23 times by name, in addition to specific mention of independence of Puerto Rico, the "military base at Diego Garcia," various pieces of congressional legislation, and innumerable indirect references using "imperialism" as a code word for the United States. By comparison, Britain is mentioned by name three times over the Falkland (Malvinas) Islands, and France twice in connection with island dependencies in the Indian Ocean. The Soviet Union is cited once in a neutral context.

While the New Delhi Summit appears not to have realigned the movement on points of substance or to reflect a fundamental break with the non-aligned radicalism of the Cuban years, there were important nuances, particularly on the economic side, and differences of tactics and style in India's approach to the presidency. India reversed the Cuban formula of placing a maximalist draft on the agenda and lobbying hard to defend it against moderate revisions. Instead, its first draft was a bland, relatively balanced document that India defended only in a few areas of direct national interest, preferring the role of noncommittal arbiter. In a movement as self-conscious as the NAM, such differences of style can foreshadow changes in direction as much as communiqués. At Havana, the contrast between an aging "old guard," represented by Tito, and Castro, as incoming chairman, was stark. In New Delhi, the roles were reversed, and Mrs. Gandhi's incisive speeches, taking the high ground on disarmament and economics, largely upstaged Castro's two-hour harangue blaming the United States for all Third World ills from malaria to terrorism. At his conclusion, none rose to applaud in the sparsely occupied hall.

A preliminary assessment of the New Delhi Summit, as implied in the initial quotation from Mrs. Gandhi, should thus probably start from the premise that style, tactics, and procedure were as important as the agreed final text. Since the Colombo Conference of 1976, non-aligned summits have struggled to reconcile essentially irreconcilable points of view, with loose consensus as a fig leaf to preserve a semblance of NAM unity. At New Delhi, the parameters within which issues were considered were further circumscribed by the most intensive prior consultations in NAM history. Whether on Afghanistan, Kampuchea, or global economic negotiations, the basic compromises could be predicted beforehand. What remained to be seen were the tone and influence of various factions over rhetoric, particularly in the Political Declaration. Understanding of these trade-offs requires a brief review of the jockeying for influence that immediately preceded the summit.

The Buildup

Pre-summit diplomacy recalled the lengthy power struggle between Yugoslavia and Cuba leading up to Havana in 1979. Yet, reflecting the movement's polarization over the preceding three years, a larger number of members were involved in what might be called a diplomatic full-court press, compacted into four months between the selection of India as chairman and the actual summit. To some degree, however, these advance meetings and bilateral consultations tended to neutralize each other, entrenching existing positions and ensuring that, despite India's relatively balanced first draft, the final result would differ little from recent positions of the NAM. Another result was increased tension, if not outright hostility, between conservative and radical extremes that carried over to the summit in outspoken verbal exchanges and propaganda. Pamphlet wars erupted in New Delhi between Iran and Iraq, and Singapore and Cuba. In one exchange, Singapore described the Havana Summit as the "lowest point of degradation" in non-aligned history and was, in turn, reviled by Cuba as a "U.S. spokesman with a Chinese accent."

Skirmishing for influence, in a lull since the Baghdad Summit was scrapped in August, began again at the October 1982 ministerial meeting in New York, which gave approval to India's deal with Iraq. In return for concessions in the wording of the New York communiqué, Cuba insisted that a separate meeting of the NACB be held in Managua a month before the summit and be devoted to Latin American issues. As the last hurrah of Cuba's presidency, it was intended to commit the movement in advance of New Delhi to a set of radical positions, particularly on Central America, thus circumscribing the capacity of moderates to seek changes during the summit.

The meeting, held from January 10–14, 1983, was also an unparalleled opportunity to indoctrinate Third World delegations, removed from Latin American issues, with the Cuban and Nicaraguan version of events in Central America. The hosts lost no opportunity to proselytize about alleged U.S. aggression, including delegate tours of the Nicaraguan-Honduran border and meetings with victims of anti-Sandinista attacks. An "anti-imperialist" rally of 80,000 Nicaraguan workers, released early from factories, was held January 12, and arriving and departing delegates passed under huge effigies of Uncle Sam and Margaret Thatcher strung up over the road. Hangers-on from the Puerto Rican Socialist party (PRSP) and the Puerto Rican Independence party (PRIP) were much in evidence, as well as an American Indian delegation committed to the "struggle against U.S. destabilization."

The Managua meeting followed the standard pattern of hammering out consensus on a final communiqué. An egregious first draft concluded with a quotation from Simón Bolívar that "the United States seems destined by providence to plague the Americas with misery in the name of freedom." The draft was toned down and most specific references to the United States eliminated, allowing moderate members to claim progress in relation to an unacceptable starting point. Yet it still condemned alleged U.S. aggression against Nicaragua and contained stinging criticism of U.S. policies in Central America. For Nicaragua, the meeting brought essentially bilateral problems with the United

States into the non-aligned forum and conferred a degree of international legitimacy on the Sandinista government.

As a tactical ploy to structure the parameters for handling Latin American issues at New Delhi, the Managua meeting succeeded brilliantly. Whole sections of its final communiqué were written without opposition into the Political Declaration of the summit. Unable in three years to gain endorsement of the "natural ally" thesis, Cuba won at Managua at least tacit acceptance for its variant form of the U.S. as "natural enemy." Banners throughout Managua proclaimed, "To be non-aligned is to be anti-imperialist," and the unwritten corollary was cleary "To be anti-imperialist is to be anti-U.S." At New Delhi, Castro could then argue in his plenary speech that the Managua meeting unequivocally identified "those responsible for the situation in Central America." As one delegate commented in frustration, moderates at New Delhi were unable to withstand the "pressures of something we have previously acquiesced in."

Pre-summit consultations among moderate NAM members, begun in November, intensified after Managua. The Indian draft, circulated in early February, posed an unfamiliar tactical question of how to preserve a basically middle-of-the-road summit declaration from wholesale radical amendments. While India had consulted closely with at least 40 members before circulating the draft, Cuba and the radical element were adamantly opposed to its relatively evenhanded treatment of the superpowers. The draft gave unusual emphasis to disarmament and economics, generally avoided contentious formulations, and referred only twice by name to the United States. A reference to Puerto Rico, while from Washington's point of view interference per se in U.S. internal affairs, was limited to support for the right of Puerto Ricans "to determine their own future."

Among the traditional non-aligned powers, leaders and senior diplomats of India, Egypt, and Yugoslavia crisscrossed the non-aligned world. India sent high-level delegations to all six previous summit capitals, President Mubarak touched base in Belgrade and New Delhi, and Yugoslav President Peter Stambolić toured Asia. Delegations from the five ASEAN states convened February 27 in Bangkok to coordinate strategy for their three members party to the NAM. By the time expert-level meetings opened in New Delhi on February 28, some 20 "like-minded" delegations had exchanged views in advance and met twice on the margins of the official proceedings to coordinate tactics. On the opposite side, radicals lost no time in following up their gains at Managua and, led by Cuba, Nicaragua, and Vietnam again proved better organized and more disciplined than the loose coalition of moderates.

Vice-President Rodriguez and Foreign Minister Malmierca of Cuba visited New Delhi separately during February to lobby for changes in the Indian draft and to pave the way for Castro.

In addition to members with global interests in the NAM, "one-issue" delegations blitzed the general membership before New Delhi, lobbying for their points of view on particular issues. Rival Iranian and Iraqi emissaries pushed their respective lines on the war. North and South Korean delegations followed one another around the world. Argentina, Guyana, Belize, Venezuela, Bolivia, Cyprus, and Libya advanced or defended against special boundary or territorial claims. Mauritian Prime Minister Aneerood Jugnauth campaigned throughout India for sovereignty over the Chagos Archipelago, including Diego Garcia. The great powers also lobbied from the sidelines as the summit approached. Chinese Premier Zhao Ziyang touched on non-aligned issues in key African capitals during January 1983, President François Mitterand of France made a state visit to India, and a senior British Foreign Office head consulted in New Delhi just before the summit. The United States and USSR followed strategies outlined in Part III of this volume.

Finally, positions at New Delhi were shaped in varying degrees by a series of meetings outside the movement in which key members participated. Most important was the Palestinian National Conference at Algiers in mid-February, which by its strident rhetoric inevitably conditioned summit language on the Middle East. A simultaneous meeting of frontline African states in Zimbabwe helped radicalize positions on southern Africa and ensured condemnation of U.S. policies there. The final language adopted at New Delhi exceeded the Harare communiqué, however, in specific condemnations of the United States. To a lesser extent, the October Commonwealth meeting in Suva, Fiji, also served as a sounding board. Finally, the Saharan war was preempted as a major issue by the meeting on February 26 of Moroccan King Hassan and Algerian President Chadli Benjedid.

By the time the summit opened, such prior soundings and contacts had revealed the relative strengths and weaknesses on most issues, suggesting where trade-offs would be made. Most delegations knew, for example, that ASEAN would not disrupt the meeting by insistence on seating Norodom Sihanouk of the exile Coalition Government of Democratic Kampuchea (CGDK), that Vietnam would drop its insistence on seating his rival, Heng Samrin, in favor of an empty seat, and that calls for specific reference to the Soviet Union in Afghanistan were little more than bluff, to be used as leverage for amendments on the Indian Ocean or elsewhere. In such negotiations, the unity of states like Cuba, Vietnam, and Nicaragua in undercutting the Indian draft was difficult for moderates to counteract. Some argued that the best defense would be an offense, and made efforts to further improve the draft from their point of view. Singapore, for example, quixotically circulated an amendment "rejecting all attempts to make the Movement the strategic reserve or the natural ally of any superpower or bloc." Yet such moderate amendments proved in most cases to be only bargaining chips, gradually relinquished in the face of concerted radical assault through the regional groups.

The Seventh Summit

Against this background, the conference opened February 28. India, despite only four months' lead time, went to great lengths to meet the logistical and security requirements of the largest gathering of heads of state and government in history. In all, 47 heads of state, 23 prime ministers or vice-presidents, and 24 foreign ministers headed delegations. Four new members—Bahamas, Barbados, Colombia, and Vanuatu—were admitted, bringing membership to 101. Of these, all were represented at New Delhi except Saint Lucia and Kampuchea, whose seat, following the precedent of Havana, was left vacant. Also present were 18 observers and 28 guest delegations from an additional 19 countries, international organizations including 15 branches of the United Nations, and various liberation groups. (See Appendix B.) A press corps of about 1,000 was on hand to cover the gathering.

On the periphery of these 143 delegations and outside the formal proceedings, there hovered additional groups, seeking to influence those inside and posing often acute protocol and security problems for India. Demonstrations by Afghan *mujahidin* resistance groups and by Tibetans promoting observer status for the Dalai Lama ended in wholesale arrests before they reached the Vigyan Bhavan conference center. Despite the presence of an official observer delegation from El Salvador, the Nicaragua-based Faribundo Martí Liberation Front (FMLF) lobbied many delegations and announced at a press conference that El Salvador would become a full NAM member following the final guerrilla victory. A five-man Chadian group claiming to represent the exile Goukouni government arrived on Libyan passports and fared less well. By chance they were spotted on the plane from Paris by members of the legitimate Chadian delegation, who protested, resulting in their forced return to Paris after 24 hours under guard. A Polisario delegation that arrived March 3 with Algerian passports was, by contrast, allowed to stay, but not admitted to the conference. Iraqi and Iranian dissident groups also sought the spotlight, with the latter staging mock Khomeini-style executions.

Such diversions added to security precautions at the summit, already tight following an abortive bazooka attack against the U.S. embassy on February 11. Nor were the risks entirely from outside, with several pairs among the non-aligned at various stages of war. Iran and Iraq, for example, could not be housed in the same hotel, according to normal alphabetical assignment, and each brought contingents of armed commandos. Official residences of both countries were ringed by sand-bagged machine gun emplacements for the summit period. All but heads of state were repeatedly frisked on entering the conference. Food for the heads of state was even subject to taste tests at three stages. According to the Indian press, the whole operation required 30,000 security personnel, 10,000 vehicles, and a conference staff of 6,000, including 218 foreign technicians hired through a London agency.

Within the closed conference complex, the meeting, as at past summits, was divided into three phases: expert or ambassadorial-level consultations on February 28–March 2, foreign ministers on March 3–5, and heads of state on March 7–12. The latter two each had unscheduled one-day carry-overs to complete the agenda. The first items of business were procedural: admission of new members and observers, formation of the 27-member Conference Bureau, selection of chairmen for key conference committees and other summit offices, and pending NACB reports. The Conference Bureau, in effect, replaces the NACB for the duration of a summit and advises the chairman in the event of procedural problems. Used effectively at Havana to endorse Castro's hard-line tactics, the bureau was hotly contested in New Delhi but did not afterward play a major role. Nevertheless, competition for its 27 seats, and particularly for chairmanship of the pivotal Political and Economic committees, reflected intense jockeying for power before the summit. Moderates engineered Yugoslavia's chairmanship of the Political Committee, but were less successful in the economic area. There, radicals like Ethiopia and Madagascar put ideology above regional loyalties in successfully urging Nigeria and Zaire to withdraw, throwing the chairmanship to Nicaragua.

Membership issues tend to be routine at a summit, with problematic applications screened out well in advance by the Coordinating Bureau. Thus, Venezuela's request to upgrade from observer to full member was withdrawn earlier in February, when it became clear that Guyana had succeeded in mobilizing African opinion against it. Honduras's application to become an observer was predictably rejected after strong opposition from Cuba, Nicaragua, and Grenada. Earlier feelers about guest status for France and Greece were also politely rebuffed. Word of France's new "opening" to the Third World reached the press, however, and was officially disavowed by an embarrassed Mitterand. Greece was finally discouraged by the prospect that, if successful, Turkey would follow suit. Thus, on membership issues, there was little new business for the summit beyond acceptance of Vanuatu's last-minute application for membership and rejection as "too late" of Luxembourg's request to be a guest. Passage of the 100 mark for membership provided a psychological boost, however, and the new members and observers, drawn largely from Latin America, strengthened the recent trend to "Latinize" the movement.

With procedural issues out of the way, meetings concentrated on reaching consensus where it was possible and identifying areas of disagreement. By virtue of the movement's composition and unique decision-making, issues tended to be channeled onto three tracks, while, as in the General Assembly, speeches largely for home consumption were delivered in plenary by all but ten delegation heads. Political issues impinging on more than one region, such as disarmament or the Indian Ocean, and Asian matters, for which there was no regional caucus, were discussed in plenary or allocated to geographically balanced working groups, along with institutional issues such as the role of the NACB or the venue of the next summit. If consensus was not reached, they were then "bumped up" to the foreign ministers and finally to the heads of state, who, in the absence of agreement, returned them to the NACB for recommendations at the next NAM meeting. Issues of Africa, Latin America, and the Middle East, by contrast, were first taken up by their respective regional groups. These, in turn, passed recommendations to the Political Committee's drafting group and eventually to the full committee, but once agreed at the regional level, language in almost every case remained inviolate. Economic issues, by nature more global and diffuse, were debated in open-ended committees and working groups, where better prepared and more economically sophisticated members like India, Algeria, and Sri Lanka tended to predominate. Economic policy, while hotly contested by India and Algeria, was in general less controversial than political issues.

Political Issues at Stake

New Delhi, like other recent summits, covered the gamut of Third World issues. Yet within each area a select few tended to be singled out as tests of strength among various groups. Of these the Asian issues, in the absence of regional consensus and perhaps because of the venue in India, dominated debate from the outset. Kampuchea, in particular, served as a lightning rod for a bitter contest, pitting the ASEAN states against Vietnam, Cuba, and India. The issue was in two parts: which, if either, rival Kampuchean delegation to seat, and the wording of a call for withdrawal of foreign forces. At Havana in 1979, the chairman had prevailed, over strident protest, in keeping the seat vacant, but that decision was later overturned elsewhere by a non-aligned majority that voted in four successive years to seat the exile government of Pol Pot at the United Nations. With the formation in 1982 of the broader CGDK, including Prince Norodom Sihanouk, the number of non-aligned states recognizing the exile coalition rose from 36 at Havana to 59. India remained the only state outside the Communist bloc to recognize the Heng Samrin regime imposed by Vietnam.

The ASEAN drive, headed by Singapore, to undo the "empty seat formula" was intended to prove that the 1979 "consensus" imposed by Cuba was "illegal" and to put radicals on the defensive by giving moderate members an issue to rally around. Their efforts paralyzed the ministerial-level meeting for three days while 61 members spoke on respective sides of the question. At the conclusion of these speeches, Indian Foreign Secretary Rasgotra predictably announced that the movement was sharply divided, and that the best option was to leave the seat vacant and refer the issue to the NACB for a report to the 1985 ministerial meeting. The outcome was thus an elaborately choreographed compromise, allowing ASEAN to maintain that there was no NAM consensus and that the Havana decision was "illegal," preventing further disruption of the summit and giving Vietnamese Foreign Minister Nguyen Co Thach room to claim the Vietnamese "could live with the Kampuchea decision, time is in their favor." The seating finally resolved, there was little disposition to fight the same battle over language on Kampuchea in the Political Declaration. Extreme amendments put on the agenda by both ASEAN and Vietnam in effect canceled each other, and the noncommittal language of India's first draft was adopted.

The Kampuchean debate also reflected uneasiness on the part of many members over recent radical campaigns to suspend or expel from the movement states considered politically unacceptable. The movement has no procedure nor precedent for suspension, although Chile has not been sent invitations to NAM meetings since the Colombo Summit as a protest agaist the overthrow of Salvador Allende. Exploiting this lack, Arab members called for Egypt's expulsion in

1979 and 1981, and at New Delhi, Libya questioned the credentials of both Egypt and Chad. Rather than, in turn, challenging the right to membership of Libya, Afghanistan, or even Cuba, moderate members hoped, by referring Kampuchea to a study group, to limit future arbitrary demands for expulsion.

Alliances during the Kampuchean debate also affected the outcome of the summit on other Asian issues. Pyongyang, part-time residence of Norodom Sihanouk, sided with ASEAN and against Vietnam. The North Korean position, perhaps reflecting a "tilt" toward China on its diplomatic tightrope between Beijing and Moscow, was also calculated to win over ASEAN and other moderate states that would otherwise oppose a call for withdrawal of "foreign [U.S.] troops" from South Korea. Withdrawn under pressure by Pyongyang at the 1981 ministerial meeting in New Delhi, this non-aligned article of faith was thus reinserted two years later, despite active lobbying from the sidelines by South Korea. Thirteen states subsequently entered reservations, however, the largest number on any single issue at New Delhi.

The time and intensity devoted to Kampuchea limited enthusiasm for a comparable fight over Afghanistan, although New Delhi was the first NAM summit since the Soviet invasion. Debate proved desultory, resulting in adoption of the 1981 language calling for "withdrawal of foreign troops" and an additional paragraph supporting two-year-old efforts by the United Nations at mediation. Ten states on both sides of the issue entered reservations on this compromise. Pakistani President Zia ul-Haq resolutely ruled out direct talks with Afghanistan, which would imply recognition of a Soviet puppet regime, despite pressure from some members to announce a "breakthrough" during the summit. Calls for reference to the USSR by name were perfunctory and apparently related to the contest over language on the Indian Ocean.

Debate over the Indian Ocean, a non-aligned preoccupation since calls for the IOZP at Lusaka in 1970, invoked, like much of the agenda, the underlying issue of the movement's relationship to the superpowers. It also revolved around New Delhi's view of the Indian Ocean region as a zone of preeminent Indian influence and the more nuanced views of its smaller neighbors. The specific question was whether and how to refer to U.S. military construction on the British-leased island of Diego Garcia without referring to 105,000 Soviet troops in the Afghan hinterland or to Soviet naval facilities in Ethiopia and South Yemen. Sri Lanka, with a stake in U.S. participation in an IOZP conference planned for Colombo in 1984, argued unsuccessfully for deletion of the reference. India resisted, and Mrs. Gandhi singled out Diego Garcia in her inaugural address. In the ensuing debate, Mauritius referred to the island's 1,800 inhabitants, relocated and compensated by Britain, as "Palestinians of the Indian Ocean." The compromise that emerged, recondite even in NAM terms, was to refer to "the military base at Diego Garcia" as a danger to the "sovereignty, territorial integrity and peaceful development of Mauritius and other states," but to do it under the heading of Mauritian sovereignty rather than of the Indian Ocean.

Also occupying general attention at the summit was the issue of mediation between Iran and Iraq. The final Political Declaration stated that disputes among member states "were aggravated by former colonial powers as the outcome of conditions of disequilibrium imposed from outside rather than any deliberate attempt on the part of fraternal states of the Movement to fuel animosities among themselves." It was, nevertheless, hard to argue that the 30-month-old war did not undermine the credibility of a movement dedicated to world peace. Yet last-minute decisions by President Saddam Hussein and President Muhammad Ali Khamenei not to attend ended hopes for mediation at the summit. Iran's continuing demands for the trial of Saddam Hussein and compensation of $50–$200 billion were, in any case, uncompromising. Handling of the Iran-Iraq issue in the declaration was also inextricable from Iraq's pursuit of the 1986 summit. In the end, the heads of state were able only to express appreciation for the unsuccessful efforts to date of the NAM Mediation Committee. A separate appeal to the two parties by the chairman was curtly dismissed by the Iranian spokesman: "We welcome Mrs. Gandhi's initiative, but our thoughts are on the battlefield."

Unlike the foregoing issues, which were widely discussed by the general membership and subject to input from states of every region, matters dealing with Latin America, the Middle East, and Africa were first debated and largely determined in narrowly focused and closed regional groups. As suggested above, Asian issues, reflecting a wide spectrum of views, generally reached the final declaration in terms differing little from the original Indian draft. The procedure—adopted at the New Delhi Summit but invoked only selectively by the political committees—that where no consensus existed, the Indian text would stand, further reinforced this tendency. Sections on Kampuchea, Afghanistan, and the Indian Ocean, while subject to some additions and revisions, retained much language verbatim in the final version. By contrast, the regional groups were more vulnerable to well-organized radical minorities, and the disposition there was to rewrite rather than revise the draft text. As at previous NAM meetings, the levels of representation on radical delegations tended to be higher than those on moderates, giving them a considerable advantage. Angola, Cuba, Ethiopia, Nicaragua, Surinam, Afghanistan, Grenada, and Vietnam all had large delegations led by the president or prime minister in New Delhi. By contrast, Indonesia, Sudan, Ivory Coast, Cameroon, Saudi Arabia, Senegal and other moderates were represented at a lower level. The latter were unable to make their views heard equally, and may have lost time by seeking cable instructions from home capitals. Since deliberations of the regional groups were closed and recommendations did not emerge until the last days of the summit, some of those lulled into a false sense of security by the Indian draft were surprised by the extent of last-minute changes.

On Latin American issues, Cuba, Grenada, Nicaragua, and Surinam made skillful use of the precedent and momentum gained at Managua. The final version, as a result, closely resembled the Managua communiqué with repeated criticism of U.S policy in Central America and tough language against Britain on the Falklands. It also restored the call for independence of Puerto Rico, albeit with 10 reservations noted, and contained the usual litany of references to Guantánamo Bay, the U.S. "blockade" of Cuba, implementation of the Carter-Torrijos treaties, and "imperialist" aggression against Grenada. Moderates in the Latin American caucus, some having justified their membership as a potential restraint to radical excess, were conspicuously silent. As at past meetings, each was occupied with its own particular desiderata or conflicting claims, and unwilling to risk support for them by taking on larger issues.

Treatment of the Middle East was similar. After PLO withdrawal from Beirut and dispersal throughout the Arab world, sympathy and support for the Palestinian cause were at a high point in New Delhi. Yasir Arafat, more than any other delegate, elicited cheers and embraces at every session. His final appeal for an eight-member NAM committee to follow up on Palestine was widely endorsed. The Political Declaration also bore the unmistakable stamp of decisions and rhetoric from the mid-February Palestinian National Conference in Algiers. Of 23 specific references to the United States in the final declaration, 13 occur in the Middle Eastern section. As at Algiers, however, there was no explicit rejection of the Reagan Peace Plan. The Arab caucus deleted, however, a reference in the Indian draft to the "right of all states in the region to existence within internationally recognized frontiers," which could imply recognition of Israel. The final version also included the United States in responsibility for the Sabra and Shatila massacres, and called for the Security Council to impose mandatory sanctions against Israel. Other changes included, at the insistence of Lebanon, broadening the call for Israeli withdrawal to cover "all non-Lebanese forces" and addition, at Iraq's request, of a separate paragraph on "Israeli aggression against Iraqi nuclear installations."

Finally, within the African group there was unanimity, despite OAU differences over other issues, on toughening the language on southern Africa. The latter remains a "motherhood" issue within the NAM, and the Africans criticized the United States for "linkage or parallelism" between a Namibian settlement and Cuban troop withdrawal from Angola, as well as for a policy of "constructive engagement" toward South Africa. They also expressed "deep concern" over efforts of the Western Contact Group, and called on the Security Council to again take up implementation of Resolution 435 on Namibia "as soon as possible."

The Economic Declaration

The New Delhi Summit occurred at an important moment for the world economy. A three-year recession in the West showed signs of abating, but developing countries continued to suffer from low commodity prices, high interest rates, and an overall slowdown in world trade. In 1981, economies of the developing world grew by an average 0.6 percent, which, with high population growth, meant a fall in per capita income for the first time in 20 years. Final statistics for 1982 promised to be worse. The NIEO package, put on the agenda at Algiers a decade earlier, seemed no closer to realization. Global negotiations, written into the Havana Declaration by Algeria, had not begun despite three years of pressure from the Third World. Cumulative debt of the Third World totaled $600 billion, and near bankruptcy in several major countries raised a real prospect of Western lenders reducing further capital flows to the Third World at a time of negative growth and average 10 percent unemployment.

The summit also occurred just before a new round of international economic negotiations, at a moment when the developing countries seemed in more than usual tactical disarray on how to secure a fair hearing from the industrialized world. Many, therefore, looked to New Delhi to provide broad guidance to the G-77 before its March–April preparatory meeting in Buenos Aires for the pivotal Sixth UNCTAD Conference on Trade, Commodities, and Raw Materials to be held in Belgrade during June and July. Forward-looking delegations also saw an opportunity to influence the economic summit meeting of the United States, Canada, Britain, France, West Germany, Italy, and Japan at

Williamsburg, in Virginia, in May and, ultimately, to resume a Cancún-type dialogue with the West. Many recalled the "catalytic" role of Algeria in setting a broad economic agenda for the Third World in 1973, and looked to India for similar direction. Crucial to the economic deliberations at New Delhi would be the contradiction between traditional non-aligned commitment to the NIEO package, including global negotiations, and the need to implement more immediate relief measures and put forward a cohesive program the West would take seriously in coming negotiations.

The resulting Economic Declaration appeared, however, to be a patchwork of compromises rather than a new or consistent statement of strategy. It resulted, in large part, from trade-offs between countries still committed to global negotiations and others seeking an acceptable formula to bury them, between OPEC and non-OPEC members, and between special lobbies like the major debtor states, the least less-developed countries (LLDC's), landlocked states, island states, and others with special needs. In the end, global negotiations were neither scrapped nor fully endorsed, but downgraded to a long-term objective. The relative priority between "immediate measures" and global negotiations was left deliberately ambiguous. India's call for a separate monetary conference represented a new element, but its scope and relationship to global negotiations remained unclear.

Particularly influential players in these negotiations were India, as host and author of the first draft; Nicaragua, as chairman of the Economic Committee; Bangladesh, as chairman of the G-77; Algeria, which continued to push for a global round; and Sri Lanka, which advocated new summit-level consultations with the West and headed a special working group. Egypt acted as spokesman for the LLDCs, and Mexico, Venezuela, and Brazil, while observers, formed a strong debtor lobby behind the scenes. The latter trio, among others, was able to restrain those who argued that an announcement of collective default would maximize Third World leverage by pointing out that it would have the opposite effect of freezing further credit. A multi-lateral financing facility for energy development, proposed by India, was relocated, at the insistence of Saudi Arabia and the Arab Gulf states, to "within existing financial institutions such as the World Bank." Typical of compromises reached was the fate of a proposed Third World bank for South–South cooperation, effectively killed by tacit agreement but given "artificial respiration" through a continuing feasibility study. In the energy area, there was less pressure on OPEC members than at Havana, and a brief section of the final declaration focused on measures to be taken by the developed countries and financial institutions.

In its treatment of non-member states, the Economic Declaration was more balanced and less polemic than its political counterpart. Mild criticism of low aid levels from the "socialist countries of Eastern Europe," included in the Indian draft, was dropped, however, in favor of a general appeal to "market or centrally directed and planned economies." It also highlighted the responsibility of "one major industrial country" for the failure to launch global negotiations. Overall, however, the 83-page declaration is repetitious and poorly organized, reflecting hasty additions and compromises in the final days of the summit. An accompanying 17-page "Action Programme for Economic Cooperation" contains 21 calls for separate follow-up conferences or series of meetings.

As an overall package, the economic documents from New Delhi probably do not serve the non-aligned well in advancing a cohesive program likely to command attention and reaction from the developed countries to which it is essentially addressed. The underlying, adversarial assumptions of Western responsibility for conditions in the Third World and of the non-aligned as victims of an "iniquitous economic system" remain unchanged. So do unrealistically high and unrealized U.N. and NAM targets for annual GNP growth, levels of official development assistance, expansion of International Monetary Fund (IMF)/International Bank for Reconstruction and Development (IBRD) lending, and voluntary contributions to the United Nations Development Program (UNDP).

A Preliminary Assessment

As chairman, India appeared more self-assured and was in a stronger international position than when it hosted the 1981 ministerial meeting. Then it was somewhat alienated from the non-aligned majority through its stand on Afghanistan, recognition of the Vietnamese-backed regime in Kampuchea, and a general perception of "tilt" toward Moscow. By 1983, however, India had projected a more balanced foreign policy with which mainstream members of the NAM could identify. Visits by Indira Gandhi to Washington in July 1982 and Moscow in September 1982 were discreetly balanced. Earlier Soviet arms deals were somewhat offset by an agreement in November 1982 to buy 40 Mirage aircraft from France and the earlier purchase of a comparable number of British Jaguar aircraft. A 1981 agreement with the IMF for a three-year extended fund facility of 5 billion special drawing rights (SDRs) also ensured a Western role in the economy.

Against this background, India's overriding interest in the Seventh Summit seemed to be in holding a smooth, well-organized conference without undue acrimony. Such an outcome could, Indians pointed out, shift attention from the movement's "inner contradictions," restore the moral posture of the NAM, and enhance its role in negotiating with the great powers. It could also avoid unsettling delicate Indian relations with the two superpowers, strengthen India's anticipated candidacy for the Security Council in 1984, and consolidate its preeminence in the Indian Ocean. India's approach may also have been subtly influenced by long-standing jealousy of China, a nation only marginally more developed, yet accepted as a great power, member of the nuclear club, and permanent member of the United Nations. A successful NAM chairmanship could, some Indians thought, be a means to similar stature. Finally, the office promised new credentials in foreign affairs for Mrs. Gandhi, the only woman to hold it other than, briefly, Sirimavo Bandaranaike of Sri Lanka. The procession of heads of state and distinguished visitors to New Delhi over the next three years would bring her nearer to the stateman's role of Jawaharlal Nehru, her father.

Domestically, the summit offered some respite for the Congress-I government from political defeats in Karnataka and Andra Pradesh states and mounting communal violence in Assam and Punjab. The relationship, if any, was indirect, however, because of the wide gulf between the conference proceedings and the general Indian population, and the latter's preoccupation with domestic issues. Within India, non-alignment itself had, however, taken on unique domestic connotations during the late 1970s. A political slogan of the Janata party from 1977–79 was "genuine non-alignment," which applied to India's relations with the great powers and its neighbors rather than to the NAM, in which it was then largely inactive. Later, when "genuine non-alignment" became a catch phrase of the movement during the transition from Cuba to India, it was discarded by Mrs. Gandhi because of its earlier connotations and use in domestic political campaigns. Responding to a question in the Lok Sabha in March 1983, she stated delphically that "when the so-called genuine non-alignment was in practice, the rest of the non-aligned world was genuinely perplexed as to our genuine intentions."

India's general approach to the chairmanship was thus one of process rather than ideology. Having trod the middle ground in the first draft, it adopted the role of referee, claiming that the final summit declarations resulted from consensus, not Indian positions for which it could be held accountable. Mrs. Gandhi studiously took the high ground of disarmament and economics in her speeches, reserving allusions like "the hood of the cobra is spread" for the nuclear threat. Yet the first draft did reflect strongly held Indian positions on Kampuchea, Afghanistan, and the Indian Ocean, and on these issues a squadron of Indian diplomats was active behind the scenes to defend the language.

India's recognition of the Heng Samrin government, probably in the context of hostility to China and support for Vietnam as a counterforce in Southeast Asia, made it imperative to avoid NAM recognition of the Sihanouk coalition. India thus preempted ASEAN pressures by a December 19 announcement, reaffirmed by Mrs. Gandhi just before the summit on February 25, that as host it would invite neither side. Once the conference began, Indian officials, with support from Cuba and Vietnam, lobbied to ensure that the speakers' list on Kampuchea was evenly divided, preventing consensus and keeping the seat empty. A list of 43 Sihanouk supporters thus dwindled on the plenary floor to about 30.

Similarly, on the Indian Ocean, New Delhi was preoccupied with U.S. military facilities at Diego Garcia as a threat to Indian influence in the region. Mrs. Gandhi reiterated to the press on February 26 that the final declaration must refer specifically to the return of Diego Garcia to Mauritius and the dismantling of the U.S. base. On Afghanistan, the Indian objective was to avoid specific mention of the Soviet Union, and in her inaugural speech, Mrs. Gandhi referred only to hopes for "early normalcy" in Afghanistan. Finally, India, having gained the chairmanship by default, had an obligation at least to be seen as supporting Iraq's revived candidacy for 1986. In each of these national objectives, Indian diplomacy clearly succeeded without appreciably harming the image of the chairman as mediator rather than lobbyist.

Beyond these limited goals, India did not attempt to manage the process of consensus or to temper language proposed by the regional groups. In the words of its conference spokesman on March 12, the final documents reflected "consensual wisdom," and it would be "wrong" to say that individual countries were responsible for any amendment. To be sure, India did little to discourage the expectations of some moderates and outsiders that the summit would mark a turning point in the movement's direction. As chairman, India also consulted closely with the Cubans, who were reassured that the draft would not be defended against regional pressure for revisions, even including the extremist package worked out at Managua.

Those like Muhiuddin Shawl, a member of the Lok Sabha from Jammu and Kashmire, who stated, "We must assert ourselves at the Seventh Summit at the cost of Russian-Indian friendship," were probably disappointed by the outcome.[36] As Mrs. Gandhi conceded in her inaugural address, "anti-imperialism still conditions our outlook." Indignation over Afghanistan, strong among some Indian intellectuals, proved secondary to political needs and the usual NAM dynamic. By not putting forward fresh ideas on the Iran-Iraq war, Namibia, Afghanistan, Kampuchea, or elsewhere, the NAM did little to meet Mrs. Gandhi's description of it as "history's biggest peace movement" or to command new attention in the West. Typical of the process was an appeal from the summit to the developed world, drafted by India to focus on disarmament and economics, but expanded by interested parties into a litany of Third World issues.

In the longer run, it appears too soon to assess the overall impact of the New Delhi Summit on the credibility and future role of the NAM. The ambiguity of its various proposals, particularly on economics, leaves considerable latitude to the chairman to coordinate and rationalize Third World priorities and strategy in dealing with the North. The importance of expanding the NACB to 74 members is also not to be underestimated in freeing the movement from a minority of radicals who were able to manipulate the bureau's procedures for three years under Cuba. Finally, the summit's place in NAM annals will also depend on the follow-up to bilateral meetings there, such as Lebanese President Amin Gemayel's talks with Syria and the PLO on troop withdrawals, and the signature on March 10, 1983, of accords setting up the Indo-Pakistani Joint Commission, agreed in advance but delayed to add luster to the summit. Assessment must, therefore, await India's success or failure in marshaling non-aligned resources behind a revitalized and more realistic Third World agenda. As a starting point, however, the summit declaration provided no clearcut mandate for the next three years, and the number of members entering formal reservations (43) was the highest in NAM history.

II

Interaction of the NAM and United Nations

7

The Non-Aligned and the United Nations

The non-aligned are losing credibility every year that passes. They survive as an entity because they are able to muster impressive voting strength in the UN and its agencies.

Sri Romesh Thapar

The United Nations is, in practical terms, the measure of non-aligned influence. While the movement's survival and growth since Belgrade is a novel phenomenon, its triennial deliberations per se have had little practical effect. Non-aligned exhortations have not affected East-West relations, which have continued to fluctuate, according to their own rhythm, between cold war and détente. Equally, commitment to decolonization, disarmament, and economic reform depends, in large part, on action by non-member states. The United Nations, thus, becomes simultaneously a fulcrum for non-aligned demands, justification for the movement's existence, and a gauge of its strength. Its parliamentary procedures provide recognition and status for voting blocs or coalitions of which the NAM, as the largest, is a principal beneficiary. While the word "bloc" remains anathema to most members, pressure to conform to the group, particularly on issues where members have no direct national interest, is strong, and helps to paper over the movement's otherwise profound divisions. As in most parliaments, logrolling is the rule, and the non-aligned routinely support fellow members in return for backing on other issues closer to home.

In the course of this political process, the two institutions have inevitably interacted, with lasting effect on both. The more significant influence has been that of the non-aligned on the agenda, institutions, and overall effectiveness of the world body. Yet the movement, too, has been channeled and shaped by its evolving role in New York. In the absence of a U.N. organization, the NAM would probably exist, but in much different form. The United Nations, despite shortcomings, forces an accommodation to dialogue and political process. While irreconcilable demands and stalemate regularly occur, compromise and behind-the-scenes moderation of demands to what is politically possible are the rule on most issues. Working within this system, the NAM has been generally pragmatic in advancing positions on issues like disarmament or North–South negotiations. The overall impact of the United Nations is, thus, to reinforce the movement's strength, influence, and moderate tendencies. A non-aligned organization outside the United Nations would probably alienate conservative members and deteriorate into a more homogeneous alliance of radical states, closer to the Soviet orbit. Their impact, while lessened, would be more confrontational toward the West, resulting in a yet more polarized world.

The influence and accomplishments of the non-aligned at the United Nations are a function of one's point of view, national interests, and expectations for the world organization. The non-aligned, for example, view their objectives as complementary, if not identical, to those of the U.N. Charter. By contrast, the United States and other Western states, outnumbered and in recent years increasingly isolated at the United Nations, view the formation of new blocs and the claimed mutuality of NAM and U.N. interests with suspicion. In fact, there is an obvious tension between the desire of great powers, responsible for most of the budget, to retain control over U.N. activities or programs and the non-aligned drive to eliminate such control. A specific example of this is U.N. funding of assistance to the PLO.

The prestige and reputation of the United Nations, particularly as reflected in the U.S. press, has declined in recent years as non-aligned power has grown within it. The two trends are not necessarily related and, almost 40 years after the San Francisco Conference and the end of World War II, memory is inevitably shorter and reliance less on the United Nations "to save succeeding generations from the scourge of war." The United Nations' share of credit for this period of peace is seldom recognized, and difficult to distinguish from imponderables of the superpower balance and nuclear deterrence. Yet a constant theme in negative press treatment of the United Nations has been that of repetitious and polemical debate, divorced from world realities and increasingly pitting a non-aligned majority against the United States and other Western states. Skepticism about the United Nations and its Third World majority is not limited to the press, and affects the institution itself. A 1981 survey of delegate attitudes, conducted by the U.N. Institute for Training and Research (UNITAR), found significant differences among delegates from developed and less developed states or, put differently, between aligned and non-aligned. The poorer the nation, the higher UNITAR found its delegates' optimism about U.N. ability to affect world crises. In many instances, non-aligned delegates ranked U.N. prospects for solving given problems twice as high as did their Western colleagues.

The United Nations is clearly the focal point for the NAM, whose members have an important stake in its welfare and existence. Almost all have permanent missions in New York where they can meet regularly or on short notice. Many members, lacking a network of embassies, also conduct most bilateral foreign business there as well. On the other hand, the existence and need for a political subgrouping of 100 states implies an ambiguous and less than total acceptance of the United Nations. Both organizations profess a global identity, but the NAM stops well short of universality. Its survival and growth thus reflect a degree of distrust of the larger organization or, as the non-aligned would say, of its failure to live up to the ideals of the U.N. Charter. In their eyes, the movement is, therefore, an essential bulwark for underdeveloped, poor, and formerly colonial U.N. members against designs of richer and imperialist colleagues.

Differing perceptions of the U.N. role and interpretations of the charter by a non-aligned majority are sources of tension within the organization and, some would argue, of its increasing immobility and paralysis. NATO states, excluded by definition from the movement, as are members of the Warsaw Pact, find themselves cast at the United Nations as defenders of the status quo and resistant to a non-aligned agenda for change. Newly elected Western governments, whether in Washington, Paris, or London, are usually eager to launch foreign policy initiatives at the United Nations, and are often frustrated. The non-aligned majority tends to put them on the defensive, seeking to limit criticism or damage to their countries on agenda items beyond their control. The non-aligned, by contrast, blame the superpowers, whose veto power in the Security Council, in their view, immobilizes the organization and frustrates the will of the majority. On this basis, they justify the efforts to revise the U.N. Charter and limit great power prerogatives designed at San Francisco to reflect postwar realities.

The inherent conflict over power, whether through influence over key committees or appointments to the U.N. Secretariat, is paralleled by deep divisions between the non-aligned and the West over substantive matters. In recent years, the issues on which the NAM is most committed at the United Nations—development, the Middle East, and southern Africa—have usually found the United States in direct opposition to non-aligned strategy, whether on North–South negotiations under U.N. auspices or economic sanctions against Israel and South Africa. Non-aligned hostility to the United States on these issues is reinforced by the movement's inherent anti-colonial and anti-Western bias, which, in turn, strengthens their determination to restructure the United Nations and reduce the great powers' role.

The result of this cycle is a climate of confrontation in which the non-aligned, through numbers, and the United States, United Kingdom, and France, through vetoes, each have blocking power. In the process, few initiatives can be mounted by either side, and the organization is less and less able to carry out the purposes stated in its charter. Continuing confrontation over a repetitious yearly agenda is not, however, in the interest of most non-aligned states. Prolonged stalemate further debases the world organization and, with it, the prestige of membership, of particular importance to smaller members. Many in the movement also recognize that it can harm U.N. effectiveness in confronting problems of underdevelopment among less developed NAM states.

Non-Aligned Views of the United Nations

Every summit meeting since Belgrade in 1961 has included an agenda item on strengthening the role of the United Nations, which the non-aligned perceive as vital to their interests. The New Delhi Summit, in fact, designated 1985 as "the year of the United Nations." The movement has three related objectives for the world organization: to maintain and strengthen its role, to restructure and "democratize" its institutions, and to maximize non-aligned leverage and voting power within it. The latter two challenge the status quo, setting in motion a power struggle within the organization probably inconsistent with the first objective of enhancing the U.N. role.

The movement's early commitment to the United Nations, charted by its founders, stemmed from a perception of it as guarantor and protector of smaller, weaker states. While the charter recognized power realities in the veto provision for permanent members of the Security Council, in all other respects U.N. membership confers equality on the sole basis of national independence. Thus, nations like Antigua and Barbuda, Dominica, and the Seychelles, with populations under 100,000, are seated on equal terms with China (over 1 billion) and India (700 million). Alphabetical seating equally makes no economic distinction between members with GNPs ranging from São Tomé and Príncipe ($19.7 million) to the United States ($2.6 trillion). For this reason, formal application for U.N. membership is usually the first priority of newly independent states, and is considered proof positive of their new status, as well as a measure of protection against annexation or attack by larger neighbors. Belize, for example, all of whose territory is claimed by Guatemala and part by Mexico, immediately joined the United Nations on gaining independence in 1981. Its future rests on U.N. membership and a British security guarantee as deterrents to annexation by Guatemala. In the case of Sikkim and Bhutan, comparable Himalayan kingdoms sandwiched between India and China, U.N. membership was arguably the margin of survival. Bhutan, a member of the United Nations since 1971 and of the NAM since 1973, remains independent, if reliant on New Delhi: Sikkim, while still preparing its U.N. application, was annexed, and in 1975, after a plebescite, became India's twenty-second state.

The stake of larger nations in the U.N. system is less immediate and clear-cut. It serves them on occasion as arbiter of last resort, sounding board for international opinion, and, at least in theory, pressure valve for world tensions. Important, and in certain crises vital, as these functions may be, larger members clearly do not, and the record suggests cannot, rely on the United Nations as a protector of national sovereignty. For them, security rests on outside arrangements, through NATO, the Warsaw Pact, ANZUS, regional agreements, or bilateral pacts. Nor do these represent, as the non-aligned often charge, failure to accept or work within the U.N. Charter, which specifically allows for regional security arrangements (articles 51–54). The United Nations has rarely been capable of effective response to situations involving a major power, whether in the 1962 Indo-Chinese war, Vietnam in the 1950s or 1970s, Czechoslovakia in 1968, or Afghanistan in 1979.

The fate of Afghanistan notwithstanding, the non-aligned perceive their greater stake in U.N. membership and stress the compatibility of the two institutions. A U.N. and non-aligned specialist like Yugoslav Ambassador Miljan Komatina, for example, writes of the "mutual permeation" of the United Nations and NAM expressed in the "congruity and complementarity of the principles and goals of the Charter with the policy of non-alignment" and "the contribution of non-alignment to the strengthening of the role of the UN."[37] The theme of identity between NAM and U.N. goals runs through the movement's documentation, and was spelled out in a separate resolution of the Lusaka Summit that recognized a U.N. "vital role in safeguarding the independence and sovereignty of the non-aligned nations."[38] It further criticized the "tendency of great powers to subordinate the work of organizations to their own interests and requirements and to bypass the world organization." The result over the years has been a non-aligned commitment to the United Nations stronger than that of most other members and an almost proprietary view of the institution. The latter manifests itself in a "we-they" atmosphere that Western diplomats soon detect in U.N. corridors or the Delegates' Lounge.

Parallel with non-aligned emphasis on the importance of the United Nations has, since the first summit, been an equal commitment to changing the shape of the world body. The Belgrade Declaration highlighted the need for revision of the charter, expansion of the Security Council and the Economic and Social Council (ECOSOC), and a "more appropriate structure" for the Secretariat. A resolution at Lusaka further pledged the non-aligned to take such unspecified measures as "will make the United Nations more effective." Under the rubrics of "democratization" and "universality," the non-aligned have consistently pushed for enlargement of U.N. bodies on the basis of geographic representation, equal participation in U.N. decision-making, and elimination of special provisions based on national power or contributions to the budget. Most NAM members would probably not distinguish between strengthening and "democratizing" the United Nations, which, if not synonymous, are for them inextricably bound together. As in the movement itself, the assumption has been that growth and maximum participation are desirable ends.

From a Western point of view, the reverse is probably true. Decision-making with no allowance for national stature ignores the reality of power and undercuts the residual influence of great powers in the U.N. process. Further enlargement of key U.N. bodies, particularly the Security Council, risks rendering them more unwieldy, subject to stalemate by bloc voting, and incapable of effective action. Finally, universality carried to its logical conclusion means that Kiribati, Tuvalu, and many as yet unnamed island mini-states are destined to join Vanuatu, Samoa, St. Lucia, and St. Vincent and the Grenadines in responsibility for controlling effects of atomic radiation, peaceful uses of outer space, and long-term rehabilitation of the Sudan-Sahel region.

Commitment to restructuring the United Nations, while a separate article of faith for the non-aligned, is closely linked to the tactical consideration of maximizing the movement's influence. Komatina equates the two goals in arguing for "a substantial opening of the world organization not only to all countries, but also to social forces, as well as giving special status to the Liberation Movements'...."[39] Here the principle of universality fuses with the non-aligned commitment to support national liberation groups and specific backing for the PLO and SWAPO. Both are full NAM members, but within the United Nations are limited to observer status in the General Assembly, which they received by "standing invitation" of its non-aligned majority. While early summits exhorted members to coordinate activities at the United Nations, recognition of non-aligned political influence evolved during the 1970s with the movement's growing numerical superiority. During that decade, non-aligned summits and declarations were increasingly viewed by both members and outsiders as harbingers of non-aligned performance in the world body.

Non-Aligned Cohesion

The degree of non-aligned unity in New York directly affects the movement's influence as an identifiable voting bloc. Yet the disarray that characterizes non-aligned policy on a variety of issues, such as war between Iran and Iraq, may equally influence the world organization by preventing consideration of disputed topics. The extent of non-aligned cohesion at any given time can be considered from several perspectives, including the control exercised by the NAM president, the tightness of its operating procedures, and the consistency of voting patterns by its members in the General Assembly and representatives on the Security Council.

A corollary to the issue of non-aligned cohesiveness is the question, sometimes asked by outsiders or even members, of how "serious is the movement, anyway." As an amalgam of 100 states, it includes a minority of dedicated activists and many more passive members who enjoy its triennial gatherings, but view the organization in fraternal rather than binding political terms. The latter, reinforced by the consensus formula, resist individual responsibility for decisions that they frequently dismiss as conference rhetoric. The image of a disciplined cadre supporting defined group interests, sometimes conveyed in academic and statistical analyses of NAM voting, is probably, therefore, misleading. The reality is closer to an amorphous political grouping regularly voting on issues of little or no interest to most members and eager to trade such votes for support on others or for group prestige. Most frustrating in this process, from a Western point of view, is the priority given to institutional loyalty and procedure over substance. Except on some security issues or matters directly affecting an individual state, the non-aligned are generally willing to forgo national positions on substantive issues in favor of membership in the movement and group exercise of power.

The effectiveness of a non-aligned organization in New York and its influence in particular U.N. bodies has varied by period and presidency. It is also affected by the personalities and motivations of a handful of key non-aligned diplomats stationed in New York. From 1973 to 1976, the Algerians were particularly effective in whipping into line NAM members taking positions contrary to a usually radical majority. President Boumedienne's authority was reinforced by the election of Algerian Foreign Minister Abdelaziz Bouteflika as president of the General Assembly in 1974. As a result, the non-aligned were able to impose whole sections of the Algiers Declaration, practically verbatim, as resolutions of the General Assembly. In the process, Algeria was able to speak credibly for the non-aligned in informal negotiations with the Western and Soviet blocs, a role that Sri Lanka continued rom 1976 until 1979 with some success, for example, in brokering divergent positions regarding the first Special Session on Disarmement (SSOD). Cuba, by contrast, forfeited such a role because of deep Western, and particularly U.S., suspicions. Binding ties to Moscow undercut Havana's ability to objectively present non-aligned policies or to attempt to moderate between conflicting East–West positions.

The president's authority also affects non-aligned operating procedures at the United Nations. Under a strong leader, drafting of important resolutions to be sponsored in the United Nations is likely to be tightly controlled within the movement, usually by one of the nine substantive working groups, and to be circulated among regional groups for support only when complete. From a bureaucratic point of view, this procedure ensures a balance of non-aligned regional participation in the process and control over tactical decisions of timing and lobbying for support. A divisive presidency, such as that of 1979–83, tends to reverse the pattern, with regional groups taking the lead in drafting resolutions and on occasion submitting them directly to U.N. bodies in advance of non-aligned consultations, in order to force the timing and to bypass or preempt the president. The non-aligned will then be forced to line up behind the resolution to preserve solidarity—for example, on an African formulation on apartheid—and the actual vote will be the same, regardless of drafting origin. Yet the latter case strains internal cooperation and prevents an orderly application of non-aligned priorities or overall strategy for a General Assembly session. On an issue like Afghanistan, where policy was paralyzed by the president's pro-Moscow line, the Islamic Conference drafted annual General Assembly resolutions that drew broad sponsorship from individual NAM members and pitted the majority against Havana and hard-core radicals.

The movement's peculiar regional makeup carries over to the United Nations with effect on its cohesiveness and, in some cases, the workings of the world body. The solidarity of African and Arab members, whose common cause on most issues began in the early 1970s, put increasing pressure on more divided Asian and Latin American delegations to endorse non-aligned positions and maximize their numerical advantage. In the process, the Asians proved generally unwilling to oppose the Afro-Arab bloc directly except on exclusively Asian issues, such as Cambodia. The Latin Americans more frequently had individual problems in applying non-aligned positions in the United Nations because of conflict with hemispheric commitments and potential friction in relations with the United States. Still, by the mid-1970s, as the NAM became more defined as a voting group in the United Nations, members like Guyana, Jamaica, Trinidad and Tobago, Argentina, and Peru found it more difficult to oppose resolutions sponsored under non-aligned auspices. This, in turn, forced other Latin American nations, such as Mexico, Brazil, and Venezuela, to pay more attention to non-aligned sentiment. By the late 1970s, outside groups like the ten-member European Community (EC-10) and the Nordic countries were increasingly reluctant to directly oppose or risk offending the non-aligned.

The New York Imprint

The concentration of so many delegations in New York leads to a momentum or group behavior frequently at variance with bilateral policies of individual states. Critics of the NAM and United Nations find in both a similar atmosphere of unreality and lack of pragmatism in tackling world problems. In part, this stems from the abstraction of most issues facing the delegates. The 140-odd agenda items for the General Assembly, many with complicated subheadings, have little direct relevance to the individual member. The smaller and less developed the state, the less time and staffing will usually be available in its capital to support a delegation in New York. The result is that delegates from most small countries, the majority of the non-aligned, are without specific instructions on many, if not most, votes. In practice, these representatives often operate with either complete discretion or loose guidelines to follow the non-aligned or regional consensus. They form the basic constituency of the NAM, 25 of whose members have populations below a million, and are most receptive to consensus positions. Even if specific voting orders are sent from home, tight deadlines or poor communications frequently prevent their receipt. The leeway thus afforded many of the non-aligned is, however, usually tempered by caution. Lacking instructions from home, the delegate from Equatorial Guinea or Belize is, for example, unlikely to be swayed by contrary U.S. and Soviet lobbying on a complex, and to him remote, issue like use of chemical weapons in Kampuchea. Under such pressure, his predictable recourse will be safety in non-aligned consensus. Similarly, when interested states, particularly great powers, lobby in capitals for support on such an issue, the home government—out of day-to-day touch with developments in New York—will often be reluctant to issue voting instructions and risk isolation from the non-aligned.

With only marginal interest in a given issue, delegates often have little incentive to vote on the merits of the case. Apart from the negative factor of avoiding isolation from the non-aligned or an exposed position vis-à-vis the superpowers, consensus offers enhanced group prestige and political capital for use on later issues. The comment of a leading African envoy in New York is typical of the dependence of individual members on the group: "... our national interests are better served within a group solution. Such weight as we carry depends on whether we act as a group. Alone, Zaire or Uganda count as nothing, unlike the United States or Britain."[40] Such a group mentality inclines members to adhere to positions taken by the summit, and frequently leads to conflict with others perhaps more directly involved and less convinced of the value of concerted non-aligned action. The premium placed by most of the non-aligned on shared colonial experience can also lead to an emotional response to political situations elsewhere that may or may not correspond to a member's own struggle for independence. In more practical terms, blind support for the NAM position on peripheral issues is usually in the expectation that other members will reciprocate on future votes of more local concern.

Membership in the NAM also provides protective camouflage for Third World regimes otherwise vulnerable to international criticism on human rights grounds. Thus, countries singled out year after year in U.N. debate and resolutions for violation of human rights almost always fall outside the NAM or other international blocs. Chile, El Salvador, and Guatemala, for example, are targets of opportunity for annual criticism in the General Assembly. While abuse of human rights undoubtedly occurs in each, comparable or more acute violations by NAM members like Vietnam, Iran, Argentina, Uganda, and Cuba escape U.N. notice. Since Third World countries not party to the NAM are mainly in Latin America, the focus of human rights activism at the United Nations is almost totally on small states of that region. Conversely, all African states belong to the NAM except South Africa, which alone on that continent is subject to regular U.N. condemnation. Non-aligned membership is thus a virtual guarantee against censure, but contributes to the existing double standard in the field of human rights.

Nor is the relationship obvious between a country's overall foreign policy and network of bilateral relations and its voting record in the United Nations. From a smaller delegation's perspective, service in New York entails a succession of votes on issues well outside the normal scope of national interest. These frequently involve pressures to support a given position from larger states, which may, at least indirectly, invoke good bilateral relations, aid, or even military support as leverage. Votes the wrong way, even on litmus issues like Afghanistan and Israel, have often provoked diplomatic protests, but have rarely altered bilateral relations and patterns of aid or trade. The latter involve a delicate balance of economic and security interests with tacit trade-offs between aid or military sales and regional stability or facilities. In a simplified case, the amount of aid and military assistance might, for example, be in approximate balance with the value of aircraft landing rights or port calls by the U.S. Navy. Voting in New York has traditionally been extraneous to these considerations, with different personnel in both countries involved in bilateral affairs and international organizations. Nor is it an easy matter to determine what weight to attach to a given U.N. vote in terms of ongoing relations between countries.

The United States and most other Western countries consequently have better relations with the non-aligned on an individual basis than in the more diffuse U.N. environment, where their influence and the impact of aid and trade are minimized. The premium placed by the United Nations on independence as the basis for association also leads to a heightened consciousness of national sovereignty when all 157 delegations are assembled. Lobbying, the rule among small countries, often becomes intervention or infringement of sovereignty if vigorously pursued by a big power. Coordination of positions and even normal consultations among otherwise friendly states can thus be subject to misunderstanding in New York.

In the resulting atmosphere, non-aligned behavior in the United Nations is freed from many of the normal constraints of national foreign policy. In the case of smaller states, dependence on outside economic and military support, even if vital to national survival, will not necessarily determine voting patterns. Francophone Africans, for example, have not hesitated to oppose France on Mayotte or, until 1977, on Djibouti, or Commonwealth members to attack Britain on the Falkland (Malvinas) Islands or, until 1981, on Belize. The dichotomy between points of view at home and in New York depends on a different nexus between states. In capitals, local needs—whether for infrastructure, import subsidization, or military hardware—predominate, structuring the relationship between donor or lender and recipient. In New York, this "real world" relationship carries over, but the needs are less immediate, and realities at home are not necessarily the main preoccupation of delegates. By contrast, the NAM and United Nations tend to approach problems at an abstract or "common denominator" level, where consensus is possible and inequalities of national power are minimized. To some Western critics, the result is an atmosphere of unreality, with delegates voting on an idealized and out-of-focus agenda. To the non-aligned, however, the separation of voting patterns from economic and military dependence is proof of the movement's ability to ensure an independent foreign policy through safety in numbers.

Further contributing to the distinct character of non-alignment in New York are the personalities and attributes of the half-dozen activists who, at any given moment, shape the movement's day-to-day focus and activities. Their individual interests can significantly affect the movement's U.N. agenda and, to the extent they reflect an identifiable common profile, also affect attitudes of the overall group. Such activists tend to come from larger and more committed NAM states like India, Yugoslavia, Algeria, Iraq, and Tanzania, but by virtue of dynamism or force of personality may include a few individuals from smaller states like Uganda and Singapore. While such a cadre of non-aligned ambassadors makes a definite imprint on the movement, its impact is, in turn, affected by the work of a second tier of NAM technicians. The latter, usually consisting of working-level career diplomats from ideologically oriented members like Sri Lanka, Algeria, and Yugoslavia, meet on an informal basis to coordinate positions for their principals.

Depending on their approach, the impact of individual NAM activists may be felt on specific issues and non-aligned positions, or on the movement's more general orientation. The single-minded focus on economic issues of Indian Ambassador Brajesh Mishra, who also served as chairman of the G-77, did much, for example, to galvanize non-aligned pressure during the late 1970s for a "global round" of negotiations with developed countries. Equally, Mishra orchestrated much of the non-aligned pressure during the 1979 and 1980 General Assemblies for further expansion of the Security Council. While Security Council enlargement remains a NAM objective, the campaign dissipated, at least temporarily, after Mishra's replacement. Equally strong, but less identified with specific issues, was the influence of Iraqi Ambassador Ismet Kittani. Selected as president of the General

Assembly in 1981, Kittani did much to reorient the movement, although he was ultimately unable to offset reaction to Iraq's continuing war with Iran and preserve Baghdad as site for the Seventh Summit.

More relevant to the movement's unique momentum in New York than these individual contributions is the collective impact of key NAM delegates. Despite the movement's obvious diversity, its activists tend to share a profile of common experience, education, and attitudes. As such, they are arguably hybrids whose national identities are in varying degree submerged in a multinational outlook. The result of higher education abroad, prolonged absence from home states, and vested career interests in international organizations is often a unique mind-set and alienation from home.

Foreign education is frequently a prelude to a career abroad, for which specialization in international organizations ensures maximum service in New York or Geneva. Recent leaders of the non-aligned have thus tended to be graduates of the Sorbonne, the London School of Economics, Oxford, or Harvard. Some, like Ugandan Ambassador Olara Otunnu, an alumnus of Oxford and Harvard Law School, have graduated from more than one. Others, like Tanzanian Foreign Minister Salim Salim, Mohamed Bedjaoui of Algeria, and Ismet Kittani, cast a wider net, including universities like Columbia, Grenoble, and Knox College. To gain admission, usually on scholarship, and to graduate from any of these schools requires discipline and intellect. A common result is often an altered vision of realities at home and determination to exert influence on a larger scale.

This emergent internationalism finds later expression in long service abroad and close association in New York or Geneva with others of the same small fraternity and orientation. Some, like Salim Salim, may remain ten years in New York, consolidating expertise and influence within the United Nations in general and the non-aligned constituency in particular. Typically, such delegates return rarely to national capitals and, in some instances, then only as stepping-stones back to larger responsibility abroad. Others, at the conclusion of tours in New York or Geneva, may move laterally into positions in the U.N. system—for instance, Mishra's appointment in March 1982 as U.N. commissioner for Namibia and Bedjaoui's election to the World Court. Their lifestyles and preferences tend toward the greater power, personal influence, and amenities of a world capital. The pattern is reinforced by both family and social ties, and commitment to children's education abroad. Further, sophistication cultivated through diplomacy in world capitals may become a liability at home, where it may be perceived as affected or Westernized.

Expertise usually puts the non-aligned activist in a position of unique authority vis-à-vis his government. Some are politicians rather than career diplomats and have unusual access at home, or are distinguished as jurists or authors. Former Ambassador Bedjaoui, long a leading non-aligned tactician, for example, combined all of these, and also sat on the Central Committee of Algeria's ruling FLN party. Other non-aligned leaders may be perceived at home as politically threatening by regimes eager, for that reason, to acquiesce in added prerogatives to keep them in exile. For professional diplomats recently at the movement's center, such as Kittani, Mishra, Salim, or B.A. Clark of Nigeria, expertise and proven influence in New York afford special indulgence from foreign ministries at home. The result for both diplomats and politicians is usually authority and leeway considerably greater than those of colleagues in the movement.

The influence on the NAM of such a cadre of leaders is strong, but difficult to measure. By contrast with conventional diplomats, posted for a single tour in New York, their focus and sphere of influence are considerably more permanent. Their stature at home also allows greater freedom of maneuver and resources to effectively lobby recalcitrant colleagues. With their internationalist outlook and professional commitment to multilateral diplomacy, they constitute a disciplined and like-minded nucleus at the movement's center. Within the arcane world of international organizations and conferences, they form an elite who have outgrown employment opportunities in their own countries and for whom the hybrid U.N. environment is also the personal reality.

Their imprint on the movement is thus to reinforce its level of abstraction and group attitudes sometimes out of step with individual capitals. Such diplomats are dedicated to the United Nations as both the focus of their own careers and the fulcrum for non-aligned efforts to alter existing political and economic structures. Imbued with parliamentary procedure, they view the NAM as a vehicle to gain control of the larger body, and constantly reinforce the movement's U.N. orientation. Faced with intractable world problems on a U.N. agenda that varies little from year to year, annual resolutions, declarations, conferences, special General Assembly sessions, and expanding committee memberships assume for them and the non-aligned an intrinsic value in the absence of substantive progress.

8

Non-Aligned Impact on the Security Council

We need to communicate to nations that their votes, their attitudes and their actions within the UN system invariably must have consequences for their relations with the US outside the UN system.

Jeane Kirkpatrick, March 1983

The Security Council is generally considered the ultimate authority and center of the U.N. system. The General Assembly can make recommendations only, while the Security Council has at least the legal power to compel and thus can, in theory, function as a strong executive, rather than purely deliberative, body. Under the charter, U.N. members must agree to accept and carry out the council's decisions and undertake to make available to it armed forces, assistance, or facilities "as may be necessary to maintain or restore international peace and security." The charter further provides for U.N. military enforcement, including "such action by air, sea or land forces" as the council may consider necessary.

While the drafters at San Francisco apparently intended these provisions to provide the muscle lacking in the League of Nations, in practice their enforcement has been increasingly unworkable in situations posing the greatest threats to world peace and security. Peace negotiations in the Middle East and Vietnam have, for example, fallen outside the United Nations. Threats to international peace and security persist, after several years, unchecked by the United Nations in Afghanistan, Kampuchea, and Iran-Iraq. In Namibia, a planned peacekeeping operation, approved in Security Council Resolution 435 of 1978, remains to be implemented and, as of early 1983, there was still no agreement on timing for a cease-fire. This is not to say that U.N. troops have not saved lives and performed gallantly as buffers in Lebanon, Cyprus, and the Golan Heights, but simply that their use since Korea and the Congo has been confined to limited and well-defined tactical situations. U.N. forces depend on the cooperation of parties to a dispute, in the absence of which they have been brushed aside or overrun, as during Israel's invasion of Lebanon in June 1982.

Recently, U.N. peacekeeping forces have been bypassed in the Sinai and twice in Lebanon, in favor of multinational forces outside the United Nations.

Given high postwar hopes for it as a bulwark of peace, it is not surprising that, of all U.N. bodies, disillusionment, even among delegates, is highest in the Security Council. A poll of 187 U.N. delegates, taken by UNITAR in 1981, gave the council a failing rating of 3.1 on a seven-point scale, with none rating it "extremely successful" (7) and only 16 percent putting it in the success categories (5–6).[41] Significantly, respondents from low-income states (1978 GNP per capita under $360) rated the council's success as 2.6, well below the 3.5 rating given by high-income states (1978 GNP per capita above $3,500). Similarly, African delegates evaluated its success at a low 2.8 and Asians (including the Middle East) at 2.5, probably reflecting the council's paralysis on Namibia and the Middle East.

The factors underlying the Security Council's performance and these low ratings are complex, and could not have been foreseen at San Francisco. Among the non-aligned, blame is assigned to the permanent members' veto power and their own "under-representation" on the council. Obstacles to the council's effectiveness most frequently cited in the UNITAR survey were lack of commitment by some members, inappropriate membership, inappropriate voting system, and lack of power to enforce decisions. Each of these explanations, selected from ten possibilities, represents different dimensions of the perception, strong among the non-aligned, that the council is controlled by superpowers frustrating the majority will.

In fact, while the permanent members have a blocking power through the veto, the non-aligned, by sheer numbers on the Security Council, can equally block a given outcome. Depending on the council's composition in a particular year, the number of non-aligned members and permanent observers represented on it fluctuates between five and eight, with an average of 6.3 since the early 1970s. With nine votes necessary to approve resolutions of the council, the non-aligned, even in years when there were only six on the council, could usually count on China or a friendly European for the additional vote necessary to block proposals. At a strength of seven, for example, from 1978 to 1980, they had blocking power without recourse to outsiders. As of 1983, participation of eight NAM members on the council ensured absolute numerical superiority.

The non-aligned presence on the Security Council is not new, although the expansion of NAM membership since the early 1970s has made the arithmetic more acute. The non-aligned have participated in the council since the movement's formation in 1961, voting with remarkable consistency on most issues. What is new since 1978–79 is the formation within the Security Council of an assertive sub-group of NAM members and permanent observers with defined procedures and a rotating monthly chairmanship of its own. This activist approach has unquestionably affected the council's operating procedures and increased non-aligned influence over its agenda, timing of meetings, and decisions taken. To date, and largely because of reluctance to cooperate with Cuba as president, non-aligned Security Council members have functioned by informal rather than institutionalized consultations with the NACB and the NAM president. The relationship could, however, eventually evolve along more formal lines, with serious implications for the council's already diminished ability to act quickly in crises. The present role within the council of the non-aligned subgroup and its evolution since 1978–79, in any case, merit closer attention.

The Non-Aligned and The Security Council

The relationship of the Security Council and the non-aligned in a sense predates the Belgrade Summit and goes back to 1950, when Egypt, India, and Yugoslavia each served as council president during critical debates on Korea. At the time of Belgrade, Egypt, Sri Lanka, and Ghana were on the council and played an active role in promoting the election, on November 3, 1961, of U Thant of Burma, a founding NAM state, as acting secretary-general. Non-aligned pressure resulted in expansion of the Security Council in August 1965 from 11 to 15 members, which added considerably to the power of non-permanent and non-aligned council members. To gain the required majority of nine, the great powers were obliged to rely increasingly on their support and, in the absence of a veto, non-permanent members for the first time could pass resolutions without supporting votes from any of the five permanent members.

In addition to the five permanent members, the Security Council's composition since the enlargement has been two from the "Western European and Others" group (WEOG), including Australia, New Zealand, and Canada; one Eastern European; three Africans; two Latin Americans; and two Asians. The breakdown of non-aligned on the council has, therefore, usually been three Africans, one or two Latin Americans, and one or two Asians. An exception was 1969, when both Latin American seats and one Asian seat went to outsiders, reducing non-aligned strength to four. Conversely, the three NAM members from Europe can tip the balance in the other direction. Yugoslavia's term overlapped in 1973 with that of two non-aligned states from both Asia and Latin America, making a majority of eight NAM members and observers. Similarly, Malta's election for a term beginning in 1983 augmented the non-aligned group for the first time to eight full members of the movement, described by Secretary-General Perez de Cuellar during the New Delhi Summit as "a highly significant proportion" able to play a "decisive role" on the Council. Theoretically, capture of a WEOG seat by Malta or Cyprus coincident with Yugoslav election from Eastern Europe and non-aligned states from Asia and Latin America could result in a controlling bloc of nine.

While the average number of non-aligned seats on the Security Council rose from 4.3 during the 1960s to 6.3 in the 1970s, non-aligned membership was not at that time an overriding consideration in General Assembly voting to fill council vacancies. When regional groups could agree on a candidate, the General Assembly, including non-aligned members, usually supported the choice. Thus, non-member Latin American states were often elected: for example, Colombia (1969–70), Costa Rica (1974–75), and Venezuela (1977–78). Likewise, Japan was elected for 1981–82, but only after agreeing to non-aligned pressure for an earlier seat for Bangladesh (1979–80). In 1979, Cuba sought to make non-alignment a qualification, basing its campaign for the Security Council on the NAM presidency, but was forced to withdraw after 157 ballots. By 1982, however, non-aligned membership had become a more critical factor in elections to the council, and communiqués of both the June NACB meeting in Havana and the October ministerial conference in New York called on members to endorse NAM candidates and specifically backed Malta. Clearly, non-aligned loyalties played a major role in sweeping victories that year by Nicaragua over the Dominican Republic and by Malta over New Zealand.

Other factors, however, also contributed to these outcomes: adverse African reaction to the South African Springboks' tour of New Zealand, lackluster campaigning by the Dominican Republic, fallout from the Falklands crisis, and delayed reaction to the earlier blocking of Cuba's candidacy. In supporting Nicaragua's candidacy, Cuba, as president of the NAM, used the full resources and power at its disposal to lobby members for the better part of a year. Desire for non-aligned votes in its campaign for a Security Council seat in 1984–85 undoubtedly contributed to Barbados' decision to join the NAM at New Delhi in 1983.

While regional and bilateral considerations have usually prevailed in elections to the Security Council, the non-aligned indirectly affected the process during the 1970s. The U.N. Charter requires that "due regard" be "specially paid in the first instance" to prospective members' contribution to "maintenance of international peace and security and to the other purposes of the organization." In recent years, this provision has been tacitly waived, and NAM representation has thus been augmented by small states such as Togo (1982–83) and war-ravaged Uganda (1981–82).

The impact of non-aligned members on the Security Council depends, of course, on their cohesion and degree of assertiveness. In general, the non-aligned have had a common view on African and Middle Eastern issues that have been the council's primary focus since the 1960s. The number of resolutions approved annually by the council has fluctuated, since the 1965 expansion, between 12 and 23, with a yearly average of 17.5. Of 280 passed by the expanded council through 1980, only 14 found one or more non-aligned members in opposition or abstention. Non-aligned support for resolutions adopted and consistency in voting was thus 95 percent. Dissenters in the 5 percent minority tended to be individual non-aligned states, particularly on Middle Eastern issues, where Arab opinion was divided. By contrast, 99 of the resolutions adopted, or 31 percent, found great powers in abstention or other members not belonging to the NAM opposed.

Other than Soviet and East European voting, which has diverged only during infrequent Yugoslav service on the Security Council, non-aligned voting patterns have been the most cohesive of any major group. By contrast, on a range of 78 council votes from 1979 to 1981, including instances when the veto was used, the United Kingdom, France, and other NATO members voted with the United States 63 percent of the time. Most divergent votes were either absentions or yes/no votes when the United States abstained, although in six cases (8 percent), there was a direct conflict.

Greater non-aligned cohesiveness and assertiveness within the Security Council have put a premium on the veto. Non-aligned numbers on the council both occasion its wider use and, by vociferous reaction, call attention to the fact. Incidence of the veto is, thus, arguably a rough measure of isolation from the non-aligned majority and of a given council's position on the East–West spectrum. Its use depends on both outside events and the tactical approach of individual great powers. Over the years, however, great powers have been reluctant to use the veto unnecessarily, underscoring their isolation, although individual governments have differed in attitudes toward confrontation.

From 1946 through 1982, 187 vetoes were cast on 160 occasions. Twenty-seven were thus simultaneous vetoes by more than one permanent member. Of the total, 112 were Soviet, 35 U.S., 22 U.K., 15 French, and 3 Chinese. While overall Soviet vetoes outnumber those of the United States by more than three to one, the pattern has been dramatically reversed in recent years. In 1975–82, the United States cast 29 vetoes to 4 by the Soviets, with 5 in 1981 and 8 in 1982. Writing in the late 1970s, the long-time Soviet ambassador to the United Nations, Yakov A. Malik, rejoiced that "now the capitalist countries became the ones in isolation, and they started to make use of the right of veto even more frequently than we had done previously."[42] Faced with this trend and non-aligned activism within the Security Council, the United States has increasingly taken the defensive position that council consideration of a given issue, whether Palestine or Namibia, would be counter-productive and damaging to initiatives elsewhere or to prospects for peace.

Formation of the Group of 7

NAM members of the Security Council became increasingly assertive and conscious of their non-aligned identity during the 1970s. At the outset, they evolved a system of informal liaison with key non-aligned states outside the council. This most often took the form of African and Arab Security Council members briefing the larger constituencies on issues before the council. While these consultations implied a measure of responsibility to the larger group, in the absence of a more formal structure, individual council members continued to act primarily on the basis of charter responsibilities and national perceptions rather than particular group affinities. Although the non-aligned usually voted together, the phenomenon of bloc voting per se was, until the late 1970s, largely confined to the General Assembly.

Between 1977 and 1979, at least four developments occurred that hastened the formation of a disciplined non-aligned organization within the Security Council. First, negotiations on Namibia were evolving into a group negotiating process in which Western states met regularly with the six "frontline" African states and Nigeria. A formal Western contact group consisting of Britain, Canada, France, Germany, and the United States emerged in 1977 as a result of Canadian and German membership on the Security Council and, led by Ambassador

Andrew Young, traveled as a group to a U.N. conference on southern Africa held that year in Maputo, Mozambique. The example of increased bargaining power through a supportive small group was not lost on the non-aligned, many of whom were across the table. Second, the issues before the council—for example, Namibia and recurrent crises in Lebanon—were in an acute phase and conducive to non-aligned activism. Third and by no means negligible, the United Nations completed construction in 1977 of new conference facilities for the Security Council that permitted adjacent and private consultations among small groups. Finally, and probably most important, the non-aligned states elected to the council in 1978 and 1979 proved to be more homogeneous and, therefore, more organizable than before.

In a movement of 100 states, the chemistry between six or seven given members is likely to be uncertain. A cooperative unit was, for example, unlikely to emerge from non-aligned members and permanent observers on the 1977 Security Council, divided between conservatives like Venezuela and Gabon and mavericks like Libya and Benin. By 1978, a more compatible subgroup of non-aligned members and observers included Bolivia, Gabon, India, Kuwait, Mauritius, Nigeria, and Venezuela. The group met regularly and was able to resolve most differences. The seating in 1979 of Bangladesh, Jamaica, and Zambia to replace India, Venezuela, and Mauritius did not alter this cooperative relationship.

During their first consultations in January 1979, the non-aligned members of the Security Council agreed to formalize the relationship by constituting themselves as the Group of Seven (G-7) with a rotating monthly chairmanship. The latter followed alphabetical order, with Bangladesh as the first incumbent, but could be altered to allow members with direct interest in a given issue to assume the leadership in months that it came before the council. Thus it became standard for Kuwait, and in later years Tunisia and Jordan, to take over for debates on the Middle East, and for one of the three Africans to coordinate on southern Africa. Changes in the order were usually made, however, only for major issues scheduled in advance, and Western delegates thus often found themselves negotiating through an African on the Middle East or a Latin American on African issues simply because that nation was chairman for the month. Lack of firsthand experience tended to limit flexibility, and diplomatic exchanges were more formal than before.

The role of monthly chairman often places an individual state in the difficult position of mediating between moderate and radical factions. Kuwait, Jordan, and Tunisia, as spokesmen, were frequently under pressure from other Arabs seeking Security Council endorsement for more radical positions on the Middle East. On particularly divisive issues, non-aligned states not on the council but with direct interest in a given subject might seek agreement among themselves before approaching the monthly chairman. Thus, for example, following the Israeli invasion of Lebanon in June 1982, Lebanon, Syria, and the PLO sought to resolve their own differences before taking a draft resolution to Jordan. In rarer cases, where there is no non-aligned consensus, the chairman cannot speak for the G-7, and expresses a national position only. Thus Commonwealth ties triumphed over non-aligned solidarity on a June 4, 1982 resolution on the Falklands, vetoed by Britain and the United States, which evenly divided the six non-aligned on the council.

The new structure, nevertheless, replaced the earlier loose consultations with a new sense of non-aligned identity on the Security Council. Kuwaiti Ambassador Abdalla Bishara, a founder of the G-7, writes of 1979 that "the importance of the non-aligned members of the Council had never been so accentuated as it was during my presidency of the Council." He credits the G-7 with "all initiatives on Southern Africa and the Middle East," and comments that "as a member of the non-aligned group of the Council, first and foremost, I made it my aim to obtain the support of the non-aligned members on any course of action I was going to contemplate."[43] British, French, and U.S. diplomats, ruminating in the Delegates' Lounge after an initial and bruising confrontation with the G-7, concluded that for the first time they were dealing with a disciplined non-aligned bloc, something previously unknown and qualitatively different on the council.

The G-7, although formed to represent the non-aligned in the Security Council and maximize their impact, has not been linked formally to other NAM organs. It does not consult the NACB on a regular basis, although it has often done so informally to establish positions and strategy on important issues before the council. In practice, the degree of briefing and liaison has varied with the orientation and personality of monthly G-7 chairmen (also referred to as presidents, coordinators, or spokesmen). Some have been scrupulous in consulting the larger body and circulating to it, in advance of other Security Council members, proposed resolutions drafted by the G-7. Others, suspicious of Cuba's presidency and radicals on the NACB, have maintained a more aloof posture.

Most would have opposed more formal bureaucratic links and, when Cuban Foreign Minister Malmierca requested a meeting with the

G-7 in November 1980, the session was deliberately limited to a briefing on non-aligned mediation between Iran and Iraq. In 1982, however, President Castro, as chairman of the NAM, advised the Guyanese president of the council, in a letter of July 3 concerning non-aligned policy toward the Israeli invasion of Lebanon, although some in the movement questioned his right to do so without prior consultations. On another occasion, the Cuban ambassador protested to the non-aligned on the Security Council that a draft resolution endorsed by them on the Middle East could not be considered a non-aligned document. Ambassaor Raul Roa-Kouri was rebuffed with a reminder that the G-7 was indeed separate from the overall movement. It was not uncommon, however, for the NACB to meet separately on matters before the council and for the NACB chairman to present a non-aligned position to the council.

Impact on Council Procedure

Formation of the G-7, reduced to G-6 in 1981–82 and expanded to G-8 in 1983, has fundamentally altered the operating procedure of the Security Council, particularly the institution of informal consultations. When a meeting is requested, the council president normally sounds out other members to ascertain their views on the timing and possible outcome of Security Council action. The next stage, if the president believes it desirable, is an informal consultation of the whole council in closed session and off the record. Such consultations, limited to a few persons from each delegation, have traditionally been a preliminary, designed to allow members to meet beforehand, in an informal atmosphere, on the agenda and parameters of a public session.

In earlier years, they tended to be brief or, in many cases, were dispensed with altogether when the president moved directly into formal session. When held, they deliberately eschewed matters of substance, and were often attended by junior diplomatic staff who merely reported back to their missions on scheduled meetings and agendas. During the mid-1970s, the number of informal consultations held each year was substantially less than the formal and public meetings—sometimes as little as 50 percent. More recently, and as a direct result of non-aligned activism, the ratio has been reversed, with closed, informal consultations held almost twice as often as public meetings.

Year	*Security Council Meetings*	*Informal Consultations*
1975	57	47
1976	113	59
1977	73	38
1978	52	113
1979	77	123
1980	77	107
1981	60	138
1982	89	163

This reversal coincided with emergence of a cohesive, non-aligned subgroup and completion of new Security Council conference rooms for both informal consultations and smaller subgroups. The latter, while available to others on request, have been virtually an exclusive preserve of the non-aligned group. Typically, when consultations of the whole council are called, the non-aligned first caucus there, frequently delaying the larger proceedings or postponing them altogether if the group does not agree. Once a common or close-to-common position emerges, informal consultations of the full Security Council usually begin on that basis, since non-aligned support is required for any resolution or decision to be adopted. Such sessions may be prolonged indefinitely as Western or Soviet delegations probe for non-aligned flexibility, seek various amendments, or strive to exploit the other side's isolation. In 1977, for example, informal consultations took up only 26 hours, compared with 116 hours in public session. By 1981, they occupied 141 hours, versus 85 hours in public.

The result has been to downgrade formal meetings, which now risk deteriorating into rhetorical statements for the record that follow a prearranged scenario. In the process, the influence of a non-aligned minority behind the scenes is maximized, and an official study of the movement by the Nicaraguan government in 1983 concluded that "the importance of the non-aligned in the Security Council is better demonstrated during informal consultations."[44] U.N. Under Secretary-General Brian Urquhart has described informal consultations that maximize the council's reluctance to meet in public as little more than "mumbling behind closed doors on issues affecting international peace and security." He concludes that if

> ...the consultation process is principally a means of escaping public disagreement and adopting an increasingly expedient and evasive approach to world problems, it may in the end reduce the

> Council to a level of impotence and disrespect from which it will not be able to recover in time the influence necessary to play a decisive role in a desperate crisis.[45]

Former Secretary-General Kurt Waldheim, by contrast, welcomed the new reliance on informal consultations as "a flexible, informal technique, shielded from premature publicity, whereby agreement can be developed and formulated through exchanges which do not become part of the public record." In this connection, he expressed belief in 1981 that "we can all be encouraged by the greater possibility of consensus which has been evident in the Security Council over the past 10 years or so."[46] Consensus, albeit at a high premium within the United Nations, is not necessarily conducive to problem-solving. The fact that 142, or 63 percent, of the 244 Security Council resolutions passed from 1970 to 1981 were adopted unanimously or without vote does not relate to peace in the Middle East or Namibia. It does reflect pressures within the council and the preference of most members to compromise toward a common denominator rather than go on record as opposing or dissociating from the majority view. Extended informal consultation offers just this opportunity to forge consensus, usually on the basis of a non-aligned starting position. Since the latter tends to evolve from existing non-aligned dogma, the prospect for innovative solutions is minimized. Waldheim's successor, Perez de Cuellar, warned in his annual report on the United Nations of September 7, 1982, that with increased use of informal consultations, "There is sometimes a risk that this process may become a substitute for action by the Security Council or even an excuse for inaction."

Ivor Richard, British ambassador to the United Nations from 1974 to 1979, notes with regret that spirited Security Council debates, which persisted into the early 1970s, have been replaced by the practice of informal consultations. He further argues that the "less formal the consultations the better."[47] In fact, the term "informal consultations" is a misnomer, and the new practice has formalized exchanges into a four-phase process of presidential soundings, subgroup meetings, closed sessions of the whole, and ratification of decisions in public. At each stage, diplomatic positions become further entrenched through coordination with others and, often, instruction from home capitals. If debate is on an issue of intense concern to the non-aligned, such as Namibia, their position and even insistence on a specific draft may have reached a "take-it-or-leave-it" point well before "informal" consultations begin. If the Non-Aligned Group is in complete agreement, it may, on rare occasions, seek to bypass informal consultations and move directly to public meetings, as during the September 16, 1982, debate on Lebanon or the September 20, 1982, session on the South African arms embargo.

Non-aligned Activism

Formation of the Non-Aligned Group has probably not affected the cohesiveness of non-aligned voting within the Security Council, which is, in any case, in the 95 percent range. On certain issues, individual states will still split from the group and vote on the basis of divergent national interests; for instance, Panama abstained when the other five non-aligned supported a January 20, 1982, resolution on measures against Israel following the Golan annexation. The group's impact is instead felt in a coordinated strategy toward the council and more effective use of its procedures for non-aligned objectives. Influence, if not control, over the agenda is important to this strategy. Of 129 meetings requested by Security Council members from 1970 to 1980, 111 or (86 percent) were called by the non-aligned. By contrast, the United States or other Western members took the initiative only seven times, and the Soviets and East Europeans almost never made requests. The secretary-general also has rarely exercised his power to call the council into session under Article 99 of the charter, although in late 1982 Secretary-General Perez de Cuellar indicated an intention to rely more heavily on this provision.

A corollary of non-aligned power to call meetings is the group's ability to block or delay debate on other issues that it considers untimely or is divided on. The non-aligned are well aware of their power to influence Security Council proceedings through delay. In a publication issued to coincide with Nicaragua's accession to the 1983 council, the Sandinista government drew attention to this role:

> Before a meeting [of the Security Council] is convoked, the non-aligned can prevent it since permanent members by tradition do not request meetings. The non-aligned thus exert their own subtle form of veto, since they can delay or prevent the holding of a meeting.... Generally, draft resolutions in the Security Council are submitted by the non-aligned. If the non-aligned do not want to do so they can cause a considerable delay.[48]

Delay may take several forms. As statistics show and the Nicaraguan government has evidently realized, other members are reluctant to call meetings and often urge the non-aligned to take the initiative in order to gain their support for subsequent Security Council action or to avoid injecting an East-West dimension into the debate. The Non-Aligned Group may resist these pressures—as, for example, when they did not wish to offend Iraq, and the council did not convene for a week following the September 1980 invasion of Iran. If others persist, the group may gain further time by going into prolonged consultations that colleagues on the council usually indulge, since non-aligned support will be required on any vote. In the process, the "tendency to avoid bringing critical problems to the Security Council," described in the September 7, 1982, report of Secretary-General Perez de Cuellar, often reaches "the point where the Council's irrelevance to some on-going wars becomes a matter of comment by world public opinion."

A refinement of shaping the Security Council agenda is the scheduling of particular issues to coincide with the monthly council presidency of states considered sympathetic to the non-aligned position or otherwise desirable. U.N. Under Secretary-General Davidson Nicol writes, for example, that "items of significance which regularly come before the Council are usually timed to coincide with a non-aligned presidency."[49] In fact, fast-breaking events like the Soviet invasion of Afghanistan and Israel's raid on Iraq's nuclear reactor cannot be held over for particular presidents, and this flexibility applies only to secondary or non-time-sensitive issues. An appeal against apartheid criminal justice might thus be scheduled together with ongoing debate on South African incursions into Angola, as happened during Panama's presidency in August 1980. A further case is renewed meetings on Namibia, called for at the New Delhi Summit and deliberately scheduled for the presidency of Zaire in May 1983.

Conversely, the non-aligned may insist on raising issues during a non-member's presidency to make a particular political point. Thus, in the last days of the last Security Council presidency of the Carter administration, in December 1980, they forced debate on a presidential appeal to South Africa over three death sentences in a bank robbery case. The purpose was clearly to maximize impact on South Africa by a statement from the U.S. as Security Council president, yet the case was then at the start of a six- to nine-month appeal process and clearly extraneous to the Security Council. Its presence on the agenda stemmed not from urgency, but from African discontent with the greater weight given to Middle Eastern issues by the council in 1980.

A similar case involving the USSR was Libya's decision to force Security Council meetings on alleged U.S. "threats and military provocations" on February 22–23, 1983, to coincide with the Soviet presidency for the month. While Sudan and Egypt agreed that the presence of the Sixth Fleet and four U.S. AWACs aircraft was necessary to offset Libya's military threat to Sudan, the Soviet Union was able to pack the speakers' list with states like Poland, East Germany, Czechoslovokia, Hungary, Bulgaria, Cuba, and Vietnam. The exercise itself was extraneous to the Security Council and aimed, on the eve of the New Delhi Summit, at portraying Libya, then a candidate for the NAM chairmanship in 1986, as a small country defending non-aligned principles against a superpower. It was also designed to gain support for a paragraph on Libya in the New Delhi Declaration. In a larger sense, however, its scheduling and that of other issues to coincide with individual presidencies reflected a presumption of inequality or even partiality on the part of different council presidents. Some, including former British Ambassador Sir Colin Crowe, have argued that this tendency is ominous for the future and "implies that Presidents are expected to bend the proceedings of the Council to suit their side."[50]

Once an issue reaches the Security Council, sheer numbers, tighter organization, location of most crises in the Third World, and the mechanism of informal consultations give the non-aligned a unique advantage. A non-aligned starting position may evolve through various amendments into a presidential draft or, more often, one simply described in the public council session as coming from consultations. The latter reflects strong pressure for consensus, and usually ensures unanimous adoption. Alternatively, proposals may emerge unscathed from informal consultations with sponsorship by specific members. Of 100 sponsored resolutions adopted between 1970 and 1981, 78 came from the non-aligned, sometimes with additional backers, and 22 from elsewhere on the Security Council. The outcome of voting is usually predictable in advance, although individual states may change position several times as a result of pressures. Few sponsors will push for a vote without a majority of nine and, unwilling to risk a public defeat, will drop a proposal quietly during consultations or seek adjournment until it can be modified to guarantee approval. The critical factor on controversial issues is usually, therefore, not the outcome, but the earlier tactical judgment by the non-aligned whether to postpone action, compromise on a given draft to avoid a veto, or force a veto to isolate one or more permanent members.

Confrontation by Veto

If consultations reveal differences between the non-aligned and a permanent member—for example, with the United States on resolutions condemning Israel or South Africa—the judgment whether to push the issue to a veto rests on several factors. Central to the decision will be an estimate of whether action by the Security Council can affect the situation, the degree of public attention, and the role of council debate in overall non-aligned strategy for handling the issue. While delegates surveyed by UNITAR rated conflict in Namibia and the Middle East as the highest U.N. priorities, only 7 percent and 2 percent, respectively, believed that the United Nations could be "highly effective" in resolving either issue. In each case, neither resolutions nor vetoes have yet altered underlying problems. High public interest, more reflected in foreign than in U.S. media, tends to make the non-aligned less flexible in compromising to avert a veto. Prospects for compromise are further reduced by emotion following a raid or attack, or by participation of foreign ministers or other senior officials.

Thus, if an issue has a high profile and is probably unresolvable in the short term, the non-aligned may perceive the publicity surrounding a veto and embarrassment to a superpower as desirable in keeping an issue before the public. If the debate is part of a pre-determined strategy to take the issue to an emergency session of the General Assembly, as in the case of Namibia in 1981, a veto is further desirable, if not inevitable from the outset. Under the "uniting for peace" procedure, first used over Korea in the early 1950s, a veto may be followed by a procedural vote (not subject to veto) to move to the General Assembly.

If an issue is not in the spotlight, however, and a positive outcome is at least possible, deliberate confrontation is less likely. Two separate cases of appeals to South Africa over convictions of African National Congress (ANC) members illustrate the point. The first, spearheaded by Mexico as group coordinator, resulted in an agreed presidential appeal on February 5, 1981, urging clemency. The second, worded along similar lines in the expectation of unanimous support, was introduced during Panama's August 1981 presidency, but was dropped in favor of individual national appeals when the United States could not go along. The non-aligned did not wish to underscore divisions within the Security Council on this issue, and Niger, as group president, did not force a vote.

No two Security Council debates present exactly the same alignments, for the flexibility of bloc and individual national positions varies with each set of circumstances and the extent of outside pressures. It is thus useful to look briefly at a few instances of the veto, one by the Soviets and three involving the United States, and the factors leading to a confrontation. While the vetoing members in each case attempted unsucccessfully to alter the outcome, their reluctance to cast a veto differed by government and according to whether the veto would be multiple or in complete isolation. Among the non-aligned, strategies varied from determination to force a veto on Namibia to a dual-track strategy on Angola designed to probe Western flexibility.

Vetoes on April 30, 1981, by the United States, United Kingdom, and France on four Namibian resolutions calling for sanctions against South Africa were a foregone conclusion. Non-aligned strategy, based on a veto and subsequent emergency session of the General Assembly, had been endorsed in January by the OAU, in February by NAM foreign ministers in New Delhi, and finally by the NACB meeting in Algiers of April 16–18. Twenty-five non-aligned foreign ministers came directly, on an Algerian government aircraft, from the NACB meeting to extended Security Council proceedings on April 21–30. Uganda, as president of the G-6, took the lead in denying, by a procedural vote and over Western and Japanese objections, the right of the South African-backed Democratic Turnahalle Alliance (DTA) to be heard on equal terms with SWAPO, an action endorsed by the OAU and NAM. When the debate concluded, Uganda, backed by the Soviet Union, East Germany, and the non-aligned, pushed for an immediate vote on sanctions against South Africa, cutting off last-minute discussion of compromise language. After the inevitable vetoes, Ugandan Ambassador Otunnu castigated "weighted votes" against the "global consensus," which, he said, undermined peace.

Security Council action against Israel during January 1982, following the Golan annexation, also resulted in a veto and emergency General Assembly session, but was less predictable because of limited time and division among the non-aligned. The need for quick reaction to the annexation precluded the careful development of strategy and non-aligned momentum that had preceded debate on Namibia. Following a unanimous Security Council resolution of December 17, calling on Israel to rescind the act of annexation, Arabs were divided, in the absence of Israeli compliance, between a tough, new resolution calling for sanctions, which the United States would oppose, and a compromise to keep pressure on Israel and avoid the veto. The former prevailed but, as a vote approached, several of the non-aligned with trade or diplomatic ties to Israel balked at compulsory sanctions. Rather than risk defeat, the resolution submitted on behalf of Syria by Jordan, as coordinator of the G-6, was modified to satisfy Zaire and Togo, ensuring nine votes.[51] The final text, which the United States vetoed on January 20, still branded Israel the "aggressor," called for unspecified mandatory sanctions, and urged states to "consider" economic measures. For Panama, which abstained, non-aligned solidarity appeared to conflict in this case with correct relations with Israel, dependence on shipping through the Panama Canal, and ambitions as a regional banking center. Yet Western solidarity was even more fractured, with Spain supporting, and the United Kingdom, France, and Ireland abstaining on, a resolution described by U.S. Ambassador Jeane Kirkpatrick as "an aberration, even a perversion of the very purpose of the Security Council."[52]

In contrast to the 1981 Namibian and 1982 Golan cases, non-aligned strategy followed a more open two-track approach in reacting to the August 1981 South African incursions into Angola. As group coordinator, Niger held in reserve a tough text calling for "comprehensive and mandatory sanctions against racist South Africa," and sought consensus on an alternative proposal for a Security Council fact-finding mission to Angola. In the absence of agreement, the text that finally emerged and was vetoed in isolation by the United States on August 31, labeled South Africa a "danger to international peace and security," thus laying the groundwork for later application of mandatory sanctions. In acrimonious debate before the vote, non-aligned ambassadors on the Security Council, in a now common practice, relinquished their seats to third secretaries and attachés when South Africa was called to speak.

Finally, the January 7, 1980, Security Council resolution on Afghanistan stands out as an example of non-aligned unanimity in forcing a Soviet veto and also going against the position of Cuba. As in the Namibian and Golan cases, the resolution affirming the "non-aligned status of Afghanistan" and calling for "immediate and unconditional withdrawal of foreign troops" was part of a strategy to move to the General Assembly under "uniting for peace." The January 7 vote of 13–2 (USSR, East Germany) was followed in two days by a procedural vote for an emergency General Assembly session of 12–2, with one non-aligned abstention (Zambia). Despite the anomaly of the movement's chairman supporting Soviet occupation of a NAM member, the non-aligned played a major role in the council debate, and Zaire cited Afghanistan's membership in the movement as a specific reason why the Soviet invasion constituted a threat to international peace. Their efforts were, nevertheless, part of a larger coalition on this issue, and 16 non-aligned states were among 52 signatories of the formal request for a Security Council meeting.

These examples should not imply that non-aligned influence is confined to forcing confrontation or blocking action by the Security Council. In fact, the non-aligned tend to be pragmatic in pursuing their own interests and open to compromises that avoid both specific action on items over which the movement is divided and vetoes on issues on which they are committed. For example, during further Security

Council meetings on Namibia in May 1983, the NAM reversed its strategy and sought a unanimous resolution rather than a veto and follow-up session by the General Assembly as in 1981. The 1983 debate, opened by Indian foreign minister Narasimha Rao as chairman of the NAM, resulted in Resolution 532, adopted by a vote of 15–0 on May 31, which called for the secretary-general to consult with all parties to the dispute. Reaction to the June 1981 bombing of Iraq's nuclear reactor by Israel was another case in which non-aligned opinion was divided on whether to push for sanctions or to enlist the United States in supporting general language condemning the raid and for "appropriate redress." Despite a stormy Arab League meeting in Baghdad on June 11 and prolonged Security Council debate on June 12–19, during which all non-aligned speakers called for sanctions, the NAM group under Tunisia's direction unanimously endorsed a milder version evolving from U.S.-Iraqi negotiations.

In another case involving Iraq, the non-aligned were more deeply divided a year before, following the September 1980 invasion of Iran. They were unwilling, on the one hand, to offend Iraq, whose ubiquitous under secretary, Ismet Kittani, positioned himself outside their consultation room, and unable, on the other hand, to meet Iran's demand for condemnation of aggression. Faced with the impossibility of devising a resolution minimally acceptable to both sides, the non-aligned argued that the Security Council should avoid public sessions in order to preserve its impartiality. In the resulting impasse, a meeting was delayed, as Baghdad consolidated initial military gains, until the secretary-general took the rare initiative of calling one. The NAM group then held extended consultations during which Iranian and Iraqi officials appeared separately before them in the informal caucus room. An eventual resolution of September 28 and a presidential statement of November 5 were confined to appeals for cease-fire, restraint, mediation, and good offices of the secretary-general. While the latter evolved into the appointment of Olaf Palme, then between terms as Swedish prime minister, as special representative and five shuttle trips, intermittent fighting continued through 1983. Nor did a later resolution of July 12, 1982, calling for a peaceful settlement, deter Iran from carrying the war into Iraq, or a resolution of October 4 induce it to withdraw.

Implications for the Council

The impact of non-aligned activism on the Security Council depends on one's perceptions and expectations of that body. From their point of view, the non-aligned have been successful in keeping Namibia and

Palestine before the public through regular recourse to the council and General Assembly. Without illusions that U.N. resolutions could lead to a breakthrough in either case, they have viewed the process as a long-term form of pressure on the West to intervene with South Africa and Israel. The approach has succeeded in heightening public awareness of the problems and, in the Namibian case, probably in drawing the United States, United Kingdom, Germany, France, and Canada directly into the negotiating process. The non-aligned maintain that, in the absence of such pressure, particularly in the Security Council, there would be little momentum to reverse the colonial status quo. From this perspective, their activism is consistent with the U.N. mandate to bring major problems to world attention and to initiate a process of dialogue.

Repetitious debate cannot, however, continue to command public attention, and has a negative impact on the Security Council, blurring the distinction between the General Assembly as a focus for world opinion and the council as an executive committee of the United Nations. Repetition further entrenches positions, and resolutions like 242 on the Middle East or 435 on Namibia become sacrosanct, with strong resistance even to the change of a comma. As circumstances evolve, they can become straitjackets, preventing further innovation or constructive adjustment. The cumulative effect of debate on the same items damages confidence in the Security Council, which, in turn, limits its real power.

While non-aligned interests in recent years have most frequently clashed in the Security Council with those of the United States over the Middle East and southern Africa, Moscow has on occasion also come under pressure. Heavy lobbying by the non-aligned secured Soviet acquiescence in resolutions on Rhodesia and a U.N. force in Lebanon that Moscow would probably have opposed otherwise. The effect of group pressure, non-aligned delegates maintain, is to raise the cost of vetoes on East–West or ideological grounds by the implicit threat of reprisals in the relations of either superpower with the Third World. The dramatic reversal since the 1970s in U.S. and Soviet use of the veto suggests that Moscow, to a greater degree than Washington, may have tailored substantive positions to relations with the Third World.

Loyalty to bloc, to which Communist and Western delegates, though in lesser numbers, are not immune, poses additional problems for the Security Council. As informal representatives of 101 members, the non-aligned face particular conflicts when council debate threatens one or more of their number, rather than castigating non-member targets like Israel and South Africa. The argument, which rarely arises in the latter cases, is then made that the council should remain silent to preserve its neutrality. Taken to the extreme, this implies that the

Security Council, despite charter obligations for international peace and security, should be a bystander until belligerents are able to agree, a military solution is reached, or a party sues for peace. Parallel U.N. and NAM initiatives also pose a potential, but more limited, issue of divided loyalties. The formation in October 1980, at the instigation of Cuba and the PLO, of a NAM "Goodwill Committee" to mediate between Iran and Iraq may, for example, have influenced initial non-aligned attitudes toward U.N. mediation.

As of 1983, non-aligned impact on the Security Council was mixed. The NAM's role in initiating action and bringing issues to the council filled an obvious vacuum. The permanent members, by contrast, seemed immobilized by the council's adverse arithmetic, superpower division on most issues, and growing shades of difference in the position of Western members. While the Non-Aligned Group still functioned only by loose liaison with the overall movement, the risk remained of a more binding relationship. The latter, forestalled by resentment of Cuba's presidency, could potentially involve supervision by the NACB, regular liaison with the NAM presidency, and an even more layered process. If so, the council's eroded response time in crisis and its reputation for impartiality would probably suffer.

Evolution of the Non-Aligned Group's role will depend, however, on developments in the overall movement, principally India's approach to the presidency and its ability to reorient the NAM along more centrist lines. While India is committed to greater Third World representation on the Security Council and has intermittently pushed for further expansion of its membership, it will be more likely than Cuba to respect the council as an institution and slower to take steps that further undermine its effectiveness. On the other hand, if, as is nearly certain, India's ambitions for a fifth term on the Security Council are realized during its three-year NAM chairmanship, the question of coordination between the chairman and the Non-Aligned Group will become academic. As of September 1983, there appeared to be no serious opposition to India's bid for a seat from 1984–86. Once on the Security Council, the chairman, who is also ex officio head of the NACB, would automatically provide regular liaison and a channel between the two bodies. The only precedent for a NAM chairman on the Security Council is Zambia in 1970, well before the Non-Aligned Group became organized on the council.

In the meantime, the non-aligned already regard the Security Council as a vehicle for their purposes rather than as a special preserve of the great powers to be avoided in favor of the General Assembly. In 1982, for example, Cyprus broke precedent by inviting Security Council President Noel Sinclair of Guyana to attend a July meeting of the NACB in Nicosia, and Nicaragua invited Togo, as council president, to attend the January 1983 NACB meeting in Managua. These invitations, turned down because of Western objections, underscored the new relationship. More significantly, growing non-aligned presence on the Security Council was particularly singled out at the March 1983 New Delhi Summit, which emphasized the desirability of "strengthening such representation in the future."

In 1983, the Non-Aligned Group was expanded by new elections to a maximum strength of eight full NAM members on the Security Council: Nicaragua, Guyana, Malta, Jordan, Pakistan, Zimbabwe, Togo, and Zaire. While this spectrum ranged from the conservative outlook of Zaire and Pakistan to the radical orientation of Nicaragua, the presence on it of activists within the NAM and United Nations, as well as its sheer numerical strength, seemed to ensure new efforts to expand the group's role. The nucleus of Nicaragua, Zimbabwe, and Malta will remain on the Security Council for two years, and could be further reinforced with the departure in 1984 of relatively moderate Togo, Zaire, and Jordan. During the 1983 Security Council's first formal meeting on January 18, to renew the mandate of the U.N. International Force in Lebanon (UNIFIL), Nicaragua made the most of its non-aligned credentials, citing the January 10–14 NACB meeting in Managua and its intention "to be spokesman and to represent the views and interests of the Movement to which we belong in every situation or dispute which may come before the Security Council." The Nicaraguan delegate, Vice Minister of Foreign Affairs Tinoco Fonseca, also foreshadowed Sandinista plans to bring Central America into the council during March 1983 by his reference to defending the "interests of Latin America and the Caribbean, where the principles of nonalignment have a natural raison d'être and where serious problems are shared by the vast majority of the Movement." His thrust was consistent with the Managua communiqué, which "urged the Security Council to give careful consideration to the Nicaraguan peace initiative."

Since 1961, the NAM has been committed to strengthening its role within the United Nations, but has focused largely on the General Assembly. Awareness of a non-aligned group on the Security Council or reference to the council in non-aligned documents has, until recently, been limited. At Nicaragua's instigation, however, the following separate paragraph was included in the Managua communiqué:

> The Ministers emphasized that Nicaragua's election to the Security Council would strengthen the Movement of Non-aligned Countries' positions and goals in that body.

Even moderates on the Security Council concede that G-8 consultations with India as NAM president will probably be closer than those with Cuba. They point out, however, that non-aligned council members will still vote according to their national interests and will not be bound by NAM declarations. From a U.S. point of view, however, an expanded non-aligned majority in itself has potentially negative implications for Western interests on the council. Instances of the non-aligned having to back off or compromise to obtain the nine votes necessary for passage will be rarer. The scope for U.S. or other Western initiatives on issues involving Soviet misconduct will probably be more limited. Prospects for initiating action and obtaining a majority, for example, on the use of Soviet chemical weapons in Afghanistan or Southeast Asia, are likely to be diminished. Subsidiary bodies of the Security Council, such as the reconstituted South African Arms Embargo Committee, on which the veto does not apply, will clearly be less manageable from a Western point of view in the hands of an absolute non-aligned majority.

The ability of the Non-Aligned Group to dominate the Security Council will continue, however, to depend on the cohesiveness of its members, and is likely to fluctuate as the mix of radical and moderate members shifts from year to year. From 1983–84, heavy-handed pressures by Nicaragua to galvanize the group around a radical nucleus on the council could polarize differences with moderates like Zaire, Togo, and Pakistan, reducing areas of non-aligned consensus. A radical assault on the Security Council could also unify its Western members and diminish instances of public disagreement among U.S. allies. While the outcome is thus uncertain, Nicaragua and Cuba are likely to push for further consolidation of the G-8 as a tool of the overall movement. The Nicaraguan government has specifically called attention to the "power that the Movement can exert in the Security Council especially if you take into account, as is almost always the case, the votes of the Socialist Camp," and has urged the G-8 to "consult the 36 members of the NACB on important issues."[53]

9

The General Assembly

Debate without effective action erodes the credibility of the Organization.
U.N. Secretary-General Javier Perez de Cuellar

The General Assembly, variously justified as a ritualized alternative to conflict or castigated as theater of the absurd, has, at least since the 1973 Algiers Summit, been home ground for the non-aligned. Their pre-eminence, to the extent they can agree, is ensured by the U.N. Charter's stipulation that "each member of the General Assembly shall have one vote." Further, the assembly's specific responsibilities for approving the U.N. budget (except peacekeeping), apportioning expenses among members, and establishing "such subsidiary organs as may be necessary" have given the non-aligned majority vast leverage over the U.N. organizational structure.

In a more general sense, however, the General Assembly lacks the authority of its convictions and remains little more than an instant sounding board for international opinion, however distorted by bloc allegiances. It may make recommendations on any issue not before the Security Council, but its innumerable resolutions are not considered binding by its members except when it serves their national interests. Thus, as pointed out by Ruth Russell, its resolutions are by definition "irresponsible."[54] Knowledge that resolutions are ultimately unenforceable has probably reinforced confrontational behavior on issues where the assembly is divided. A "conflict model," as developed by Kurt Jacobsen in his quantitative analysis of the General Assembly, consists of rhetorical speeches for "the public gallery," competition on roll-call votes, bloc sponsorship of resolutions, and debate in plenary rather than committee sessions.[55] By contrast, consensus resolutions tend to emerge from informal consultations at the committee level and broad inter-group sponsorship.

In recent years, the number of General Assembly resolutions approved without recorded vote by consensus or acclamation has risen steadily, reaching 58 percent of resolutions adopted during the 1981 regular General Assembly session and 54 percent in 1982. The trend does not, however, necessarily indicate a shift from conflict to consensus models, since the number of non-substantive resolutions commemorating events or dealing with procedural items has also risen sharply. So has the number of non-specific resolutions dealing with abstract general principles. Consensus on such issues does not necessarily indicate that the assembly is working effectively to articulate differences and resolve real-world conflicts. On the contrary, in Jacobsen's phrase, the assembly may well be "a self-perpetuating consensus former" where consensus becomes not a means, but an end in itself.[56]

Recorded votes, by contrast, are a better indication of behavior in the General Assembly, since contested issues are more likely to mirror real-world problems. Analysis of non-aligned voting provides a profile of the movement's cohesion on different types of issues, unity in relation to other groups within the U.N. system, and relative agreement with the positions of Washington and Moscow.

Trends in the General Assembly

While the non-aligned have maximized influence on the Security Council through an increasingly organized majority, their power is still neutralized by the veto right of permanent members. In the General Assembly, by contrast, the only limitation to absolute non-aligned control is the movement's own cohesion. As the Security Council has become increasingly paralyzed on Third World issues by U.S. and other permanent member vetoes, the non-aligned have more frequently forced southern African and Middle Eastern questions into the General Assembly through the device of emergency special sessions.

Failure by the council to agree on and implement a course of action also has blurred distinctions between the council and the assembly, leaving both as debating forums for the most part devoid of practical effect. Further, the proliferation of agendas and "special," "emergency special," and "resumed" General Assembly sessions has, in recent years, made the assembly almost a year-round process rather than the traditional 13-week event, thereby altering its relationship to the Security Council. In the resulting tension between the two organs, the non-aligned, resentful of the veto, have generally sought to enlarge the assembly's mandate at the expense of the council.

As in the NAM, expanded U.N. membership has been accompanied by comparable growth in annual agendas. In 1955, 66 items were inscribed on the General Assembly agenda, and 142 in 1982. Inevitably, debate and resolutions on these items have required more time than the traditional General Assembly period from September to December. During the regular 1981 session, 330 resolutions were adopted by the General Assembly plenary, and 344 in 1982. Since 1978, all regular General Assembly sessions have had to resume the following year, often running several more months to complete their agendas. While the practice occurred often during the Cold War and other times of tension, it is now standard. The U.N. Charter provides for additional or "special sessions" of the assembly to be called on 15-day notice at the request of the Security Council or a majority of the General Assembly. During the first 30 years, six such sessions were held, and another six in 1975–82. The latter, all initiated by the non-aligned or G-77, dealt with the Middle East, Namibia, disarmament, and the NIEO.

More significant in terms of the General Assembly's role vis-à-vis the Security Council has been increasing use of the emergency special session (ESS). This procedure, known as "uniting for peace" and crafted by Secretary of State Dean Acheson in 1950, following paralysis of the council from 1946 to 1950 by multiple Soviet vetoes, was designed to break deadlocks in the council over issues involving a threat to or breach of peace or an act of aggression. It brings the assembly into emergency session on 24-hour notice at the request of nine council members or a majority of the assembly after a veto or failure by the council to obtain the necessary majority. Five such sessions were held before 1967 and four have been held since 1980. The early cases, except for the Suez crisis in 1956, were triggered, as foreseen by the United States, over Soviet vetoes in crises such as Hungary and the Congo. While Soviet action also led to the January 1980 emergency General Assembly meeting on Afghanistan, the last three such sessions—on Palestine in 1980, Namibia in 1981, and the Golan annexation in 1982—have all followed U.S. vetoes. Each also has been a clear-cut initiative of the non-aligned group, which appears to perceive the "uniting for peace" mechanism as special leverage in spotlighting Third World issues in a forum beyond reach of the permanent members.

The Seventh ESS on Palestine, described by a senior U.N. official as a "pre-arranged emergency," was, in fact, decided on the previous year, at PLO insistence, during the Havana Summit. A subsequent U.S. veto on April 30, 1980, of a non-aligned Security Council resolution on Palestinian rights provided a pretext for this ESS, although the meeting was not requested until July. At its conclusion, the non-aligned, again led by the PLO, further prevailed in adopting a formula whereby the Seventh ESS would not be formally closed and could be reconvened at any time by request of the members. This device provided an open-ended authority that the non-aligned decided to exploit two years later, during an April 1982 NACB meeting in Kuwait. As a result, four reconvened sessions were held during the remainder of 1982. Resumption after two years proved little more than a continuation of the earlier pre-arranged emergency, and the sessions were again left open-ended, giving the General Assembly a pretext to convene at any time on issues of the Middle East. Similarly, the Eighth ESS on Namibia was delayed five months on convenience rather than emergency grounds following three Western Security Council vetoes on April 30, 1981.

Use of the ESS for other than immediate crises or threats to the peace is a departure from its intended function and has tended to blur the distinction between the special session and the ESS, debasing the latter. From a non-aligned perspective, however, the modified procedure offers both the greater prestige and public attention of an emergency session and new flexibility to reclaim issues of concern from a veto-prone Security Council. In a broader sense, virtually continuous sessions of the General Assembly provide a more permanent base for the non-aligned within the U.N. system. The General Assembly president, often a key non-aligned leader, now retains active office throughout the year rather than mere titular authority when the regular General Assembly concludes. In April 1982, for example, the assembly president set a precedent by attending the Baghdad NACB meeting on Palestine specifically "in his capacity as President of the General Assembly." The subsequent president, Imre Hollai, a Hungarian, represented the assembly at both the Managua NACB meeting in January and the New Delhi Summit in March 1983.

As the non-aligned grew to be a majority of the General Assembly, the percentage of General Assembly presidents from the movement kept pace. Today, the movement's preponderance in the assembly would probably ensure continuous non-aligned incumbents if the presidency did not rotate by geographic region. From 1946 to 1961, however, only six countries that later became members of the NAM held the office. From 1962 to 1970, there were four non-aligned presidents of the assembly, and from 1971 to 1981, six. Of the latter, two—Shirley Amerasinghe of Sri Lanka and Abdelaziz Bouteflika of Algeria—derived added stature from their countries' concurrent chairmanship of the NAM. Other recent presidents have included such major figures in the movement as Salim Salim of Tanzania and Ismat Kittani of Iraq. Despite its pervasive influence, however, the NAM, unlike the OAU, Arab League, Islamic Conference, and other groupings, has never requested formal observer status in the assembly, but would probably do so if a decision were reached to form a permanent

NAM secretariat. In the absence of staff personnel, all NAM members, including SWAPO and the PLO, already have access to the assembly.

In practical terms, the NAM enjoys full support from the General Assembly staff apparatus with or without observer status. Its closed sessions are held, free of charge, in U.N. meeting rooms, with simultaneous translation, full U.N. conference services, and documentation. Since 1978, all major non-aligned communiqués and declarations, many of substantial length, have been printed, at the NAM president's request, and distributed on General Assembly stationery to all U.N. members. In addition, special services, funded from the regular U.N. budget, have been provided on request to meet particular NAM needs. In 1982, for example, a specially tailored U.N. seminar on conference techniques and management was arranged for an Iraqi delegation involved in preparations for the ill-fated Baghdad Summit.

Alignments Among the Non-aligned

While General Assembly resolutions may lack binding force and through repetition no longer command world attention, the variety of issues considered and the sheer number of resolutions adopted continue to provide an index of non-aligned and international opinion at a given point in time. Computers have facilitated tabulation and use of this data, permitting, for example, analysis of non-aligned voting patterns in relation to those of the United States and Soviet Union. The findings for recent years underscore the coincidence of interest within the General Assembly between the Soviet Union and the non-aligned, as well as the relative isolation of the United States. Generalizations as to cause and effect are more difficult, however, and the explanation of parallel voting on most issues by the non-aligned and the Soviet bloc may lie more in Moscow's strategy of courting Third World opinion at the United Nations than in non-aligned affinity for the Soviet system.

Comparative data on coincidence of voting by the non-aligned or other groups with the United States or the Soviet Union is not absolute, for there are several areas of predictable East–West agreement within the United Nations. Washington and Moscow, for example, commonly vote together on resolutions involving the U.N. budget or efforts to revise the charter. Thus, a given country's record of 95 percent agreement with Moscow does not necessarily imply only 5 percent coincidence with the United States. On 341 recorded votes from the Thirty-Seventh General Assembly, Moscow and Washington voted "yes" or "no" together 20.2 percent of the time, and during 1981 agreed 17.6 percent of the time on 287 votes. Using a smaller data base, agreement between the two was estimated at 20.6 percent in 1979 and 12.5 percent in 1980.[57]

Use of a "yes" or "no" basis for comparison does not take account of abstentions and absences, although it reflects an act of will or participation, and corresponds to the General Assembly definition of "members present and voting" (General Assembly Procedural Rule 127). As a result, the ranking of countries by agreement with the United States or USSR should be regarded as approximate in the case of smaller countries with high rates of absence. Of 287 votes during 1981, Antigua, for example, was "present and voting" only about 15 percent of the time, and on those occasions had 62.5 percent agreement with the United States and 68.2 percent with Moscow. Dominica, which missed all votes, had zero agreement with both.

With these caveats, examination of voting in 1981 and 1982 reveals an overwhelming disparity in the coincidence of non-aligned votes with those of the United States and USSR. Of the total 341 General Assembly votes in 1982, the United States voted "yes" or "no" on 271, for which non-aligned support ran from a high of 35.2 percent (St. Lucia) down to 9.3 percent (Grenada). The median was 20.6 percent support from Zambia, Bahrain, and Mali; average NAM support for the United States on all votes was 20.4 percent. Rank ordering of the NAM in terms of coincidence of voting with the United States (Appendix D), showed the following "friends" at the top: St. Lucia (whose top ranking was probably skewed by 171 absences and 12 abstentions), Morocco (31.8 percent), Lebanon (31.5 percent), Malawi (31.4 percent), Singapore (30.8 percent), and Somalia (30.6 percent). Preceding Grenada at the bottom were, almost without exception, Soviet client states: Vietnam (10.3 percent), Cape Verde (10.4 percent), Cuba (10.5 percent), Mozambique (11.2 percent), Laos (11.4 percent), Afghanistan (11.5 percent), Ethiopia (12.2 percent), and South Yemen (12.4 percent).

Comparison with the Soviets on 302 votes for which they were "present and voting" in 1982 reverses the rank order with minor variations (Appendix E), but reveals dramatically higher levels of vote coincidence with the non-aligned. Only one of 94 NAM members belonging to the United Nations in 1982 (St. Lucia) fell below a vote coincidence of 75 percent with Moscow (71.6 percent). Ten states were above 90 percent, with a median of 82.6 percent, and average NAM support of 83.4 percent, slightly down from 84.9 percent in 1981. Particularly striking at the top of the list were slavish support levels from Seychelles (100 percent, skewed by 252 absences), Vietnam (98.2 percent), Laos (97.7 percent), Afghanistan (95.3 percent), and Cuba (93.5 percent). Allegiance in these percentiles on such a broad range of votes clearly represented willingness to side with Moscow and against non-aligned consensus on Afghanistan and a number of other issues.

An alternative measurement is to compare voting records on a smaller cross section of U.N. votes that clearly impinged on U.S. interests. Compared with the broad range of items, non-aligned votes on issues for which the United States mounted a full lobbying effort were cast with specific knowledge of the importance attached to them by Washington. They are thus perhaps more indicative of relative East–West influence within the General Assembly. For this purpose, ten votes during both the 1981 and the 1982 General Assembly were identified in a monitoring system devised by the Department of State; they included such key issues as Kampuchea, Afghanistan, El Salvador, the neutron bomb, the Middle East and South Africa. Soviet agreement with the United States was 10 percent in 1981 and 11.1 percent in 1982. Despite individual country differences, NAM voting on the ten "key" votes followed the overall pattern. Average non-aligned agreement with the United States was 22 percent in 1981 and 37.4 percent in 1982.

A third index of "alignment" or orientation on the East–West spectrum is useful as a middle ground between the limited ten-vote sample and the totality of 341 votes, which inevitably includes miscellaneous and irrelevant issues. The list of ten votes was expanded for this purpose to a larger selection of over 100 important political and economic issues on which recorded votes were taken during the 1981 and 1982 General Assemblies. The latter excluded most procedural and U.N. "housekeeping" issues, thereby reducing the level of Soviet/U.S. agreement to 7 percent in 1981 and 8.3 percent in 1982, and providing a more clear-cut indicator. Of these 118 votes in 1982, the non-aligned voted with the United States an average 13.2 percent of the time and with the Soviets 88.6 percent. The comparable figures for 1981 were 11.2 percent and 88.4 percent.

While percentages of non-aligned agreement with East or West vary according to the vote samples used, the pattern and composition of states clustered at upper and lower limits of each list are remarkably consistent. Variations in the actual figures are, in fact, predictable from the size of the sample and type of issues selected. Inclusion among the ten votes in 1982, for example, of five significant but statistically atypical defeats for the Soviet Union (Afghanistan, Kampuchea, Puerto Rico, Israeli credentials, and chemical weapons) ensured a relatively higher average level of non-aligned agreement with the United States (37.4 percent). So does inclusion of closely contested rather than lopsided votes and under-representation of Middle Eastern and southern African issues. Conversely, greater U.S./Soviet agreement on all votes (20.2 percent) results in higher non-aligned coincidence with the United States than on the selected vote sample where Soviet disagreement with Washington was 91.7 percent in 1982 and 93 percent the preceding year.

Two conclusions may be drawn, neither surprising in light of the movement's radicalization in the 1970s and its pervasive anti-colonial bias. First, on the broad range of issues before the General Assembly, non-aligned interests and voting patterns were more nearly parallel to the Soviet Union than to the United States. This convergence, while implying no particular non-aligned affinity for the Soviet system, isolates the United States on many issues within the assembly and limits the scope for furthering U.S. policies through active involvement in that institution. Second, the percentage of support for Moscow by a small cadre of Soviet clients within the NAM is nearly triple that of the most devoted U.S. allies. Virtually undeviating support for Soviet positions by five to ten states is assured, while the United States at best receives 30 percent support from a small number of the more conservative NAM members.

Given the number of General Assembly votes on issues of southern Africa, the Middle East, disarmament, and the world economy, which in a loose sense can be said to have colonial overtones, the movement's anti-Western voting profile is a logical extension of its institutional preoccupations. Coincidence on the majority of issues with the Soviet position is, therefore, not necessarily a measure of Soviet influence or control. For most NAM members, it results in greater part, from differences with U.S. and other Western positions on specific issues and underlying post-colonial mistrust. The dependent variable is more likely to be the Soviet vote on issues dear to the NAM, by which Moscow can exploit existing polarization and seek to increase its opportunities in the Third World. An exception to this hypothesis is the group of outright Soviet supporters in the NAM, whose percentiles of agreement with Moscow bespeak overt control.

Non-Aligned Cohesion

To what extent are voting patterns of the non-aligned a result of membership in the movement rather than a reflection of Third World attitudes not unique to the NAM? The colonial legacy is shared by many non-member states that might be expected to vote along similar lines, indicating that the movement per se is not a dominant factor in U.N. voting behavior. In fact, there is clear-cut differentiation between the performance on all vote samples of the non-aligned and of Third World states outside the movement. Measuring performance relative to the United States on the ten most important General Assembly votes in both 1981 and 1982 by awarding a point for each vote in agreement and subtracting one for each vote opposed highlights this difference. Thus, on a possible scale of +10 to −10, the 24 non-NAM developing countries of Latin America and Asia averaged +3.25 in both years, while the average non-aligned rating was −1.8 in 1981 and −1.6 in 1982.

A difference of this order between states with similar interests on most economic, decolonization, and other issues tends to reinforce the view that bloc loyalty and selective membership influence voting. While presence within the NAM of an organized radical or pro-Soviet minority will inevitably lower the group rating in relation to the United States, non-NAM developing states outnumber even the most conservative of the non-aligned in the positive ranges of +5 and above. It is sometimes claimed that radical countries of the Third World join the NAM while more pro-Western states do not. Yet the presence in the movement of conservatives like Saudi Arabia, Morocco, Singapore, Pakistan, and Colombia suggests that pressure within the NAM, rather than simple self-selection, accounts for these statistics.

Within the movement, there was slight variation between regional components. On the larger cross-section of "important issues," the African states voted with the United States, on average, 8 percent of the time in 1981 and 13.5 percent in 1982. In both cases, their support closely paralleled that of the overall NAM. Latin American members of the non-aligned agreed with the United States on 9.5 percent of the votes in 1981 and 21 percent in 1982. By contrast, the United States received 15.3 percent and 31.7 percent support from non-NAM Latin American nations during 1981 and 1982. Asians and Middle Eastern members voted with the Untied States just under 8 percent of the time in 1981 and 16 percent in 1982, compared with 16 percent and 24 percent support from Asians outside the movement. Finally, the three European members (Yugoslavia, Cyprus, Malta) were lowest, with 4 percent support for the United States, compared with an average 44 percent from Western Europe and 5 percent from Eastern Europe.

Consistency of non-aligned voting predictably varied on all voting samples by type of issue. Votes on core questions of decolonization tended to be unanimous while divisions showed up on issues more peripheral to the non-aligned or where the context was clearly

East–West rather than North–South. Non-aligned cohesion was greatest on geographic issues where its regional subgroup was unified and least on Asian and Latin American votes lacking a regional consensus within the NAM. Thus, within the cross section of ten key votes in both 1981 and 1982, NAM members "present and voting" were unanimous in opposing or deploring the neutron bomb, nuclear collaboration with South Africa, the Golan annexation, and U.S. extradition of an accused terrorist to Israel.

On Asian issues, by contrast, there tended to be less agreement. The non-aligned were in only 83 percent agreement on Afghanistan in 1981 and 84 percent in 1982. In 1981, 80 percent supported a ban on chemical weapons in Southeast Asia, with 81 percent voting for it in 1982. On Kampuchea, 79 percent voted for withdrawal of foreign forces in 1981 and 80 percent in 1982. Only 53 percent could agree on the wording of a 1981 resolution on Guam. Finally, on Latin American issues, 89 percent agreed in 1981 to appeal against intervention in El Salvador, and 90 percent did so in 1982. Only 50 percent of the non-aligned "present and voting" opposed the 1982 resolution on the colonial status of Puerto Rico.

The pattern holds true with a larger data base, and on the larger selection of "important votes" non-aligned members voting "yes" or "no" were close to unanimity on Middle Eastern, southern African, and disarmament resolutions. Even nuclear or near-nuclear members did not oppose a NAM consensus against such weapons, despite high priority given to national development programs. Inter-bloc differences were apparent, however, on a range of Latin American votes dealing with Chile, Guatemala, and El Salvador, as well as on resolutions dealing with Bermuda, the British Virgin Islands, and Montserrat. As a general rule, differences were greater on votes with a specific and limited focus, and less or non-existent on more generalized or global issues. Non-aligned voting on economic issues, for example, was unanimous in all but a few cases.

The degree of voting discipline the movement can command is thus strongest on issues that have traditionally been its primary focus. The weight of non-aligned dogma on Middle Eastern, southern African, disarmament, and economic issues is sufficient that votes against the consensus pose a question of institutional identity and maximize peer pressure on the dissenter. Exceptions to this occur when NAM extremists occasionally push for more radical formulations than the consensus will bear, but this process of adjustment normally takes place at NAM ministerial and summit meetings, and does not often affect voting in the General Assembly. Cuba's miscalculation on September

24, 1982, in pushing for a vote to put Puerto Rico on the agenda, for example, gained support from only 19 hard-core NAM radicals. In most cases, however, non-aligned states whose national interests conflict with the radical consensus will not oppose it on a recorded vote. Non-aligned calls for comprehensive, mandatory sanctions thus are not opposed by states bordering on South Africa like Botswana, Swaziland, and Zambia, whose fragile economies would be shattered if trade and transport were cut off. Members like India, Iraq, Argentina, and Pakistan, committed to joining the nuclear club, must for the same reason regularly denounce the nuclear menace.

While non-aligned discipline precludes outright opposition on most core issues, opprobrium is not as strong in the case of absences and, to a lesser extent, abstentions. The rate of absenteeism is, in any case, high for practical reasons among members with small or even part-time delegations. Four members (Seychelles, Equatorial Guinea, Belize and St. Lucia) were absent for at least 50 percent of all recorded votes during 1982. Such chronic absenteeism provides camouflage for other members with policy reservations to avoid taking a stand. Annual condemnations, sponsored by the NAM, of relations between Israel and South Africa thus find among the absentees a minority with trade dependence on South Africa or diplomatic relations with one or both states.

On more peripheral issues, there is greater scope for flexibility by individual members. On the U.S. proposal for International Civil Service Commission (ICSC) appointments in 1981, Ivory Coast, Liberia, Morocco, Niger, Senegal, Singapore, Togo, and Trinidad and Tobago diverged from the group in offering support. Similarly, it is not unusual for Cuba, Afghanistan, Vietnam, and Laos to vote with the Soviet Union (and United States) on issues like the budget. In such cases, votes run counter to non-aligned thinking, but not on issues that have been a major focus of the movement's rhetoric. The area in which non-aligned voting is most vulnerable to East–West pressure is probably, therefore, confined to issues outside the movement's traditional focus. The latter, of course, tend to be marginal in a United Nations whose overall agenda increasingly coincides with that of the NAM.

Comparison of non-aligned voting consistency with that of NATO and the Warsaw Pact places the NAM between the two big-power voting blocs. As defined by Thomas Hovet, Jr., a voting bloc in U.N. terms is "a group of states which meets regularly in caucus and the members of which are bound in their votes in the General Assembly by the caucus decision."[58] The strength of the non-aligned bond varies by issue, but tends to be compelling for many of those that have dominated the General Assembly in recent years. Unlike the Warsaw Pact, however, loyalty to bloc is more nuanced. On all votes in 1982, the Warsaw Pact voted with the Soviet Union an average of 98.4 percent of the time, down slightly from 99.2 percent agreement in 1981.

Country	*Percentage of Agreement*	*Number of Votes*	*Abstentions*	*Absences*
Byelorussia	100	302	0	0
Ukraine	100	302	0	0
Czechoslovakia	100	298	2	2
Hungary	100	297	2	3
Bulgaria	100	295	4	3
East Germany	100	298	2	2
Poland	100	289	8	5
Romania	87.2	274	13	15

NATO, by contast, voted with the United States during 1982 an average of 64 percent of the time, with a wide range from 80.1 percent British support down to 33.2 percent from Greece.

Country	*Percentage of Agreement*	*Number of Votes*	*Abstentions*	*Absences*
United Kingdom	80.1	206	65	0
West Germany	76.6	192	78	1
Belgium	74.4	199	72	0
Luxembourg	73.7	186	70	15
Canada	70.7	191	80	0
France	68.8	199	70	2
Italy	67.9	187	82	2
Netherlands	66.8	199	71	1
Denmark	60.3	189	82	0
Norway	59.8	184	86	1
Iceland	58.4	178	77	16
Portugal	57.3	192	73	6
Turkey	44.6	233	32	6
Greece	33.2	211	56	4

Voting cohesion within the NAM falls between the two superpower blocs but surprisingly, in view of the 98 U.N. members involved as of 1983, is considerably closer to the discipline of the Warsaw Pact than to the loose consensus of NATO. There is, however, no single member that can serve as a yardstick for NAM voting, and cohesion can best be judged by comparison with a core group of member states. On all 341 votes during the 1982 General Assembly, the non-aligned voted with Yugoslavia 97.6 percent of the time, with India 96.5 percent, with Singapore 95.8 percent, and with Cuba 94.5 percent. On all 287 votes during 1981, NAM voting coincided with that of Yugoslavia 98.2 percent of the time, with India 97 percent, with Singapore 92.3 percent and with Cuba 92.1 percent. India and Yugoslavia were selected to represent key founding members and chairmen of the NAM, and Singapore and Cuba as ideological poles of the movement.

The average 96.1 percent vote agreement with these four states in both 1981 and 1982 tends to confirm the NAM as the most cohesive large bloc in the U.N. system. Moreover, on the more potentially divisive sample of "important" votes, the non-aligned voted with India 97 percent of the time in 1981 and 97.7 percent in 1982, with Yugoslavia 96.4 percent and 97.8 percent, with Singapore 93.7 percent and 92.1 percent, and with Cuba 91.5 percent and 92 percent. The average voting consistency of the non-aligned on these selected votes was, thus, 95 percent over a two-year period.

The clustering of these percentiles in the mid-nineties also suggests that the bitter rivalries during Castro's presidency and the running feud between conservative and radical subgroups have not substantially affected voting within the United Nations. To be sure, non-aligned vote support for Cuba was 3 percent lower on all votes in 1982 than that for Yugoslavia. Yet the difference is slight when measured against average support for the United States of 64 percent from its NATO allies. To the extent that NATO is, therefore, classified as a voting bloc, which most non-aligned perceive it to be, the movement itself, by virtue of greater voting cohesion and membership, clearly falls within the definition.

10

Non-Aligned Impact on the UN Structure

We [the non-aligned] have contributed to the realization of the universality of the UN and to the strengthening of its role and importance.

Marshal Tito, 1979

The United Nations today differs radically from the fledgling structure of the late 1940s. Its present focus, balance of power, and decentralization would come as a shock to those at San Francisco. Yet the institution was never intended to be immutable and frozen to fit realities of 1945. Articles 108 and 109 of its charter provide mechanisms for constitutional change, but these are cumbersome and depend on unusual agreement of two-thirds of the General Assembly and all five permanent members of the Security Council. In practice, such amendments have been rare, and sweeping changes in the U.N. structure have been accomplished by more subtle, informal means, often under pressure from the non-aligned and Third World majority.

Pressure for change in the United Nations and resistance to it both stem from the basic incompatibility between "universality"—the principle of equal participation by all sovereign states—and the concept of special responsibility on the part of major world powers. The dichotomy was underscored by admission of 35 new states in the early 1960s, and in his report to the General Assembly of 1965 the secretary-general called for re-examination of membership criteria in light of the emergence of mini-states and micro-states. A Security Council committee of experts was eventually set up in 1969 to study implications for the United Nations of some 65 independent or still non-self-governing prospective members with populations under 300,000 (50 of these had under 100,000 inhabitants).

The United States proposed to give mini-states all rights of membership save the vote and the right to hold office, while freeing them from financial burdens. After desultory discussion of the U.S.

and other formulas, all anathema to the non-aligned, the committee lapsed into inactivity. In the absence of agreement, the only solution appeared to be for permanent members to use their veto authority on grounds that the mini-states were not able to fulfill the requirements of U.N. membership. Ultimately, however, the permanent members concluded that the public posture of the largest states vetoing admission of the smallest and poorest was politically untenable. The United States and others, by acquiescing in admission of Bhutan in 1971 and Grenada in 1974, in effect conceded the principle.

A corollary of universality is that the U.N. structure be equally responsive to all its members without regard to size, power, or population. On this basis, the developing countries, through the NAM and G-77, gradually concluded that their major preoccupations differed from the organizational focus envisaged in the charter. Problems of decolonization and development, while glimpsed at San Francisco, clearly were secondary to peacekeeping and political issues. In the intervening years, the balance has been redressed through a proliferation of new autonomous agencies and sub-organs shaped by Third World members to be responsive to their perceived needs. Budgetary power vested in the General Assembly has allowed the majority to prevail over potential resistance from major contributors in this restructuring process. The resulting network of development-oriented bodies like UNCTAD, the U.N. Industrial Development Organization (UNIDO), and the U.N. Development Program (UNDP) and of political organs like the Center Against Apartheid, the Committee on Palestinian Rights, and the Council on Namibia bespeak Third World influence in the United Nations.

Beyond influence within the formal or constitutional U.N. structure, the developing and non-aligned members have perhaps had more profound impact through informal institutions that have effectively relocated the seats of decision-making. Schematically, the United Nations is an elaborate edifice of expert bodies, ad hoc committees, commissions, standing committees, and main committees, each deliberating and forwarding information and recommendations to principal decision-making organs. The NAM, the G-77, and regional caucuses are extraneous to the organizational diagram and not recognized in the charter. Yet meetings of these groups, provided by the U.N. Secretariat with interpreters and conference services, comprise a major percent of those held at U.N. Headquarters. Decisions taken at them often determine the majority position in regular U.N. organs, which consequently become hostage to these behind-the-scenes and closed sessions. As in the Security Council, positions staked out in advance tend to predominate, except that in the case of the General Assembly and its seven main committees, they can and usually do represent an absolute majority.

The impact of coordinating majority positions outside the regular U.N. framework is to limit dialogue and possibilities for compromise inherent in the normal committee process. If reached in advance, a common position of most NAM members will, by simple arithmetic, prevail in the assembly, and there is no incentive for other than rhetorical exchanges. In the process, power shifts away from the formal committees, some of which become nearly superfluous. The existence of irregular or hidden power centers also contributes to Western, and particularly U.S., perceptions that the United Nations is less and less relevant. In practical terms, these informal structures tend to reduce the effectiveness of Western participation in the decision-making process, and thus Western commitment to its results.

The West, which has no similar coordinating mechanisms, as a group often trails or appears to trail behind the latest position of the NAM, the G-77, or the African caucus. While the ten members of the European Community coordinate to some degree, the larger WEOG grouping, to which the United States is invited as an observer, limits its discussion to precedural and U.N. staffing issues. An exception for economic issues is Western coordination in the OECD or its New York variant, the Vinci Group, and on disarmament, in the so-called Barton Group.

The convergence of non-aligned influence in New York creates a distinctly new approach to power based on the arithmetic of national sovereignty rather than economic, military, or even population factors. Former U.S. Ambassador to the United Nations Patrick Moynihan quotes Secretary-General Waldheim as saying that "some people were shocked to see the UN reflect the 'entirely new balance in the world,' as compared to the founding days of 1945." As distinct from the "true balance of power," Moynihan notes that Waldheim was referring to the "emergence of the notion that a majority of votes in the General Assembly in itself conferred a certain kind of power, which now 'they' had and 'we' didn't."[59]

Both the NAM and the G-77, in any case, recognize and thrive on this "entirely new balance," which is accentuated by the U.N. parliamentary structure. For this reason, they have resisted Western attempts to redress the New York balance by shifting North–South negotiations elsewhere. The 1975 Paris Conference on International Economic Cooperation (CIEC) foundered and was dissolved in 1977. More recently, the developing countries insisted at Cancún in 1981 that the long postponed "global round" be held under U.N. auspices and in New York. They have continued to resist Western proposals to open it under the OECD in Paris or anywhere else.

The primary focus of the non-aligned, and indeed of most diplomats in New York, has been parliamentary procedure and the deliberative organs of the United Nations. At the conference tables and in the lobbies, officials are busy negotiating the wording of resolutions, seeking to control and shape the resulting verbiage to suit their countries' or groups' interests. A less visible aspect of the United Nations is, however, the work of the permanent secretariat, headed by the secretary-general, which includes varied good offices, peace-keeping operations, economic development, refugee assistance and the specialized agencies. In these areas, the secretary-general usually receives quiet support from both the Western powers, the non-aligned and in many cases the Soviet bloc. Such behind-the-scenes cooperation often has important political results, as in the case of the secretary-general's May 1983 report on WHO findings which defused allegations about the "poisoning" of school girls in the occupied West Bank.

The capacity of the secretary-general to perform such objective and impartial functions is, however, restricted by non-aligned rhetoric in the deliberative bodies which reduces confidence in the overall organization. Moreover, mandates for the secretary-general in the form of U.N. resolutions have in recent years become increasingly imprecise, leaving little basis for decisive action by the United Nations. The non-aligned, while attributing broad problem-solving responsibilities to the secretary-general, have usually failed to provide him with the necessary political leverage. The permanent secretariat, while distinct in an institutional sense, is thus by no means exempt from NAM-induced changes elsewhere in the U.N. structure.

The restructuring, "democratization," or evolution of the United Nations is a continuing process, usually pitting developing against developed states. The objectives of the former are common to the NAM and the G-77, which coordinate and reinforce respective positions. Their campaign includes an elaborate exercise to review the charter and, in their view, strengthen the United Nations by bolstering powers of the General Assembly and curbing those of the Security Council through enlarged membership and limitations on the veto. Like the major powers before them, they seek not enhancement of the system but control of the levers of power for their immediate ends. A less formal, but equally determined, struggle is in progress over control of the budget, key U.N. committees, and personnel appointments to the Secretariat.

Charter Review

Since 1945, there have been three amendments to the U.N. Charter, each expanding membership of principal organs to accommodate new states and their desire for broader geographic representation. The Security Council was enlarged from 11 to 15 members, effective August 31, 1965, and the Economic and Social Council (ECOSOC) was twice expanded, from 18 to 27 in 1965 and to its present 54 members in 1973. To be adopted, each change was ratified by two-thirds of the membership and all permanent members of the Security Council, "in accordance with their respective constitutional processes." In the United States, this meant advice and consent of the Senate before the president ratified amendments.

From the non-aligned perspective, these enlargements were not so much permanent ceilings as steps toward "democratizing" or opening up U.N. organs to membership on a purely geographic basis. They point out that while the 1946 Security Council included 22 percent of the original U.N. members, the expanded council in 1983 represents less than 10 percent of the membership. Pressures are, therefore, again building to enlarge this and other organs. While the non-aligned have yet to agree on a new target for Security Council membership, they have in the past supported ECOSOC membership for all U.N. states. Western countries, particularly the permanent members, having gone along with earlier enlargements, have been reluctant to support further erosion of their own position and of these bodies' residual efficiency. Their resistance has centered on forestalling a two-thirds vote of the General Assembly, which would then isolate permanent members failing to ratify a proposed amendment.

Apart from these specific amendments, a more general assault on the U.N. Charter, led by the non-aligned, began in the early 1970s. Latin American, Asian, and African delegations argued in the General Assembly for an overall review of the charter and were adamantly opposed by the Soviet bloc, including Cuba, which maintained that the charter was sacrosanct. The United States, United Kingdom, and France expressed reservations about a general review, but agreed to consider amendments on a case-by-case basis. In 1972, 13 non-aligned states urged abolition of the veto as "irrelevant" to the modern world, and the following year, 3 African states argued for elimination of permanent membership on the Security Council. Debate on revising the charter sharpened somewhat in 1974 as Africans reacted with anger to vetoes by the United States, United Kingdom, and France of a non-aligned resolution calling for expulsion of South Africa from the

United Nations. In their insistence on reopening the charter, the Africans were joined by Latin Americans eager to include in it a clear-cut definition of aggression and by others, like Japan, with aspirations to permanent membership on the Security Council.

The result of this malcontented coalition was a General Assembly vote of 85–15 to set up the 42-member ad hoc Committee on the Charter. The action was taken over strong Soviet objections in the Sixth Committee (legal), and came at the end of the turbulent 1974 assembly, which followed the Algiers Summit and OPEC price rises. It also coincided with Grenada's admission and lack of further resistance to the idea of universality. From the outset, the ad hoc committee's focus was on limiting the veto power and role of permanent members. It was expanded to 47 members in 1975 and, by lopsided vote, given added status as the Special Committee on the Charter of the United Nations and on the Strengthening of the Role of the Organization.

In subsequent years, the Special Committee has submitted annual reports to the General Assembly, been renewed by overwhelming majorities, and held publicized special meetings at Manila in 1980 and at Geneva during 1982. While its accomplishments have so far been modest, because of the unanimity of permanent members needed to amend the charter, it has served to clarify non-aligned goals for structural reform. As the Moroccan delegate noted with resignation in 1981, efforts to limit or abolish the veto were a "purely theoretical exercise, since those empowered under Article 108 of the Charter to change that right were the very ones who enjoyed it." The 1983 New Delhi Summit, nevertheless, singled out the Charter Review Committee for special support and called on the non-aligned to further coordinate their activities.

While high turnover among non-aligned delegates has led to covering much of the same ground year after year, the Special Committee on the Charter had by 1982 identified a range of 54 proposals with varying degrees of support. In general, these fell into three categories: abstractions such as treaties on non-use of force or peaceful resolution of disputes, measures to strengthen the role of the General Assembly, and measures to diminish, at least from a Western perspective, the role of the Security Council. The inconsistency of efforts to curb the council's scope in a committee charged with "strengthening the role of the organization" mirrors the tensions between universality and special responsibility, majority and minority within the United Nations.

Among measures to strengthen the General Assembly, non-aligned committee members have argued for more frequent emergency sessions when the Security Council fails to respond to threats to peace (that is, when a veto is cast), more extensive fact-finding mechanisms, and the assembly's right to formulate "specific proposals concerning the practical activities of the Security Council." By contrast, proposals for the council, if implemented, would gravely weaken it by further increasing membership, extending the veto to one or two non-permanent members by rotation according to region, holding council meetings away from New York "in regions where threats to peace arise and where solution of disputes is the most necessary and urgent," and avoiding council decisions that "do not have the consent" of states directly interested in questions under discussion. The impact of these proposals would be staggering, particularly the cost and inefficiency of shuttling the council from region to region in a world of simultaneous, multiple crises. To date, only two Security Council meetings have been held outside New York: in Addis Ababa from January 28 to February 4, 1972, and in Panama from March 15 to March 21, 1973. In early 1981, the non-aligned on the council pushed unsuccessfully for a session in Algiers to coincide with the April NACB meeting there on Namibia.

A further set of proposals made in the Charter Review Committee deals specifically with the "unanimity rule," shorthand for the permanent members' right of veto. These contain measures to designate certain issues as procedural and not subject to veto, to make the determination of procedural issues itself "procedural," and to exempt from veto issues relating to maintenance of peace, inalienable rights of peoples to self-determination and disputes to which a permanent members is party. Most issues of the Middle East and southern Africa could, of course, be pigeonholed in one of the latter three categories. The emphasis on procedural issues as a way to limit the veto reflects a hope that Security Council members will themselves revise the "provisional" rules of procedure, thus obviating the need for amendment of the charter. A document submitted in 1981 by Egypt "on behalf of the non-aligned countries of the Special Committee," numbering 23, had this in mind in stressing the need to examine "areas where application of the rule of unanimity should be limited."

The USSR and East European committee members have remained adamantly opposed to these demands. The United States and most other Western nations have been equally resistant to assaults on the veto, but more flexible in considering procedural issues. Willingness by the United States and ten WEOG members on the committee to continue the dialogue has probably helped to avoid General Assembly resolutions on the unanimity rule and a showdown on amendments to the charter. From 1979 to 1982, Libya introduced annual resolutions specifically on the veto, but was in each case defeated on procedural motions. In the longer run, however, commitment to restructuring the United Nations is likely to lead to confrontation with the permanent members of the Security Council as the non-aligned become frustrated by lack of progress in the committee, described by the Indian delegate in 1979 as a "burial ground" for proposals.

Another forum for airing these differences is discussion in the Security Council itself, initiated in early 1983 by a non-aligned majority of eight, of the secretary-general's September 1982 proposals for U.N. reform. Corridor debate at the New Delhi Summit on expanding the council, requiring two or three vetoes to block resolutions, and making the NAM chairman ex officio a permanent member, foreshadowed new demands for revision of the charter.

The U.N. Budget

Third World pressure for expanded programs and resistance from major donors, faced with recession in the early 1980's, has inevitably led to conflict on the budget. Calculated in two-year cycles, the regular U.N. budget for 1982–83 was $1.5 billion (less than the GNP of the Netherlands). While perhaps not large in absolute terms, the figure, which does not include peacekeeping operations, specialized agencies, and voluntary contributions, is the latest in a spiral over which major contributors, like the United States, have less and less control. The General Assembly, controlled by a non-aligned majority, ultimately approves the budget and sets the level of assessments levied on member states, which has risen about 80 percent in the past 5 years. Major donors, over whose objections the last four budgets have been approved, have little recourse other than the unpalatable step of withholding assessments, in violation of obligations under the charter. An exception is peacekeeping, such as U.N. forces in Lebanon and elsewhere in the Middle East, which must first be approved by the Security Council. Following the 1973 Arab-Israeli war, the permanent members agreed, under pressure from the non-aligned, who in that case endorsed the concept of special responsibility, to pay a 15 percent surcharge on their regular assessments to support peacekeeping.

The U.N. budget, which has grown 700 percent since 1963, is divided as follows: 40 percent for economic, social, and humanitarian activities; 40 percent for administration and support services, including conferences; and 20 percent for "other" uses, such as legal and political activities. Annual short-term deficits have grown by over 30 percent per year from 1977, to $303 million in 1982. These are largely caused by the Soviet Union, China, and many small countries that deliberately withhold all or part of their assessments, although most delinquents avoid falling more than two years behind because, at that point, voting rights are suspended. Soviet, Ukrainian, and Byelorussian arrearages on mandatory peacekeeping and regular budget assessments, for example, were estimated by the U.N. at $168.8 million as of January 1, 1983. The Soviet Union, Ukraine, Byelorussia, Mongolia, Bulgaria, and East Germany further compound the crisis by insisting on making partial payments and voluntary contributions in useless, non-convertible currencies. For purposes of comparison, the United States paid 24.45 percent of all assessed and voluntary U.N. collections during 1980, while the USSR (including the Ukraine and Byelorussia) paid only 4.27 percent.

The cumulative result, in the words of Kurt Waldheim's Report on the U.N. Financial Emergency to the 1981 General Assembly, has been a "steady erosion and deterioration of the Organization's financial position." The secretary-general also summarized bleak prospects for borrowing on the open market and from members or for issuance of U.N. bonds. Faced with this financial crisis, the General Assembly has dithered. A special committee, established in 1975, was unable to agree and reported back, in essence, that the problem was serious, but that no solution was in sight. On December 10, 1980, the assembly acted to earmark proceeds from the sale of commemorative postage stamps. The stamps, released during November 1982 in Geneva, New York, and Vienna, were optimistically expected to generate net revenue of $2 million, about 0.5 percent of the projected deficit for that year.

Faced with these deficits and unchecked U.N. spending, the United States and other major donors have put strong pressure on the secretary-general for zero-growth budgeting, the principle that increases in a given area must be offset by equivalent reductions elsewhere. Kurt Waldheim, in whose ten-year tenure the regular budget tripled, obliged by issuing such a directive in 1981, undoubtedly aware that great power support would be vital for his re-election later that year. The result was a 1982–83 budget with, the United Nations maintained, real growth under 1 percent. Yet the claim rested on scaled-down projections for inflation and exaggerated estimates of the dollar's value against foreign currencies. Under the circumstances, the United States, for the first time in December 1981, voted against the U.N. regular budget, although it had twice in recent years opposed supplemental appropriations. The Soviet Union, Eastern Europe, the United Kingdom, West Germany, and Japan joined in opposing the resolution, which was approved by a vote of 120–15–6. A revision of the 1982–83 budget was approved on December 21, 1982, by a similar majority of 117–14–12. While, for the first time since 1955, the dollar amount was less than the previous year, the "savings" came from revised inflation and exchange rate figures, and reflected a 5 percent growth in real terms. It was, therefore, again opposed by the United States and other major donors.

The non-aligned, despite Soviet and Western appeals for budgetary restraint, have not grasped the seriousness of the fiscal situation, and have a vested interest in channeling more money into U.N. programs and activities oriented to the Third World. They form an active bloc within the Fifth Committee (administrative and budgetary), which forwards final budget recommendations to the General Assembly for almost automatic approval. The power over U.N. budgets, which the non-aligned have gradually assumed, is part of a larger strategy, in concert with the G-77, to gain similar control over the budgets and development programs of other international agencies, primarily the IMF, the IBRD, and their affiliates. The latter, while making major concessions in the late 1970s, have remained relatively impervious to pressures to eliminate voting weighted according to contributions and to admit the PLO and liberation organizations.

Control over multi-lateral budgets will remain, however, a central demand in the North–South negotiations and the focus of non-aligned and G-77 efforts in New York. Their majority was evident in a General Assembly vote of 121–3 (United States, United Kingdom, West Germany) on October 20, 1982, to cut off IMF credits to South Africa. While the vote will have no practical effect, it underscores Third World pressure to substitute political for economic criteria in decision-making by the international financial institutions.

Within the United Nations, consideration of the budget is channeled through a three-step committee process. The secretary-general's budget, prepared by the U.N. Office of Financial Services, is given for review to the standing 16-member Advisory Committee on Administrative and Budgetary Questions (ACABQ). The latter, composed of financial experts and individuals elected by the Fifth Committee, considers overall funding levels and recommends reductions to the Fifth Committee. Simultaneously, the separate Committee on Program and Coordination (CPC) prepares recommendations based on program content. Both are considered by the Fifth Committee, whose proposed budget is then ratified by the General Assembly.

Non-aligned influence over the process has grown with erosion of the ACABQ. In earlier years, the latter's recommendations for financial restraint, from experts acting in an individual rather than national capacity, were usually unchallenged. Recently, however, they have been increasingly overridden by non-aligned members of the Fifth Committee, which has become more politicized and reluctant to heed technicians' advice. Addressing this issue, the U.S. delegate asked the committee rhetorically on December 18, 1981: "How can such behavior by this Committee fail to invite redoubled efforts by others to undermine the ACABQ?" Many of the non-aligned also favor merging the ACABQ and the less powerful CPC, on the theory that greater focus on program content would promote higher funding levels. In 1981, India first floated this proposal, which, from a Western perspective, would remove a further vestige of restraint from the budgetary process.

On a more informal level, non-aligned delegations are able to make common cause with Secretariat officials, many themselves from the Third World and, in any case, committed to program expansion and increased funding. Occasionally, the collusion is blatant, as during the late 1970s, when senior officials of the Law of the Sea (LOS) Conference and the Third World-oriented Center for Transnational Corporations took to the Fifth Committee floor to lobby against ACABQ budget cuts. Also in 1981, the Division of Narcotic Drugs and the Department of Public Information were publicly criticized by the U.S. delegation for lobbying in the General Assembly against the proposed budget of the secretary-general. In practice, however, such interference is usually not necessary. Non-aligned delegations are in daily working contact with the Secretariat staff of bodies like the Council for Namibia and the Center Against Apartheid. Discontent with evolving budget recommendations is soon registered, and can thus be acted on at an early stage.

Just as important as the budget itself is who pays for it, worked out by a scale of assessments formulated in the General Assembly. The United States is assessed at the maximum rate of 25 percent, which in 1980 amounted to $349 million, for assessed contributions to the regular budget, peacekeeping, and specialized agencies. In addition, the United States provided $508 million on a voluntary basis, for a combined 24.5 percent of all 1980 assessed and voluntary contributions to the United Nations. For the years 1983–85, the assessed U.S. share will be greater than the combined assessments of 147 member states and 2.5 times that of all the non-aligned states. In the same period, the following ten major donors will pay 75.1 percent of the U.N. budget: United States (25 percent), USSR (10.5 percent), Japan (10.3 percent), West Germany (8.5 percent), France (6.5 percent), United Kingdom (4.7 percent), Italy (3.7 percent), Canada (3.1 percent),

Spain (1.9 percent), and the Netherlands (1.8 percent). Among oil-rich states, Saudi Arabia pays .86 percent (estimated at $6.7 million for 1983), Libya .26 percent (estimated at $2 million), and Iraq .12 percent (estimated at $940,000).

Many of the latter complain that new oil revenues may put them in a higher bracket. For this reason, Algeria sponsored a resolution, adopted by the General Assembly in 1981, to assist countries with rapid GNP growth by stretching out the base period on which assessments are calculated from seven to ten years. The Algerian resolution also provided that the least-developed countries would, notwithstanding an ongoing review of national contributions, be guaranteed that "their individual rates of assessment should not in any way exceed the present level." The revised assessment scales, effective from 1983, incorporated this approach, although oil-producing countries were forced to absorb modest increases to offset reductions for the USSR and Eastern Europe. Along the same lines, Cuba sponsored resolutions, adopted in both 1981 and 1982, requiring the secretary-general to report on alleged U.N. losses due to "inflation and monetary instability in the developed countries." These were clearly meant to lay the groundwork for higher levies against the West to offset alleged losses from inflation. In the U.S. case, the present ceiling of 25 percent, well under the assembly's formula for U.S. "capacity to pay," was negotiated in 1972 as a result of strong congressional interest.

The end result of these initiatives for the United States and other major donors is increasingly a situation where the United States must pay as directed by the majority or violate the charter by withholding contributions. After decades of East European misconduct and non-aligned casualness about paying bills, the United States began, in the early 1980s, a modest program of withholding funds for activities of which it strongly disapproved. In 1980 and 1981, the United States withheld, in accordance with congressional legislation, the estimated portion of its assessment that would have been used to finance Secretariat offices dealing with Palestinian affairs ($191,775 and $211,125, respectively). It also registered disapproval through a program of phased deferrals on payments for the regular budget and major cutbacks, beginning in fiscal 1983, on voluntary contributions. These measures were in response to growing public and congressional concern that the United Nations was, in effect, imposing on the United States a regimen of international taxation without adequate representation. In a period of recession, both the Carter and the Reagan administrations were under pressure from Congress to reduce funding for the United Nations or face the threat of mandatory legislation to do so. The Helms Amendment of August 3, 1978, did, in fact, briefly cut off use of U.S. dues to the United Nations for technical assistance.

By the 1982 General Assembly, the U.S. delegation was engaged in an across-the-board struggle for zero-growth budgets within the United Nations and its specialized agencies. American diplomats insisted on amendments to any resolution with "financial implications" that specified that they would be implemented "only to the extent that they can be financed without exceeding the level of resources approved in the 1982–83 program budget." As the U.S. delegate stated on December 20, 1982, in explaining a vote against the revised budget, "We reject the notion that the UN is immune from the economic climate in which it exists."

The new emphasis led to virtually complete U.S. isolation in 1982 on pork barrel issues within the United Nations, such as construction of a new OAU headquarters in Addis Ababa. A further test case was the LOS Treaty, which, as of early 1983, the United States had not signed (along with West Germany, the United Kingdom, and others). These states were, nevertheless, still assessed for costs, including a well-publicized December 1982 conference at Montego Bay, Jamaica. Pointing out that the United States was being called on to finance preparations for a seabed mining program that it had specifically opposed, President Ronald Reagan announced on December 20, 1982, that the United States, alone among U.N. members, would withhold its 1983 share, estimated at about $500,000.

Within the United Nations, only one of the financial amendments introduced by the United States was adopted, but the campaign served notice of U.S. determination to limit U.N. growth at the taxpayers' expense and, in a practical sense, may have restored some authority to the process of ACABQ budget review. Other major donors supported the effort, and U.S. Ambassador Jeane Kirkpatrick was accompanied by the Soviet and British ambassadors during a November 18, 1982, call on U.N. Secretary-General Perez de Cuellar to urge budgetary restraint. While the Soviet Union welcomed the U.S. initiative, it nevertheless often acquiesced in increased costs in cases where opposition could entail Third World opprobrium.

Like everything at the United Nations, insistence on zero growth involved trade-offs with other important principles. Rigid application would, for example, have required voting against the annual call for troop withdrawal from Afghanistan because of the estimated $127,000 costs of U.N. shuttle diplomacy, and opposing the equally desirable resolutions on Kampuchea and chemical weapons because of program costs. While exceptions were made in these cases, they highlight the contradiction between a policy of no growth and selective reliance on the United Nations where it supports American interests. The tension between recessionary donor economies and U.N. bureaucratic growth is likely to produce increasingly sharp confrontation between the United States and the U.N. majority during the mid-1980s.

Secretariat Staffing

Non-aligned pressure to strengthen geographic criteria for U.N. staffing, like that for bigger budgets, intensified with greater membership and organization during the 1970s. General Assembly President Abdelaziz Bouteflika of Algeria is reported to have noted, at the conclusion of the 1974 assembly, that "the only thing left now to decolonize is the Secretariat." The remark goes to the core of non-aligned thinking about the Secretariat and the United Nations in general. The predominance of North American and West European professional staff during the first decades of the organization was seen as a legacy of colonialism.

Article 101 of the charter provides two conflicting criteria for staff recruitment: The "paramount consideration" shall be the "necessity of securing the highest standards of efficiency, competence and integrity"; and "Due regard shall also be paid to the importance of recruiting the staff on as wide a geographical basis as possible." Over the years, the non-aligned have placed increasing weight on the second criterion, also challenging the assumption that the "highest standards" for efficiency or competence are necessarily Western. In pressing for change in the personnel area, they have usually been joined by the Soviets and East Europeans, and often by Germany and Japan, which as a legacy of World War II are still under-represented.

Third World influence over staffing was underscored at the top of the pyramid by election in December 1981 of a non-aligned secretary-general, Javier Perez de Cuellar of Peru, despite professed U.S. and Soviet agreement on Kurt Waldheim as the "least unacceptable choice." The campaign, which depended on Chinese cooperation in vetoing the Waldheim candidacy, revealed both regional divisions in the NAM and momentum through successive subgroup and NAM endorsements. Foreign Minister Salim Salim of Tanzania was backed for the job in varying degrees by the OAU Summit in July 1981 and, during September, by the NAM ministerial meeting in New York and the Arab League in Tunis. Faced with vetoes by the United States on multiple ballots, Salim withdrew on December 10 to "give real possibilities for other candidates from the Third World to be considered." While the designated NAM candidate lost, the principle of a Third World secretary-general was conceded, and Perez de Cuellar won easily the next day. Although the election eventually divided Africans and Latin Americans, who, anticipating Salim's withdrawal, turned to candidates of their own, the non-aligned were united on the principle of a Third World secretary-general and, with Chinese help, prevailed. The exercise, according to the *New York Times*, again caused Washington "to appear as the obstacle to Third World aspirations."[60]

The secretary-general is the only Secretariat position filled by voting, although the G-77 at one point pushed to elect the director-general for development and international economic cooperation in order to ensure an incumbent from the developing world. While the United States, Soviet Union, and, to a lesser extent, France, the United Kingdom, and Canada have always exerted strong pressure for appointments to specific senior jobs, Third World states have focused instead on "desirable ranges" or quotas for their nationals. To increase the turnover of available jobs, they oppose all "inherited" positions, insist on mandatory retirement at age 60, and favor fixed terms over permanent appointments. In the economic area, they have pressed for decentralization to increase the authority of regional commissions, for which up to 75 percent of personnel are recruited from the region involved.

The formula for recruitment to the 3,350 higher or professional-level U.N. posts has undergone changes in response to building pressures for geographic distribution. In the early years, secretaries-general and Western delegations were opposed, on grounds of efficiency, to mathematical formulas or the automatic "right" of any member to jobs in the Secretariat. By 1957, Ceylon argued in the General Assembly for national quotas, but settled for a resolution calling for "appropriate" job preference for under-represented states. In 1962, the assembly approved a formula setting national quotas on the basis of financial contributions, regional population, and membership, with up to five jobs for each U.N. member.

Subsequent general assemblies have debated the relative importance of these factors, gradually scaling down the weight attached to contributions. The 1970 assembly repeated the call for preference to "qualified candidates of under-represented countries" or, as Norman Graham and Robert Jordan put it, for an international "affirmative action" program.[61] In 1976 and 1980, the allocation of jobs on the basis of membership alone was increased. The 1980 resolution provided, further, that 40 percent of vacancies during 1981–82 be given to unrepresented states and that "no posts shall be considered the exclusive preserve of any member state." It also called for consideration by the 1986 assembly of parity, in determining quotas, between membership and contribution factors, which many developed countries supported simply to postpone the issue for six years.

As a result, by January 1, 1983, U.N. professional positions were allocated on the basis of 57.2 percent by contribution to the regular budget, 35.6 percent by membership, and 7.2 percent by regional population. Although this represented a considerable reduction from the 100 percent weight once given to contributions, it continued to provide between 414 and 560 positions to the United States, largely on the basis of paying 25 percent of the budget. While the United States remained well within its ceiling, with 504 nationals on the professional staff as of mid-1982, many of the leading states within the NAM were in excess of their national quotas. As of June 30, 1982, these included Algeria, Ethiopia, Iraq, Sri Lanka, Egypt, Tanzania, Syria, Argentina, Bangladesh, Ghana, Nigeria, Sierra Leone, Tunisia, Uganda, and India, with the last at double its national quota. The smaller NAM members Gabon, Bahrain, Equatorial Guinea, São Tomé and Príncipe, Djibouti, Bhutan, Maldives, Guinea-Bissau, St. Lucia, Kuwait, Qatar, and Surinam remained without representation.

The effect of insistence on national quotas has been less to limit the role of Western nationals than to undercut the concept of an international career civil service. As the latter developed under the League of Nations, it was based on subordination of national loyalties to the larger organization and service of international peace. In practical terms, the idea rested on a civil servant corps committed to a long-term career and not subject to countries of origin for instructions or advancement. Secretary-General Perez de Cuellar advised his staff along these lines on January 12, 1982, that it is "wholly inadmissible that Secretariat staff should seek or receive instruction from governments or authorities outside the UN."

Yet the impact of heightened national consciousness and quotas among the staff erodes higher loyalties, and ultimately the impartiality on which the United Nations must depend for survival. The 1980 General Assembly's injunction, for example, to fill 40 percent of professional vacancies with given nationalities and to "increase the representation of developing countries in senior and policy-formulating posts" risks creation of "fast track" nationalities, thus corroding morale and belief in promotion by merit. The inevitable result is increasing recourse to national governments for redress and further politicization of the system. This process will be accelerated by retirement during the mid-1980s of most of the first generation of U.N. career officials.

Insistence on fixed terms rather than permanent appointments is particularly damaging, over the long run, to a career civil service. For the non-aligned, however, it offers access to more positions and training for government personnel. The Soviets and East Europeans have insisted on fixed terms as a means of controlling exposure of personnel to Western life. As of January 1, 1983, only one of 176 professional-level Soviet employees of the United Nations had a permanent appointment. In addition, all but the highest-ranking Soviet personnel are obliged to live with Russian diplomats in a controlled compound at Riverdale, New York, and are, for all purposes, indistinguishable from government apparatchiks. One-third of both Soviet U.N. employees and members of its diplomatic mission are, in any case, reliably estimated to work directly for the KGB. When the senior Soviet at the United Nations, Arkady Shevchenko, defected in 1978, Moscow acted to shorten from five to three years the terms of his successors, under secretaries-general Sytenko and Ustinov.

Non-aligned and Soviet pressure has resulted in an increase in fixed-term appointments from 20 percent in the early years to 40 percent by 1983. A 1981 U.N. inspection report, drafted by, inter alia Soviet Inspector Alexander S. Bryntsev, recommends specific measures to ensure that "in the future the majority of the staff subject to geographical distribution would have fixed-term appointments." Such a shift would further damage the concept of an impartial U.N. officer corps. Morale at Turtle Bay has already suffered from the "under-development syndrome" of geographic selection without, in every case, requisite qualifications. A predominance of fixed-term appointments, as well as overall staff frustration with U.N. effectiveness, would complete the process.

Control of Key Committees

In addition to the principal U.N. organs and seven main committees of the General Assembly, there are approximately 100 subsidiary bodies, committees, and commissions drawn from U.N. member states. These range from the Committee on Enhancing the Effectiveness of the Principle of Non-Use of Force in International Relations to the U.N. Conference for the Promotion of International Cooperation in the Peaceful Uses of Nuclear Energy (UNPICPUNE). Both the NAM and the G-77 have pressed hard to increase or "democratize" the membership of these bodies. While enlargement of subsidiary committees can be justified as mirroring the growth in U.N. membership to 157, it has made the work of smaller committees more cumbersome, causing many to subdivide into new working groups. Enlargement also inevitably strengthens the tendency within committees toward majority or bloc positions, and reduces the influence of both individual experts and states, including the great powers.

While membership of most subsidiary bodies remained constant during the first years of the United Nations, the 1960s and 1970s brought a proliferation of new organs and enlargement of existing ones, particularly in the decolonization, disarmament, and budgetary areas. The once unchallenged ACABQ, for example, was expanded in 1971 and 1977 to its present 16 members. The key Committee on Contributions, which considers assessment scales and arrearages, was enlarged in 1968, 1972, and 1976 to its present 18. Similarly, the Decolonization Committee grew in 1962 and again in 1979 to 25, and the Special Committee Against Apartheid in 1965 and 1970 to 18. Such shifts tend to alter the balance, giving control to the developing world majority. The committees on apartheid, Palestinian rights, Namibia, and international development strategy are, for example, routinely chaired by members of the non-aligned. The 45-member ad hoc Committee on the Indian Ocean has been chaired, from its inception, by Sri Lankans.

Non-aligned influence in certain areas is strengthened by the uneven distribution of Third World staff throughout the Secretariat. The latter tend to gravitate to areas of particular interest, such as the Trusteeship and Public Information departments. They also comprise much of the staff of committees dealing with southern Africa and the Middle East. The United States and Soviet Union, to be sure, are equally insistent on placing their nationals in specific jobs and, despite growing reactions against "inherited" posts, have each preserved an under secretary-generalship. To some extent, however, their mutual efforts, unlike those of the non-aligned, tend to offset each other. The resulting network of fiefdoms, described by Theodor Meron as "Balkanization of the Secretariat," is in this sense advantageous to the non-aligned.[62]

Non-aligned committee power has also been enhanced by Western tactical disarray. By an informal understanding, not incorporated in the U.N. Charter, permanent members of the Security Council, have traditionally had the prerogative to sit on any U.N. body or committee for which they choose to be candidates. Known as the Permanent Members' Convention, the practice was observed without exception until the late 1970s, guaranteeing participation of great powers, except China, which did not exercise the privilege, in all major areas of the United Nations. In return for this tacit acceptance of special responsibilities, the permanent members agreed not to seek office on committees, thereby allowing smaller states to become chairmen, vice-chairmen, and rapporteurs.

As committee membership, under non-aligned prodding, became increasingly based on geographic distribution, observance of the convention came to depend on forbearance of other Europeans in deferring to the permanent members. Given shifts in their relative power since World War II, the Germans and Nordics have grown increasingly restive with the claimed priority of France and the United Kingdom to European committee seats. Faced with limited seats and growing ambitions of their own, states like Germany, Finland, and Spain were, by the early 1980s, unwilling to forgo their own candidacies in favor of France and Britain. The result was a breakdown of the convention in which Western permanent members, including the United States, could no longer take committee memberships for granted. The convention had, in any case, long been viewed as alien and offensive by the non-aligned, who saw in WEOG divisions an opportunity to further "democratize" U.N. subsidiary organs.

Unraveling of the convention began in the mid-1970s with the exclusion of France from the Human Rights Commission. In 1980, Britain was ousted from the ACABQ after more than three decades of service and from the Committee on Contributions. In 1981, four permanent members' places were lost: the United States and United Kingdom on the International Civil Service Commission, the United States on the Statistical Commission, and the USSR on the Commission on Narcotic Drugs. The latter was unusual, however, in that Moscow, with only occasional mild jockeying from Yugoslavia or Romania, can count on deference from its satellites for East European committee seats. The convention's demise is, therefore, at much greater cost to the United States, France, and Britain.

By 1983, the United States was actively lobbying, like any other country, through demarches and diplomatic notes in New York, Washington, and foreign capitals to retain a voice in major U.N. committees. More seriously, its exclusion from certain bodies called into question the extent of Washington's future cooperation with them. While the United States regained a seat on the International Civil Service Commission, effective January 1, 1983, as the result of an understanding with Belgium, even a one-year absence from the commission was a matter of grave concern to policy-makers already questioning American support for the world organization. Nor was the outlook clear for continued U.S. tenure on other U.N. bodies. By early 1983, the United States, Spain, Australia, and France were competing for three seats on the Human Rights Commission, and the United States was one of 11 WEOG candidates for five seats on the Commission on Narcotic Drugs.

11
The UN Agenda

Within the United Nations, the non-aligned countries have imposed themselves as an irreplaceable factor in the work of the world organization and through it also in international relations.

Lazar Mojsov

The preceding chapters have examined non-aligned influence on specific, if nevertheless major, components of the United Nations. What, however, has been the cumulative impact, and how can it be measured in a political institution vulnerable to pressure from all sides, Third World and superpowers alike? As the majority at the United Nations has been transformed since 1945 from developed Western states to the Third World, enlargement of the institution's agenda has been inevitable, to reflect new concerns of a different majority. As Ruth Russell observed in 1970, the decade of the 1960s marked a shift in U.N. priorities to economic development, decolonization, and racial equality.[63] While desirable and, in a broad sense, each linked to world peace and security, these goals were a departure from more traditional approaches to international order shaped by diplomatic failure in two wars and the League of Nations. Moreover, they were of secondary concern to the developed countries most involved in the outcome at San Francisco.

The new realities of non-aligned voting strength and revised U.N. priorities obliged older members to undergo, during the 1970s, a process of adjustment or, in Jacobsen's phrase, "resocialization."[64] Western members were forced to relearn rules of the club, scaling back operating habits and expectations based on transitory postwar power. Yet compromise was compensated by the ongoing "socialization" of Third World states, many outside democratic traditions, adjusting for the first time to U.N. parliamentary practice. The rationale for Western acquiescence thus remained that the United Nations still represented a moderating influence, an escape valve for tensions, an alternative to war.

The new priorities, accelerated by the asymmetry between Third World and Western members, tended, however, to exclude the latter.

Economic development rested, in the majority view, on trade concessions and transfer of resources and technology from rich to poor. Western states, facing recession in the early 1980s, reacted to this one-way street by offering far less than demanded by an increasingly clamorous majority. Emphasis on decolonization also separated the United States and the rest of the West from the non-aligned. NATO membership and a Eurocentric policy well into the 1970s tended to identify Washington with the colonial powers, despite its origin as a colony, progress toward civil rights, and role in pressing the British, French, and Dutch to decolonize. Lack of similar U.S. pressure for change in Portuguese colonial policies during the late 1960s and early 1970s was particularly alienating to Africans who did not share U.S. views on the overriding importance of the Azores bases in geopolitical terms.

The changes in New York, however, were gradual, as U.N. parliamentary routine translated consensus of the growing majority into a foundation of resolutions affecting the overall U.N. agenda and approaches to specific problems. Awareness in Washington of this subtle transformation was limited for most of the period by East–West perceptions and was experienced primarily in mounting frustration with U.N. sluggishness. When the trend became unmistakable, the public appeared surprised that most of the world considered the United States out of step, and reaction in Washington was embattled. Former Ambassador Moynihan wrote in 1978:

> The real problem is very different, and vastly ominous. It is that the United Nations has become a locus of a general assault by the majority of the nations in the world on the principles of liberal democracy which are now found only in a minority of nations, and for that matter a dwindling minority.[65]

Parallel Agendas

What had occurred, however, was less an assault on liberal democracy than a progressive standardization of NAM and U.N. agendas, using parlimentary democracy to carry it out. To be sure, the non-aligned closely monitor the General Assembly agenda, incorporating many of its items in their own meetings in order to develop cohesive positions for use in New York. Yet the two agendas are mutually reinforcing, and most items first identified at NAM conferences find their way onto the U.N. agenda and are then routinely carried over year after year. In relation to the U.N. system as a whole, the movement functions much like its component parts in New York, which meet as informal or hidden power centers in advance of the Security Council or General Assembly.

NAM summit, ministerial and Coordinating Bureau conferences regularly meet around the world to take decisions that are then upheld by the majority at the United Nations. The bureau, for example, met during April 1982 in Kuwait and determined to call for a resumed ESS on Palestine, which was convoked the same month in New York, affecting all 157 U.N. members. The resulting General Assembly resolution was squarely based on the "program of action" developed at Kuwait. Outsiders to the movement are excluded from this initial process, and even those with "official observer" status in the movement are barred from working sessions where policy is formulated. By the time a General Assembly begins, substantive positions of the non-aligned have been reached, and politics and power within the U.N. context become the paramount considerations.

By 1983 the degree of NAM influence over the U.N. agenda and procedures was apparent in the non-aligned initiative to transform the Thirty-Eighth General Assembly into a special meeting of heads of state to address "problems facing the world," particularly development and disarmament. First proposed at the New Delhi Summit, the idea of using the General Assembly as a global summit meeting to increase pressure on the superpowers was subsequently put forward by the new NAM Chairman. In letters of March 28, 1983, Mrs. Gandhi urged U.N. members to attend the 1983 UNGA at the summit level as a "collective manifestation of political will." While initial response from the major powers was cautious, a large number of non-aligned leaders were expected to attend. The proposal, irrespective of its merits, represented a clear-cut initiative by the non-aligned to define U.N. priorities at closed meetings outside New York and then determine how, when, and at what level they should be taken up by the larger body. The proposal was also intended to renew under India's chairmanship the movement's role as mediator between East and West by promoting a first meeting between President Reagan and Chairman Andropov under NAM auspices.

The process of reaching non-aligned consensus also telescopes momentum back to smaller and smaller groups or even individual countries or liberation movements. The regional groups within the movement endorse positions that the NAM accepts and then takes to New York. Within the former, a few activists are likely to hold sway over the less involved majority. Thus, within the Arab League, for example, PLO or Syrian radicals may well predominate, overcoming decreasing resistance from moderates at each stage of the process. Conference declarations also allow individual NAM members to stake out collective positions that can later be cited to reinforce or justify national policies.

Argentina perceived this in pressing for non-aligned endorsement, during the August 1975 ministerial meeting at Lima, of its claims in a then obscure dispute over the Falkland (Malvinas) Islands. In the absence of Argentine inhabitants on the islands, the Lima Declaration made an express exception to non-aligned dogma on "self-determination of peoples" and "strongly supported" the "just claims of the Argentine Republic." Once on the books, the position was reaffirmed at subsequent meetings and, following Argentina's invasion of the islands on April 2, 1982, Buenos Aires was able to cite chapter and verse to stiffen non-aligned opposition to the "illegal situation" caused by Britain. From a British point of view, the Lima Declaration irrevocably prejudiced the potential vote of two-thirds of the U.N. membership and precluded use of the General Assembly in a settlement of the problem.

The losers in this process are clearly those outside the transmission belt of resolutions from regional groups to the non-aligned plenary and on to the General Assembly. In the words of one senior Secretariat official, it is "simply too late" to substantially influence the majority of non-aligned positions once they have reached the final stage in New York. Once there, non-aligned technicians at the staff level are active on the various NAM contact groups for key issues, and on working and drafting units within U.N. committees to incorporate positions reached earlier by their ministers or heads of state.

Foreign ministers of the NAM have met in New York at the beginning of the General Assembly every year since 1969. Their purpose is to coordinate the translation of non-aligned positions into U.N. doctrine. For example, such a meeting during September 1979 "reaffirmed the urgent and vital need to translate into action and decisions, the resolutions and Program of Action" just adopted at Havana. A non-aligned communiqué then singled out 20 "priority" items on the General Assembly agenda to be "approached consistently with the principles indicated at non-aligned summit conferences and other meetings."

The great majority of substantive items before the United Nations have been addressed in some form in prior non-aligned declarations or resolutions if they have not, in fact, been duplicated on the formal NAM agenda. The result is a standardized agenda for international conferences that, while including most world problems and conflict situations, is by no means comprehensive or necessarily balanced. Minimized in its formulation are situations, whether between Iran and Iraq, Uganda and Tanzania, or Libya and Chad, that find the non-aligned in disarray. Yet the agenda, despite defects, structures and politicizes the approach to international affairs of the United Nations and many of its programs and autonomous groups, from the Decade for Women to UNESCO.

Underlying U.N. consideration of a given item are a number of basic resolutions that structure and define the parameters of particular issues. Of more than 5,000 resolutions passed over the years by the General Assembly, most are soon forgotten, but a small number are constantly cited and reaffirmed in subsequent decisions. These foundation documents or philosophical underpinnings have frequently evolved from the NAM or have been adopted and reinforced by it. The trend began at Bandung, when principles adopted there and derived from the Panchsheel were written into a U.N. resolution of December 1957 on "peaceful and neighborly relations between states."

More important, the Third World rallied in 1960 around seminal Resolution 1514, adopting the Declaration on the Granting of Independence to Colonial Countries and Peoples and calling for an "end to colonialism in all its manifestations." This document, over the years, has served as a touchstone for the NAM, and a committee, established the following year to implement it, has been dominated by members of the movement and has spearheaded their efforts in the decolonization field.

In the economic area, the Declaration and Program of Action for the New International Economic Order, adopted during the Sixth Special Session in 1974, endorsed as U.N. doctrine a non-aligned package worked out at Algiers. The Charter of Economic Rights and Duties of States, adopted over U.S. objections later in the year, sought to legitimize nationalization to redress the imbalance of developing countries, which had 70 percent of the world's population and 30 percent of its income.

Running through these and other foundation documents of the United Nations, which have shaped subsequent resolutions in their respective areas, is a common thread of anti-colonialism central to the movement's identity and survival. A measure of insensitivity to free enterprise and liberal democracy, as understood in the West, is also apparent in a significant number of these documents. Problems as diverse as development, disarmament, the Middle East, and Namibia are framed as results of colonial exploitation. Insistence on this dimension both gives the Third World majority a moral highground in dealing with former colonial powers, among whom the United States is grouped, and tends to polarize U.N. debate.

From a non-aligned perspective, the anti-colonial focus is both a deeply felt product of experience and a vital rallying point and source of strength within the movement and the United Nations. It explains the continued predominance in both bodies of anti-colonial rhetoric and resolutions in 1983, when the decolonization process is virtually complete. Excepting Namibia, remaining colonies are limited to a handful of island dependencies, mostly in the Pacific and the Caribbean. The U.N. Decolonization Committee lists 17 still under colonial administration, with a combined population of 787,095. The smallest of these populations, such as Pitcairn with 60 people and the Cocos (Keeling) Islands with 435, are considerably outnumbered by the bureaucracy of U.N. delegations, interpreters, and staff who monitor their progress.

The principle of self-determination, running through all these documents but mentioned only twice in the U.N. Charter among the general "purposes" and goals of the organization, has taken on a more restrictive and exclusively anti-colonial meaning through interpretation by the non-aligned. Originally framed as a universal process toward self-government, with independence as only one of several possible outcomes based on "the freely expressed wishes of the peoples concerned," the principle is today seldom invoked outside the context of decolonization. In the process the "right" to self-determination is limited to colonial peoples and not ascribed to those living within existing states, regardless of their expressed wishes.

Interpreted in this manner and reiterated in every declaration of the non-aligned, self-determination becomes not a universal principle, but a weapon for use against the West. Commitment to independence as the only outcome of self-determination explains regular invitations to the *independentista* parties of Puerto Rico to attend NAM meetings, despite their appeal to only 6 percent of the island's electorate. It also explains non-aligned support for national liberation movements as the sole legitimate representatives of their people, often regardless of their limited local followings.

Given U.N.achievement in decolonization, it was inevitable that anti-colonial feeling would find expression in other areas. The more radical of the non-aligned have campaigned since the Belgrade Summit to bring the Commonwealth of Puerto Rico into the U.N. decolonization machinery, but have shown no comparable enthusiasm to take on Soviet occupation of the Baltic Republics and other territories. South Africa's system of apartheid, a direct affront to the movement's African majority, is also an obvious target. That it is equally an affront to all that the United States claims to stand for has not yet been appreciated by the non-aligned. Former General Assembly President Lazar Mojsov of

Yugoslavia writes that the fight against racial discrimination became "an extension of the struggle to end the system of colonialism."[66] Common cause between African and Arab countries extended the anti-colonial focus to Palestine, cementing this linkage by a decade of non-aligned and U.N. resolutions equating Zionism and racism, a formulation that was first developed at the Algiers Summit and subsequent NACB meetings.

Economic and development themes, which occupy the lion's share of U.N. system-wide resources, have equally drawn strength from shared anti-colonialism. The standard non-aligned explanation for problems of the developing countries and the imbalance between North and South has been the legacy of colonialism. Present economic structures are blamed on "neocolonialism," and the United States, as the largest economy, is particularly singled out as "imperialist." Research centers have been established in both the NAM and the United Nations to monitor transnational corporations, viewed by many in the Third World as agents in a process of recolonization. The developed or status quo countries have, in fact, clearly failed to remedy inequalities of the present structure, and multi-national corporations have often transgressed against national sovereignty of both home and host countries. Yet a priori definition of development as a colonial issue obscures other underlying causes of economic frailty, some, like oil-pricing, originating in the Third World itself. Concentration on perceived Western "guilt" for the world economy also has largely absolved the Soviet Union of responsibility to assist.

Even U.S.–Soviet disarmament takes on colonial overtones from a non-aligned perspective. Nuclear dominance by the superpowers is viewed by many within the NAM as a monopoly to exclude the Third World from power. While committed to reducing U.S. and Soviet power, they also fear bilateral arms negotiations as a potentially hostile condominium. The non-aligned further link disarmament with development, on the assumption that arms reduction would release major sources of capital for economic assistance to the Third World. Peripheral non-aligned involvement in a forum without power to compel serious negotiations has probably tempted superpowers to rhetoric rather than negotiation.

Starting at Belgrade in 1961, the non-aligned called for a world disarmament conference in order to participate in the process. The Colombo Summit refined the demand to a General Assembly Special Session on Disarmament (SSOD), and two were held at non-aligned insistence in 1978 and 1982. As a result, U.N. committees with non-aligned majorities have been reorganized in New York and Geneva. General positions on disarmament now often move from a NAM summit through a 21-member working committee, including 16 NAM members, to the 40-member Committee on Disarmament in Geneva, back to the First Committee in New York, and finally to resolutions of the General Assembly.

Ideally, the non-aligned would favor multi-lateral disarmament negotiations under the United Nations or imposition of non-aligned deadlines for such objectives as a test ban and reduction of strategic arms. Yet the process has probably distracted attention from Strategic Arms Reduction Talks (START), Mutual Balanced Force Reductions (MBFR), Intermediate Nuclear Forces (INF), and other bilateral negotiations that, while without major results to date, represent the more practical approach. The second SSOD in 1982, despite worldwide attention, broke no new ground, with results described by General Assembly President Kittani as "too few and too insubstantial." The non-aligned were unable to agree on a final statement, with considerable acrimony over whether to exempt conventional weapons, in growing demand throughout the Third World, from proposed arms reductions.

Beyond New York

The cumulative impact of the non-aligned on the U.N. agenda has been to concentrate the world organization's attention and resources on issues of priority to the movement. While this leverage is always greatest in the politicized environment of U.N. Headquarters in New York, non-aligned summits, starting with Lusaka in 1970, have also called for implementation of NAM decisions within the "specialized agencies and all international bodies." The spillover of non-aligned influence to international agencies in Geneva, Vienna, Rome, and elsewhere has, however, been limited by the technical nature of some of these bodies. Most, like the Food and Agriculture Organization (FAO), the World Health Organization (WHO), the U.N. Human Rights Commission (UNHRC), the International Telecommunications Union (ITU), and the World Meteorological Organization (WMO), are seen as vehicles for translating into the Third World context resources and technology for agriculture, health, refugee assistance, and communications . They can thus be of direct benefit to developing countries, most of which perceive that confrontation with Western donors over political issues could jeopardize continued contributions. Such cost-benefit analysis, reinforced by U.S. and other Western diplomacy, has over the years made technically oriented agencies generally more resistant to politicization. Where institutional benefits to the Third World are less clear-cut, however, confrontation over extraneous political issues has been intense and frequent.

Confrontation between Western members and the non-aligned bloc, as in New York, is usually over both substance and institutional control. At the substantive level, core issues from the non-aligned agenda have increasingly framed debate within the specialized agencies. In more politicized bodies, plenary speeches are today virtually indistinguishable from those in the General Assembly. In others, political issues of southern Africa and the Middle East are debated in terms of health, agriculture, and labor. At a deeper level is the same struggle between donors and the majority for control of the institutions. The United States, for example, has historically taken the minimalist approach that technical agencies should be confined to standard-setting and, where necessary, international regulation, with only a secondary role in technical assistance. The non-aligned, by contrast, favor a major role for the specialized agencies in development. The conflict again is an irreconcilable one of votes against money.

Outside New York, the distinction between the NAM and the G-77 becomes less clear-cut, with little differentiation in positions on technical issues within the specialized agencies. Its exclusively economic focus and status as an official negotiating body make the G-77 the more logical Third World caucus in most of these forums. Its separate presidencies are also better organized to deal at the expert level with the FAO in Rome, UNIDO in Vienna, UNCTAD in Geneva, and UNDP and North–South negotiations in New York. Yet, within the G-77, the non-aligned have often prevailed, even in the more technical agencies, in injecting NAM positions and, to a certain extent, political issues. For example, in the years following the Algiers Summit, South Africa was systematically excluded by the non-aligned majority from major U.N. agencies including the FAO, ILO, and WHO.

The PLO gained observer status during the same period at plenary meetings of the major agencies. By the late 1970s, political issues, while couched in terms of the various agencies, routinely appeared on otherwise technical agendas. Thus, pro-forma debate occurs at each WHO assembly on health conditions in Arab territories occupied by Israel, and labor conditions in these areas are regularly considered in the ILO. Third World delegates to the Law of the Sea Conference argued against "present-day colonialism of the seas."

On a more technical level, during the World Administrative Radio Conference (WARC) in 1979, the non-aligned pursued general goals stated in the Havana Summit Declaration and, for the first time, caucused at the initiative of India, Iraq, and Algeria to campaign for a non-aligned chairman. Within the WHO, a NAM caucus has met since 1977 before each annual assembly, and members of its Coordinator Country Group on Health, including Cuba and Yugoslavia, have been active on substantive issues. During the May 1982 WHO Assembly, an Arab effort spearheaded by Cuba to suspend Israel's voting rights was dropped only in the face of a threatened walkout by the United States. Non-aligned health ministers caucused, however, on May 6 to issue a separate statement on the Falklands attacking the "stubborn and insensate position of the UK."

Within the FAO, Arab radicals overcame African and Latin American resistance to enforce Egypt's probationary status following Camp David by forcing the "temporary" closure of FAO regional offices in Cairo during the FAO biennial conferences of 1979 and 1981. In the ILO, non-aligned pressure gained observer status for the PLO in 1975 and was behind condemnations of Israel that contributed in large part to U.S. withdrawal from the organization during 1977–81. The NAM also caucused separately on southern African issues, including a declaration on apartheid, during the 1981 ILO Conference.

In recent years, the question of Israeli membership has become the most disruptive political issue within several of the specialized agencies. The PLO, Syria, and other radical Arab delegations have attempted for many years, in the General Assembly, to lay the groundwork for expulsion, with resolutions asserting that Israel "is not a peaceloving member state." While they have been unsuccessful to date, and failed decisively on a procedural vote of 74–9 during the 1982 General Assembly, Israel has come under greater pressure in the specialized agencies.

On September 24, 1982, a non-aligned majority within the International Atomic Energy Agency (IAEA) voted to withdraw Israel's credentials, implementing a decision taken at the June meeting of the NACB in Havana. The campaign was extended to the ITU during the October 1982 plenary meeting in Nairobi, where Israel's expulsion was narrowly averted by a vote of 61–57. Suspension of American participation and funding for the IAEA and certainty of similar action against the ITU if Israel were expelled undoubtedly affected the outcome, as did maximum diplomatic leverage including personal calls to many leaders by the U.S. secretary of state. Ayatollah Khomeini's offer to make good the loss of U.S. funding ultimately proved less than convincing to some of the non-aligned in light of Iran's arrearages to the ITU.

Such digressions into the political sphere, while well publicized, have been for the most part peripheral to the technical work of these agencies. Some, like the International Civil Aviation Organization (ICAO) in Montreal, have been even more impervious to the intrusion of diplomats and political items from New York. By contrast, non-aligned influence has been greatest in international conferences and bodies with a more abstract mandate, where the benefits or resource transfers to developing countries are less tangible. In such forums, there has been little incentive among moderate states to resist political inroads by the non-aligned. Within the U.N. Environmental Program (UNEP), for example, developing states have shown uneven interest in ecological preservation, and the May 1982 Nairobi Conference became in part a new forum to press demands for the NIEO, disarmament, and increased Western economic aid.

The July 1980 U.N. Conference on the Decade for Women at Copenhagen was a textbook case of this dynamic. Concern with the status of women, while professed by all, has been strongest in the West. In fact, opposition to women's rights in the Muslim world probably contributed to politicization as a way to divert attention from women's issues to Palestine. The non-aligned majority at Copenhagen had little of a tangible nature to gain from the Decade for Women. Individual delegates were committed to women's rights, but tended to be from private life and unfamiliar with political trade-offs of the United Nations and NAM. They were thus vulnerable to an organized lobby of non-aligned activists that forced through its own political agenda, unrelated to women's issues.

Non-aligned delegations met well in advance at Baghdad during May 1979, and their positions were further elaborated in New York by a NAM majority on the preparatory committee for Copenhagen. In particular, the Baghdad meeting insisted on involvement of women in liberation movements and special attention to Palestinian and black South African women. The last two cases were singled out at a time when 17 million Iranian women were being returned to medieval segregation and several hundred million women in other non-aligned countries remained circumscribed by tribal or religious custom.

At Copenhagen, a small group of NAM radicals, comprising Syria, Cuba, Algeria, India, and the PLO, introduced amendments on southern Africa and the Middle East, including the now standard equation of Zionism and racism. The PLO was present in every caucus room, and hijacker and terrorist Leila Khalid was invited, at NAM insistence, to address the overall gathering. The conference was thus politicized from the outset, and ended July 31 without consensus on a program for the second half of the decade. African efforts to restrain more radical NAM colleagues were brushed aside as politics prevailed over women's issues. The "important role" of the non-aligned at Copenhagen was nevertheless praised by heads of state at the subsequent New Delhi Summit, and by early 1983 preparations were already underway for a meeting of the NAM before the next women's conference at Nairobi in 1985.

UNESCO, with its general mandate of "collaboration among nations through education, science and culture," has also been susceptible to pressures from the non-aligned, who form a bloc of 23 on its 45-member Executive Board (due for expansion to 51 in 1983). The concept of a New World Information Order (NWIO), shaped by Muhammad Masmoudi of Tunisia in the early 1970s, has been endorsed and enlarged at all subsequent meetings of the NAM. The movement's positions have in turn been cited in the preambular sections of every UNESCO resolution on the NWIO. Within UNESCO, NAM members including Yugoslavia, India, Iraq, Tunisia, and Cuba have joined observers such as Mexico and Venezuela to lobby for governmental control of the press, including licensing of journalists and other restrictions, unacceptable to the United States, on freedom of the media.

The organization has also been vulnerable to Third World political pressure, and the United States and ten other Western states withdrew from a 1975 UNESCO meeting that equated Zionism and racism in the guidelines for mass media. Western opposition and the weakness of an information order excluding Western media have so far prevented adoption of an overall action program, but in 1976 the movement established a separate Non-Aligned News Agencies Pool to advance NWIO objectives and eventually serve as a single, intergovernmental news service throughout the Third World. The seventh meeting of the pool, at Pyongyang, North Korea, during May 1982, reported that 86 NAM agencies had joined but only about 50 were participating in news-sharing arrangements coordinated by Tanjug, the official Yugoslav service. Annual resolutions of the General Assembly, initiated by 41 NAM states on the 67-member Committee on Information, call for U.N. and international support for the pool.

Confrontation within UNESCO over the NWIO poses the same basic dilemma of sovereign versus real power in international decision-making. The NWIO or the Law of the Sea (LOS) Treaty are equally subject to question if consensus does not encompass states with the most developed news media or the technology and capital for seabed mining. Demands for an information order, complemented by Soviet initiatives on government responsibility for the media, will nevertheless persist, and have become a NAM "article of faith." Furthermore, codification of Third World principles into "international orders" like the NIEO, the NWIO, and the New Scientific and Technological Order (NSTO) received new impetus at an August 1982 UNESCO conference in Mexico City, when NAM delegates called for the New World Cultural Order (NWCO).

The U.N. Human Rights Commission (UNHRC) in Geneva has, over the years, probably been even more politicized than UNESCO. The non-aligned have until recently tended to view the UNHRC process as one of damage limitation, since conditions in some Third World countries have often made them prone to infringe on human rights. With 21 of 43 seats on the commission as of 1983, the NAM offered protection from criticism on human rights grounds. UNHCR investigations, like similar debates in the General Assembly, often focus, as a result, on Latin America, where NAM influence and membership are least, and tend to reserve criticism for states outside the movement like El Salvador, Guatemala, and Chile.

For this reason, maltreatment of its Indian population by Nicaragua or of political prisoners by Cuba has never reached the UNHRC agenda. The tendency to single out a few Latin American states for regular condemnation has eroded the commission's reputation and led to charges of a double standard. Nor have non-aligned members of the UNHRC been willing to speak out on obvious human rights violations in Poland. A Western-backed resolution of March 8, 1983, was supported only by Colombia, Gambia, Senegal, and Togo. It was strongly opposed by India, Cuba, Libya, Nicaragua, Yugoslavia, Mozambique, Tanzania, and Ghana, which were simultaneously championing, at the New Delhi Summit, harsh criticism of the human rights situations in Israel and South Africa.

Beyond transferral of human rights criticism to non-member states, the commission has served the NAM as another forum for attacks on Israel and South Africa. During the 39th annual UNHRC meetings at Geneva in February–March 1983, discussion focused almost exclusively on Israel, "colonial and racist regimes in Southern Africa," and Chile. Repetitious resolutions on human rights in "Israeli-occupied Middle East territories" and in South Africa have been adopted year after year, and non-aligned commission members caucus regularly on such issues during the annual UNHRC six-week meeting. A further NAM initiative has been to broaden the definition of human rights well beyond traditional Western concepts of civil and political rights to include economic, social, and cultural rights as well as development, defined in the New Delhi Summit Declaration as "a human right" and the "prerogative of nations as of individuals comprising them." Introduced in a modest form by Senegal in 1979, the "right to development" was radicalized as a vehicle to advance the NIEO, incorporated in subsequent NAM declarations, and in 1982 translated into a resolution of the General Assembly sponsored by Cuba and India.

The spillover of non-aligned political issues to agencies and bodies outside New York has thus been uneven, with technical benefits to the developing world as a restraint, in some cases, to inroads from New York. Western discipline in keeping these agencies within their mandates remains important, and the temptation to score political points in these forums on issues like Afghanistan and Poland risks opening the door to a wider and unmanageable agenda. Strong leadership by the heads of several agencies, as well as the infrequency of plenary meetings in bodies like the ILO and WMO, have somewhat limited their vulnerability to an outside agenda. The key restraining element thus far has, nevertheless, been power of the developed countries over the budget, in the form of contributions to technical activities of direct benefit to the Third World. Where this relationship does not exist, political issues tend to predominate. The next World Women's Conference, planned for Nairobi in 1985, may well be no less contentious, although the West has now had warning enough to organize a strategy of its own.

While the power of the purse has been a restraining factor in some agencies, that discipline, too, is eroding as voluntary contributions decline in a period of recession, and plenary debate in most agencies increasingly parallels that in the General Assembly. Nor are Western donors, themselves beneficiaries of the technical agencies, usually in a position to make good on threats to withhold support. In an agency like ICAO, for example, an annual contribution of about $5 million preserves U.S. influence in setting international airfield safety specifications. The yearly return on this investment to U.S. avionics suppliers is estimated at about $1 billion. The confrontation between the West and the non-aligned within the specialized agencies, slower to develop than in the United Nations itself, thus mirrors the larger challenge to the international structure and dominant interests emerging from World War II. The United States has argued over the years for a narrow technical mandate for the specialized agencies that maximizes the leverage of donors. The Third World, by contrast, is committed to expanding the agencies to encompass a non-aligned political agenda and massive resource transfers consistent with the NIEO.

The Cumulative Impact

Within the United Nations itself the restraining influence of major contributors has been largely lost and, for most members of both institutions, NAM and U.N. objectives are seen as identical. Yugoslav Ambassador Miljan Komatina writes with conviction that "for the UN, the activities of the non-aligned countries contribute a source of dynamism, direction, democratization, efficiency, reaffirmation and strengthening of its role in the world." He concludes that the "non-aligned countries have become the basic influential component of the democratization of the UN."[67] Most observers would agree that, by sheer numbers and the voting consistency they have increasingly demonstrated, the non-aligned are now the "basic influential component."

Yet the judgment that their new power contributes to efficiency and strengthening of the world institution is not widely shared outside the movement. The process of consolidating non-aligned influence and synchronizing the NAM and U.N. agendas has admittedly been played out within a parliamentary framework. States, many of which lack such traditions, have mastered rules of procedure to gain control. Yet the process of stretching and bending rules to change the institution, critics would argue, has resulted in a herniated structure unable to function as intended. Defenders of the NAM point out, however, that the line between creative procedural development and abuse is a fine one, and that, during an earlier period, U.S. innovations such as "uniting for peace" and bloc voting trod a similar tightrope.

In case after case since the early 1970s, the non-aligned have won on points of NAM principle by using a majority to reinterpret or alter established U.N. practice. Redefinition of the ESS from a crisis management device to a broad mandate for intervention by the General Assembly is a case in point. On specific issues, the majority has not hesitated either to disregard clear requirements of the U.N. Charter or to devise new formulas without formal amendment to it. In December 1978, a non-aligned majority voted down by 38–70 a U.S. resolution to identify as an "important question," requiring a two-thirds majority for passage, an Iraqi motion calling for a military and nuclear embargo against Israel. Yet Article 18.2 of the charter clearly designates an issue involving "international peace and security" as an "important question." The non-aligned thus achieved victory at the cost of trivializing the issue. The protection against temporary passions of the majority, afforded by the "important question" clause, has increasingly been overriden by the non-aligned, who view the procedure as anti-majoritarian and elitist.

Similarly, since December 1975, the PLO has been invited to address the Security Council under a special formula devised by the non-aligned that provides "the same rights of participation as those conferred on member states that are invited to participate pursuant to Rule 39." The latter rule applies to U.N. members only, and to gain legitimacy for the PLO, the non-aligned rejected the only other applicable provision for members of the Secretariat or "other persons" with relevant information (Rule 37). The new formula, outside the charter, has been adopted by procedural vote over solitary U.S. objections during all subsequent sessions on the Middle East.

Cuba's efforts, endorsed by NAM declarations, to inject Puerto Rico into the United Nations is another case of circumventing U.N. practice. Removed by a General Assembly resolution of 1953 from the list of "non-self-governing territories" for which the United Nations is responsible, Puerto Rico has since been the target of a long-term Cuban and NAM "decolonization" campaign, clear interference in U.S. internal affairs. Using a majority in the Decolonization Committee, which has no mandate for Puerto Rico, Cuba attempted in 1981–82 to shoehorn the island onto the General Assembly agenda and, despite resounding defeat by the assembly in 1982, will continue to agitate on this issue.

Arbitrary use of U.N. procedures by the non-aligned is further evident in the annual exclusion of South Africa from the General Assembly. In 1974, non-aligned members of the Credentials Committee, led by Senegal and Tanzania, voted not to accept the delegation's credentials and were upheld by a plenary vote of 98–23. This exclusion, ritualized in subsequent years, perverts the clear-cut mandate of the Credentials Committee merely to verify that individuals representing member states are bona fide representatives authorized by their government to do so. Regardless of shared distaste for apartheid, the committee is not mandated to make political judgments about the government of South Africa or any other U.N. member. A procedure, subject to veto by the permanent members, exists for depriving states of U.N. membership, but the non-aligned ignored the process, thus violating the charter to exclude South Africa from a General Assembly in which it had no influence anyway.

Such use, or misuse, of existing procedures, combined with lack of clarity in many resolutions passed by the majority, often undercuts the credibility and functioning of the U.N. Secretariat. The Secretariat is, for example, charged with putting into effect a plan for independence and impartial elections in Namibia; yet a General Assembly resolution of December 12, 1973, sponsored by the non-aligned, endorsed

SWAPO as the "authentic representative of the Namibian people." Later resolutions call it the "sole and authentic" representative, although SWAPO, while the largest, is only one of several potential parties to an election. The designation has given Pretoria both grounds to question U.N. impartiality and a pretext to further delay implementation of any plan for Namibia. The G-6 compounded the problem by procedural votes in the Security Council during April 1981 that denied the Democratic Turnahalle Alliance (DTA), another Namibian party, the right to speak while seating SWAPO.

A more subtle effect of non-aligned influence has been widespread acceptance within the United Nations of the consensus mechanism. In listing major non-aligned achievements in the United Nations, Komatina writes that "non-aligned countries particularly contributed to the democratization of the system of consensus."[68] While adoption of resolutions by consensus is a standard procedure of the General Assembly, generally designed to save time when there is near unanimity of opinion, its use has increased significantly in recent years, and other versions of consensus, closer to NAM practice, have appeared within the United Nations. Specifically, the concept of consensus as an alternative to a roll-call vote has been replaced in many committees of the United Nations with the non-aligned formula of decision by consensus only, without recourse to voting. Following the Algiers Summit in 1973 and establishment or reorganization of U.N. committees under non-aligned pressure during the mid-1970s, adoption of texts by consensus only became the modus operandi in key committees dominated by Third World delegations. The practice was not opposed by the United States or other Western states, which initially saw in it a means to avoid the isolation of being outvoted by the non-aligned majority on every issue.

Consensus, however, is a loose concept and, even in the general definition of former U.N. Legal Counsel Erik Suy as "the adoption of a text without a vote and by no objection," is subject to varying interpretation.[69] The 1979 Havana Declaration, for example, admits that "consensus has a certain indefinable quality hard to express in words although we all know instinctively what it means." It is not surprising, therefore, that the practice of consensus is not uniform from one committee to the next. Some, like that on outer space, do not in fact reach consensus without the full agreement of all members. Others, like the Committee on Decolonization, routinely refer to the General Assembly consensus resolutions passed over the objections of a small Western minority. As in the movement, it was probably inevitable that some committee chairmen would disregard objections from individual governments in order to force through a false or pseudo consensus by abusing powers of the chair.

Widespread use of consensus at the United Nations at worst forces acquiescence without a vote in positions of the majority, which are then presented as agreed by all through use of the term "consensus." The practical result is to further downgrade the force and even the legal value of U.N. decisions. An arbitral tribunal appointed by the International Court of Justice found in a dispute of January 19, 1977, between Libya and Texaco Overseas Petroleum that U.N. resolutions have varying legal value, "depending on the type of resolution and conditions attached to its adoption and its provisions."[70] A consensus supported only by non-industrialized states, such as that cited by Libya to confer rights to nationalize natural resources, clearly was not binding, in the arbitrator's view.

The result of non-aligned influence on the U.N. agenda and procedures has, in these instances, probably been to impair rather than strengthen the institution. Yet responsibility for the overall state of the United Nations and the power vacuum into which the non-aligned have expanded also lies with the major powers. The U.N. structure rests on a tenuous balance between the Security Council and the General Assembly, with the council as a counterweight or ballast to the less predictable tendencies of a majority in the General Assembly.

The relationship, however, is premised on the possibility of agreement among the permanent members and their willingness, when necessary, to vote together on enforcement measures, under Chapter VII of the charter, to maintain international peace and security. With the ineffective exceptions of an arms embargo against South Africa and a general embargo against Rhodesia, superpower disagreement has blocked mandatory U.N. action in every instance. As a practical matter, certainty in advance that one of the great powers will veto rules out U.N. enforcement as an option in most crises. In the words of Secretary-General Perez de Cuellar's September 7, 1982, report on the United Nations, the system of collective security envisaged by the charter presupposes "at the minimum, a working relationship among the permanent members."

Paralysis of the Security Council on matters of enforcement at the core of the U.N. system has prompted the majority in the General Assembly to assume additional responsibility by any procedural means at hand. The process has been geared to advancement of a non-aligned agenda on specific issues rather than a structural concept of what the United Nations should be. The result, therefore, has been to weaken a system already flawed by superpower division, enlarging the area of overlapping responsibility, and confusion among its major organs. Within the many agencies and subsidiary bodies of the assembly, set up to meet development needs, there are equally blurred lines of authority and increasing acrimony among rival bodies. Blame for this state of affairs cannot be clearly assigned between a cohesive, non-aligned lobby and the divided superpowers. Increased U.S. use of the veto, not only in cases involving Chapter VII of the charter but in other instances as well, combined with long-standing Soviet practice, has probably contributed to the process of unraveling. The absence of restraint, in short, has been relatively widespread.

The identification of the United Nations primarily with interests of the Third World and the alignment of its agenda with that of the NAM raises important issues of its credibility among states not party to the movement. Even in technical fields, there have been allegations that analyses and data are often altered or suppressed to avoid conflict with Third World positions—for example, on LDC growth rates and the inflationary impact of oil prices. Harvard economist Hendrik Houthaker stated, for example, "I don't pay much attention to UN research today because I know much of it is propaganda."[71] Whether or not such sweeping statements are wholly valid, they contribute to decreased respect, support, and vigor in the U.N. system. Within the political sphere, the pervasive, anti-colonial orientation of the United Nations, reinforced by the non-aligned, enforces a one-dimensional approach to problems of the post-colonial era. States outside the movement are, therefore, often reluctant to bring problems or threats to peace into the U.N. framework, preferring to seek outside mediation, as Britain did initially in the Falklands crisis.

The tendency to politicize rather than solve problems is both a dynamic of large groups like the NAM and an outgrowth of the movement's history and sense of identity. Formed in reaction to the Cold War and then-massive influence of the superpowers, the shared negative experiences of colonialism and underdevelopment were, for most, the common bond. The movement's self-image and cohesiveness evolved in reaction to outside forces perceived as hostile. Agreement was thus more easily reached on resolutions to condemn, to deplore, or to decry—common verbs in U.N. parlance—than on realistic solutions requiring compromise by all sides.

The negative anti-colonial focus of the movement has been sustained as a rallying point for its diverse membership, while differences of political and economic outlook tend to preclude agreement on innovative solutions. There has been no detailed non-aligned plan, for example, for the Middle East or Namibia, but ringing, ritual denunciation at all NAM meetings of Israel, South Africa, and Western states for failure to resolve these issues. Within the United Nations, there has been consistent non-aligned pressure to abolish the veto, eliminate special prerogatives of permanent members, and strengthen the General Assembly as a locus of non-aligned power, but limited willingness to compromise or accept restrictions on freedom of the majority. While the NIEO is sometimes cited as a comprehensive non-aligned plan for change, it too is an uncompromising document based on Western acquiescence in Third World demands rather than on dialogue.

To the extent that compromise and real negotiation are blocked, whether by non-aligned or superpower intransigence, the United Nations is clearly diminished. Its annual march through a standardized agenda and condemnatory resolutions appears increasingly marginal to events of the mid-1980s. Despite international law and annual resolutions on peaceful settlement of disputes, the 1982 invasion and recapture of the Falklands seem little different from events in those islands 150 years ago. Pivotal events, critics argue, are simply not affected by an annual 29,000 hours of U.N. meetings or the 700 million pages of official documents produced in 1982. Shaped by two world wars, the United Nations nevertheless remains the only international framework outside military alliances for averting a third. Yet the growing disaffection of many members offers little reassurance about its ability to respond in a future crisis. To be sure, valuable technical services, whether malaria eradication or food research, continue under U.N. auspices. In the long run, however, a worsening political climate and continued confrontation in New York could threaten donor support for these as well.

III
The Non-Aligned and the Superpowers

12

The Soviet Union and the NAM*

While the running dogs of the USSR are proud of being running dogs of the USSR, the running dogs of the US have their tails between their legs.

A Non-Aligned Diplomat

The Non-Aligned Movement, at least at its inception, was defined by its relationship to the superpowers. The objective was acceptance of the NAM by Moscow and Washington on its own terms and outside the Cold War context. Inevitably, however, East–West perceptions have shaped approaches to the NAM by both superpowers, which have lobbied to involve the non-aligned in various issues well outside the Third World. There is, furthermore, an inconsistency between the non-aligned goal of reducing East–West tensions and the greater leverage afforded to many NAM members by U.S.–Soviet competition for influence. The alternation of periods of détente and renewed tension has shown that outside intervention in the Third World occurs during both, and possibly with greater frequency when East–West relations are best. Some within the NAM, therefore, view détente not as desirable but as a "condominium of superpowers who are carving out the world into new spheres of influence."[72]

The Non-aligned and the Superpowers

While the movement's orientation has evolved from East–West issues to a primary focus on anti-colonialism, the relationship with the

*For a more comprehensive treatment of Soviet policy toward the Non-Aligned Movement, see James F. Grant, "The Soviet Approach to the Non-Aligned Movement," individual research paper prepared for the National War College (1980), on file in the Library of the National Defense University, Washington, D.C.

superpowers has remained an area of ambiguity and division among members. As an organization, the NAM seeks recognition and special attention from the superpowers along with an enhanced role in the United Nations. Members nevertheless reject individual accountability for NAM positions, using the group rationale to divorce positions on international issues from bilateral relations with either superpower. The line between the attention and respect demanded of superpowers by the movement and real or imagined intervention is also ambiguous, and fluctuates by issue and alignments within the NAM. Diplomacy toward the non-aligned must, thus, thread a path between often simultaneous accusations of neglect and interference.

The related question of the movement's balance or equidistance between East and West has been largely superseded by anti-Westernism inherent in an agenda of colonial and related issues. Where once equidistance may have been used by some members to justify a new and separate identity, the movement's survival and growth since the early 1960s have now made the concept, never officially endorsed by the movement, marginal. Although Cuba's overt campaign to align the NAM with Moscow clearly strained the consensus, there is now little pretense to a median position between East and West.

The United States is routinely castigated by name in communiqués of the non-aligned while, as of mid-1983, the Soviet Union has virtually escaped critical reference. Nor would the "evenhanded" references to both superpowers, unsuccessfully urged by moderates during meetings in 1982 and early 1983, necessarily represent equidistance or true balance. References to 105,000 Soviet troops in Afghanistan or backing for Vietnamese occupation of Kampuchea might be paired, for example, with allegations of U.S. colonial domination of Puerto Rico or condemnation of the presence of U.S. military advisers in El Salvador, thus giving equal weight to both.

Competition between superpowers, nevertheless, maximizes non-aligned influence both at the United Nations and in seeking economic or military support. The threat to "turn to the other side" is an effective strategy for aid only if superpower competition exists. Thus, seeking to limit U.S. support for Britain, Argentina hinted throughout the Falkland crisis at probable military aid from Moscow, and countless NAM states have alternated between military suppliers. While non-aligned dogma is committed to disarmament and reduction of tensions, the Soviet threat is usually cited first by members seeking Western aid.

Moscow and Washington, in theory, have a mutual interest in limiting this kind of leverage, which has led both to underwrite inexhaustible economic and military demands of selected Third World states. Both, in fact, initially viewed the NAM with nearly identical skepticism, but yielded in later years to mutual suspicion and competition for influence in the Third World. Cold War rigidity left little sympathy in Washington, Moscow—or even Beijing—for the idea of a non-aligned or neutralist group of states. Josef Stalin's concept of a world in "two camps," divided between socialism and imperialism, left no alternative in the inevitable class struggle. Similarly, Secretary of State John Foster Dulles's faith in Western moral superiority left no margin for non-alignment, which he labeled "immoral." Speaking in June 1949, Mao Zedong declared that there was "no third road, nor could there be a foreign policy which took a sharp turn away from both the Western alliance system and the Soviet bloc."[73] All three looked on non-aligned or uncommitted states as potential allies of the other two.

From similar starting points of skepticism and distrust, U.S. and Soviet assessments and strategy toward the NAM have been markedly different. The United States, whose two-way trade with the Third World is ten times that of the Soviet Union and whose economic assistance is four times higher, has concentrated on bilateral ties rather than blocs. Moscow, with fewer channels and less leverage—excluding concentration countries like Cuba, South Yemen, Ethiopia, and Vietnam—has perceived larger blocs, particularly the NAM, as a vehicle to undercut Western bilateral ties in the Third World. As a result, Soviet diplomacy toward the non-aligned in recent years has sought to reinforce the movement's anti-colonial orientation and negative stereotypes of the U.S. and the rest of the West. The United States, by contrast, has been on the defensive, seeking to moderate non-aligned positions critical of specific American interests, whether related to Puerto Rico, Israel, Diego Garcia, or elsewhere.

These differing approaches have inevitably shaped non-aligned perceptions of the United States and USSR. The Soviet posture of general support and encouragement for NAM positions has fostered an image of Moscow as sympathetic toward non-aligned interests, although not for most members a "natural ally." The United States, by seeking to "limit damage," has more often been in the role of complaining or cajoling on specific issues, leaving an impression of opposition or indifference, if not actual hostility toward the NAM. For Moscow, with limited resources of aid and trade in the Third World, the process has been one of astute posturing. Trends within the NAM, at least since the Algiers Summit, have been largely inimical to the West, virtually offering Moscow a "free ride." This and subsequent chapters examine how U.S. and Soviet approaches have diverged at important turning points within the movement and the implications for non-aligned relations with the superpowers.

Soviet Views

With Stalin's death in 1953, the Soviet Union adopted a more active diplomatic strategy in the Third World. Moscow endorsed the Panchsheel principles in early 1955 and, although excluded from the conference itself, commented favorably on the results of Bandung. In contrast with silence from Washington, Soviet President Kliment Voroshilov and other officials sent greetings to Bandung and, in its aftermath, worked closely with the Chinese to gain a foothold in the new grouping. Their effort to do so through the Afro-Asian People's Solidarity Organization (AAPSO) has been described as a "parody of and the parasite on the Bandung spirit," but nevertheless reflected a new Soviet strategy of involvement in the Third World.[74]

Suspicion of states differing from the Soviet model, characteristic of the Stalin era, gave way to the realization that the anti-colonial focus of emerging states could be of direct benefit to Moscow. Capitalizing on this, Premier Nikita Khrushchev put forward in the General Assembly, during October 1960, a strongly anti-Western declaration calling for immediate independence of all "colonial countries and peoples." While the declaration eventually adopted as Resolution 1514 was based on an Afro-Asian draft, the episode foreshadowed Soviet strategy for the next two decades of siding with the Third World and isolating the United States and the rest of the West by emphasis on anti-colonial and anti-imperialist rhetoric.

Despite this campaign for influence in the Third World, the Non-Aligned Movement appeared initially to Moscow as more of a threat than an opportunity. By 1961, the Soviets were somewhat disillusioned with lack of Third World support at the United Nations for Soviet positions on the Congo crisis, Lebanon, and replacement of the secretary-general with a "troika system." The movement's early emphasis on an independent role between East and West represented an imponderable to the Soviets that provided few clues to its later anti-Western orientation. Nor was it then clear that the NAM represented more than one of several transient groupings in the fluid international conditions of the early 1960s. A further negative factor for the Soviets was the early preeminence among the non-aligned of Yugoslavia which constituted a direct challenge to Moscow in Eastern Europe and within the Third World. In these circumstances, Moscow showed little enthusiasm for the Belgrade Summit, manifesting its indifference by detonation of an atomic test on the eve of the conference.

Soviet ideological rigidity also worked against a precipitous embrace of the NAM by Moscow. Yugoslav Foreign Secretary Mojsov has described Soviet aims for the movement as a process of "ideological differentiation" by which "reactionary countries" would be culled out, leaving a "revolutionary core" as natural allies of Moscow.[75] The logical extension of this approach, as Mojsov points out, is Afghan puppet leader Babrak Karmal's redefinition in 1980 of "real non-alignment" to include Soviet armed intervention.

Yet, at the outset, Moscow remained cautious about endorsing new countries of uncertain orientation, and was obviously concerned by inclusion at Belgrade of conservative states like Saudi Arabia, Tunisia, Morocco, and Ethiopia. This reserve resulted, during the early 1960s, in an essentially negative approach to the movement whereby, like the United States, Moscow sought to limit damage to its interests rather than to exploit the NAM to advance global policies. As late as 1968, the Soviets were lobbying vigorously behind the scenes to dissuade President Tito and others from calling a new summit that, Moscow feared, might focus on the invasion of Czechoslovakia.

Sino-Soviet relations have also been a long-standing factor in Soviet perceptions of the NAM. Close ties with Beijing initially tilted Moscow toward the Bandung grouping, where Chinese influence was strong and might eventually prevail in admitting the Soviet Union. As Sino-Soviet differences developed into an open rupture beginning in 1959, the prospect of a second Bandung, dominated by China, became a threat to Moscow. By comparison, the rival NAM, even with Yugoslavia's pre-eminent role, seemed preferable. By the Cairo Summit, Soviet press coverage of the movement was generally favorable, and Pravda reported afterward, on November 1, 1964, that "The Soviet Union evaluates highly the policy of non-alignment to military blocs pursued by several countries, supports Afro-Asian solidarity, and is for cooperation among all revolutionary forces."[76]

Thus the movement, by default, became a vehicle to limit Chinese gains in the Third World, and Soviet writers have regularly attacked alleged Chinese influence in the NAM as vehemently as that of the United States. Bondarevski and Sofinski, for example, accuse Beijing of trying to "disfigure" the movement by reinforcing North–South divisions rather than the cleavage between socialists and imperialists.[77] The Chinese, for their part, have worked over the years to undercut Soviet influence in the NAM and were active among the non-aligned during Cuba's 1979–81 presidency on issues such as the Soviet-backed invasion of Kampuchea by Vietnam. Prior to the Havana meeting, they had publicly questioned Cuba's non-aligned credentials and called on NAM members to change the summit venue and expel Cuba from the movement.

More important, however, in changing Soviet policy toward the NAM was the movement's radicalization in the early 1970s as decolonization and economic issues replaced the earlier focus on Cold War themes. The new stridency of non-aligned rhetoric against the West coincided with Soviet objectives to undercut Western influence in the Third World, and Moscow soon turned its attention to further sharpening the movement's anti-colonial and anti-imperialist thrust. CPSU First Secretary Leonid Brezhnev, for example, rejoiced at the outcome of the Algiers Summit: "For our part, we have every respect for the anti-imperialist program drawn up in Algiers, and we wish the participants in the Movement of Non-Aligned Countries success in putting it into effect."[78]

By 1973, the NAM had clearly become, in Moscow's view, a positive mechanism to be used both to isolate the United States and to gain acceptance for Soviet global aims. From that point, Soviet praise of non-alignment became progressively more fulsome, and by the 1976 Colombo Summit, Brezhnev was emphasizing identical Communist Party of the Soviet Union (CPSU) and NAM orientations:

> As has been repeatedly emphasized in important documents of the CPSU, the Soviet Union highly values the anti-imperialist, anti-colonialist, and anti-racist orientations of the Non-aligned Movement....[79]

By September 1, 1981, the first officially designated "Day of Non-alignment," congratulatory messages from non-members were received only from the Soviet Union, Bulgaria, China, Czechoslovakia, Mongolia, Poland, and East and West Germany.[80]

Re-evaluation of the movement and of the opportunity posed by anti-colonialism in the Third World coincided with and reinforced a more flexible overall approach by Moscow toward the NAM, the United Nations, and individual Third World states. In the Stalin era, Soviet strategy had focused on creation of local Communist parties rather than relations with Third World governments. By the 1960s, however, Moscow increasingly realized that exclusive reliance on orthodox Communist parties limited its opportunities for penetration of the Third World.

Soviet strategy shifted, therefore, to support for nationalist regimes and liberation movements. The new approach was also compatible with growing Soviet interest in the NAM, since ideology no longer prevented the Soviets from working with non-aligned states like

Algeria, which were then deeply anti-Western but differed from the Soviet model. In return for broader access, Moscow dropped insistence on local party cadres, acquiescing in the dissolution of parties in Egypt and Algeria and standing aloof from factional disputes among India's three Communist parties. Although two were later abrogated (Egypt and Somalia), Moscow signed treaties of friendship between 1971 and 1983 with 15 non-aligned states. These represented a notable departure from Soviet practice and the first such ventures outside the Warsaw Pact. All contain provisions for mutual respect of non-alignment.

To rationalize such departures from orthodoxy, Soviet "intellectuals" reinterpreted the theory of "non-capitalist development," attributed to Lenin, to mean that "pre-capitalist societies of the Third World could evolve directly into socialism without otherwise inevitable class struggle."[81] This ideological legerdemain was given official sanction by the 1956 CPSU Congress and used to justify Soviet support for nationalist leaders like Nasser and Ben Bella. Within the framework of Third World states proceeding along the path to socialism, the movement came to be viewed in Moscow as a necessary, but transitional, phenomenon to be rendered obsolete by the emergence of a unified world socialist order. From this point of view, Soviet support for the NAM became a "prerequisite for the class struggle at the international level," which would be supportive of the Kremlin's anti-capitalist objectives and linked to an "overall socio-economic transformation of the Third World along communist lines."[82]

In the United Nations as well, the Soviets began in the mid-1970s to temper ideology with pragmatism in voting with the non-aligned bloc on a range of "colonial" and economic issues. For the most part, this did not involve deliberate decisions by the Kremlin to change the Soviet position on a given issue to correspond to that of the NAM majority but, rather, the politics of posturing. Strident non-aligned criticism of the United States and the rest of the West on issues of the Middle East, southern Africa, and economic reform, which dominate the U.N. agenda, coincided closely with Soviet long-term goals. What has distinguished Soviet diplomacy since the Algiers Summit, however, has been the careful and often disingenuous tailoring of Soviet positions to give the impression of an identity of interest with the non-aligned.

An example drawn from among many is Soviet support of non-aligned proposals for an Indian Ocean Zone of Peace (IOZP). The plan, which would close down U.S. and British bases at Diego Garcia, would also block further Soviet use of naval facilities at Massawa, Aden, Perim Island, Mukalla, Assab, Socotra, and the Dahlak Islands. Yet, knowing that agreement is highly unlikely, Moscow has consistently backed the plan in order to win non-aligned favor, particularly from India as it takes over the chairmanship, and to draw attention away from Afghanistan and to the U.S. presence at Diego Garcia. Foreign Minister Andrei Gromyko's remarks to the General Assembly on October 1, 1982, are typical of such posturing:

> We can well understand the legitimate concern of the coastal states of the Indian Ocean over the expansion of the United States military presence there. It is literally growing before our very eyes, also threatening the security of the USSR from the South. We cannot help drawing our own conclusions from this. The Soviet Union endorses the idea, put forward by the non-aligned countries, of turning the Indian Ocean into a zone of peace.

Gromyko's words encapsulate Moscow's message to the non-aligned: support for NAM positions, mutuality of Soviet and non-aligned interests against a common threat, the United States as an aggressive, hostile power, and implicitly, the legitimacy of Soviet military force.

Deference to the movement and non-aligned positions has been a recognizable theme in recent Soviet statements at the United Nations. Alone among permanent members, Soviet delegate Richard Ovinnikov singled out the eight non-aligned members on the Security Council for fulsome praise during the new council's first meeting on January 18, 1983. Ovinnikov highlighted non-aligned contributions to "improving the international situation and to eliminating and preventing crisis situations." He also noted pointedly that "membership on the Security Council of eight states representing the Non-aligned Movement lays upon them a special responsibility and makes it possible for them to play an important role in the Council's activities...."

Ovinnikov's public support for the G-8 and the absence of similar statements from Western members of the council reinforces the conclusion that the non-aligned bloc dynamic tends to favor Soviet over Western interests on the council. Outgoing members of the 1982 Security Council have, in fact, commented privately that formation of a non-aligned group in frequent confrontation with the West is a "free ride" for the USSR. In their view, it is only infrequently necessary for the Soviets to intervene when the non-aligned show signs of what Moscow regards as undue flexibility or compromise. In such cases, they seek, through the PLO, Cuba, or others, to stiffen the NAM position, or themselves introduce disruptive amendments.

Perhaps most revealing of the new priority attached to the NAM by Moscow was the first foreign policy address of CPSU Secretary-General Yuri Andropov. Speaking to the Central Committee plenum only ten days after his appointment, Andropov highlighted Soviet support for the non-aligned at the outset of his speech. While President

John Kennedy's inaugural address made passing reference to non-alignment, posturing for non-aligned support has been notably absent from U.S. presidential statements and underscores the difference in approach. Andropov also singled out Soviet relations with the incoming NAM chairman:

> The importance of the group of states which created the Non-aligned Movement is growing in international life. With many of them the Soviet Union has all-round friendly ties which benefit both sides and make for greater stability in the world. One example of this is the Soviet Union's relations with India. Solidarity with the states which have gained freedom from colonial oppression, with the peoples who are upholding their independence has been and remains one of the fundamental principles of Soviet foreign policy.

Soviet Clients in the NAM

As Moscow reassessed its policy toward the Third World and the NAM, its tactics to gain influence with selected members also went through a period of trial and error. Initially, the largest and most powerful countries, capable of shaping the movement's course, were singled out for special attention. India, Egypt, Indonesia, and Algeria were recipients of large-scale Soviet military and economic assistance, and their leaders called regularly in Moscow, where the more compliant were rewarded with Lenin Peace Prizes. Uneasy rapprochement was even achieved with Marshal Tito of Yugoslavia, vindicating, to the chagrin of Soviet hard-liners, Belgrade's independent course.

While Soviet relations warmed significantly with each of these states, reaching peaks in Cairo and Djakarta in the later years of Nasser and Sukarno and during the Ben Bella regime in Algeria, the size and complexity of these states made them resistant to Soviet control. Although conscious of Moscow's influence, each pursued essentially independent policies in the NAM. Algeria's strong leadership served Soviet interests by setting the movement on a more radical anti-Western course, but the causes lay in Algeria's liberation struggle and national orientation. None of these states were ultimately prepared to be used as proxies, thus, for the time, denying Moscow a direct voice or input within the movement.

In the non-aligned context, Cuba presented a different target of opportunity. While invited to the Belgrade Summit, largely because of Third World reaction to the Bay of Pigs invasion, it remained on the NAM periphery. Acute economic problems and fear of U.S. invasion made it particularly vulnerable to Soviet influence. There is reason to believe that Cuba would initially have preferred a Soviet military guarantee of its security, even at the cost of possible expulsion from the NAM.[83] In 1968, virtually alone among the Third World, Cuba endorsed the Soviet invasion of Czechoslovakia, and by the end of the decade, Moscow had turned increasingly to Havana as a channel of influence into the NAM. Soviet military aid, purchases of Cuban sugar at prices well above the world market, and supplies of oil well under the world price increased significantly in these years. Havana's economic dependence became nearly total after the disastrous crop failure of 1970, and in 1972 Cuba joined the Soviet-controlled Council for Economic Mutual Assistance (CEMA). By 1982, twenty-three years after Cuba's revolution, its economy continued to depend on an esimated $4 billion a year in Soviet aid, equivalent to 25 percent of Cuba's GNP, and its ruble debt to Moscow stood at $9 billion. In that year, Moscow bought 44 percent of the Cuban sugar crop at a price 42 percent above the world market and supplied 95 percent of Cuba's oil needs at 40 percent of the OPEC price.

With Cuba as the model and chosen instrument, Moscow broadened its base in the movement to include other hard-core radicals outside the movement's mainstream but dependent in varying degrees on Soviet support. Admission at the 1976 Colombo Summit of Vietnam, North Korea, Angola, and the PLO widened the circle, as did installation of "revolutionary" regimes in Ethiopia and Afghanistan. Soviet officials, having actively promoted many of these changes, closely monitored their impact on the movement and commented approvingly on the addition of Vietnam and North Korea, "which have held high the banner of anti-imperialist struggle."[84]

By the 1980s, the core of radical NAM members, clustered around Cuba and for the most part heavily dependent on Soviet aid, had grown to about a dozen states. Based on opposition to a General Assembly resolution calling for troop withdrawal from Afghanistan, these included on November 29, 1982: Afghanistan, Angola, Cuba, Ethiopia, Grenada, Laos, Libya, Madagascar, Mozambique, South Yemen, Syria, and Vietnam. While a few of these states have been erratic in voting patterns and allegiances, most constitute a core group of Soviet supporters within the NAM and United Nations. Some, as noted in Chapter 8, vote as consistently with the Soviets as members of the East European bloc. Two, Cuba and Vietnam, belong to CEMA.

In the aggregate, the group represents an evolution in Soviet strategy toward the NAM away from concentration on the largest states and toward reliance on smaller, but more controllable, members. To be sure, the Soviets have continued to cultivate close relations with larger states like India, but within the non-aligned context Cuba et al. have been the primary vehicle in recent years. The vulnerability of these countries to Soviet influence and their ability to act quickly as a small, but disciplined, cadre within the movement have more than offset their lack of size and stature. Nor has Cuba attempted to disguise the relationship. Fidel Castro proclaimed at the Algiers Summit, "I want to remind you that Cuba is a socialist country, Marxist-Leninist, whose final goal is communism." Six years later, at Havana, he stated, "We are very grateful to the Soviet people" and "to the glorious October Revolution because it ushered in a new era in human history...."[85]

With a reliable client state within the movement, for the first time, Moscow's goal became the fostering of the impression of identity between Soviet and non-aligned interests. Soviet diplomatic and senior officials lost few opportunities to drive home this linkage. Speaking at a banquet given in his honor by Indian President Neelam Sanjiva Reddy in December 1980, Brezhnev referred to "the solidarity front of socialist and non-aligned countries, a front which stands in opposition to the aggressive forces of imperialism and restrains their actions aimed at peace, freedom and the independence of peoples." The preferred vehicle for Soviet penetration of the NAM was the "natural ally" thesis, first put forward by Cuban delegates at the 1970 Lusaka Summit and personally endorsed by Fidel Castro three years later at Algiers. His Algiers speech echoed CPSU Secretary Brezhnev's dictum to the summit that the "socialist states and the Soviet Union" should be accepted as the "natural and most reliable allies" of the non-aligned.[86]

The formulation, dutifully put forward again by Cuba at the Colombo and Havana summits, was never adopted, but is evidence of Moscow's campaign for respectability in the Third World. By identifying themselves with non-aligned positions on national liberation and exploiting the emotional residue of colonialism, the Soviets hoped to expand and legitimize their presence in the Third World, particularly in the military sphere. Muted Third World reaction to increased Soviet or surrogate military force in Africa, southwest Asia, Indochina, and Central America is evidence of the strategy's partial success. Notice of this expanded presence has been confined within the movement to occasional, oblique warnings against "hegemony" and an appeal at the New Delhi Summit for the United States and USSR to resume negotiations on the Indian Ocean, broken off by the United States in 1980 over Afghanistan.

Cuba's chairmanship of the NAM increased the scope for Soviet influence, but probably fell short of Moscow's aims. With the "natural ally" thesis again rejected at Havana, Castro was still able to push through strongly anti-U.S. and anti-Western positions on most international issues. The Havana Summit was the high-water mark of non-aligned radicalism, and advanced Moscow's objective of isolating the United States and portraying developed Western countries as enemies of the Third World. In subsequent months, Cuba was able to use the non-aligned chairmanship to limit damage to Moscow from its invasion of Afghanistan and to promote support for the Vietnamese occupation of Kampuchea.

While the majority of the non-aligned split with Moscow and Havana on these issues at the United Nations, Cuban influence prevented meetings on either subject or critical reference to the Soviet Union in official declarations of the NAM. The same documents, however, continued to single out the United States for blame on a wide spectrum of issues. The persistence and strengthening of anti-Western themes within the movement, despite clear violation of its central principles by Moscow, was probably due in large part to effective action by Soviet clients. Cuba and others were able to make adroit use of general resentment by the non-aligned of U.S. policy on North–South issues, the Middle East, and southern Africa.

In any case, the presence within the NAM of a core of client states prepared to block consensus on positions damaging to Moscow or inconsistent with Soviet foreign policy is a major tactical advantage for the Soviets. Although the relationship of most of these states to Moscow is generally known, they nonetheless can lobby non-aligned colleagues in a manner that the Soviets or other Warsaw Pact states could not. Moscow is able to coordinate positions and convey guidance to these states well in advance of NAM conferences and, once they have begun, to rely on them to carry out instructions by appropriate division of labor. Within the United Nations, the relationship is obvious and provides Moscow with a claque of Third World supporters on any issue. Soviet orchestration of its clients is frequently undisguised—as, for example, on December 8, 1982, when the United States delivered a strong attack in the First Committee on use of lethal Soviet chemical weapons in Afghanistan, Laos, and Kampuchea. The Soviet delegate walked to the back of the room, handed the Afghan chargé a prepared speech, and Afghanistan soon launched a rebuttal based on use of American defoliants ten years earlier in Vietnam.

Soviet officials monitoring ministerial or summit meetings have equally easy access to client delegations without concern that their presence will be exploited as interference in non-aligned affairs. Moscow does not, therefore, need to lobby worldwide with the general

NAM membership to make its positions known and can limit public initiatives to protocol greetings and a few, carefully chosen interventions. By contrast, periodic U.S. demarches in non-aligned capitals can be, and often are, exploited as superpower interference. The Soviets have not hesitated, however, to lobby hard with states outside the core group on certain issues when their influence is threatened. During preparations for the Havana Summit, for example, when Cuba's prospective leadership was challenged, albeit ineffectively, by moderates, Moscow weighed in hard with states like India and Yugoslavia to limit opposition. At the summit itself, Soviet delegates worked behind the scenes to seat the Kampuchean delegation headed by Heng Samrin.

Soviet use of surrogates to influence the movement became apparent to rank-and-file members during Cuba's presidency. The obvious discipline and prior coordination with which a small band of states regularly outmaneuvered the majority to shape the consensus and control key NAM committees could not long escape notice. Traditional guardians of non-aligned ideology expressed concern, and by the end of Castro's term, the phenomenon of an aligned minority was widely debated in private among NAM members. Yugoslav Ambassador Komatina charged specifically, in April 1982, that "a small group of non-aligned countries is linking itself ever more closely with the Warsaw Pact." He noted, further, that these states belong to "consultative groups of the socialist community" at the United Nations, attend military maneuvers of the Warsaw Pact, and "approve a priori the foreign political moves of the leading Bloc power, including actions involving intervention against the non-aligned countries."[87]

Awareness of Soviet leverage over the movement through client states also led to increasing cohesion among a grouping of about 20 "like-minded" states, considered moderates in the NAM context, which met regularly during 1981–83 as a counterweight to the Cuban group. For many of these countries, the movement still represented a fragile bulwark against Soviet intervention, and Cuba's campaign to legitimize invasions of Afghanistan and Kampuchea as defense of non-alignment ran counter to their national interests.

Limits of Soviet Control

Moscow's foothold in the NAM, and through it in the United Nations, has led some to portray these institutions' frequent hostility to the United States and the rest of the West as results of Soviet diplomatic initiative and skill. Yet Soviet influence remains narrowly based and dependent on loyalty of a small core of states. These have been effective up to a point in mobilizing the more passive larger group, but remain outside the mainstream and, in some cases, themselves are politically vulnerable. The moment of maximum Soviet leverage during Cuba's presidency revealed clear limits to the power of proxies. Explicit linkage of non-aligned and socialist interests was rejected even at Havana, and the hard-line tactics there of Soviet client states eventually prompted moderates to regroup. The pendulum swung partially back at meetings in New Delhi during 1981 and 1983 as Cuban leadership weakened and passed to India.

Soviet channels into the movement are thus an important tactical advantage, but no guarantee of ability to control the final product. Non-aligned condemnations of the United States and the rest of the West have clearly advanced Soviet interests in the Third World, but Moscow's role in the process has probably been more that of beneficiary than shaper of events. Continuation of the anti-colonial focus and resentment of Western economic superiority ensured the movement's anti-U.S. orientation, from which Moscow could only benefit. The Soviets have sought, through proxies and directly, to encourage these trends, but the sources were indigenous to the Third World. The influence of Soviet clients within the movement has been exaggerated by some U.S. policymakers unwilling to accept non-aligned hostility as in large part the result of post-colonial bitterness, opposition to specific U.S. policies, and discrepancies of wealth.

The transition from Cuban to Indian leadership, although not marked by a shift away from anti-colonial and anti-imperialist rhetoric in the New Delhi Declaration, will be an interesting test of Soviet relations with the NAM. The impact of Soviet clients on non-aligned decision-making is likely to gradually diminish over the three years of India's chairmanship. While Moscow has developed broad ties—including massive aid and equipment supplies and 2,000 Soviet economic and 500 military advisers in the country—India's size and diversity make it resistant to overt Soviet influence in the NAM or bilaterally.

As if reflecting uneasiness in Moscow, the New Delhi Summit was preceded by unusually intense Soviet efforts to mobilize its resources in the movement. Raul Castro held extensive pre-summit consultations in Moscow, and Soviet aircraft conveyed the leaders of Cuba, Grenada, and Surinam to New Delhi with a stopover in Tashkent. President Samora Machel of Mozambique and Nicaraguan junta coordinator Daniel Ortega Saavedra also made quiet, but obligatory, stops in

Moscow en route to the summit. Others, like Libyan Vice-President Abdul Salam Jalloud, consulted in Moscow immediately after the summit.

Sensing a possible shift in non-aligned orientation, the Soviet press and think tanks concentrated on the movement as the Seventh Summit approached. Most railed, like TASS on January 29, against the "blind alley of equidistance," and Gennady Chufrin of the Oriental Studies Institute reiterated the standard line that Moscow should not bear "equal responsibility" for "ex-colonial handicaps" of the developing world. By mid-February, Soviet media were openly attacking the Indian draft declaration and recalling the "success" achieved at Managua. On the eve of the summit, February 27, an *Izvestiya* article by K. Geyvandov described the movement as founded on "the ruins of the colonial system" and claimed that "99 percent of the misfortunes which the member states of the NAM are suffering from are the result of the policies of imperialism, racism and Zionism." Geyvandov also attacked moderates within the NAM as "apologists of imperialism," and predictably concluded that the USSR is the "natural friend and ally of the non-aligned."

On the covert level, KGB agents were active in the six weeks before the summit in attempts to discredit the United States and maintain the leverage of Soviet clients in the NAM. A prime example was a carefully forged letter, attributed to Ambassador Jeane Kirkpatrick, that appeared in Communist newspapers of India and Nicaragua and included a plan "to Balkanize India and to destroy its influence in the Third World and elsewhere." More effective, however, was a campaign, conducted by the client cadre but orchestrated in Moscow, to portray India's more balanced draft declaration for the summit as a concession by Indira Gandhi to Washington, agreed during her July 1982 visit. Such charges, picked up by the Communist Party of India (CPI), resulted in greater pressure for radical revisions to the draft.

Moscow's underlying concerns and covert efforts did not interfere with continued posturing on the official level. Andropov and Mrs. Gandhi exchanged letters before the summit, and well-publicized fraternal greetings from the Presidium of the Supreme Soviet and USSR Council of Ministers were echoed by similar messages from leaders of East Germany, Czechoslovakia, and Romania. A 15-man Soviet delegation, including senior officials of the CPSU, covered the summit, and their detailed reporting permitted the Moscow Oriental Studies Institute to issue a preliminary positive reaction on March 11, even before the New Delhi Summit concluded. Following this cue, Radio

Moscow intensified broadcasts to the Third World on the summit, dwelling on its condemnations of the United States and linking these to extraneous elements like joint U.S.–South Korean military exercises and the sixteenth anniversary of the My Lai massacre.

In the period following the New Delhi Summit, Moscow's ability to command non-aligned sympathy through a policy based largely on posturing will depend on the movement's substantive orientation. As the movement's anti-colonial thrust was accentuated in the early 1970s, Soviet diplomacy sought to emphasize anti-Westernism, to the exclusion of other elements. The priority attached since 1973 to North–South economic issues, for example, met an uncertain response in Moscow. On one hand, it conveniently focused the Third World on Western guilt for colonialism, with the United States, as the largest economy, portrayed as principal villain. It also provided a much-cited rationale to avoid the costs of development: "The Soviet Union has repeatedly stated that it does not intend to bear responsiblity for the plunder of the young states, committed by the colonialists and the present-day neo-colonialists."[88] At the same time, emphasis on development threatened the Soviets, not party to the World Bank or IMF and unable to play a major role, with exclusion if North–South negotiations ever gained momentum. Their absence from the 1981 Cancún Economic Summit between key representatives of developed and developing states underscored Moscow's potential isolation from such a dialogue. From a Soviet point of view, it was therefore of utmost importance to reinforce the linkage between colonialism and existing economic problems. The Yugoslav theoretician of non-alignment, Leo Mates, sums up thus:

> In some instances, the accusation boils down to "colonialism" being the main cause of the lack of development, and the accumulation of wealth in the developed countries. Quite naturally and, one would say, almost automatically, this definition of the problems and direction of activities led to close links with the Soviet Union and the countries associated with it.[89]

To be sure, the Soviets have made extravagant claims to offset their disadvantage in the economic area. Foreign Minister Gromyko asserted, for example, in the General Assembly on October 1, 1982, that the Soviet Union is doing as much as, if not more than, any developed country in the field of economic assistance to the Third World. Yet, using the OECD definition of official development assistance (ODA), net Soviet disbursements amounted to only $1.6

billion in 1980 (.14 percent of Soviet GNP). By comparison, net ODA was .27 percent of the U.S. GNP and, among the Development Assistance Commission of the OECD, the donor average was .34 percent. Furthermore, Cuba and Vietnam accounted for 75 percent of all Soviet aid, with most of the remainder going to North Korea, Afghanistan, Kampuchea, and Laos. Excluding this core group, Soviet aid to the developing world was only .02 percent of its GNP in 1982. Soviet aid to non-Communist LDCs has always been low, and on a net basis has actually been negative since 1980. Within the Third World, all but 11 client states are today repaying Moscow more in principal and interest than they receive annually in new aid.

Given limits to its influence in the movement and inability to restrain, particularly in other world forums, the reaction of NAM members to Afghanistan and Kampuchea, Moscow has sought to reinforce non-aligned positions that serve its interests and to downplay others. In particular, the Soviets continue to use the anti-colonial fervor of the NAM as a way of distracting attention from their own misconduct. Soviet Ambassador Oleg Troyanovsky charged on November 24, 1982, that the annual General Assembly debate on Afghanistan was

> ...obviously aimed at distracting attention from really burning international issues, such as averting the threat of nuclear war, curbing the arms race and eliminating dangerous sources of conflict in the Middle East, in the southern part of Africa, in the South Atlantic, and the eradication of the vestiges of colonialism.

The continuing deadlock between the Third World and the West over the Middle East and southern Africa has allowed the Soviets to cater to Third World opinion and largely camouflage projection of their own military force throughout the world. As long as these issues dominate the international agenda, the Soviets will probably retain considerable advantage over the West among both the non-aligned and the U.N. majority. The late Soviet ambassador to the United Nations, Yakov Malik, commented that "...the situation became easier due to an increase in the number of United Nations members from developing countries. Their position generally coincided with ours."[90] In his view, "The reason for this was that at practically every session of the General Assembly the Soviet Union would introduce important new motions reflecting the interests of the developing countries."

Continued preoccupation by the non-aligned with southern Africa and the Middle East is perceived in the Kremlin as essential to undercutting U.S. influence in the Third World. The linkage of racism and Zionism evident in non-aligned documents since 1973 originated in Moscow, and Soviet propaganda in the Third World has long played on the theme of "racist" U.S. support for South Africa and Israel. In exploiting post-colonial fears, particularly in Africa and the Middle East, the Kremlin mobilizes a vast army of academic institutes and Third World centers to reinforce diplomatic resources. The outpouring of propaganda materials from these parastatal organs is orchestrated to promote Soviet solidarity with the non-aligned and U.S. responsibility for major world problems.

Specialists like Vasiliy Solodovnikov of Moscow's African Institute, ambassador to Zambia since 1976, become interchangeable with regular Soviet diplomats. Solodovnikov was previously a propagandist for the Soviet Society for Friendship with African Peoples and the Soviet Afro-Asian Solidarity Committee. Organs such as these provide funding for pro-Soviet publications throughout the Third World. Just before the New Delhi Summit, at a time when India was promoting a return to centrist NAM principles, more than a dozen books appeared in New Delhi and Bombay extolling Moscow as a "natural ally" and Cuba as its disciple. These were complemented by TASS pamphlets distributed free in New Delhi on Soviet maritime interests in the Indian Ocean and by a series of pro-Moscow seminars organized by "non-aligned" specialists like G. Bondarevski.

Massive as these human and institutional resources are, their thrust is negative, and depends on continuing sources of world tension and conflict for which the United States can be blamed. The rhetoric of Marxism-Leninism has in general generated little enthusiasm in the Third World or, for that matter, in the Soviet Union itself after more than 60 years. Breakthroughs in either southern Africa or the Middle East would deprive Moscow of a major propaganda weapon. By early 1983, with agreement for U.N.-supervised elections in Namibia and withdrawal of foreign troops from Lebanon both elusive but not beyond possibility, Soviet propaganda focused increasingly on Central America as a third area of U.S. vulnerability.

The United Nations, of course, is a unique forum to influence Third World opinion, and Soviet diplomacy in New York makes common cause with the non-aligned to the extent possible. While Moscow has tended to be at least as conservative as the United States on matters of basic U.N. reform and financing, it portrays itself, like the non-aligned, as a revisionist force opposed to a postwar international order established by the West. The United States is thus cast as the primary obstacle to change, and the USSR, while protecting its veto power, often sides with the non-aligned in challenging the U.N. status quo.

Courtship of the non-aligned has led to greater Soviet flexibility, and unyielding vetoes in the early years gave way to a less doctrinaire approach, leaving the United States in most frequent opposition to Third World resolutions. Superpower use of the Security Council and General Assembly has also been reversed, with the Soviet Union almost invariably backing non-aligned demands for special sessions of the General Assembly and the United States, in contrast with the Korean War period, seeking to confine sensitive issues to the Security Council. Soviet media reflect this new reliance on the General Assembly majority, and now describe the United Nations as "an impressive force" while dismissing resolutions on Afghanistan or Kampuchea as "farfetched questions."[91]

Yet Afghanistan and Kampuchea continue to bedevil the Soviets at the United Nations in the form of repeated, hostile majorities of the General Assembly. Afghanistan, in particular, underscored for Muslim members of the non-aligned the expansionist nature of Soviet aims in the Third World. Nor, during the 1982 General Assembly, was Moscow able to effectively exploit the crisis in Lebanon or prevail in its efforts to inscribe Puerto Rico or the Trust Territories of the Pacific Islands on the agenda. Several resolutions, such as those on chemical weapons and treatment of Soviet peace groups, were decidedly not to Moscow's liking. Such failures suggest that the claimed identity of Soviet and non-aligned interests remains more propaganda than fact. To be sure, a minority of client states continue to perceive Moscow as their "natural ally" and a majority of members regard Soviet positions as more sympathetic to the movement than those of Washington. The latter perception stems, however, from policy differences with the United States rather than from Soviet diplomacy. Without these differences, the non-aligned would probably tend, in the words of one Indian diplomat, toward the more equidistant position of "a pox on both your houses."

There remain built-in limitations to an uncritical NAM embrace of the Soviet Union. While anti-colonialism of the non-aligned has served Moscow well in undercutting the West, their inherent nationalism has equally been an obstacle to penetration. Soviet inroads, whether in Egypt, Somalia, Sudan, or Algeria, have often been short-lived. As Francis Fukuyama concludes, nationalism in the Third World is fundamentally xenophobic, placing limits on outside manipulation of local politics.[92] By 1983, the Soviet Union had consolidated strategic footholds in the Caribbean, the Indian Ocean, Afghanistan, and Southeast Asia, but lacked broad influence throughout the Third World. Soviet intervention during the late 1970s in Afghanistan, Ethiopia, and South Yemen to replace already pro-Moscow regimes with even more hard-core cadres seemed to reflect basic distrust of nationalism and lack of direct control. It also further discredited the theory of "non-capitalist development," again in disfavor with Kremlin ideologues as Third World nationalism proved resistant to a world order made in Moscow and the NAM itself could no longer be viewed as a passing stage en route to socialism.

In more practical terms, "expanding political ambitions in the Third World, initially boosted by military instrumentalities, are in the longer run subject to being undermined by Moscow's limited economic capabilities."[93] Having established the degree of dependence necessary for direct control, Moscow in the mid-1980s has only limited resources available elsewhere. In this light, its posturing among the non-aligned may be regarded as a low-cost strategy to compensate for failure to develop broad bilateral relations with the Third world.

13
The United States and the Non-Aligned

The United States began for the first time to look at non-alignment with eyes misty with affection.

India Today, March 15, 1983

U.S. policy toward the Non-Aligned Movement, to the extent that it has been articulated or coherent, has fluctuated among periods of neglect, attempted rapprochement, and active rebuttal or confrontation. While the movement's radicalization since the early 1970s and repeated condemnations of U.S. policy have largely shaped American reactions to it, other factors have also played a role. U.S.–Soviet relations and the perception of Soviet inroads within the movement have clearly been a cause for concern. From 1979 to 1983, the ambiguities and emotionalism surrounding U.S.–Cuban relations further complicated acceptance by Washington of the movement's claims to be non-aligned. Disillusionment with the United Nations has also limited sympathy in the United States for its Third World majority represented by the Non-Aligned Movement. Finally, the alternation of Democratic and Republican administrations has led to shifts and discontinuities in policy toward the non-aligned.

Underlying the fluctuations in U.S. policy has been the same ambivalence that many members exhibit toward the NAM: whether it is a gathering place for Third World leaders to meet and exchange ideas without responsibility for what is said or a serious grouping of sovereign states whose declarations reflect national positions and are generally binding. If the former, a range of options from indifference to indulgent interest seems indicated. In the latter case, however, the assumption that NAM positions have direct bearing on members' bilateral relations and U.N. voting requires a response of stricter accountablity, linking performance in the NAM to members' relations with the United States. The non-aligned, of course, view such linkage as interference or subversion of the NAM, but those with friendly ties to the United States would be quick to protest if Washington endorsed attacks on them comparable with those against the United States in the NAM.

Uniquely U.S. perspectives also come to bear on the non-aligned, explaining some of the emotionalism surrounding discussion of the NAM in Washington policy circles. From a conservative viewpoint, the movement's claimed strength in numbers is not consistent with notions of an international order based on power in any traditional sense. Weight in international relations depends on a calculus of economic and military strength, leaving a movement based on assumed moral authority and unable to enforce its decisions in a distinctly ambiguous category outside the conservative frame of reference. Reactions to its often strident demands range on a emotional level from confusion to anger. Different ambiguities, perhaps more subliminal, shape liberal views of the movement. Demands from small, poor, and formerly colonized countries tend to reinforce a syndrome of liberal guilt, touching on Vietnam, conspicuous consumption in a world of poverty, and perceptions that the United States itself was wrenched from Indians, Eskimos, and Mexicans. Diffuse guilt, however, cannot be quantified, and translates into uneasiness and indecision toward the NAM.

On a practical level, another cause of uneven U.S. policies has been the problem of effectively dealing with both triennial NAM summits around the world and day-to-day operations of the non-aligned bloc in New York. This anomaly has on occasion led to a vacuum in the division of responsibility for non-aligned affairs between the Department of State and the U.S. Mission to the United Nations. The latter reports to the State Department in a formal sense, but the presence of a cabinet officer at its head gives it unique authority. Over the years, working relations have tended to be uneven, often depending on the personalities and relationship of the secretary of state and the U.N. ambassador. In practice, however, much responsibility for non-aligned affairs has devolved to New York, particularly in periods when the permanent representative has taken a personal interest in the NAM.

The Early Years

Cold War rivalries and mistrust of Soviet and Chinese activities in the Third World marked U.S. reaction to the emergence of new states during the 1950s and 1960s. The policy of containment, adopted by Washington to halt Soviet expansionism in the postwar period, frequently spilled over into the Third World and was inconsistent with the basic thrust of non-alignment. Military intervention by the Eisenhower administration in Iran (1953), Guatemala (1954) and Lebanon (1958), as well as pactomania of the Dulles era, were seen as menacing by states moving toward a definition of non-alignment. CENTO and SEATO, in particular, brought the Cold War to the Third World. Under John F. Kennedy, intervention in Cuba and emphasis on counter-insurgency and special forces tended to tarnish initiatives like the Alliance for Progress or Peace Corps. Finally, the long U.S. involvement in Vietnam corresponded with the formative, first decade of the NAM and limited U.S. opportunities for common cause with the non-aligned.

This historical context shaped the approach of successive U.S. administrations to early Third World meetings beginning with Bandung. The Eisenhower administration saw in Bandung a vehicle for extension of Chinese, and ultimately Soviet, influence, and opposed the conference from the outset. Washington, nevertheless, encouraged friendly states in attendance—Pakistan, Turkey, and the Phillipines to rebut criticism of the West. Secretary of State Dulles, in a frequently quoted speech of June 9, 1956, labeled the idea of non-alignment or neutrality as "an immoral and shortsighted conception," equating it with "indifference to the fate of others."[94]

Thus, even before the movement took form in 1961, U.S. policy was negative toward the concept of a third political grouping outside the prevailing bipolar framework. The Belgrade Summit, however, seemed preferable to Bandung, excluding as it did the Chinese and enhancing Yugoslavia's independence from Moscow. President Kennedy, therefore, sent an encouraging message to the conference that read in part:

> The peoples represented at Belgrade are committed to achieving a world of peace in which nations have the freedom to choose their own political and economic systems, and to live their own way of life, and since our earliest beginnings this nation has shared that commitment.

Reaction in Washington to the summit was nevertheless negative, based on positions taken on a range of Cold War issues. Failure to condemn Soviet violation of the moratorium on atomic testing or to take a firm position on the Berlin Wall while criticizing the United States, for example on Guantánamo, tipped the scales against the nascent NAM. Secretary of State Dean Rusk characterized U.S. official reaction to the press on September 22, 1961: "...our attitude toward the policies and positions of those at Belgrade was mixed before they went there and it was mixed after they came back."[95]

In subsequent years, the Department of State took the position in public that "genuine" non-alignment was not contrary to U.S. interests. In private, however, there was concern that the concept was potentially dangerous to U.S. interests and, in particular, conflicted with the network of regional treaties and special relationships on which American security interests were then based. In the 1956 speech quoted above, Secretary Dulles referred to security treaties concluded with 42 states as a cornerstone of U.S. global policy. A circular message of July 1964 from the State Department to American embassies abroad warned specifically:

> Except where the US is involved in a series of defensive alliances, genuine non-alignment is not incompatible with present US interests (although such a concept certainly is inconsistent with the avowed goals of Communist governments and movements throughout the world). At the same time, Communists and so-called neutralists must be prevented from exploiting non-aligned concepts, slogans, and activities in such a way as to weaken present alliances, and to increase Communist prestige, influence and penetration.

The potential threat posed by the movement to U.S. interests was considered gravest in Latin America, where outside involvement, it was thought, could undermine the special relationships embodied in the Monroe Doctrine and the Organization of American States (OAS). Early Third World gatherings had been exclusively Afro-Asian, but expanded at Belgrade to include Cuba, as well as observers from Brazil, Bolivia, and Ecuador. Prospective further enlargement at the Cairo Summit in 1964 was cause for concern in Washington, and U.S. diplomats lobbied in several Latin American capitals against attendance. Such efforts were unsuccessful, however, and in addition to Cuba, nine Latin American states attended the Second Summit as observers.

Lack of success in these early contacts led Washington policymakers to conclude that U.S. ability to influence or work constructively with the movement was limited. Following Cairo, a period of general neglect by Washington paralleled drift within the NAM itself and the Vietnam era. The United States, unlike the Soviets, sent no unofficial observers to meetings of the NAM, no further presidential or official messages, and made no attempt to rebut periodic non-aligned declarations. Cold War perceptions of the movement had persisted under the

Kennedy and Johnson administrations, otherwise committed to improving relations with the developing world through aid, more regular contacts, and the Peace Corps. There was, thus, little acknowledgment of the NAM, which was not yet viewed as a lasting phenomenon. The Bay of Pigs and Cuban missile crisis also limited enthusiasm for dealing with an organization of which Cuba was a founding member.

As the movement expanded and became more stridently anticolonial, apparent indifference by the United States was viewed by the African majority as lack of commitment to decolonization and national aspirations of new states. This perception, encouraged by Cuba and others, was reinforced by Third World suspicion of NATO and U.S. interventions in Indochina, Cuba, the Dominican Republic, Lebanon, and the Congo. A minority within the U.S. government, including its representative on the U.N. Trusteeship Council, Mason Sears, perceived the implications and potential opportunities for the United States inherent in Third World nationalism. Sears argued in memoranda of 1954 and 1956 to Dulles, and 1959 to Secretary of State Christian Herter, for open U.S. support for these aspirations while new nations were still in a formative stage.[96] His and other appeals did not, however, prevail in the Cold War atmosphere of that era.

Instead, the impression grew among the non-aligned that the United States was on the wrong side of colonial issues and that progress toward decolonization would be made only over opposition from Washington. By the late 1970s, this perception was so strong that even clear U.S. support for independence of Zimbabwe and efforts for a solution in Namibia did not alter opinion in the movement or limit its anti-imperialist rhetoric. Tanzanian President Julius Nyerere charged in 1977, for example, that "America has continued to look at African affairs through anti-communist spectacles and to disregard Africa's different concerns and priorities."[97] In the politically charged forum of the NAM, such suspicions contributed to U.S. isolation and willingness by most members to go along with a consensus condemning U.S. policy on a range of issues. At Colombo in 1976, some even argued for addition of "Kissingerism" to the litany of evils against which the NAM must guard.[98]

Confrontation

Neglect of the Non-Aligned Movement ended with the Algiers Summit of 1973. In its aftermath, the developed countries were faced with concerted demands for the NIEO and convulsions in the world oil market. The Sixth Special Session on Raw Materials and Development that followed in New York in 1974 left the United States isolated on many issues from the Third World and even European allies. Reassessment of the Non-Aligned Movement and U.S. policy toward it also coincided with recognition of changes in the United Nations and reduced U.S. influence. In this connection, Secretary of State Henry Kissinger complained regularly about "alignment of the non-aligned," and Ambassador John Scali attacked "tyranny of the majority" in a speech to the General Assembly in December 1974.

Kissinger was, nevertheless, forced by the oil price shock and the Algiers Summit to recognize the movement's impact and adjust U.S. policy to take it more fully into account. Speaking at New Delhi in October 1974, he avowed that "the United States recognizes non-alignment" and that "our relations with the non-aligned countries are another pillar of our foreign policy." With some foreboding, he continued: "It is a corollary of this, however, that bloc diplomacy of any kind is anachronistic and self-defeating. We see a danger of new patterns of alignment that are as artificial, rigid and ritualistic as the old ones."[99]

The result of continuing review in Washington was a new tactic, both toward the NAM and the United Nations in general, of rebutting charges against the United States forcefully and in full. This approach was particularly evident during the 1975–76 term of Daniel Patrick Moynihan as U.S. ambassador to the United Nations. Moynihan writes: "The tactic, initiated at this Mission on instruction of the President [Gerald Ford] and the Secretary of State [Henry Kissinger], has been to respond to attack by counterattack."[100] Underlying the Moynihan strategy were two assumptions: that the Non-Aligned Movement was hostile to U.S. interests and that, as the largest political bloc at the United Nations, it was vulnerable to breakup if directly attacked. Moynihan had concluded that "In the 1970s the non-aligned nations have consistently supported international action which has had the effect or would have the effect of slowing American growth."[101] In support of his argument that the movement could be destroyed, he quotes a memorandum of February 1976 to Secretary of State Kissinger from Assistant Secretary of State for International Organizations Samuel Lewis, to the effect that non-aligned solidarity had reached a peak with the Sixth Special Session and now had "nowhere to go but down." The memo concluded, "The logic of the situation, therefore, is with us."[102]

Confrontation involved regular rebuttal by the U.S. delegation of criticism or hostile positions in the General Assembly and myriad committees of the United Nations. The result was heated rhetoric and increased acrimony on both sides. In the post-Vietnam and post-Watergate period, the Moynihan policy was perceived domestically as standing up for U.S. interests against a hostile Third World majority, and struck a responsive chord among Americans disillusioned with the United Nations. It failed, however, to significantly alter positions of the non-aligned or bring about the movement's demise. As an avowed policy objective, the dissolution of the NAM was probably self-defeating, although Moynihan claimed in a telegram, released on January 28, 1976, to have made progress "toward a basic foreign policy goal, that of breaking up the massive blocs of nations."[103] The cable continued: "The non-aligned or Group of 77, or whatever, are groups made up of extraordinarily disparate nations, with greatly disparate interests. Their recent bloc-like unity was artificial and was bound to break up." The movement did not break up, however, although mutual suspicion between the non-aligned and Washington grew by confrontation. The policy probably contributed as well to the objective of NAM radicals and the Soviets to portray the United States as number-one enemy of the Third World.

Rapprochement

By mid-1976, confrontation had evolved into a more restrained U.S. approach toward the non-aligned, based on persuasion and quiet diplomacy. Consultations with selected non-aligned states in their capitals and by Moynihan's successor, William Scranton, at the United Nations were substituted for plenary rhetoric and threats of reprisal in bilateral relations. The revised U.S. strategy coincided with the end of Algeria's presidency and a period of relative moderation under Sri Lanka. The United States took a more active role in consulting with non-aligned members in advance of the Colombo Summit and sent a State Department officer as an unofficial observer of the proceedings. This more moderate approach, adopted late in the Ford administration, may have contributed to the increased number of reservations entered at Colombo on anti-American sections of the Summit Declaration on issues such as Panama, Puerto Rico, Korea, and the Middle East.

The Carter administration continued efforts toward rapprochement with a presidential message, requested by Yugoslavia, to the non-aligned foreign ministers' conference at Belgrade in 1978, the first such U.S. greeting since 1961, although the Soviets had sent high-level messages to all since the 1964 Cairo Summit. The Carter initiative was part of a larger effort to improve relations with the developing countries and encourage awareness of human rights. Improved dialogue with the Third World majority, a cornerstone of this policy, was emphasized in speeches of Secretary of State Cyrus Vance and personal diplomacy by Ambassador Andrew Young at the United Nations.

Within the State Department and National Security Council, a series of interagency meetings were held in the period prior to the Havana Summit to craft a more constructive approach to the movement. The purpose was to devise a strategy; not just to limit damage to United States interests, as in the past, but to find alternatives to confrontation over North–South issues and to limit opportunities for Soviet exploitation. Strategies studied by Washington policymakers and discussed with the British and other NATO allies included plans for more concerted lobbying to offset Cuban and Soviet momentum before Havana. Success depended, however, on a more active role in the movement by states friendly to the United States, and consideration was even given to encouraging membership by moderate Third World states outside the movement, particularly in Latin America.

Agreement could not be reached, however, on a comprehensive policy toward the non-aligned. The stumbling block remained unresolved doubts whether, even with the most carefully crafted diplomacy, the movement could play a positive role in terms of U.S. interests. Skeptics argued that its continuing anti-colonial bias ensured hostility and restricted Western diplomacy to damage limitation. Quiet contacts, nevertheless, continued in selected NAM capitals on specific issues of concern to the United States. An American diplomat was assigned to cover the 1978 ministerial meeting at Belgrade and the 1979 session of the NACB in Colombo that led up to the Havana Summit. Informal conversations between U.S. diplomats and counterparts in the NAM centered on the need for moderation on issues that Cuba was expected to exploit at the summit, including the equation of Zionism and racism, Puerto Rico, Guantánamo, the Panama Canal, and U.S. troops in Korea.

In effect, the United States had chosen a moment of maximum Cuban and Soviet influence over the movement to attempt to redress what Washington perceived as non-aligned bias. The atmosphere at Havana allowed little scope for the United States or even friendly non-aligned states to affect the proceedings or moderate strident criticism of the United States. Fidel Castro charged in his opening address that "Yankee imperialists" had obtained a draft of the Havana Declaration (freely circulated by NAM members in New York) and "made feverish diplomatic contacts" to rewrite it or block the summit in Cuba.[104] Two U.S. Foreign Service officers, assigned as unofficial observers to follow the meeting, were kept under close surveillance by Cuban intelligence but nonetheless, charged the official daily, *Granma*, ran a "NATO spy ring."

Increased U.S. attention to the NAM lent plausibility to Castro's adept exploitation of the Soviet brigade episode as an American effort to sabotage the Havana Summit. By apparent coincidence, U.S. intelligence documenting maneuvers by a Soviet brigade in Cuba had leaked on the eve of the summit to a technical journal, *Aviation Week and Space Technology.* Senator Frank Church of Idaho, then facing a losing campaign for reelection, seized on the issue to demand "immediate removal of all Russian combat troops from Cuba."[105] Reaction, complicated by an intense campaign in progress for ratification of the SALT II Treaty, was strong in Washington, and National Security Adviser Zbigniew Brzezinski publicly labeled Castro a "Soviet puppet." The timing and inexplicable U.S. reaction to the presence in Cuba,for at least a decade, of a Soviet brigade convinced NAM delegates that the incident was a propaganda ploy to discredit Cuba and the Sixth Summit. Typical of non-aligned reaction, Yugoslav Foreign Secretary Mojsov described the episode as an "unwieldy and clumsy drive aimed at compromising Havana as the venue of the Summit."[106]

Controversy over the brigade underscored the contradictions between hopes of the Carter administration for improved relations with the developing countries and presidency of the major Third World political body by a Soviet client state. Cuba's success in achieving a new peak of strident opposition to Western policy could only call into question further attempts to work constructively with the non-aligned. Efforts to improve bilateral relations with Cuba, including an exchange of modest interest sections in 1977 and release during the summit of Puerto Rican terrorists convicted of armed attacks on the U.S. Congress, also had failed because of Cuba's refusal even to consider reduction of troop levels in Africa.

The summit and related issues of the brigade and U.S.–Cuban relations received heavy coverage in American media, and in its aftermath negative public opinion toward Castro was applied equally to the NAM. Official reaction by White House and State Department spokesmen to the summit was uniformly negative, and policymakers, not for the first time, concluded there was no real prospect for influencing non-aligned behavior. Seizure of American hostages by Iran deepened the perception of U.S. weakness and, while non-aligned states like Algeria were vital mediators, there remained little enthusiasm in an election year for building new bridges to the NAM. The Soviet invasion of Afghanistan, which weakened Cuba's grip on the movement, also, paradoxically, turned U.S. attention away from the Third World and NAM. Underlining, as it did, Soviet ability to project military power, Afghanistan left a foreign policy based on improved relations with the Third World vulnerable to charges of weakness and irrelevance.

Confrontation Again?

Ironically, as the Non-Aligned Movement entered a period of potential change in the aftermath of Afghanistan and the transition to a new NAM chairman, U.S. policy returned to a primary focus on East–West issues, solidarity of the Western alliance, and military strength. The electoral mandate of the Reagan administration to reverse the erosion of American influence abroad did not preclude dialogue with the Third World such as the Cancún Summit, but the initial priorities in foreign affairs lay elsewhere. Moreover, renewed attention to Soviet expansionism led many in Washington to view with suspicion, and perhaps to overestimate, the degree of Cuban and Soviet influence on the movement. Tentative efforts of the Carter administration toward rapprochement with the non-aligned, coming at a moment of maximum inflexibility and anti-Westernism, clearly had not succeeded. In this area, as elsewhere, a new administration sought to differentiate its policies from those of its predecessors.

The February 1981 ministerial conference in New Delhi provided grounds for an initial assessment of the movement. The meeting was the first major gathering of the non-aligned since the Havana Summit, and the Reagan administration's first exposure to the NAM. The results at New Delhi were moderate by the standards of Havana and, at a press briefing on February 17, 1981, the State Department spokesman praised the call for troop withdrawals from Afghanistan and Kampuchea while dismissing positions taken on the Middle East as "absurd formulations."

While the Havana Summit had generated intense comment and reaction in Washington, the decision to comment on lesser ministerial meetings reflected a renewed willingness to react and, if necessary, to rebut direct criticism. To stay informed on non-aligned developments, the practice was continued of assigning diplomats to cover non-aligned meetings, but officials, including the author, who traveled to New Delhi in 1981 and 1983 adopted a low profile and confined themselves to reporting on major decisions of these meetings. Two such officers, assigned to augment the small U.S. mission in Havana during a June 1982 meeting of the NACB, were denied entry visas by Cuba.

Recent contact with the non-aligned as a group has, however, been largely centered in New York, where U.S. isolation at the United Nations was ascribed in part to hostility of the Third World majority, often shaped by positions of the NAM. Initially, officials of the Reagan administration at the United Nations followed a policy of not dealing directly with or even referring to the NAM in order not to further enhance and legitimize its status in the U.N. system. Instead, American delegates attempted to work with regional groups or directly with individual countries. Yet group dynamics at the United Nations were by then too strong, and the integration of regional groups within the structure of the NAM too advanced, to reverse these trends. Evidence was clear-cut of increasing non-aligned cohesion in General Assembly voting and activities on the Security Council.

By 1982, both U.S. and Soviet representatives were regularly referring in the General Assembly to NAM declarations and non-aligned positions on various issues. In right of reply to Cuba, U.S. Ambassador Kenneth Adelman, for example, twice challenged Castro's claim to speak for the non-aligned. Soviet Permanent Representative Oleg A. Troyanovsky cited with approval the Havana NACB decision of June 1982 "to put an end to the outflow of financial resources from developing countries through transnational corporations." Only in the Security Council was there a concerted effort by the United States to consult with members on a individual or regional basis, in order not to further galvanize the non-aligned group.

Faced with the need to deal with the non-aligned in the conduct of routine U.N. business, U.S. Ambassador Jeane Kirkpatrick attempted to curb unbalanced criticism of the United States by holding individual states responsible for consensus positions of the NAM. The test case was a non-aligned communiqué of September 28, 1981, resulting from the annual ministerial meeting in New York to coordinate non-aligned strategy before the General Assembly. Such meetings and resulting declarations are not usually considered major events in the NAM, and attendance tends to be sporadic because of concurrent proceedings in the United Nations.

While admitting its anti-American bias, one Asian diplomat contended that the communiqué was "just not important enough to fight over."[107] Yet for Senator Moynihan, it represented "the most supinely pro-Soviet, anti-American, anti-democratic pronouncement ever adopted by these 93 nations."[108] Its contents, drafted by Cuba and circulated as an official General Assembly document to all U.N. members, led Kirkpatrick to respond astringently by letter of October 6 to 64 non-aligned members with which the United States has relatively good relations and, in most cases, bilateral aid programs. At the same time, U.S. embassies in those capitals were instructed to express official displeasure and urge governments to dissociate from the communiqué.[109]

The Kirkpatrick letter (Appendix G) pointed out that the 21-page declaration criticized the United States no less than "nine times by name and dozens of times by implication" while refraining from mention of the Soviet Union despite "continuing military occupation of Afghanistan, Kampuchea and Chad—all with the support of the USSR." The letter further took exception to charges of U.S. aggression against Libya and efforts to "destabilize" Grenada and Nicaragua, and stated that the offending communiqué had "no more claims to being truly non-aligned than does the Permanent Mission of Cuba which issued it." The crux of Kirkpatrick's argument was that such "base lies and malicious attacks on the good name of the United States" did not represent an "accurate reflection" of most governments' positions, and that they should, therefore, dissociate from this and future unbalanced NAM positions.

The Kirkpatrick letter was the first instance of the United States initiating an on-the-record written exchange with the movement. It thus represented official recognition of the organization's role and the attention paid it by the United States, as well as a challenge to individual members to reconcile contradictory bilateral and multilateral behavior. Reaction to it varied among recipients and non-recipients. Some, like Malawi, Saudi Arabia, St. Lucia, and Tunisia, pointed out their absence from the meeting. Others claimed to have noted reservations orally to Cuba, while 22 states reported that they had dissociated in writing. Some frequent supporters of the United States were, however, unwilling to dissociate because of internal or regional pressures. Others expressed private frustration about being put on the spot when, they claimed, private negotiation in advance could have moderated the document.

Among the radical fringe, the letter was exploited as American interference in the NAM, and Cuban officials handed out copies in the U.N. Delegates' Lounge. The Cuban official daily, *Granma*, charged on October 29 that America's "hysterical, cynical and blackmail policy against the NAM" was due to "increasing influence of the NAM in the world forum, especially in the United Nations, where the NAM has given more than one defeat to the adventurous and hegemonistic aggressiveness of the Yankee imperialists."

As a one-time warning, the Kirkpatrick letter had two positive effects. It helped to persuade the non-activist majority of the movement that NAM positions should be considered in a wider context, including relations with the United States. It also demonstrated that the United States takes the movement seriously and treats its positions as the considered product of mature and sovereign states. As a regular tactic, however, confrontation risks enhancing the status of the movement and reinforcing its anti-Western bias. Being called on the carpet also can antagonize U.S. supporters in the movement, whose efforts to restore a measure of balance after the Cuban years are complicated by confrontation with Washington.

Subsequent communiqués from NAM meetings during 1982 at Kuwait, Havana, and Nicosia, Cyprus, were equally strident in criticism of the United States, but were within the NACB context and largely devoted to regional issues. A more valid test of the Kirkpatrick strategy was the next ministerial meeting in New York, on October 4–9, 1982. Its final communiqué specifically condemned the United States in five instances, but in less harsh terms than before. Moderates, well aware of U.S. scrutiny and probably anxious to retain or increase their share of U.S. aid, played a more prominent role, but were unable to delete the offending references or insert balancing criticism of the Soviet Union. Nevertheless, the modest improvement in 1982 probably reflected the earlier U.S. intervention, as well as further deterioration in Cuban control of the NAM.

From the U.S. perspective, a particularly unfortunate concession, extracted by Cuba at the October 1982 meeting in return for acquiescing in somewhat more moderate language, was the agreement to hold a special NACB meeting in Nicaragua during January 1983. The Managua meeting was a dilemma for Washington. It was sure to provide a forum for radicals to undercut any gains from the Kirkpatrick letter and from a more than usually constructive General Assembly, at which non-aligned majorities had thwarted Cuban and Soviet ploys to embarrass the United States over Puerto Rico and Micronesia, passed resolutions on chemical weapons, and voted for withdrawal of foreign troops from Afghanistan and Kampuchea. Managua also gave the Sandinista regime, as we have seen, a captive NAM audience before which to castigate U.S. policy in Central America.

Faced with these prospects, the tactical choice for Washington was between ignoring Managua as a minor NAM meeting without long-term significance and mounting a diplomatic campaign of damage limitation.

Activism prevailed, and worldwide efforts were undertaken to point out inaccuracies and lack of balance in Nicaragua's draft communiqué and to encourage moderate members to attend in order to offset the influence of a radical minority. While some countries begged off on the basis that Latin American issues were remote to their interests and that New Delhi would be a more important proving ground for the NAM, in the end 116 delegations, including 87 member states, attended. Managua was the largest extraordinary meeting of the NACB to date, stretching facilities and far exceeding Nicaraguan expectations of 50–70 delegations. Yet intensive lobbying was based on an unrealistic assessment of U.S. ability to influence the results and ended up by giving the meeting an importance it would not otherwise have enjoyed.

It was impossible to keep such widespread demarches secret, and the Sandinista press had a field day with distorted accounts of U.S. "subversion," front-paging as proof of American interference the text of an alleged aide-mémoire delivered by the U.S. ambassador in Buenos Aires.[110] The single Foreign Service officer assigned to cover the meeting was repeatedly cited in the press for "pressuring NAM delegations." Efforts by the American ambassador in Managua to get across that normal diplomatic contacts did not constitute an "attempt to sabotage the meeting" were largely unheeded.[111] Washington's response to press inquiries showed clear disappointment with the results:

> We regret that certain members of the Non-aligned Movement have seen fit to use the Coordinating Bureau's meeting in Managua as a forum for propaganda against the United States and to attempt to impose a philosophy inimical to the basic precepts of non-alignment. While we want to study the document further, the US considers that the communique does little to advance a constructive approach to the complex problems it addresses.

The Managua episode showed once again the difficulty of countering propaganda by countries like Cuba, Nicaragua, and Vietnam within the closed confines of a NAM meeting. In a controlled environment like Managua, there is no counterbalance to the radical litany of U.S. aggression and imperialism. Delegates were not told, for example, that the small number of American military advisors then in Central America posed no threat to the 75,000-man Nicaraguan army and militia, which were advised by 2,000 Cuban and Soviet-bloc military and security personnel. Nor was it possible to remind them that in the first 18 months of the Sandinista revolution, the United States provided more aid than all other countries combined, and more than U.S. aid over a decade to the Somoza regime. Or that, while claiming to want negotiations with the United States, Nicaragua has broken off contact whenever they appeared imminent. In other words, the deck is stacked at such meetings, and even states closely allied with the United States tended to accept Nicaragua's accusations at face value in the atmosphere of Managua.

The six weeks between Managua and the New Delhi Summit provided little time for a new round of diplomatic efforts. In any case, the more balanced draft declaration, circulated on February 14 by India, while still containing many positions anathema to Washington, provided less ground for complaint, lulling moderates and outsiders alike into a false sense of security. In the interim, American diplomats continued to stress in contacts with the non-aligned and in public statements that the United States may not always agree with NAM positions, but respects the principles of non-alignment. The latter, they stressed, require avoidance of unfairness or bias toward non-member states. Consultations along these lines were held prior to the summit by Under Secretary of State Lawrence Eagleburger in Belgrade and by Assistant Secretary of State Gregory Newell in New Delhi and other Asian capitals. The hope was clearly that New Delhi would herald a reassertion of centrist leadership and that, if the United States were attacked by name, Moscow would equally be cited for occupation of Afghanistan and other violations of non-aligned principle. Without such balance, critical reference to U.S. policy in Central America, Puerto Rico, or Diego Garcia seemed to Washington patently unfair.

In light of consultations among the non-aligned and hopes that the Seventh Summit would set a new pattern for the movement over the next three years, a decision was taken to follow the Kennedy and Carter precedent of a presidential letter to the meeting. Writing to Mrs. Gandhi as the incoming chairman on February 16, 1983, President Reagan underscored that the United States shares the ideals of non-alignment as "fundamental guidelines for relations among states" (Appendix F). Citing Kennedy's message to the Belgrade Summit, Reagan's letter stated that "The United States remains as committed today, as in 1961, to the principles upon which non-alignment is based."

During the actual summit, three Foreign Service officers augmented the U.S. Embassy staff in New Delhi, although they were depicted in the Communist press as a high-level delegation of 12.[112] Their efforts were directed at following the closed proceedings from afar in order to provide Washington with a timely assessment of their outcome. There was, in any case, no prospect for outsiders or even members of the NAM to alter the outcome once regional groups sent back a totally rewritten political declaration, reminiscent of Managua, through the political committees to the heads of state.

Few with whom the United States had consulted in advance spoke up in any regional group. Some argued that President Reagan's decision in early March to seek $60 million in emergency military aid to El Salvador made it impossible to argue effectively for moderation. Based on past performance, there is little evidence that those who claimed this would otherwise have played a more assertive role. The press announcement was, nevertheless, widely cited by the Nicaraguan "Foreign Minister," Rev. D'Escoto Brockman. There were also concurrent U.S. initiatives viewed favorably by non-aligned moderates such as the Reagan letter to Indira Gandhi, a concurrent presidential letter of February 14 to General Ershad of Bangladesh as chairman of the G-77, and U.S. support for a 50 percent increase in IMF country quotas.

The Decision-making Process

The preceding summary of U.S. policy since the early 1960s toward the non-aligned is one of fluctuation and multiple turning points. The Non-Aligned Movement has, to be sure, changed and evolved during this period, but swings in the U.S. policy pendulum have not necessarily corresponded to developments within the NAM. Some, such as the Carter administration's attempted rapprochement at a moment of maximum Cuban and Soviet influence, have been poorly synchronized and have stemmed from pressures and policy disputes within the U.S. government rather than careful assessment of the NAM. In Washington, unrelated foreign policy issues often become hostage to internal bureaucratic rivalries. In the late 1970s, polarization between advocates and opponents of the SALT II Treaty clearly impinged on policy toward the NAM. Supporters of SALT II, for example, protected themselves in policy debates by a less conciliatory posture toward the Third World. The issues were also inextricably linked in a U.S. campaign year by Castro's presidency of the NAM and publicity surrounding Soviet troops in Cuba.

Optimism, perhaps unfounded, that the United States as a superpower can and should play an active role in the major Third World political grouping has tended to affect policy toward the non-aligned. Yet over the years, U.S. initiatives, lacking a coherent framework, have concentrated piecemeal on specific issues or crises. In the aftermath of the Algiers Summit, for example, Third World solidarity caught the United States by surprise, and generated intense and sometimes contradictory reactions. Similarly, the prospect of a summit in Havana and Cuban domination of the NAM led to intense review of U.S. options. Yet such crisis management, endemic to Washington, risks becoming a purely internal bureaucratic process designed to demonstrate that a particular office or department is "on top of the problem." The NAM, with summits every three years and relative lulls in between, is itself episodic and encourages an erratic policy toward it. If, between summits, there has been a change of U.S. administrations, awareness of the NAM tends to be diminished and swings of the policy pendulum greater.

Faced with an impending summit of the NAM, whether at Havana, Baghdad, or New Delhi, and nearly certain condemnation of the United States on issues ranging from Puerto Rico to the Middle East, the usual bureaucratic response has been a "package" of actions intended to "cover all bases." Components might well be consultations on the NAM with NATO allies, briefings for Congress, embassy demarches in selected NAM capitals, presentation of U.S. views on the likely agenda to a wider spectrum of NAM members, and public reaction to non-aligned declarations.

Such a package provides reassurance that the problem is in hand, but may be little more than a series of disconnected conversations without a unifying strategy or practical effect on events. Patchwork demarches also cast the outsider in a suspect and carping role of constantly lecturing NAM members on what positions to take. U.S. interventions are frequently resented and, in a world where real influence is often image, tend to be ineffectual. Missing from such an approach is a coordinated response to basic questions about the NAM: whether a strong Third World political grouping is, on balance, in U.S. global interests; what U.S. influence within it could realistically be; and whether U.S. policy should attempt to moderate and enhance the movement or to reduce its impact in favor of bilateral relations, regional groups, or other international forums.

A separate and important dimension of policy toward the NAM is represented by Congress and the intersection of U.S. public opinion with foreign policy. In the U.S. system, decisions on strategy toward a bloc such as the non-aligned nations cannot be taken in a vacuum by the executive branch. U.S. economic assistance, received in some form by the majority of NAM members, involves congressional responsibilities and close supervision of the appropriations process. Details on the behavior of aid recipients in New York, within both the NAM and the

United Nations, are frequently more publicized and more available to Congress than facts on economic development in individual countries. Lack of congressional backing for the United Nations and pressures to reduce foreign aid, particularly in a period of recession and cutbacks in domestic programs, further heighten reaction on Capitol Hill to strident criticism by recipients of U.S. aid.

Although the September 1981 ministerial meetings were considered routine by the non-aligned, their location in New York and the publicity surrounding the Kirkpatrick letter prompted a strong congressional reaction. Senator Moynihan introduced an amendment to the 1982 Foreign Aid Bill to deny economic or military assistance to any non-aligned state that did not dissociate itself in writing from the communiqué. A modified version, adopted 88–0 by the Senate, called on the president "to take into account," when acting on future aid requests, whether a country had disavowed the document. The final legislation, not requiring specific reporting by the president, cleared both the House and Senate, and was signed by President Reagan on December 5, 1981.

In practice, a mandatory cutoff of aid would probably have been difficult to enforce, since reservations taken on the communiqué were never published officially by the NAM and could not be verified in all cases. The amendment nevertheless represents a warning shot by the Congress. While there is no evidence to date of aid reductions because of performance in the NAM, State Department officials testifying before congressional committees were subsequently questioned on repudiation of the communiqué in connection with new aid requests. As Senator R.W. Kasten, Jr., of Wisconsin said during debate on the amendment, its purpose was to "put countries on notice that we will look at their attitudes in international forums and the cheap shots at the US will have a cost in the future." Senator Moynihan pointed out, further, that for donor countries, "it is not unreasonable to expect not to be vilified by the receiver, not to have vicious lies stated by the country one is wishing to assist." The amendment nevertheless provoked accusations of outside interference in NAM decision-making. Reaction in Havana, predictably, went further:

> This action can't be seen as only directed as blackmail against those who agreed with a certain document, but rather as a cynical and powerful weapon with a greater goal: that of trying to undermine NAM unity, that of modifying its efficiency by buying off a government here and there, that of blunting its anti-imperialist edge.[113]

As a warning, the Moynihan amendment has not worked, judging from subsequent unrestrained criticism of the United States in NAM documents. The philosophy it embodied is, nevertheless, rooted in growing unpopularity of foreign aid with the taxpayer and popular resentment of aid recipients perceived as "biting the hand that feeds them." The possibility of more binding future legislation thus cannot be excluded. It would essentially be an attempt to accomplish by legislative means what diplomacy has clearly failed to achieve.

As with other blanket legislation in foreign affairs, explicit linkage of aid levels and performance in the NAM or United Nations would almost certainly be cumbersome. It would also alienate many countries, pushing them further toward the Soviet Union. Across-the-board legislation unavoidably limits the diplomatic flexibility needed to maintain and strengthen U.S. interests in a changing world. Countries generally well-disposed toward the United States, like Sudan, Jamaica, Kenya, Jordan, Malaysia, and Nigeria, were unable or unwilling, for varying reasons, to disavow the 1981 ministerial declaration. Mandatory action against such states, which share important interests with the United States, would undercut U.S. influence in strategic regions that the Soviets are seeking to penetrate. Nor is it likely that rhetoric in the NAM can be muted by congressional legislation. The absence of U.S. constituencies for foreign aid and the United Nations nevertheless, ensures continuing close scrutiny by Congress, particularly when the foreign aid bill is under consideration on Capitol Hill. This watchdog function introduces a further imponderable in decision-making related to the NAM, but is also essential to keep diplomacy in tune and responsive to the pubic will.

14

The Future of the NAM

Its past is one of which we can be justly proud, its present condition does it no credit, and finally, if it persists in its present course, its future will be one of shameful oblivion.

S. Rajaratnan, March 1983

Returning to the distinction between non-alignment as a concept and as an institution, made in Chapter 1, the two have fared differently since the early 1960s. Former Indian Prime Minister Morarji Desai redefined non-alignment, during a February 27, 1983, symposium at the Indian International Center, as simply meaning "that states should judge everything on merit and settle disputes by discussion and negotiation, not by resort to force." In these broad terms, it remains as relevant today as when it emerged following World War II, and continues to provide a philosophical framework and middle ground for states not directly party to the struggles of East and West.

Much can happen, however, between an idea and its institutional implementation. Bureaucratic and political pressures, if unchecked, can so transform a general concept like non-alignment that the resulting institution bears little relation to its founders' intent. Thus, while the theory of non-alignment remains universally applicable, the movement's failure to live up to it has eroded confidence in the NAM. As at the United Nations, repetition of anti-colonial and NIEO rhetoric to avoid real issues dividing the membership has introduced a phoniness that corrodes the original sense of mission and unity.

As the movement enlarged and institutionalized, it became the province of government bureaucrats more concerned with NAM procedure, consensus, and organizational issues than with new ideas or perspectives. Bureaucracy and rote replaced the intellectual renewal that characterized Bandung, Belgrade, and even Algiers. In the words of M.S. Rajan, "It would seem that short of a multilateral treaty (like the UN Charter) spelling out in legal terms the constitution, purposes, functions etc. of the Movement, and a permanent secretariat (like the UN Secretariat or the Commonwealth Secretariat), the Non-aligned

Movement has acquired the features of an international organization."[114] In appealing for an infusion of new thought, Dr. Soedjatmoko of the U.N. University in Tokyo speaks of the "intellectual impotence" of the South and concludes that "the non-aligned lost confidence in their own pluralistic vision of global solidarity that first brought them together."[115]

Bureaucratic hardening of the arteries has complicated and postponed the movement's adjustment to a changed world, requiring new priorities of its members. In part, this has also been a result of success in bringing the colonial era to an end and in guaranteeing the survival of newly independent states. To be sure, colonial empires were already collapsing under their own weight and demands of the postwar period. Yet the NAM accelerated pressure on the remaining, recalcitrant few. Despite U.N. resolutions calling for an "immediate end" to colonialism, its demise came faster than anyone would have predicted in 1961, depriving the movement in a short time of its central mission. Some subsequently argued that, having achieved its goal, it should be disbanded and that further costly summits, largely duplicating meetings at the United Nations, today have little purpose.[116]

Proposals to disband, except those made by Burma in 1979, were, however, in large part facetious and neglected the important psychological dimensions of membership. Over the years, the movement had provided a platform for leaders like Julius Nyerere and Kenneth Kaunda who otherwise might not have gained such international attention and stature. For them and others, it was a convenient vehicle to project the needs and concerns of smaller countries onto a world stage. Through the NAM they had a collective impact on Western thinking, not in mediating on disarmament or East–West issues, but in structuring the agenda, terms of dialogue, and ways of thinking about relations between North and South. The 1980 Brandt Commission Report, *Programme for Survival,* unmistakeably reflected the idiom of the Third World and broad exposure by its authors to positions of the non-aligned.

Yet, overall, non-aligned influence on the West—except for specific and focused pressure for decolonization—has tended to be diffuse and without tangible benefit to the Third World. In the absence of clear-cut non-aligned priorities, individual members have often been unable to separate the movement and its objectives from their own national preoccupations. Otherwise scholarly Indian accounts of the origins of non-alignment, for example, often simply retrace India's own historical development, starting with positions of the Indian National Congress in 1885. By the same token, the end game of summits became for members to lobby for NAM endorsements of national objectives. Argentina would go to meetings determined to win the larger group to its side in the conflict with Britain, and Bolivia to enshrine, as it did at the New Delhi Summit, its claim aginst Chile for an outlet to the Pacific. Yet such national campaigns were often irrelevant or even in conflict with the movement's broader aims. For example, since Falklanders have unanimously opted for continued association with Britain, NAM backing for Argentina's claim was inconsistent with long-standing support for self-determination.

The emergence by the late 1970s of regional groups as the basic decision-making units of the NAM was an extension of the failure to distinguish between national and non-aligned objectives. By political trade-offs and agreement to support each other's claims, states could more easily gain approval for national goals in the smaller regional groups. By the same principle, a regional package of assorted national claims and positions would be accepted without challenge by other regional groups eager to preserve intact their own positions. In the process, Arab, African, and Central American foreign policy became ipso facto that of the Non-Aligned Movement as a whole. Yet given the movement's diversity and inherent pluralism, the expectation of a common foreign policy is, in the words of M.S. Rajan, "not only absurd on the face of it but also subversive of freedom and equality among the members of the group, which is the essential foundation of non-alignment."[117]

To be sure, representing two-thirds of the U.N. community, the non-aligned could be expected to have a majority of the world's problems. Yet the movement, like NATO confronting the perennial problems of Greece and Turkey, has been externally oriented and ill-prepared to resolve differences within. Issues, perhaps manageable in a bilateral context, tend, as at the U.N., to be recast by the majority along ideological lines. Superpower reaction to the contradictions inherent in NAM summit declarations has tended toward posturing designed to win non-aligned support at no cost from the Soviet Union and indifference or disappointment from the West.

External Changes

The NAM, as we have seen, originated in reaction to a particular historical moment, characterized by the emergence of a large number of former colonies into a bipolar world split between East and West.

Non-aligned doctrine, which evolved in the early years and continues to be regularly reaffirmed, defined the movement and its role largely in relation to the two superpowers. The world, in the meantime, moved into a multipolar phase, and by the end of the century power will have evolved even further from the superpower framework on which the NAM is based. The present five-cornered power structure of the United States, USSR, EC-10, Japan, and China introduces new complexity, with different risks and options for the Third World. The ideological and military division between East and West remains, but the interplay and balance with other power centers is infinitely more subtle, and must be understood by a movement seeking to engineer world peace.

Within the Third World, the reappearance of China, after years of introversion, has already raised basic questions. Beijing perceives its role as "defender of Third World interests," but to date has lacked the necessary diplomatic and economic resources and has stood outside the established groupings of the NAM and G-77. Yet its ambition to assume the mantle of Third World leadership is clear. Premier Zhao Ziyang's trip to Africa in January 1983 was in sharp contrast with that of his predecessor, Zhou Enlai, two decades earlier. Zhao was not preaching the Maoist gospel of revolt against established governments; instead, he was seeking to work with them to cement ties between China and the Third World. Even in pro-Soviet capitals like Addis Ababa, Maputo, and Luanda, Beijing is now actively competing to offset the influence of Moscow.

Chinese strategy toward the Third World is not parallel, but tangential, to the NAM. As B. Vivekanandan points out, China belongs to the Third World, and not the NAM, because it is specifically "aligned against imperialism and hegemonism," and thus uncomfortable with non-aligned theories of either equidistance or natural alliance.[118] As a practical matter, non-aligned fears of domination by the Chinese giant would preclude NAM membership, and periodically rumored feelers from Beijing have, therefore, come to nothing. China's role on the periphery of the movement is, nevertheless, likely to represent a powerful force and alternative model for some members. While Chinese policy will continue to be based on relations with Washington and Moscow, its role and standing in the Third World offer leverage with both. The theory of "double hegemonism," evolved by Beijing in 1982 to treat the United States and USSR as equal threats to the peace, rests in large part on strengthened ties to the Third World.

Nor is the multipolar phenomenon entirely external to the movement. States within the NAM itself will probably emerge, if not as superpowers, then as major political, economic, military, and nuclear forces in their region. The emergence of states like Iraq and Iran was accelerated during the 1970s by OPEC success in forcing up oil prices and by the reliance of NATO and Warsaw Pact members on arms transfers to improve their own balance of payments and to gain influence in the Third World. India, long concerned by China's power, has already developed industrial, agricultural, and nuclear bases for the future. Its ambition for influence throughout an expanded Indian Ocean region may or may not prove consistent with purely non-aligned goals. As other regional centers of power emerge within and outside the NAM, there will be conflicting trends to avoid isolation by clinging to the movement, and to drift toward regional or more narrowly focused groupings.

The result of these new complexities and pressures is likely to be a period of prolonged adjustment within the NAM. The apparatus of decision by consensus and cumbersome summits, however, works against change, and the tendency to date has been to adhere to past "consensual wisdom." Rather than explore divisive causes of economic and structural weakness in the Third World, members have been content to blame outside forces, the United States, as the most developed economy, being a primary target. Yet at a given point, real-world problems impinge and demand solution. If the movement is to survive as more than a nostalgic, fraternal order, it must confront its inner contradictions and provide responses more relevant to the general membership.

Economic differences, in particular, have exacerbated the political gulf between moderates and radicals in the movement. During Cuba's presidency and the radicalism of the NIEO decade, moderates were generally outmaneuvered and ineffective in representing their positions within the NAM. Political conservatism combined with reliance on free markets to isolate Singapore, Malaysia, Indonesia, Saudi Arabia, Kuwait and others from radicals advocating state-controlled economies. By 1983, however, pressures for a more pragmatic and issue-by-issue approach, rather than insistence on an ideological package, offered some hope that such countries could play a stronger role.

The major challenge to non-alignment thus will not be to reach a paperwork consensus on irreconcilable political issues, but to forge solidarity on the basis of a new, more realistic economic package. As Ambassador C.B. Muthamma pointed out at the Indian International Center in February 1983: "At £4^{50} per loaf of bread in Ghana, there is no point preaching about the virtues of non-alignment." Singapore, Saudi Arabia, and the states of the Persian Gulf are already moving away from the developing countries and into the developed column. The least-developed countries, which lack natural resources, will fall further behind in relative, if not absolute, terms. In the process, differences of national interest and perspective are likely to become more acute as balance sheet realities cause middle-level states to resist demands of the least-developed. At the September 1981 Paris Conference of Least Developed States, for example, countries like India and Pakistan proved reluctant to assume the costs of concessional aid to the LLDC majority.

Growing realization that economic interests differ within the Third World will put increasing pressure on oil-producing members. Oil pricing, supported in 1973 as a weapon to press LDC demands, has in the succeeding decade damaged rather than aided most Third World economies. Admittedly, there has been quiet dialogue between OPEC and non-OPEC members despite the movement's failure to take a public stand. Discussions over oil, which surfaced in 1979 at UNCTAD V in Manila, continued behind the scenes at the Havana Summit and ultimately led to some OPEC concessions to Third World oil importers. Yet these measures and bilateral aid from countries like Saudi Arabia and Iraq by no means offset the second oil price shock of 1979–80 and the subsequent recession, which badly eroded the Third World balance of payments. The position of the non-aligned has also been complicated by the wholesale recycling of OPEC revenues to U.S. banks and back to the LDCs as commercial loans.

Use of oil as a "weapon" against the North has always depended on OPEC willingness to channel excess profits to the South and on the ability of producers to transcend immediate national interest in reaching agreed price and production levels. By late 1982, both assumptions had proved false, and concepts such as Julius Nyerere's oil-fueled "strike fund for the South" seemed bankrupt.[119] Lowered oil prices in 1983 promised some relief to Third World importers, but for many the gains were more than offset by diminishing aid from the oil producers. In the longer run, doubts about members' mutuality of interests threaten to engulf the NIEO itself. After ten years of rhetoric, the alliance of oil producing states like Algeria, Saudi Arabia, Kuwait, and Iraq with the least-developed states seems more tenuous as economic realities threaten a further subdivision into Third and Fourth Worlds. In this light, the insistence of OPEC countries on tying all Third World economic demands to an ever receding package of global negotiations appears to be little more than a tactical ploy to avoid separate energy talks with either the North or the oil consumers of the South.

The Immediate Future

Against this background, India began its term as chairman in a climate of general cynicism and frustration with the effectiveness of international institutions. Such an environment offered the hope that, to break the impasse, parties would show more flexibility in talks between North and South, but also the risk that repetition of the same formulas would further discredit the NAM and the United Nations. The usual response of both organizations to real-world problems has been to call an international conference. Yet meetings have tended to result in more meetings, not solutions. As Mrs. Gandhi said on assuming the non-aligned chairmanship, "Despite Ottawa, Versailles and Cancún, the dialogue between the developed and the developing has not yet begun." More cynically and only in part true, the problems themselves provide a raison d'être for international bureaucracies, which have an inherent, if unacknowledged, interest in their continuation within acceptable limits, rather than in solutions.

Non-aligned rhetoric has tended to lock members into positions that since the early 1970s have not produced results. Stalemate is not, however, in the interests of the developing countries, many of which are now prepared to reappraise the feasibility of the NIEO and to negotiate on specific aspects on which progress is possible. Others will continue to react strongly against efforts to redirect or moderate the movement's thrust. The outlook is, therefore, for a period of transition under Mrs. Gandhi's leadership and possibly a strained, less supportive relationship with the G-77 as both institutions go through a period of trial and error. Pressures to develop a separate or even joint secretariat as a tangible way of demonstrating unity are likely to increase.

The role of chairman during this transition will be quite simply to hold the NAM together, mediating to the extent possible between its two extremes. Cuba's failure to do so tore the fabric of the movement, and will be followed by a period of healing various wounds and institutional rebuilding. India's success or failure in lowering the rhetoric and general temperature of the movement will demonstrate whether the Cuban era was a temporary aberration or will be the rule as meaningful consensus becomes harder to reach on any issue. A yardstick of India's performance will be the approach taken toward the movement by Cuba as leader of the radical faction and by Singapore as one of Havana's most outspoken critics within the NAM. Their ad hominem exchanges grew increasingly shrill during Cuba's chairmanship and spilled over at the New Delhi Summit in a vitriolic war of pamphlets. At the root of these exchanges was Cuba's injection into the NAM of purely East–West issues sure to exacerbate tensions in a pluralistic movement and to reopen old debates over the relationship of the non-aligned to the superpowers. A further yardstick will be the movement's ability to lure back Burma, which resigned at the peak of rhetorical excess in Havana, and to attract major states of the Third World like Brazil and Mexico.

The challenge for India, already committed to keeping East–West tensions out of the NAM, will be to define more precisely what are Third World, as distinct from East–West, issues. This, in turn, requires realistic priorities in dealing with the former and discipline to prevent the intrusion of East–West matters in the packages inevitably put forward by the various regional groups. Put differently, the movement must reach consensus on which issues fall within, and are susceptible to application of, non-aligned principles, rather than continuing to assume that NAM doctrine is simply an amalgam of its members' foreign policies.

To be fair, the chairman's role in streamlining the movement to meet realities of the late twentieth century is severely limited. There is no existing mechanism, as proven by the New Delhi Summit, to provide an overall, unifying vision or to ensure that the product of the NAM is more than the sum of its parts. Fear of evolving into a bloc and opposition to well-defined institutional procedures have meant that institutionalization, inevitable as the NAM grew to over 100 members, was largely random and unplanned.

The growing force of regionalism within the movement, for example, skews it toward a lopsided structure and political orientation. Recent non-aligned meetings have shown the collective power of 51 African members, which they are increasingly willing to use. Since the group includes a majority of least-developed members of the NAM, a more active role is likely to include insistence on special concerns of these members. A more outspoken African lobby is also a restraint to the power of the chairman and traditional activists like Algeria, Yugoslavia, and even Cuba, and may lead to conflict with other groups in the movement. The alliance of African and Arab members, for example, will be subject to strain as Africans realize that they no longer need Arab support to prevail, and that economic interests of the two groups are often contradictory. Arabs, having co-operated to secure expulsion of South Africa from the General Assembly, will equally be frustrated by the Africans' failure to endorse similar action against Israel, as in October 1982. Symbolic of probable tensions to come between Arab and African groups were those that flared briefly during Security Council meetings between March 22 and April 5, 1983, over Chad's complaint against Libya. More broadly, the campaign to seat the

SDAR on which a tenuous compromise was reached by the OAU at Addis Ababa in June 1983 has increasingly divided Arabs and black Africans.

In the near term, a modus vivendi will be reached between the ambitions and vast diplomatic resources of India and the movement's essentially unmanageable procedures. A semblance of unity will be restored and factional bickering of the Cuban period will be less visible. Those with a stake in the movement will, like the Lok Sabha resolution of March 23, 1983, be able to hail "the unity and international role of the non-aligned community" and to claim that its meetings "strengthened the hands of all those who stand for independence, peace, disarmament and development."[120] There will, however, be strong resistance to new departures involving any sacrifice of national and regional interests.

Members will continue to approach the NAM as a platform from which to lobby for their own objectives. Innovation or unique Third World approaches to global problems will continue to be rare. Jaipal, for example, points out the anomaly that since the early 1960s the movement has never confronted one of the major threats to political stability and the future of mankind that stems in large part from within its member states: unchecked population growth.[121] As co-recipient in 1983 of the first U.N. award for progress in population control, Indira Gandhi will be sensitive to the issue but probably unable to generalize her concern among 101 members. Ultimately, however, willingness to confront such a reality will test the caliber and vision of the movement's leadership.

A Movement in Search of a Vision

Non-alignment, as we have seen, continues to mean different things to different members of the NAM. The common bond is not ideology, military security, economic self-interest, or politics. It is, rather, psychological reassurance and a sense of common identity formed in most cases through the twin experiences of colonialism and underdevelopment. The NAM provides a unique forum for Third World states, many still evolving toward a sense of nationhood, to meet in an environment they control. It is the only organization where former colonial powers are excluded de facto from membership, and its meetings give free rein to the complex of continuing resentments and insecurities still shared by formerly colonized nations. The exclusion of the developed countries from non-aligned proceedings is a source of pride and reassurance to most members. The spectacle of U.S., French, British, Japanese, and other diplomats waiting outside the security perimeter of closed meetings for scraps of information is, not surprisingly, greeted with general amusement and enjoyment. By contrast, signs of indifference to the NAM, particularly by the great powers, are met with anger and hostility, as detracting from collective self-esteem.

Thus, non-aligned gatherings, by their very nature, take place in an environment corresponding not to the real world, but to the members' vision of what it ideally should be. As noted at New Delhi by the delegate of Vanuatu, statements and decisions can be made in the NAM without fear that they "could result in undesirable relations" with the superpowers. Consensus can be reached, as if in a vacuum, without concern whether a country's position is consistent with the stand it takes elsewhere. Many smaller members thus frankly explain to outsiders that while they took this or that stand in the NAM or even the United Nations, it does not mean anything or reflect their national position. A case in point is consensus at Managua and New Delhi for independence of Puerto Rico after most of the NAM had voted a few months before in New York, 70–30, not to declare the island a colony. By the same token, members see no contradiction between strident political attacks on the United States and appeals elsewhere in the same summit declaration for increased economic assistance.

Such inconsistencies reflect a basic tension between views of the NAM as a fraternal order without serious consequence and as a sober grouping of sovereign states, between reality and unreality. International influence as a serious world movement is, of course, the rationale articulated for the NAM by its adherents. Yet, to be taken at face value by outsiders, this interpretation assumes a degree of self-discipline in putting its own house in order yet to be demonstrated by the NAM. For its global vision to be credible, the movement must take firm steps to end conflict between Iran and Iraq, Ethiopia and Somalia, Libya and Chad, and some 30 other simmering wars or hostile claims between members.

Failure to reconcile these differences has led to frequent predictions of the movement's impending dissolution. Yet critics have vastly underestimated its solidarity as a club of last resort, meeting real, if intangible, needs of its membership. Its summits have been held, for the most part, on schedule; its membership has quadrupled; and its influence at the United Nations has grown. Non-alignment has proved to be a popular orientation for domestic reasons, and members undergoing basic political change have, with the exception of Burma, retained non-alignment as a cornerstone of foreign policy. Thus, for example, Indonesia repudiated the Sukarno era but not membership in the NAM, in which he was intimately involved. Association on an equal basis in such a large grouping, whatever its drawbacks, clearly continues to provide reassurance and a measure of protection for otherwise fragile Third World states.

The movement's rhetorical and declarative approach to international affairs is, furthermore, uniquely adapted to its majority of newly emergent states whose behavior is shaped by ruling elites rather than integrated national interests. The major concern of these elites, whether military or civilians, is usually to maintain the sociopolitical structures which keep them in power. To do so, it is convenient, and often politically essential, to blame external factors for their countries' intractable problems. Non-aligned declarations are, therefore, used to reinforce and legitimize regimes without broad support at home. Ruling elites have a direct political stake in NAM dogma, which places the causes of underdevelopment, economic dislocations, and poverty outside the Third World, absolving them of responsibility. Since the policies of Western countries are visible and their economic relations with most of the non-aligned are substantial, if not overwhelming, the United States and its allies have been the primary scapegoats in this process.

The benefits of membership thus outweigh the fact that the movement is an uncongenial forum for many members put on the defensive by anti-colonial rhetoric and radical positions to the left of their national policies. Such members would, for example, probably feel more at home in a conference of world neutralists including selected Europeans, but are not strong enough or sufficiently insulated from world affairs to abandon the field to potential enemies. Even Saudi Arabia, whose conservative orientation conflicts to some degree with many non-aligned positions, finds its continued presence necessary to monitor and offset the stratagems of potential foes. States with specific disputes find NAM membership essential to represent their point of view. Thus, Somalia lobbies to explain claims to Ethiopia's Ogaden region, and Morocco works to offset Algeria's position on the Sahara. Failure to do so forfeits the issue, and North Korea fully exploits South Korea's absence to push demands for withdrawal of U.S. troops and unification.

In spite of factional division, warfare between members, and the unraveling identity of Third World economic interests, the Non-Aligned Movement is likely to lurch along from summit to summit, as it has since 1961. Its loose procedures leave room for members to pick and choose from it what they will, ignoring the rest. In the short term, India's chairmanship provides reassurance and continuity for members who began to question basic premises under Cuba. Yet, unless outside events or self-discipline within the movement itself provide a new rationale, the NAM will probably play a smaller role in the formation of members' overall foreign policy. As international relations, particularly in the economic sphere, become more complex, specialized functional, regional, religious, and economic groups will proliferate and command increasing attention on given issues. Important states, like Nigeria and Indonesia, already participate in a broad range of regional, oil, and specialized economic bodies. Complex interaction in so many international forums will necessarily reduce the fraction of a member's foreign policy that is determined within the NAM.

The course of the NAM will, nevertheless, continue to have major significance for the United Nations and its viability during the final decades of the century. In the short term, a non-aligned majority could again precipitate a direct challenge to the United Nations over the issue of Israeli membership, although Latin American and African members have so far refused to go along with such action because of potential harm to the United Nations. Both Republican and Democratic U.S. administrations have warned that Washington would take strong action if Israel were expelled, which could take the form of cutting off contributions and boycotting the General Assembly.

In the longer term, the lack of cohesion within the NAM will have a continuing, negative impact on the United Nations. As further differences develop within the movement, consensus in the United Nations will become more important as evidence of non-aligned unity and continued existence. To gain agreement, however, an even higher level of abstraction and symbolism will be required, with resolutions based on broad generalities and avoiding controversial specifics. The result will make implementation of mandates by the Secretariat nearly impossible, and will further immobilize the world organization. High levels of abstraction will not appear to outsiders as a relevant response to world problems or conflict situations, and will increase Western disenchantment with the United Nations. Negotiations on major world issues will, more and more, be channeled outside the institution. The success of the non-aligned in substantially setting the U.N. agenda through closed meetings outside its framework will compound frustration of other countries that pay the major share. In the United States, the growing gap between major financial support and minimal influence at the United Nations will spill over into increasingly bitter press and public criticism, and more intensive congressional review of U.S. participation. If the process is unchecked, the United Nations risks falling into increasing disuse until, like the League of Nations, a world conflagration reveals it to be without power or relevance.

15

Toward a New Approach

The Third World, in its relations with the North, is like a trade union in its relations with employers. It is trying to make unity serve as a compensating strength so as to create a greater balance in negotiations.

Julius Nyerere, 1982

A number of broad, related conclusions about the NAM's evolution, present influence on the United Nations, and susceptibility to U.S. and Soviet influence emerge from the preceding pages. Briefly summarized, they provide a starting point for consideration of a more consistent, long-term U.S. approach to the non-aligned.

Since the mid-1970s, the non-aligned have exerted a fundamental and still growing influence on the structure and agenda of the United Nations. As the largest political bloc within it, the non-aligned view the United Nations as the focal point for their influence. U.S. policy toward the movement is, therefore, inextricably linked to American strategy and national objectives at the United Nations. While the United Nations affects American interests in a much broader context, its effectiveness as a vehicle of U.S. policy is in large part determined by attitudes of the non-aligned toward the United States.

The functioning and structure of the Non-Aligned Movement are less and less relevant to the problems of the late twentieth century and the national needs of its members. Regional, political, and economic disparities of 101 members reduce consensus to a high level of generality, limiting the movement's ability to take positive action or to put forward realistic proposals. Its bias, reflecting political realities of its membership, tends to be toward criticism rather than strong leadership.

The Soviets are well ahead of the United States in access to the NAM through client states, but do not exert a controlling influence on the overall movement. Cuba's presidency revealed limits to radicalization of the movement both in general philosophy and on specific issues like Kampuchea, Afghanistan, Egyptian membership, and Cuba's bid for a Security Council seat. Soviet influence is thus not sufficient explanation for U.S. difficulties with the non-aligned.

Anti-Westernism is kept alive within the NAM by a post-colonial outlook and continuing stalemate on southern Africa, the Middle East, and North–South economic issues. While U.S. approaches to the non-aligned have been largely in reaction to presumed Soviet and Cuban gains, a major force within the movement has been opposition to Western policy rather than affinity for Moscow.

As a U.S. policy, neither rapprochement nor confrontation has had the intended effect on non-aligned behavior and attitudes. Although U.S. ability to affect non-aligned positions is limited, action by Washington has often had the negative effect of intensifying the movement's anti-Western course. The declaration drafted for the abortive Baghdad Summit was probably correct in claiming that efforts "aimed at disparaging the Movement, weakening its unity and reducing its international influence" have on balance strengthened the NAM.

Acceptance of the NAM

These conclusions also suggest that the movement, in some form, is here to stay, and that U.S. policy should begin by providing no pretext to keep it in its present anti-Western mode. From a non-aligned perspective, the movement's purpose is to safeguard the independence and nationalism of Third World states. Yet this same nationalism, while often requiring forbearance and sensitivity in bilateral relations, is a cornerstone of Washington's foreign policy and world view. Nationalism, by contrast, represents a threat to the Soviets, for whom the NAM itself is only a transitional step to world socialism. The rhetoric and thrust of Third World nationalism may be expected, however, to evolve with longer experience of independence. The movement is today in a period of transition as are most individual members, still preoccupied with problems of nation-building, formation of viable economies, and survival in the twentieth century. The present collective attitudes of the NAM necessarily reflect this post-independence phase.

In an earlier, less interdependent world, the United States went through a comparable period in which survival was thought to depend on avoidance of "entangling alliances." The central concept of non-alignment, articulated by Nehru as "avoiding foreign entanglements by not joining one bloc or the other," is "strikingly similar."[122] Richard B. Morris goes further in noting a "disposition toward non-alignment" in revolutionary America and in describing George Washington's Neutrality Proclamation of April 22, 1793, as a "classic formulation of the great rules of non-alignment in words that might have been voiced by a

Nehru of India or a U Nu of Burma."[123] For both revolutionary America and the non-aligned, the overriding goal was avoidance of economic or other dependence on foreign powers through self-sufficiency. As Indira Gandhi put it in her closing address to the Seventh Summit: "Non-alignment embodies the courage and strength of self-reliance. Alignment denotes dependence."

Dependence, however, remains at the core of relationships between the United States and the non-aligned. As one Indian professor asked rhetorically during a February 27, 1983, seminar on non-alignment at New Delhi, "What self-respecting member would accept something and give nothing back in return? Acceptance of something not given to other members creates suspicion." For the United States, now in the role of global banker, Third World preoccupation with dependence is a major challenge to diplomacy.

The best that can be hoped for is a generally shared concept of fairness, evolved through careful dialogue. To achieve it, the consistency and tone of U.S. policy are as important in dealing with the Third World as agendas and the content of negotiating "packages." It is the abrupt, and to outsiders arbitrary, shifts in U.S. policy, whether on Law of the Sea or the alternation of rapprochement and confrontation toward the NAM, that smaller nations find most threatening and confusing.

The Substantive Impasse

What are the issues on which progress could lead to broad improvement in U.S. relations with the non-aligned? They are the Middle East, Namibia, world recession, and reduction of the $600–800 billion spent annually on arms while basic human needs are unfulfilled. Solutions to each are vital to the United States, and have been objectives of both Republican and Democratic administrations. To be sure, progress in these areas will not *per se* alter the confrontational rhetoric of the NAM which is deeply rooted in the institution and responsive to political needs of its members. It may, however, cause some of the non-aligned to reassess positions that have become rote over the past decade.

The United States in the 1980s is in a position of global responsibility for many situations that, like the Middle East and southern Africa, are beyond its control. Yet responsibility both limits Washington's ability to posture for Third World support and entails opprobrium when intractable problems do not yield to quick solution. A substantive role also demands unwelcome caution, for missteps in the Middle East could affect the security of Israel and vital U.S. interests; in Namibia, they could strengthen the hand of reactionary elements in South Africa. Yet it is precisely the direct involvement of the United States in seeking solutions to these problems that gives Moscow an opportunity to foment trouble from the sidelines, whether through arms supply or support for dissident groups.

As long as stalemate continues over southern Africa, the Middle East, and economic reform, the movement is likely to remain in a time-warp of anti-Westernism. Repeated confrontation tends to solidify blocs within the United Nations, where, in the extreme, they undermine all dialogue, preventing points of view and even delegations from being heard. When Israeli Prime Minister Begin, for example, addressed the General Assembly on June 18, 1982, 102 nations, including most of the NAM, left the hall.

Blocs are not new to the United Nations and, in fact, were pioneered by the United States in the early 1950s, when it was possible to line up a majority of Latin American and European supporters for American initiatives. Yet today, the formulation of bloc positions away from New York prevents the unraveling and exploration of substantive differences from which new ideas and solutions might evolve. Ritual denunciations year after year stifle diversity and a more tolerant world view, which are major U.N. strengths. The United States should, therefore, endorse rather than cut short the airing of differences, encouraging the non-aligned themselves to come to grips with basic problems for which no solution is without costs and sacrifice. Premature challenge on agendas or terms of reference before substantive issues are fully joined permits refuge in rhetoric, criticism, and bloc positions. By contrast, discussion on a full range of issues brings into the open contradictions among oil producers and importers, rival regions, LDCs and countries at the point of takeoff, conservative and radical regimes. Failure to engage also concedes a monopoly on morality to theoreticians of Western and colonial guilt for all world problems.

Even the non-aligned are not optimistic about quick progress on issues dividing the United Nations. Solutions involve multiple steps that may not be completed within this century. In southern Africa, free and internationally recognized elections in Namibia, to which the United States has been committed since 1977, are an essential first step. Differences with the non-aligned over the related issue of Cuban troops in Angola do not detract from commitment to that goal. A settlement in Namibia would undercut NAM radicals, far from that troubled region, who have opposed negotiations and called for sacrifice of others against

South Africa's superior military force. In the Middle East, progress toward Palestinian autonomy remains essential to involve moderate elements of the polarized Arab world and break the cycle of violence. As in southern Africa, the causes of violence go back generations, but involve a small number of states directly affected by the outcome. Thus, within the framework of Security Council resolutions, it is possible for the United States and its Western allies to pursue solutions directly with the parties. The United Nations forms a backdrop to Western mediation in both Namibia and the Middle East. In default of other intermediaries, the Third World chorus will be anti-Western in case of failure but will accept solutions agreed by those directly involved.

Solution to these problems will be slow, and the benefits from progress at each stage should not be overestimated. Partial solutions are unlikely to result in a steamroller of credit for the West. Rhodesian independence did not alter the basic equation or attitudes on southern Africa, although it may have bought a measure of tolerance for Western efforts on Namibia. Similarly, elections in Namibia, once held, will shift attention to the persistence of apartheid in South Africa. Yet progress—whether in implementing Resolution 435 in Namibia, troop withdrawal from Lebanon, or Palestinian autonomy—is required to sustain Third World confidence in the West's continuing commitment. Tangible steps like previous Western initiatives in the Rhodesian negotiations, establishment of UNIFIL in Lebanon, and creation of the Contact Group make it politically easier for Third World leaders to meet the West halfway. They also highlight the irrelevance of the Soviet Union to solution of the basic issues. Failure to move ahead, by contrast, gives opportunities to Moscow and locks the NAM into a radical mode.

In breaking the present impasse, the United States must be prepared to exert strong leadership, consulting with European allies although knowing that their support will be wavering and less than complete. The EC-10 and other Europeans are more vulnerable than the United States to pressures of the non-aligned both because of greater economic dependence on Third World markets and raw materials and, in many cases, because of internal domestic politics. Typically, Western European governments take pains to find positive content in declarations of the NAM, generally ignoring the anti-Western themes. Italian Foreign Minister Emilio Colombo claimed, for example, in Pakistan on March 28, 1983, that the Seventh Summit had "reconquered" the true spirit of non-alignment.

The non-aligned also exploit differences between the United States and Europe, singling out for praise in the New Delhi Declaration "the advanced European stand on the problems of the Middle East and

Palestine," as well as the French initiative "to seek negotiated political solutions in Central America." Europeans like Austrian Chancellor Bruno Kreisky and President Willy Brandt of the Socialist International justify these efforts as providing the non-aligned with an alternative to East or West and thereby offsetting Soviet gains, although bilateral access to oil and markets must also loom large. There is no evidence, however, that Brandt's and Kreisky's overtures to Yasser Arafat of the PLO and to liberation movements of southern Africa have done more than strengthen those groups, to the detriment of rivals more friendly to the West. As Leopold Senghor complained to the Socialist International in 1977, "You always go to help those who claim to be Marxist and progressive."

The U.S. approach must be based, by contrast, not on compromise and lip service to national liberation, but on real convergence of interests with the non-aligned. In the mid-1980s, the independent Third World grouping envisaged by founders of the NAM clearly coincides with U.S. interests. The rapid and virtually complete dismantling of colonial empires during the 1960s has been followed by expansion of Soviet force beyond the USSR's borders into Afghanistan and Indochina, and to the more remote nations of Ethiopia and Cuba. The non-aligned theory of survival through strength in numbers is essentially defensive and aimed against expansionist powers. For countries near the Soviet border, non-alignment is, in fact, a theoretical response to the Brezhnev doctrine legitimizing Moscow's right of intervention. The existence of strong and independent countries in a pluralistic world environment, to which both the non-aligned and the United States are committed, is clearly inconsistent with a Soviet policy based on exploitation of weakness to gain control.

The Economic Dimension

Economics brings us back to sensitivities about dependence in a movement and among states committed to independence. The preferred term today is "interdependence," which is often a euphemism to avoid the implications of dependence, neocolonialism, or less than complete control over national destiny. It is hard to argue that the well-being and even the survival of economies in the North and the South are fully interdependent. In reality, the linkage is at most partial, and far less in the North than in the South. The greater vulnerability of the South makes some degree of dependence, cutting against the grain of Third World nationalism, a fact of life in relations with the North.

Given the growing economic gap and negative growth in many Third World states, the United States is unlikely ever to fully satisfy demands largely created by its worldwide image of high consumption and standards of living. Both the Brandt Commission and the White House report on prospects for the year 2000 suggest that there will be continued deterioration in the environment and global quality of life, and that demands of the poor upon the rich can only increase. Some would conclude from this that U.S. assistance can be only a palliative, prelude to greater demands, and that ultimately there is no basis for dialogue. Yet interdependence is valid to the extent that an outright rupture would have incalculable consequences for both North and South. A degree of inequality and dependence is likely to be a fact of international life for the foreseeable future, if not a permanent condition, requiring forebearance and cooperation on both sides.

Two developments have converged in the mid-1980s, presenting both acute danger and hope for a more cooperative, pragmatic relationship between North and South. The first is the worldwide economic crisis, from which Third World states have suffered most and will be the last to feel the effects of recovery. As economists point out, the elements for a global financial crash exist in the massive indebtedness of the Third World and Eastern Europe.[124] In Latin America, economic growth was negative in 1982 for the first time in 40 years and consumer prices rose by 80 percent, the highest annual increase on record. In Africa, 17 countries had acute food shortages in 1982, average economic growth was minus 1.4 percent, and foreign exchange reserves fell below the level of one month's imports. By 1983, even a stalwart of the non-aligned like Yugoslavia was struggling with $19 billion in foreign debt of which $4.5 billion was due that year.[125]

Under such pressures for immediate relief, the second development has been erosion of the Third World consensus behind the NIEO and global negotiations. Even the second Brandt Commission report admits that the "process of negotiation between North and South has itself become an obstacle to progress on the crucial issues."[126] From a Western point of view, the NIEO has always boiled down to "a unilateral transfer of resources from the developed countries to the developing ones."[127] Global negotiations as a strategy to implement this transfer have raised both extravagant expectations and exaggerated fears.

As the non-aligned are themselves beginning to realize, the NIEO has always been based on the unworkable premise that "financial revolution could be brought about by giving decision-making power on loans to borrowers rather than to lenders," with the inherent risk of lenders "quitting these organizations."[128] As the revolution has failed to materialize, doubts have increased; even the Cuban theoretician and assistant minister of foreign affairs, Ricardo Alarcon, admits that both the NIEO and CERDS "will continue to be permanent aspirations systematically frustrated."[129] While NAM declarations regularly blame the United States for this "systematic frustration," the basic point at issue has been lender responsibility for bank policy. Differences over agendas and preliminary conferences have been minor compared with those over control of institutions like the IMF and the World Bank.

Exploration by the United States of the new climate resulting from these developments should begin, as with a general posture toward the non-aligned, with recognition of areas of common interest. Economic cooperation among developing countries coincides with broad American interests. Rational growth in the Third World reduces political instability and opportunities for outside penetration. It is no coincidence that Soviet gains have been in economically backward Ethiopia, Cuba, and Vietnam, while self-sustaining economies in the developing world have usually been capitalist. Greater integration of developing economies adds to competition in some areas with the United States, but represents an overall enlargement of the world market and a larger slice of the planetary product for all.

The process further tends to exclude the Soviet Union, which has few trade linkages to the developing countries. Compared with an estimated 19 percent for the United States, the USSR accounted for only 2 percent of Third World trade during 1981, and has little to contribute to the development process. Like the Marshall Plan, development of the Third World offers better hopes of stability, expanded trade, and lessened confrontation over economics, all of which outweigh differences as growth places political relationships on a more equal footing. Unlike the Marshall Plan, the process involves creation of skills, infrastructure, and traditions, rather than recovery, and is infinitely slower and more complex. If pursued too rapidly, as in Iran, the results may be chaotic and unpredictable.

In recognizing these broad areas of common interest, both sides must also identify more clearly than before where U.S. and Third World interests diverge. The assumption current, for example, among some Third World economists that massive U.S. capital flows to the South would be repaid with interest via increased exports to new markets and are, therefore, no more than self-interest needs reexamination. To the extent that the recipient's development plan is based, like India's, on import substitution the world market will not grow; and there is, in any case, no assurance that resulting purchases will not be made in the East, giving Moscow the benefits of U.S. "self-interest."[130] Furthermore, the majority of both government and private loans to the Third World are for immediate imports or day-to-day government financing.[131] These have no long-term effect on capital formation or expansion of world markets and serve neither the borrower, who is caught in a new spiral of debt, nor the lender, whose money is at risk.

Such different perceptions of self-interest reflect different diagnoses of underlying problems. The non-aligned blame economic ills on external factors, seeking to offset them by massive resource transfers and changes in the international financial institutions. If, however, as many Westerners believe, the causes of stagnation in the Third World are mainly within inefficient economic and social structures, increased liquidity without structural adjustment would be inflationary and compound existing problems.

In working toward less confrontational relations with the South, the objective must be replacement of demands for unilateral transfer of resources with a sense of shared responsibility and recognition of indigenous as well as external causes of economic failure. While this has proved to be an elusive goal to date, in a receding world economy there is clear scope for leadership by the largest single economy, whose recovery, more than all else, shapes that of the developing world. By 1983, a rapidly strengthening U.S. economy appeared to make such a role possible. The vehicle for U.S. initiatives will probably continue to be sector-by-sector talks on trade, commodities, money, finance, and economic interdependence in small groups representing developed and developing states and in existing larger forums like UNCTAD and GATT.

In these talks U.S. willingness to discuss and, in some measure, respond to Third World economic needs will lead to improvement in bilateral ties, since perceived U.S. hostility or recalcitrance has in the past branded states cooperating with the United States as sellouts. The four-year impasse over terms of reference for global negotiations created an impression that the United States did not take developing countries seriously, and thus ceded to others the role of shaping events. Opposition before controversial issues like energy could be explored has tended to isolate the United States while France and others of the EC-10 gained credit in the Third World for potential support, safe in the knowledge that U.S. opposition would make real concessions moot.

A more pragmatic dialogue with the developing countries, on the other hand, will permit a U.S. voice in shaping the philosophy of

North–South relations. The premise, fostered by the non-aligned, of Western guilt for economic failures has not been adequately challenged. In the words of the late Algerian President Houari Boumedienne:

> Europe and the United States have plundered the national wealth of the Third World. We should consider whatever contribution the industrialized countries make to be a simple restitution of a tiny part of the debt contracted by their odious exploitation.[132]

or of Tanzanian President Julius Nyerere:

> In one world, as in one state, when I am rich because you are poor, and I am poor because you are rich, the transfer of wealth from the rich to the poor is a matter of rights; it is not an appropriate matter for charity.[133]

Such attitudes yield slowly to acceptance of national responsibility for economic performance and development. Selective aid and regular dialogue are, however, the means to redirect attention toward raising economic output and away from redistributing wealth. In the process, U.S. aid becomes not "reparations" for past inequity, but a partnership involving responsibilities on both sides, linked in a general sense to bilateral relations and shared objectives. Engagement along these lines also pre-empts economic demands as a traditional rallying point for radicals, and deflects to Moscow the Third World's hostility toward bystanders in the development process.

U.S. Tactics Toward the NAM

Evolution in non-aligned thinking about the United States, as we have seen, will probably depend in part on progress in the Middle East, southern Africa, and world economic reform. In the meantime, tactical options range from working quietly with non-aligned leaders to seeking to maximize disaffection of NAM members with the movement as an institution to serve their interests. In the past, warnings, such as the Kirkpatrick letter of October 1981, have sometimes been effective in causing smaller countries to think twice before subscribing automatically to declarations of the NAM. Yet extended, as in the Moynihan years, into a policy of concerted attack on the movement's existence, the result has been a beleaguered and anti-U.S. reaction.

Without pretexts to blame the United States for essentially their own problems, the non-aligned would be under more pressure to address the movement's internal contradictions and ambiguities. The inference, however groundless, of U.S. hostility or interference allows radicals to keep the movement on a negative and reactive course. Without it, there can be no justification for avoiding a more disciplined and rational application of non-aligned principles to members and outsiders alike. Resolution of the contradictions that have corroded the movement is a problem for the non-aligned that the United States should follow with interest but not attempt to control. Ultimately, the evenhandedness with which non-aligned principles are applied will determine the movement's relevance and the degree of attention it commands from outsiders. In the meantime, consistency should be the goal of U.S. policy toward it.

Direct diplomacy with member states is also an important adjunct of an overall approach to the NAM. Bilateral channels can often be used to reach understandings not possible in a larger gathering. The difficulty, however, is in translating such private agreement into on-the-record support at the United Nations or, put differently, in enforcing a linkage between bilateral and multilateral behavior. Within the NAM, bilateral relations can be, and often have been, used at cross-purposes by the United States. Among the smaller and less developed members, dependent on outside aid and military assistance, positions on key issues in the NAM and United Nations are sometimes vulnerable to pressure from suppliers. Where pressure is exerted, however, the reaction is uniformly negative from larger, less vulnerable members, who view it as undermining the movement's existence. Exploitation of bilateral ties to break non-aligned consensus on key votes at the United Nations antagonizes influential states like Algeria, India, Yugoslavia, and Iraq. Compared with the safety in numbers enjoyed by regular NAM supporters of the Soviet Union, the Latin American, African, or Asian member who yields to Western pressure on a U.N. vote tends to be the exception that stands out from the NAM majority and is held up as a victim of U.S. intervention.

A long-term approach, not compatible with pressure on the weaker states, is to seek improved relations with leading members, outside the Soviet sphere, who in large part shape the movement's course. While countries like Algeria and India distinguish between a bilateral agenda and anti-Western rhetoric in New York, there is little doubt that expanded relations and understanding with the United States could in time bring at least modest dividends in the NAM.

Improvement depends, however, on sustained effort, careful evaluation of common interests, and more frequent initiatives like the July 1982 visit of Prime Minister Indira Gandhi to Washington. A corollary is regular diplomatic contact with a larger spectrum of NAM states, not in the form of pressure prior to votes but a a means toward broader understanding of mutual positions. Such access is vital to offset Cuban and other hostile propaganda with the facts, as perceived in Washington, on critical areas like Central America.

A cohesive approach to the NAM would also include regular, behind-the-scenes U.S. support for regional subgroups when there is a coincidence of interest. The U.S. Mission in New York has, for example, played an important role in supporting ASEAN opposition to Vietnam's occupation of Kampuchea and efforts of the Islamic Conference to seek withdrawal of Soviet troops from Afghanistan. In both cases, momentum from the smaller groups carried the movement and the United Nations. A secondary role of this kind involves sharing of information and quiet lobbying, but not transforming an issue into East–West confrontation. Since many, if not the majority, of non-aligned positions evolve unchanged from subgroups, quiet dialogue at that level is often possible before decisions are made.

The objective of quiet diplomacy, based on acceptance of limits to U.S. influence on the NAM, should not be destruction of the movement, in any case beyond American power to achieve. Instead, it should keep options open as the NAM enters a period of transition and adjustment to conflicting demands of its membership. As it evolves in different form or conceivably dissolves from internal causes, the United States should avoid prolonging the present anti-Western phase by tactics of confrontation. Without a credible Western or "imperialist" threat, the non-aligned will have to adjust to the real concerns of members or face competition from more effective Third World groups.

Although the ideal of an independent and genuinely non-aligned grouping remains desirable from an American perspective, the ability of the United States to affect the adjustment process is by no means certain. Running through all U.S. approaches to the NAM has been the unresolved question of whether members well disposed to the United States can play an active role in challenging clients of the Soviet Union and promoting a more geniune form of non-alignment. Even intermittent periods of relative neglect by Washington have rested on an assessment that the anti-Western bias of the NAM is so strong that moderates cannot raise effective challenge to issues portrayed as colonial by non-aligned doctrine. Rapprochement, by contrast, has been based on encouragement of moderates to reassert control and, by superior numbers, to shape non-aligned demands and rhetoric along more pragmatic lines. Linkage of performance in the NAM to relations with the United States is a variation intended to strengthen moderates with the implied carrot and stick of bilateral assistance.

In contrast with the Soviet Union, the United States has no reliable channel into the movement in the sense that its supporters would betray national or broad, non-aligned principles if called on to do so. The United States could not achieve, and has not sought, the tight control exercised over a small minority by Moscow. Some members commented after the New Delhi Summit that the United States should have "arranged" for countries to speak in its defense; in fact, of 90 plenary speeches lasting 54 hours, 15 singled out the USSR for praise while none stood up for the United States. "Arrangements" of the kind suggested, however, are clearly easier where the relationship is authoritarian, and at the same time are profoundly subversive of the NAM.

The majority of the non-aligned, roughly those receiving the Kirkpatrick letter, look more to the West than the East in bilateral relations because of trade, education, and cultural patterns. A smaller number, such as Singapore, Pakistan, Egypt, Zaire, and Morocco, are branded by Cuba and the Soviet Union as "proxies" of the United States or the West. Cuba even argued in a pamphlet circulated at New Delhi that "Singapore aspires to be the Troy Horse (sic) within the Movement of Non-aligned countries." Yet, while these states share many mutual interests with the United States, their performance in the NAM and United Nations does not support such allegations. In the General Assembly, their positions coincide with Washington well under 30 percent of the time (Appendix D), and within the movement their influence is concentrated on selected issues of prime importance to them, not on generalized defense of Washington. Pakistan, threatened by Soviet invasion next door, has thus focused on Afghanistan; Singapore has taken the lead on Kampuchea; and Egypt has fought to preserve its own membership after Camp David. It is important to remember that Singapore and other moderates actively opposed to Cuba see themselves not as ideological extremists or defenders of Western values, but as guardians of the original principles of non-alignment. For them, the main objective has been to prevent the "hijacking" of the NAM by Soviet proxies, not to advance or defend U.S. interests. The issue for U.S. policymakers will, therefore, continue to be not creation of Soviet-style assets, but a longer-term approach to the survival of anti-colonial attitudes based on reducing unnecessary areas of conflict with the United States and strengthening the tendency toward genuine non-alignment.

Related Tactics in the U.N.

Public opinion in the United States has not traditionally viewed the United Nations with the tolerance accorded Congress and other political institutions. Reaction tends to be polarized between outright dismissal and idealized commitment, with detractors in a majority as the United Nations evolves further from its origins in 1945. Criticism has centered on costs to the taxpayer at a time when the United States is isolated on most votes and a frequent object of strident condemnation. The United Nations is no longer widely seen as a significant contributor to the solution of world problems, but as a place where issues become politicized by outsiders and more difficult to resolve. In a larger sense, the United Nations is a convenient scapegoat for frustration, particularly among conservatives, about American inability to relate effectively to the outside world during the late twentieth century. The difficult interaction between a political process with the variables and delays of American-style democracy and the world at large is only magnified at the United Nations.

Defenders tend, by contrast, to focus on earlier aspirations for the United Nations that often no longer apply as concerns of a new majority have taken precedence. Ambassador Moynihan reacted strongly to what he called the "standard Orwellian inversion of meaning" at the United Nations, the distortion of facts to suit preconceptions frequently at variance with an actual situation.[134] Such abuse of language, perfected, as Moynihan pointed out, in totalitarian countries, undermines logic, accountability, and, in the end, effectiveness of the United Nations. Challenge to it, however, involves nearly constant confrontation with the majority of delegations that do not share American traditions of precise use and consequences of language. Most delegations at the United Nations do not have the benefit of legal counsel on their small staffs and do not necessarily regard language, whether in constitutions, charters, or resolutions, as a safeguard to their rights. The prevailing assumption in the Delegates' Lounge is, rather, that rhetoric in the world body is largely symbolic, and should not be taken literally. As one Arab diplomat noted, it is engrained in the culture of many non-aligned countries, particularly in the Arab world, to employ tough language in public and reserve compromises for private negotiations.

As a result, public declarations, whether in the NAM or the United Nations, tend to be discounted.

Differing uses of language reflect differing approaches to the United Nations itself. A casual approach to language lends itself to the kind of posturing at the United Nations routinely engaged in by the Soviets and many of the non-aligned. Diatribes by "microphone revolutionaries" like Libya, Cuba, and Nicaragua are basically a corruption of language. It is standard for these countries to counter whatever charges are made against them by accusing others of precisely their own wrongdoings. In a world body already saturated with words, the result is indifference to truth and falsehood alike.

Strict constructionists, including the United States and Great Britain, by contrast, have tended to view the United Nations in essentially legal terms, paying close attention to nuances of language and often opposing otherwise acceptable resolutions because of difficulty with a few words. Such an outlook has led to increasing disregard of the General Assembly, where language is imprecise and non-binding, and concentration on the Security Council, where precision is ultimately enforceable by veto. Yet even there, the perfect can be enemy to the good, and a time-consuming focus on every word by busy senior officials often leads to delays that make the Washington policy process seem inept compared with that of small or less pluralistic states. Particularly dramatic "failures of communication" were President Carter's 1980 switch of votes on the Middle East and voting instructions received too late during the Falkland crisis in 1982.

To the non-aligned, who place less premium on language, whether of the U.N. Charter or of new resolutions, the United Nations is more a political and historical process than an institution with defined responsibilities. More than two-thirds of its members, including most of the non-aligned, were not present at San Francisco, and are committed to restructuring the United Nations to reflect their concerns and participation. For them, non-Western cultural approaches to language often coincide with a political interest in obfuscation. The Universal Declaration of Human Rights and the U.N. Charter itself are essentially Western documents infused with Western values. Non-aligned control of an international system shaped by such values frequently involves deliberate ambiguity on the part of states not committed to them. Why, the non-aligned ask, should the developed minority have a monopoly on innovation? Thus, a procedure like "uniting for peace," improvised by the United States in the 1950s to enhance the power of the majority, has been broadened to suit a later and different majority.

From the U.S. perspective, such changes are clearly for the worse, but the process is not reversible, and by the mid-1980s, attempts to put the genie of "one state, one vote" back in the bottle are obsolete. A more diffuse and less controllable United Nations often does not serve U.S. interests, but insistence on the status quo only ensures confrontation at unequal odds. More than the United States, members of the EC-10 have shown pragmatism in adjusting to the change, since they have less at stake and can, perhaps, afford to be more cynical and to rely on the United States to resist changes that would harm them as well.

A more pragmatic approach to the United Nations involves redefinition of objectives there. It has clearly functioned imperfectly as a forum to resolve disputes, particularly those involving superpowers. Nor is any nation wise to rely on it as a guarantor of sovereignty. Yet the major powers have not themselves worked toward these objectives. Their ambivalence is evident in reluctance to endorse strong, and consequently less than controllable, leadership of the United Nations. Compromise candidates rather than activists have emerged as secretaries-general since Dag Hammarskjold because of inherent distrust of supranational authority. U.S. and Soviet military strength and alliances also bespeak lack of trust in a U.N. preventive role.

The benefits to the United States of membership in the United Nations have been real, but far more modest. It has been an inconspicuous place to meet for quiet contacts impossible elsewhere. During the Berlin airlift, the Cuban missile crisis, and the seizure of hostages in Iran, quiet diplomacy was possible there behind the scenes. At times of tension, U.S.–Soviet conversations have occurred on the margins of the United Nations that would not have been possible in more formal and publicized bilateral settings. Nations with which the United States has no diplomatic ties, like Iran and Vietnam, also can be contacted in New York directly or through third parties on vital issues like return of the hostages and an accounting of Americans missing in Vietnam. The U.N. principle of universality provides a moral basis for dealing with such countries whose policies and actions are otherwise repugnant to the United States. When universality is breached, however, as by the illegal expulsion of South Africa or attempts in 1982 to expel Israel, this rationale is threatened.

The Security Council, despite shortcomings, remains the only recognized international body capable of establishing outlines for peaceful settlement of disputes. A solution in Namibia, still elusive in late 1983, would build on previously agreed U.N. resolutions. The Camp David Agreements evolved from a foundation of Security Council resolutions on the Middle East. The Security Council also has served to control the escalation of crises that have been brought to its attention at an early stage. Finally, the specialized agencies have played a major role in eradication of disease, refugee assistance, food research, setting standards for international air safety, and regulating international health codes and postal exchange. Such programs, too complex to be shouldered by individual states, remain an important partnership between developed and developing states in which the United States can, and should, quietly benefit from its leading role.

Withdrawal by the United States or even dissolution of the U.N. system would not alter the present impasse on issues of the Middle East, southern Africa, and economic development, all of which require collective resources for solution. Instead, the international community would be divided into hostile blocs even less likely to communicate effectively. Non-participation forfeits the opportunity to make U.S. views known, and the United Nations would be far less manageable from outside. Opponents capitalize on such mistakes; and the Soviet Union, for example, is unlikely to withdraw again from the Security Council after that body agreed, in Moscow's absence, to a U.N. force in Korea. On a smaller scale, the United States and United Kingdom probably would not, in hindsight, repeat the error of abandoning the Decolonization Committee to Cuba and the Eastern bloc.

A flexible U.S. approach toward the United Nations involves picking and choosing carefully which issues to pursue in the world body. Those likely to become politicized by the majority can be channeled elsewhere. Thus, real disarmament negotiations will continue to be conducted directly with the Soviets in START, MBFR, and INF; many economic decisions will remain centered in the OECD, World Bank, and other international financial institutions; and selected Latin American issues will be dealt with in the OAS. While these subjects will still be raised in New York, discussions there can in most cases be treated as symbolic and essentially non-binding. The United States would, in any case, continue to insist on its point of view and veto power on issues of clear and immediate principle, but not necessarily seek confrontation on matters of secondary interest.

On larger issues like the Arab–Israeli conflict and global negotiations, U.S. positions in the United Nations are shaped by strong public involvement. On such matters, any amendment to agreed wording at the United Nations—for example, in Resolution 242 of 1967, on the Middle East—is charged with domestic political consequence. In other cases diplomatic flexibility without compromise of basic principles can reduce the number of issues on which the United States is isolated. This does not mean acquiesence, but more frequent abstention or non-participation in place of quixotic efforts to set the standard. In this way, respect for U.S. authority is likely to be greater when its representatives speak firmly on points of real principle.

A modified—some would say more casual—approach to the United Nations is not, however, a simple tactical adjustment of foreign policy, but is closely linked to public opinion and domestic politics. Located in New York, the United Nations provides a window on foreign policy—however distorted or divorced from the reality of particular situations—for domestic opinion. Its biases and frequent condemnations of the United States, reported in U.S. media almost to the exclusion of positive elements, contribute to public and congressional perceptions of an adversary relationship. Unlike an American embassy abroad, the U.S. Mission to the United Nations is frequently at the intersection of foreign policy and domestic opinion. Popular commitment to Israel and the concern of U.S. media with the New World Information Order directly shape behavior in the United Nations and will continue to do so. Within these limits, however, modification of official and public expectations for the United Nations and the U.S. role in it is possible, but requires a gradual and sustained process of education.

Acceptance of U.N. proceedings as a continuing process with, for the most part, symbolic rather than literal significance opens the door to different uses of the United Nations. The concentration of 157 states as members and 6 as observers is an unparalleled political forum and source of information. U.N. informality offers easy access to top diplomats of the developing countries, who are usually more open to dialogue and attention in New York than in their own capitals. Their numbers invariably include diplomats marked for rapid advancement, and an unusually high proportion have gone on to become foreign ministers. Such contacts should be closely coordinated with U.S. objectives and programs in each country, rather than focused exclusively on lobbying for U.N. votes, which, with the exception of a few litmus issues, tend not to be of lasting importance. Use of the United Nations on less than the multi-lateral level can be an important adjunct to bilateral diplomacy and useful in building support for U.S. regional policies. France, Japan, Australia, and others appear to have been more adept than Washington at balancing official U.N. proceedings with quiet pursuit of such foreign policy goals.

A broader approach does not necessarily downplay the United Nations itself or its objectives, but only the importance of rhetorical debate and repetitious tests of voting strength. As regional groups have gained power, the United Nations has, in any case, become less useful as a forum for expression of U.S. values as ideology. The cabinet-level designation of the U.S. ambassador to the United Nations may therefore today give undue prestige and publicity to a body where the United States is regularly outvoted. It is also an anomaly not considered necessary by any of the other 156 members. Appointment of professional diplomats is probably in the long run more consistent with scaled-down U.S. expectations, objectives, and participation in the United Nations. On the other hand, a "political" ambassador with a domestic constituency and ties to the White House will probably be required, at least for the near term, to justify and "sell" U.S. participation in the United Nations to an increasingly skeptical Congress and public.

It is easier to describe than prescribe, and the foregoing has not attempted to make specific recommendations, but to suggest outlines of a general U.S. approach to both the NAM and the United Nations to ease the present sterile confrontation. The remedies proposed, essentially diplomatic in nature, seek to increase areas of shared interest between the non-aligned and the United States and to resolve problems such as Namibia and the Middle East which have been used as leverage against the West. The confrontational approach of the non-aligned is, however, deeply ingrained and will at best adjust slowly to changes in the international situation. Both the United States and the majority of the non-aligned, nevertheless, have a broad stake, not shared by the Soviet bloc, in solution to these problems. In light of this, the movement's arrested development in an anti-colonial and anti-Western mode must be seen in part as a failure of U.S. policy over the past two decades. A challenge for the mid-1980s will, therefore, be to devise a well integrated and consistent U.S. approach to the NAM and the U.N. By 1983, the non-aligned have fundamentally altered the structure and agenda of the United Nations, and historic U.S. patterns of behavior and perceptions of the organizations are no longer relevant. The U.N. process remains valuable, however, and dialogue there can still change perceptions on both sides, eroding ideology with an appreciation of interrelated problems.

NOTES

1. Socialist Republic of Vietnam, *The Non-Aligned Movement: History—Present Problems* (Hanoi: Information and Press Dept., Ministry of Foreign Affairs, 1981).

2. Interview of President Nasser with Hanz Fleig of Hamburg TV, 1961. Published in Gamal Abdel Nasser, *On Non-Alignment* (Cairo: Information Administration, Ministry of National Guidance, 1966), p. 17.

3. Warren Hoge, "Bogota Begins Seeking 'New Partners' Among Non-aligned," written interview with Colombian President Belisario Betancur Cuartas, *New York Times*, Jan. 9, 1983, p. E5.

4. G.H. Jansen, *Non-alignment and the Afro-Asian States* (New York: Frederick A. Praeger, 1966), p. 41.

5. Ibid., p. 72.

6. Jyoti Sengupta, *Non-alignment—Search for a Destination* (Calcutta: Naya Prakash, 1979), p. 49.

7. Eugene Berg, *Non-alignement et nouvel ordre mondial* (Paris: Presses Universitaires de France, 1980), p. 22.

8. Peter Willetts, *The Non-Aligned Movement* (New York: Nichols Publishing Co., 1978), p. 12.

9. Jansen, op. cit., p. 296.

10. Fouad Ajami, "The Fate of Non-Alignment," *Foreign Affairs*, Winter 1980–81, p. 383.

11. Felix R.D. Bandaranaike, "History of Non-alignment as a Force for Peace and Stability in a Divided World," in U.S. Bajpai, ed., *Non-alignment: Perspectives and Prospects* (New Delhi: Lancers Publishers, 1983), p. 22.

12. Willetts, op. cit.

13. Nicaraguan Ministry of Foreign Affairs, Office of Multi-lateral Organizations, *The Movement of Non-aligned Countries—an Indispensable Force in the Anti-Imperialist Struggle* (Managua: Office of Multi-lateral Organizations, Ministry of Foreign Affairs, 1983), p. 10.

14. Bandaranaike Centre for International Studies, *Non-Aligned Conferences: Basic Documents*, (Colombo: Gunaratne and Co., 1976), p. 52.

15. Robert A. Mortimer, *The Third World Coalition in International Politics* (New York: Praeger Publishers, 1980), p. 28.

16. Bandaranaike Centre for International Studies, op. cit., p. 95.

17. Nicaraguan Ministry of Foreign Affairs, op. cit., p. 82.

18. Z.A. Bhutto, *The Third World: New Directions* (London: Quartet Books, 1977), p. 19, quoted in S.C. Gangal, "Non-alignment and the Third

World: Convergence and Divergence," in K.P. Misra, *Non-alignment: Frontiers and Dynamics* (New Delhi: Vikas Publishing House, 1982), p. 193.

19. John Graham, "The Non-Aligned Movement After the Havana Summit," *Journal of International Affairs* 34, no. 1 (Spring/Summer 1980): 157.

20. *Addresses Delivered at the Sixth Conference of Heads of State or Government of Non-Aligned Countries* (Havana: Editorial de Ciencias Sociales, 1980), p. 147.

21. Rikhi Jaipal, *Non-alignment: Origins, Growth and Potential for World Peace* (New Delhi: Allied Publishers Ltd., 1983), p. 130.

22. Jansen, op. cit., p. 287.

23. M.S. Rajan, "Non-Alignment: The Dichotomy Between Theory and Practice in Perspective," *India Quarterly*, Jan.–Mar. 1980, p. 46.

24. Ibid., p. 48.

25. Sushil Kumar et al., "Cooperation among Non-Aligned Countries," *Foreign Affairs Reports*, Apr.–May 1980, p. 75.

26. A.C. Shahul Hameed, *In Pursuit of Peace: On Non-alignment and Regional Cooperation* (New Delhi: Vikas Publishing House, 1983), p. x.

27. Ibid., p. xviii.

28. Peter Willetts, *The Non-Aligned in Havana* (New York: St. Martin's Press, 1981), p. 37.

29. Bandaranaike Centre for International Studies, op. cit., p. 13.

30. Edvard Kardelj, *Yugoslavia in International Relations and in the Non-Aligned Movement* (Belgrade: Socialist Thought and Practice, 1979), p. 188.

31. M.S. Rajan, "Institutionalization of Non-alignment," in K.P. Misra, ed., *Non-alignment: Frontiers and Dynamics* (New Delhi: Vikas Publishing House, 1982), p. 55.

32. A.W. Singham, *The Non-aligned Movement in World Politics* (Westport, Conn.: Lawrence Hill, 1978), p. 227.

33. Hameed, op. cit., p. xi.

34. George Kennan, letter to the author dated Nov. 22, 1982.

35. Shanti Swarup, "Non-alignment, Mobilization and Capability," in K.P. Misra, ed., *Non-alignment: Frontiers and Dynamics* (New Delhi: Vikas Publishing House, 1982), p. 52.

36. Muhiuddin Shawl, statement at Seminar on Non-alignment: Options for the New Delhi Summit," New Delhi, Indian International Center, Feb. 27, 1983.

37. Miljan Komatina, "Policy and Movement of Non-Alignment and the United Nations," *Review of International Affairs*, Oct. 5, 1981, p. 11.

38. Bandaranaike Centre for International Studies, op. cit., p. 41.

39. Komatina, op. cit., p. 12.

40. Bernard D. Nossiter, "The UN Role: Mudslinging or Consciousness-Raising," *New York Times*, Jan. 30, 1982.

41. Thomas M. Franck et al., *An Attitude Survey: Diplomats' Views on the United Nations System* (New York: UNITAR, 1982), pp. 8–14.

42. Davidson Nicol, *Paths to Peace* (New York: Pergamon Press, 1981), p. 175.

43. Ibid., pp. 68, 72.

44. Nicaraguan Ministry of Foreign Affairs, op. cit., p. 93.

45. Brian Urquhart, "International Peace and Security," *Foreign Affairs*, Fall 1981, pp. 14–15.

46. Nicol, op. cit., p. x.

47. Ibid., pp. 245–47.

48. Nicaraguan Ministry of Foreign Affairs, loc. cit.

49. Davidson Nicol, "The Non-Aligned Group in the Security Council," *Review of International Affairs*, Feb. 20, 1980, p. 16.

50. Nicol, *Paths to Peace*, p. 96.

51. "US Vetoes UN Resolution on Golan Annexation," *New York Times*, Jan. 21, 1982, p. A13.

52. Ibid.

53. Nicaraguan Ministry of Foreign Affairs, loc. cit.

54. Ruth B. Russell, *The General Assembly: Patterns/Problems/Prospects* (New York: Carnegie Endowment, 1970), p. 54.

55. Kurt Jacobsen, *The General Assembly of the United Nations: A Quantitative Analysis of Conflict, Inequality, and Relevance* (Oslo: Universitetsforlaget, 1978), p. 43.

56. Ibid., p. 57.

57. Vladislav B. Tikhomirov, *Quantitative Analysis of Voting Behaviour in the General Assembly* (New York: UNITAR, 1981), p. 42.

58. Thomas Hovet, Jr., *Bloc Politics in the United Nations* (Cambridge, Mass.: Harvard University Press, 1960), pp. 30–31, (quoted in Sydney Bailey, *The General Assembly of the United Nations* (New York: Frederick A. Praeger, 1964), p. 24.

59. Daniel Patrick Moynihan, *A Dangerous Place* (New York: Berkeley Books, 1980), pp. 123–24.

60. "Someone Is Trying to Fire Dr. Waldheim," *New York Times*, Nov. 1981, p. E5.

61. Norman A. Graham and Robert S. Jordan, *The International Civil Service* (New York: Pergamon Press, 1980), p. 13.

62. Theodor Meron, *The United Nations Secretariat* (Lexington, Mass.: Lexington Books, 1977), p. 197.

63. Russell, op. cit., p. 5.

64. Jacobsen, op. cit., p. 174.

65. Moynihan, op. cit., p. 209.

66. Lazar Mojsov, *Dimensions of Non-Alignment* (Belgrade: Medjunarodna Politika, 1982), p. 55.

67. Komatina, op. cit., p. 12.

68. Ibid., p. 13.

69. Erik Suy, "The Meaning of Consensus in Multilateral Diplomacy," in Robert J. Akkerman et al., *Declarations on Principles—a Quest for Universal Peace* (Leiden: Sijthoff, 1977), p. 472.

70. Louis Henkin, et al., *International Law, Cases and Materials* (St. Paul, Minn.: West Publishing Co., 1980), pp. 108–11.

71. *Business Week*, July 20, 1981.

72. Remarks by T.N. Kaul, in K. Kamalanathan, *National Seminar on Non-Alignment* (Tirupati, India, Sri Venkateswara University Press, 1977), p. 189.

73. Swarup, op. cit., p. 58.

74. Jansen, op. cit., p. 252.

75. Mojsov, op. cit., p. 246.

76. James F. Grant, "The Soviet Approach to the Non-Aligned Movement," individual research paper (1980) prepared for the National War College, on file in the library of the National Defense College, Washington, D.C., p. 67.

77. G. Bondarevski and V. Sofinski, *Le non-alignement: Ses amis et ses adversaires dans la politique mondiale* (Moscow: Academy of Sciences of the USSR, 1978), p. 6.

78. Rais A. Tuzmukhamedov, *Soviet Union and Non-Aligned Nations* (Bombay: Allied Publishers, 1976), p. 65.

79. Zafar Imam, "Soviet View of Non-alignment," in K.P. Misra, ed., *Non-alignment: Frontiers and Dynamics* (New Delhi: Vikas Publishing House Ltd., 1982), p. 453.

80. Jaipal, op. cit., p. 149.

81. Devendra Kaushik, "Soviet Perspectives on the Third World: Ideological Retreat or Refinement?" *The Non-aligned World* 1 (Jan.–Mar. 1983): 87.

82. Imam, op. cit., pp. 466–68.

83. William M. LeoGrande, "Evolution of the Non-Aligned Movement," *Problems of Communism*, Jan.–Feb. 1980, p. 39.

84. Tuzmukhamedov, op. cit., p. ix.

85. LeoGrande, op. cit., p. 42; *Addresses Delivered at the Sixth Conference ... of Non-Aligned Countries*, p. 6.

86. Grant, op. cit., p. 85.

87. Miljan Komatina, "Non-Alignment: Differences and Disputes," *Review of International Affairs*, Apr. 5, 1982.

88. Tuzmukhamedov, op. cit., p. 10.

89. Leo Mates, "The Movement Is Facing Discord and Trial," in U.S. Bajpai, ed., *Non-alignment: Perspectives and Prospects* (New Delhi: Lancer's Publishers, 1983), p. 55.

90. Nicol, *Paths to Peace*, p. 175.

91. Vladimir Petrovskiy, *Soviet Journal of International Affairs*, Apr. 1982.

92. Francis Fukuyama, "A New Soviet Strategy," *Commentary*, Oct. 1979.

93. Robert H. Donaldson, ed., *The Soviet Union in the Third World: Successes and Failures* (Boulder, Colo.: Westview Press, 1981), p. 378.

94. Commencement address by Secretary of State John Foster Dulles, delivered at Iowa State College, June 9, 1956, reprinted in *New York Times*, June 10, 1956.

95. *New York Times*, Sept. 23, 1961, quoted in B.K. Shrivastava, "The United States and the Non-aligned Movement," in K.P. Misra, ed., *Non-alignment: Frontiers and Dynamics* (New Delhi: Vikas Publishing House, 1982), p. 436.

96. Mason Sears, *Years of High Purpose: From Trusteeship to Nationhood* (Washington, D.C.: University Press of America, 1980), pp. 95, 135.

97. Julius Nyerere, "America and Southern Africa," *Foreign Affairs*, Summer 1977, p. 671.

98. Jaipal, op. cit., p. 118.

99. Henry Kissinger, speech to Indian Council on World Affairs, New Delhi, Oct. 28, 1974.

100. Moynihan, op. cit., p. 310.

101. Daniel Patrick Moynihan, *Counting Our Blessings—Reflections on the Future of America* (Boston: Little, Brown and Co., 1980), p. 49.

102. Moynihan, *A Dangerous Place*, p. 309.

103. Quoted from Jan. 23, 1976, circular cable from Ambassador Moynihan to Secretary Kissinger and all U.S. embassies, *New York Times*, Jan. 28, 1976, p. 8.

104. *Addresses Delivered at the Sixth Conference... of Non-Aligned Countries*, p. 4.

105. Robert Shaplen, "A Reporter at Large: Alignments Among the Non-Aligned," *The New Yorker*, Oct. 22, 1979, pp. 157–58.

106. Mojsov, op. cit., p. 239.

107. Bernard D. Nossiter, "US as Whipping Boy," *New York Times*, Oct. 5, 1981, quoted in *The Congressional Record* 127, no. 151 (Oct. 22, 1981).

108. Letter, dated Oct. 21, 1981, from Daniel P. Moynihan to colleagues in the U.S. Senate.

109. U.S. State Department, "Report to Congress on the Non-Aligned Countries Regarding the Communiqué of September 28, 1981," submitted in accordance with Section 720(B) of P.L. 97-113, Jan. 28, 1982.

110. *El nuevo diario* (Managua), Jan. 6, 1983.

111. *Barricada* (Managua), Jan. 13, 1983.

112. *The Patriot* (New Delhi), Mar. 4, 1983; *Barricada* (Managua), Mar. 2, 1983.

113. Editorial in *Granma*, Oct. 19, 1981.

114. Rajan, "Institutionalization of Non-alignment," p. 43.

115. Soedjatmoko, "Non-alignment and Beyond," *The Non-aligned World* 1 (Jan.–Mar. 1983): 9, 17.

116. U.S. Bajpai, ed., *Non-alignment: Perspectives and Prospects* (New Delhi: Lancers Publishers, 1983), pp. x–xi.

117. Rajan, "Institutionalization of Non-alignment," p. 475.

118. B. Vivekanandan, "Non-alignment and the Chinese Perspective," in K.P. Misra, ed., *Non-alignment: Frontiers and Dynamics* (New Delhi: Vikas Publishing House, 1981), p. 475.

119. Swaminathan S. Aiyar, "Scrapping Global Negotiations," *The Indian Express*, Mar. 8, 1983, p.

120. *The Times of India,* Mar. 24, 1983, p. 9.

121. Jaipal, op. cit., p. 152.

122. A. Appadorai, "Non-alignment: Some Important Issues," in K.P. Misra, ed., *Non-alignment: Frontiers and Dynamics* (New Delhi: Vikas Publishing House, 1981), p. 10.

123. Richard B. Morris, *The Emerging Nations and the American Revolution* Harper and Row, (New York: 1970): quoted in Attar Chand, *Non-aligned World Order: Ideology, Strategy, Prospects* (New Delhi: UDH Publishers, 1983), p. 181.

124. Samir Amin, "After the New International Economic Order: The Future of International Economic Relations," in U.S. Bajpai, ed., *Non-alignment: Perspectives and Prospects* (New Delhi: Lancers Publishers, 1983), p. 207.

125. *Newsweek,* Mar. 21, 1983.

126. Brandt Commission, *Common Crisis: North-South Cooperation for World Recovery* (London: Pan Books, 1983), quoted in *The Financial Times* (London), Feb. 9, 1983.

127. A.K. Das Gupta, "Non-alignment and the International Economic Order," in K.P. Misra, ed., *Non-alignment: Frontiers and Dynamics* (New Delhi: Vikas Publishing House, 1981), p. 137.

128. Aiyar, op. cit.

129. Ricardo Alarcon, "Significance of the Movement of the Non-aligned Countries," *Review of International Affairs,* Nov. 5, 1981, p. 9.

130. Das Gupta, op. cit., p. 140.

131. Amin, op. cit., p. 208.

132. *Newsweek,* Sept. 15, 1975, p. 37, quoted in Grant, op. cit., p. 93.

133. Charles Krauthammer, "Rich Nations, Poor Nations," *The New Republic,* Apr. 11, 1981, p. 20.

134. Daniel Patrick Moynihan, *The Congressional Record,* 97th Cong., 1st sess. 127 (October 22, 1981), p. 5.

Selected Bibliography

Books

Addresses Delivered at the Sixth Conference of Heads of State or Government of Non-Aligned Countries. Havana. Editorial de Ciencias Sociales, 1980.

Bailey, Sydney. *The General Assembly of the United Nations*. New York: Frederick A. Praeger, 1964.

Bajpai, U.S., ed. *Non-alignment: Perspectives and Prospects*. New Delhi. Lancers Publishers, 1983.

Bandaranaike Centre for International Studies. *Non-Aligned Conferences: Basic Documents*. Colombo: Gunartatne and Co., 1976.

Bandyopadhyaya, Jayantanuja. *North over South*. New Delhi. South Asian Publishers, 1982.

Berg, Eugene. *Non-alignement et nouvel ordre mondial*. Paris: Presses Universitaires de France, 1980.

Bondarevski, G., and V. Sofinski, *Le non-alignement: Ses amis et ses adversaires dans la politique mondiale*. Moscow. Academy of Sciences of the USSR, 1978.

Brandt Commission. *Common Crisis: North-South Cooperation for World Recovery*. London. Pan Books, 1983.

Castro, Fidel. *The World Economic and Social Crisis*. Havana. Publishing Office of the Council of State, 1983.

Chand, Attar. *Non-aligned Nations: Arms Race and Disarmament*. New Delhi: UDH Publishers, 1983.

———. *Non-aligned Solidarity and National Security*. New Delhi: UDH Publishers, 1983.

———. *Non-aligned States: A Great Leap Forward*. New Delhi: UDH Publishers, 1983.

———. *Non-aligned World Order: Ideology, Strategy, Prospects*. New Delhi: UDH Publishers, 1983.

Colard, Daniel. *Le mouvement des pays non-alignes*. Paris. La Documentation Française, 1981.

Committee on Foreign Relations, U.S. Senate. *Proposals for UN Reform, Report Pursuant to Section 503 of the Foreign Relations Authorization Act, Fiscal Year 1978 (Public Law 95-105)*. Washington, D.C.: U.S. Government Printing Office, 1978.

Crabb, Cecil V., Jr. *The Elephants and the Grass: A Study of Non-Alignment*. New York: Frederick A. Praeger, 1965.

Donaldson, Robert H. ed. *The Soviet Union in the Third World: Successes and Failures*. Boulder, Colo.: Westview Press, 1981.

Finger, Seymour Maxwell. *Your Man at the UN: People, Politics and Bureaucracy in Making Foreign Policy*. New York: New York University Press, 1980.

Franck, Thomas M., John P. Renninger, and Vladislav B. Tikhomirov. *An Attitude Survey: Diplomats' Views on the United Nations System*. New York: UNITAR, 1982.

Gal, Choidogin. *Socialist Community and Non-alignment*. New Delhi: Allied Publishers, 1979.

Gopal, Krishnan. *Non-alignment and Power Politics*. New Delhi: V.I. Publishers, 1983.

Goryanov, Mikhail. *Two Ways of Looking at the Indian Ocean*. Moscow: Novosti Press Agency, 1981.

Graham, Norman A., and Robert S. Jordan. *The International Civil Service*. New York: Pergamon Press, 1980.

Gupta, Vijay. *India and Non-alignment*. New Delhi: New Literature, 1983.

Hameed, A.C. Shahul. *In Pursuit of Peace: On Non-alignment and Regional Cooperation*. New Delhi: Vikas Publishing House, 1983.

Hansen, Roger D. *Beyond the North-South Stalemate*. Overseas Development Council, New York: 1979.

Iman, Zafar. *Towards a Model Relationship: A Study of Soviet Treaties with India and Other Third World Countries*. New Delhi: ABC Publishing House, 1983.

India, Government of. *Two Decades of Non-alignment: Documents of the Gatherings of Non-aligned Countries, 1961–1982*. New Delhi: Ministry of External Affairs, 1983.

Jacobsen, Kurt. *The General Assembly of the United Nations: A Quantative Analysis of Conflict, Inequality, and Relevance*. Oslo: Universitesforlaget, 1978.

Jaipal, Rikhi. *Non-alignment: Origins, Growth and Potential for World Peace*. New Delhi: Allied Publishers, 1983.

Jaisingh, Hari. *India and the Non-aligned World: Search for a New Order*. New Delhi: Vikas Publishing House, 1983.

Jankowitsch, Odette, and Karl P. Sauvant, eds. *The Third World Without Superpowers: The Collected Documents of the Nonaligned Countries*. Dobbs Ferry, N.Y.: Oceana, 1978.

Jansen, G.H. *Non-alignment and the Afro-Asian States*. New York: Frederick A. Praeger, 1966.

Jawatkar, K.S. *Diego Garcia in International Diplomacy*. Bombay: Popular Prakashan, 1983.

Kamalanathan, K. *National Seminar on Non-Alignment*. Tirupati, India: Sri Venkateswara University Press, 1977.

Kardelj, Edvard. *Yugoslavia in International Relations and in the Non-Aligned Movement*. Belgrade: Socialist Thought and Practice, 1979.

Khan, Rasheeduddin. *Perspectives on Non-alignment*. New Delhi. Kalamkar Prakashan Ltd., 1981.

Lall, K.B. *Struggle for Change*. New Delhi: Allied Publishers, 1983.

Martin, Laurance W. *Neutralism and Non-alignment: The New States in World Affairs*. New York: Frederick A. Praeger, 1962.
Mates, Leo. *Nonalignment Theory and Current Practice*. Belgrade: Belgrade Institute, 1972.
Menon, M.S.N. *No to Exploitation*. New Delhi: Mahajan Publishing House, 1983.
Meron, Theodor. *The United Nations Secretariat*. Lexington, Mass.: Lexington Books, 1977.
Misra, K.P. *Non-alignment and Neutralism*. New Delhi. Indian Council for Cultural Relations, 1982.
———. *Non-alignment: Frontiers and Dynamics*. New Delhi. Vikas Publishing House, 1982.
Mojsov, Lazar. *Dimensions of Non-Alignment*. Belgrade. Medjunarodna Politika, 1982.
Mortimer, Robert A. *The Third World Coalition in International Politics*. New York: Praeger Publishers, 1980.
Moynihan, Daniel Patrick. *A Dangerous Place*. New York: Berkeley Books, 1980.
———. *Counting Our Blessings—Reflections on the Future of America*. Boston: Little, Brown and Co., 1980.
Nasser, Gamal Abdel. *On Non-Alignment*. Cairo: Ministry of National Guidance, 1966.
Nicaraguan Ministry of Foreign Affairs. *The Movement of Non-Aligned Countries—An Indispensable Force in the Anti-Imperialist Struggle*. Managua: Nicaragua. Office of Multi-Lateral Organizations, Ministry of Foreign Affairs, 1983.
Nicol, Davidson. *Paths to Peace*. New York: Pergamon Press, 1981.
———. *The United Nations Security Council—Towards Greater Effectiveness*. New York: UNITAR, 1982.
Nord, Lars. *Nonalignment and Socialism*. Uppsala. 1974.
Orbis Press Agency. *Non-aligned Countries*. Prague: Orbis Press Agency Publishing, 1982.
Petkovic, Ranko. *Non-Alignment in the Contemporary World*. Belgrade. Medjunarodna: 1980.
———. *Non-Alignment*. Belgrade: STP, 1979.
———. *Non-Alignment and the Big Powers*. Belgrade: Jugoslovenska Stvarnost, 1979.
———. *Non-alignment—An Independent Factor in the Democratization of International Relations*. Belgrade: Socialist Thought and Practice, 1979.
Rao, T.V. Subra. *Non-alignment in International Law and Politics*. New Delhi: Deep and Deep Publications, 1981.
Rothstein, Robert L. *The Third World and US Foreign Policy*. Boulder, Colo.: Westview Press, 1981.
Russell, Ruth B. *The General Assembly: Patterns/Problems/Prospects*. New York: Carnegie Endowment for International Peace, 1970.

Saini, M.K. *Aspects of Non-alignment*. New Delhi: Kalamkar Prakashan Ltd., 1981.

Sauvant, Carl P. *Changing Priorities on the International Agenda*. New York: Pergamon Press, 1981.

———. *The Group of '77*. New York: Oceana Publications, 1981.

Saxena, Munish N. *Non-aligned Movement in the Eighties*. Moscow: Novosti, 1982.

Sears, Mason. *Years of High Purpose: From Trusteeship to Nationhood*. Washington, D.C.: University Press of America, 1980.

Sengupta, Jyoti. *Non-alignment—Search for a Destination*. Calcutta: Naya Prakash, 1979.

Sharma, Soumitra. *Development Strategy and Developing Countries*. New Delhi: South Asian Publishers, 1983.

Singapore Ministry of Foreign Affairs. *Havana and New Delhi: What's the Difference?* Singapore: National Printers Ltd., 1983.

Singham, A.W. *The Non-aligned Movement in World Politics*. Westport, Conn.: Lawrence Hill, 1978.

Socialist Republic of Vietnam. "The Non-Aligned Movement: History—Present Problems," Hanoi: Information and Press Dept., Ministry of Foreign Affairs, 1981.

Subrahmanyam, K. *Indian Security Perspectives*. New Delhi: ABC Publishing House, 1983.

Sud, Usha. *Decolonization to World Order*. New Delhi: National Publishing House, 1983.

Tandon, J.C., Sunita Batra, and Regina Muley. *Non-alignment: A Bibliography*. New Delhi: Lancers Publishers, 1983.

Tewari, Udai Narain. *Resurgent Tibet*. New Delhi: Selectbook Service Syndicate, 1983.

Tikhomirov, Vladislav B. *Quantitative Analysis of Voting Behaviour in the General Assembly*. New York: UNITAR, 1981.

Tuzmukhamedov, Rais A. *The Soviet Union and Non-Aligned Nations*. Bombay: Allied Publishers, 1976.

Vohra, Dewan C. *Economic Relevance of Non-alignment*. New Delhi: ABC Publishing House, 1983.

Vukadinovic, Radovan. *Non-Aligned Countries and Detente*. Belgrade: Jugoslovenska Stvarnost, 1979.

Willetts, Peter. *The Non-Aligned Movement*. New York: Nichols Publishing Company, 1978.

———. *The Non-Aligned in Havana*. New York: St. Martin's Press, 1981.

Articles

Ajami, Fouad. "The Fate of Non-Alignment." *Foreign Affairs*, Winter 1980–81.

Akinyemi, A. Bolaji. "Non-Alignment Today." *Review of International Affairs*, Mar. 5, 1980.

Alarcon, Ricardo. "Significance of the Movement of the Non-aligned Countries." *Review of International Affairs*, Nov. 5, 1981.

Bissel, Richard. "The Fourth World at the UN." *The World Today*, Sept. 1975.

Bondarevski, G. "Non-aligned Movement and the Pernicious Theory of Equidistance." *Soviet Review*, Aug. 27, 1979.

Bose, Pradip. "The Non-aligned Movement and Its Tasks." Paper presented at Indian International Center Seminar on Options for the New Delhi Summit, Feb. 27, 1983.

Bulajic, Krsto. "Cooperation Among Non-Aligned Countries." *Review of International Affairs*, Feb. 20, 1980.

Chavan, Yeshwantrao B. "Non-alignment in the Eighties." *Mainstream*, Mar. 1983.

Chisti, Sumitra. "Non-aligned India's Economic Relations with the Socialist Bloc." *The Non-aligned World* 1 (Jan.–Mar. 1983).

Chopra, Maharaj K. "Non-alignment: Military Dimension." *Problems of Non-alignment* 1 (Mar.–May 1983).

Corea, Ernest. "Non-Alignment: The Dynamics of a Movement." *Behind the Headlines*: (Canadian Institute of International Affairs,) June 1977.

Damodaran, A.K. "An Agenda for Non-alignment." *Mainstream*, Mar. 1983.

Eilan, Arieh. "Soviet Hegemonism and the Nonaligned." *The Washington Quarterly*, Winter 1981.

Fernando, B.J. "The Non-Aligned Movement: Democratic in Spirit and Practice." *Review of International Affairs*, Feb. 5, 1980.

Golob, Ignac. "Non-Alignment and Detente." *Review of International Affairs*, Sept. 20, 1981.

Graham, John A. "The Non-Aligned Movement After the Havana Summit." *Journal of International Affairs* 34, no. 11 (Spring/Summer 1980).

Grant, James F. "The Soviet Approach to the Non-Aligned Movement." Individual research paper prepared for the National War College (1980). On file in library of National Defense University, Washington, D.C.

Ijewrey, Dr. "Nigeria and Non-Alignment." *Review of International Affairs*, Feb. 5, 1980.

India, Government of. "Non-alignment: A Blueprint for Peace." New Delhi Ministry of External Affairs, 1983.

Jarrin, Edgardo Mercado. "Non-Alignment and the Conflict Between North and South." *Review of International Affairs*, Sept. 20, 1981.

Jawaharal Nehru University. "Non-alignment: Tasks and Issues." New Delhi: Delhi University Press, 1983.

Jawatkar, K.S. "Issues Before the New Delhi Summit: Relevance of Non-alignment." Paper presented at India International Center Seminar on Options for the New Delhi Summit, Feb. 27, 1983.

Joshi, Nirmala. "The Soviet Union and the Non-aligned Countries: Natural Allies?" *Problems of Non-alignment* 1 (Mar.–May 1983).

Kashkett, Steven B. "Iraq and the Pursuit of Non-alignment." *ORBIS*, Summer 1982.

Kaushik, Devendra. "Soviet Perspectives on the Third World: Ideological

Retreat or Refinement?" *The Non-aligned World* 1 (Jan.–Mar. 1983).

Keenleyside, T.A. "Prelude to Power: The Meaning of Non-Alignment Before Indian Independence." *Pacific Affairs*, Fall 1980.

Kijun, Edvard. "The Non-Aligned Countries and Nuclear Energy." *Review of International Affairs*, Aug. 5–20, 1980.

Komatina, Miljan. "What Lies Ahead of the Non-Aligned." *Review of International Affairs*, June 5, 1980.

———. "Policy and Movement of Non-Alignment and the United Nations." *Review of International Affairs*, Oct. 5, 1981.

Larabee, F. Stephen. "The Soviet Union and the Non-aligned." *World Today*, Dec. 1976.

LeoGrande, William M. "Evolution of the Non-Aligned Movement." *Problems of Communism*, June 1980.

Mates, Leo. "Role of the Founders in the Movement of the Non-Aligned." *Review of International Affairs*, Sept. 20, 1981.

Mehta, Jagat S. "Non-aligned Principles and Non-Aligned Movement." *Mainstream*, Mar. 1983.

Minic, Milos. "Unity on the Authentic Principles of Non-Alignment." *Socialist Thought and Practice*, Jan. 1980.

———. "The Activity of Non-Aligned Countries in the Struggle for World Peace." *Review of International Affairs*, Feb. 20, 1980.

———. "The Policy and Movement of Non-Alignment in the 1980s." *Review of International Affairs*, Sept. 20, 1981.

———. "The Forceful Presence of Non-Alignment in the World." *Review of International Affairs*, Dec. 20, 1981.

Mishra, Pramod Kumar. "South Asian Responses at Non-aligned Summits from Belgrade to Havana." *Problems of Non-alignment* 1 (Mar.–May, 1983).

Misra, K.P. "The Conceptual Profile of Non-Alignment." *Review of International Affairs*, July 5–20, 1980.

———. "Burma's Farewell to the Non-Aligned Movement." *Asian Affairs*, Feb. 1981.

Muij, D. "Seventh Non-Aligned Summit Postponed." *Review of International Affairs*, Sept. 5, 1982.

Mujezinovic, Dzevad. "Non-Alignment and Crisis in Asia." *Review of International Affairs*, Dec. 5, 1980.

Murthi, C.S.R. "Between the Summits." *The Non-aligned World*, 1 (Jan.–Mar. 1983).

Nair, V.M. "Havana Summit Shows up Non-Aligned Divisions." *The Round Table: The Commonwealth Journal of International Affairs*, Jan. 1980.

Naryanan, K.R. "Non-Alignment, Independence and National Interests." *Review of International Affairs*, Sept. 20, 1980.

Nick Stanko. "Action Forms of the Non-Aligned Movement and Advancement of Democratic Relations Within its Framework." *Review of International Affairs*, Dec. 20, 1981.

Nicol, Davidson. "The Non-Aligned Group in the Security Council." *Review of International Affairs*, Feb. 20, 1980.

Novak, Andrej. "The Non-Aligned in the 1980s." *Socialist Thought and Practice*, July–Aug. 1980.

Nujoma, Sam. "The Non-Aligned Movement and the Struggle for National Liberation in Southern Africa." *Review of International Affairs*, Sept. 20, 1981.

O'Brien, Conor Cruise. "Non-alignment." *New Statesman*, Apr. 8, 1966.

Ogene, F. Chidozie. "The Impact of the International System on the Non-Aligned Movement." *Review of International Affairs*, Sept. 20, 1980.

Petkovic, Ranko. "International Conference on Non-Alignment in Lagos." *Review of International Affairs*, Feb. 20, 1980.

———. "Indo-Yugoslav Symposium on Non-Alignment." *Review of International Affairs*, June 5, 1980.

———. "The Authentic Principles of Non-Alignment." *Review of International Affairs*, Sept. 20, 1981.

———. "Non-alignment Is not in Crisis." *Mainstream*, Mar. 1983.

Pilon, Juliana Geran. "Through the Looking Glass: The Political Culture of the UN." *(The Heritage Foundation,)* Aug. 30, 1982.

Rajan, K.P. "Soviet Union and Law of the Sea. *Problems of Non-alignment* 1 (Mar.–May 1983).

Rajan, M.S. "Non-Alignment: The Dichotomy Between Theory and Practice in Perspective." *India Quarterly*, Jan.–Mar. 1980.

———. "Non-Alignment: The New Delhi Conference and After." *Southeast Asian Affairs* (Institute of Southeast Asian Studies, Singapore), 1982.

Rana, A.P., Sushil Swarup Kumar, and S.D. Shanti Muni. "Cooperation Among Non-Aligned Countries. Evolution, Principles, Forms and Outcomes." *Foreign Affairs Reports: Indian Council of World Affairs*, Apr.–May 1980.

Ranganathan, A. "India and the Non-aligned Movement." Paper presented at India International Center Seminar on Options for the New Delhi Summit, Feb. 27, 1983.

Rao, P.V. Narasimha. "Adherence to the Principles and Aims of Non-alignment." *Review of International Affairs*, June 5, 1980.

Sarajcic, Ivo. "Non-Alignment, Independence and National Interests." *Review of International Affairs*, Aug. 5–20, 1980.

Sauvant, Karl P. "The Non-aligned Movement and the Group of 77." *The Non-aligned World* 1 (Jan.–Mar. 1983).

Seth, V.S. "Non-alignment and the Crisis Situation in the Horn." *Problems of Non-alignment* 1 (Mar.–May 1983).

Shaplen, Robert. "A Reporter at Large: Alignments Among the Nonaligned." *The New Yorker*, Oct. 22, 1979.

Shaplen, Robert A. "A Reporter at Large: The Paradox of Non-alignment." *The New Yorker*, May 23, 1983.

Singh, Dinesh. "Non-Alignment and New International Economic Order."

Review of International Affairs, Sept. 20, 1981.

Soedjatmoko. "Non-alignment and Beyond." *The Non-aligned World* 1 (Jan.–Mar. 1983).

Sondhi, M.L. "Select Bibliography on Non-alignment." Paper presented at India International Center Seminar on Options for the New Delhi Summit, Feb. 27, 1983.

Subrahamanyam, K. "Non-alignment Under Stress." *Strategic Analysis,* Dec. 1980.

_______ . "Non-alignment and Defence." *Strategic Analysis,* Mar. 1981.

Tyabji, Badr-ud-Din. "Non-alignment: From What and for What?" *Problems of Non-alignment* 1 (Mar.–May 1983).

Vrhovec, Josip. "The Advance of Non-aligned Policy." *Socialist Thought and Practice,* 1978.

Glossary

AAPSO	Afro-Asian Peoples' Solidarity Organization
ACABQ	Advisory Committee on Administrative and Budgetary Questions
ANC	African National Congress
ANZUS	Australia, New Zealand, United States
ASEAN	Association of South East Asian Nations
CENTO	Central Treaty Organization
CERDS	Charter of Economic Rights and Duties of States
CGDK	Coalition Government of Democratic Kampuchea
CIEC	Conference on International Economic Cooperation
COMECON/ CEMA/ CMEA	Council for Economic Mutual Assistance
COMINFORM	Information Bureau of Communist Parties and Workers
CPC	Committee on Program and Coordination
CPI	Communist Party of India
CPSU	Communist Party of the Soviet Union
CTB	Comprehensive Test Ban
DTA	Democratic Turnahalle Alliance
EC-10	European Community (10 members)
ECDC	Economic Cooperation Among Developing Countries
ECOSOC	Economic and Social Council
ESS	Emergency Special Session
FAO	Food and Agriculture Organization
FMLF	Faribundo Marti Liberation Front
FRETILIN	Revolutionary Front for the Independence of East Timor
G-6/7/8	Group of 6, 7 or 8 Non-Aligned on the Security Council
G-77	Group of 77
GATT	General Agreement on Trade and Tariffs
GDR	German Democratic Republic

IBRD	International Bank for Reconstruction and Development
ICAO	International Civil Aviation Organization
ICSC	International Civil Service Commission
IMF	International Monetary Fund
INF	Intermediate Nuclear Forces
IOZP	Indian Ocean Zone of Peace
ITU	International Telecommunications Union
LDC	Less-Developed Country
LLDC	Least Less-Developed Country
LOS	Law of the Sea
MPLA	Popular Movement for the Liberation of Angola
MBFR	Mutual Balanced Force Reductions
NACB	Non-Aligned Coordinating Bureau
NAM	Non-Aligned Movement
NATO	North Atlantic Treaty Organization
NEFO	New Emergent Forces
NIEO	New International Economic Order
NSTO	New Scientific and Technological Order
NWCO	New World Cultural Order
NWIO	New World Information Order
OAS	Organization of American States
OAU	Organization of African Unity
ODA	Official Development Assistance
OECD	Organization for Economic Cooperation and Development
OPEC	Organization of Petroleum Exporting Countries
PLO	Palestine Liberation Organization
PRIP	Puerto Rican Independence Party
PRSP	Puerto Rican Socialist Party
SDAR	Saharan Democratic Arab Republic
SEATO	South East Asia Treaty Organization
SSOD	Special Session on Disarmament
START	Strategic Arms Reduction Talks
SWAPO	South-West Africa Peoples' Organization

TNF	Theater Nuclear Forces
UNCTAD	U.N. Conference on Trade and Development
UNDP	U.N. Development Program
UNEP	U.N. Environmental Program
UNESCO	U.N. Educational, Scientific, and Cultural Organization
UNHCR	U.N. High Commission for Refugees
UNHRC	U.N. Human Rights Commission
UNIDO	U.N. Industrial Development Organization
UNIFIL	U.N. International Force in Lebanon
UNITA	National Union for the Total Independence of Angola
UNITAR	U.N. Institute for Training and Research
UNPICPUNE	U.N. Conference for the Promotion of International Cooperation in the Peaceful Uses of Nuclear Energy
WARC	World Administrative Radio Conference
WEOG	Western Europe and Others Group
WHO	World Health Organization
WMO	World Meteorological Organization

Appendix A
Membership of the Nonaligned Movement: July, 1983

Afghanistan (1961)+
Algeria (1961)+
Angola (1964)+
Argentina (1973)
Bahamas (1983)+
Bahrain (1976)+
Bangladesh (1973)+
Barbados (1983)+
Belize (1983)+
Benin (1964)+
Bhutan (1973)+
Bolivia (1979)+
Botswana (1970)
Burundi (1964)+
Cameroon (1964)+
Cape Verde (1976)+
Central African Republic (1964)+
Chad (1964)
Colombia (1983)
Comoros (1976)
Congo (1964)+
Cuba (1961)+
Cyprus (1961)+
Djibouti (1979)
Ecuador (1983)+
Egypt (1961)+
Equatorial Guinea (1970)+
Ethiopia (1961)+
Gabon (1973)
Gambia (1973)
Ghana (1961)+
Grenada (1979)+
Guinea (1961)+
Guinea-Bissau (1976)
Guyana (1970)+
India (1961)+
Indonesia (1961)+
Iran (1979)+
Iraq (1961)+
Ivory Coast (1973)
Jamaica (1970)+
Jordan (1964)+
Kampuchea (1961)
Kenya (1964)+
Korea (Pyongyang) (1976)+
Kuwait (1961)+
Laos (1964)+
Lebanon (1961)
Lesotho (1970)
Liberia (1964)
Libya (1964)+
Madagascar (1973)+
Malawi (1964)
Malaysia (1964)+
Maldives (1976)
Mali (1961)+
Malta (1973)+
Mauritania (1964)+
Mauritius (1973)
Morocco (1961)+
Mozambique (1976)+
Nepal (1961)+
Nicaragua (1979)+
Niger (1973)
Nigeria (1964)+
Oman (1973)+
Pakistan (1979)+
Palestine Liberation Organization (1976)+
Panama (1976)+

Peru (1973)+
Qatar (1973)
Rwanda (1970)
Saint Lucia (1983)
São Tomé and Príncipe (1976)
Saudi Arabia (1961)
Senegal (1964)+
Seychelles (1976)+
Sierra Leone (1964)+
Singapore (1970)+
Somalia (1961)+
South-West Africa People's Organization (1979)+
Sri Lanka (1961)+
Sudan (1961)+
Surinam (1979)+
Swaziland (1970)+
Syria (1964)+
Tanzania (1964)+
Togo (1964)+
Trinidad and Tobago (1970)+
Tunisia (1961)+
Uganda (1964)+
United Arab Emirates (1973)
Upper Volta (1973)+
Vanuatu (1983)+
Vietnam (1973)+
Yemen (Aden) (1970)+
Yemen (Sana) (1961)+
Yugoslavia (1961)+
Zaire (1961)+
Zambia (1964)+
Zimbabwe (1979)+

+Indicates membership in NACB as expanded at the March 1983 New Delhi Summit.

Dates in parentheses are for first NAM summit attended as a full member. The present list does not include Chile, which has boycotted the movement since being sharply criticized at the 1976 Colombo Summit. Although still formally a member, since there is no mechanism for expulsion, it is not invited to attend meetings.

Appendix B
Permanent Observers and Official Guests of the NAM at New Delhi Summit, March 1983

Permanent Observers

- ANC
- AAPSO
- Antigua and Barbuda
- Brazil
- Costa Rica
- Dominica
- El Salvador
- League of Arab States
- Mexico
- OAU
- Organization of the Islamic Conference
- Pan Africanist Congress of Azania
- Papua New Guinea
- Philippines
- Socialist Party of Puerto Rico
- United Nations
- Uruguay
- Venezuela

Official Guests

- Austria
- Dominican Republic
- Economic and Social Commission for Asia and the Pacific
- FAO
- Finland
- The Holy See
- International Committee of the Red Cross
- International Conference on the Question of Palestine
- Portugal
- Romania
- San Marino

Spain
Sweden
Switzerland
U.N. Ad Hoc Committee on the Indian Ocean
U.N. Commissioner for Namibia
U.N. Committee on the Exercise of the Inalienable Rights of the Palestinian People
UNCTAD
U.N. Council for Namibia
UNDP
UNESCO
UNIDO
U.N. Special Committee Against Apartheid
U.N. Special Committee on Decolonization
World Food Council
WHO

Appendix C
Chronology of Major Non-Aligned Meetings

Apr. 18–24, 1955	Afro-Asian conference at Bandung, Indonesia
July 17–21, 1956	Meeting of Presidents Tito and Nasser and Prime Minister Nehru at Brioni, Yugoslavia
June 5–12, 1961	Preparatory meeting at Cairo, Egypt
Sept. 1–6, 1961	First Summit Conference at Belgrade, Yugoslavia
Oct. 5–10, 1964	Second Summit Conference at Cairo, Egypt
Apr. 13–17, 1970	Preparatory meeting at Dar es Salaam, Tanzania
Sept. 8–10, 1970	Third Summit Conference at Lusaka, Zambia
Apr. 8–12, 1972	Foreign ministers' meeting at Georgetown, Guyana
May 13–15, 1973	Preparatory meeting at Kabul, Afghanistan
Sept. 5–9, 1973	Fourth Summit Conference at Algiers, Algeria
Aug. 25–30, 1975	Foreign ministers' meeting at Lima, Peru
Aug. 16–19, 1976	Fifth Summit Conference at Colombo, Sri Lanka
July 25–30, 1978	Foreign ministers' meeting at Belgrade, Yugoslavia
Jan. 26–Feb. 2, 1979	Extraordinary meeting of NACB at Maputo, Mozambique
Sept. 3–9, 1979	Sixth Summit Conference at Havana, Cuba
Feb. 9–13, 1981	Foreign ministers' meeting at New Delhi, India
Apr. 16–18, 1981	Extraordinary meeting of NACB at Algiers, Algeria
Sept. 24–28, 1981	Pre-UNGA Non-aligned ministerial meeting in New York
Apr. 5–8, 1982	Extraordinary meeting of NACB at Kuwait, Kuwait

May 31–June 4, 1982	Preparatory meeting of NACB at Havana, Cuba
July 15–17, 1982	Extraordinary meeting of NACB at Nicosia, Cyprus
Oct. 4–9, 1982	Non-aligned ministerial meeting in New York City
Jan. 10–14, 1983	Extraordinary meeting of NACB at Managua, Nicaragua
Feb. 28–Mar. 2, 1983	Preparatory experts' meeting for Seventh Summit, New Delhi, India
Mar. 3–5, 1983	Preparatory foreign ministers' meeting for Seventh Summit, New Delhi, India
Mar. 7–12, 1983	Seventh Summit Conference at New Delhi, India
Oct. 1983 (tentative)	Special meeting of Non-aligned Heads of State and Governments during the 38th General Assembly
Sept. 1983	Special meeting of Non-aligned Heads of State and Governments during the 38th General Assembly
Aug. 1985 (tentative)	Foreign ministers' meeting at Luanda, Angola
1986	Eighth Summit Conference at site to be designated in 1985

Appendix D

Coincidence of Non-Aligned Voting with the United States on 271 General Assembly Roll-Call Votes on Which the United States Voted "Yes" or "No": 1982

Member	Plen.	1st	2nd	3rd	4th	5th	6th	Spec.	Over.	Votes	Abstn.	Absnt.
St. Lucia	36.5	0.0	**	66.7	50.0	33.3	**	**	35.2	88	12	171
Morocco	28.9	55.6	0.0	61.1	25.0	37.5	0.0	17.6	31.8	233	17	21
Lebanon	26.9	58.3	0.0	50.0	0.0	25.0	**	22.2	31.5	168	25	78
Malawi	30.3	65.2	0.0	16.7	0.0	37.5	0.0	20.0	31.4	153	97	21
Singapore	28.8	55.2	0.0	28.6	25.0	50.0	20.0	20.0	30.8	211	33	27
Somalia	26.3	61.5	0.0	50.0	0.0	40.0	0.0	17.6	30.6	216	27	28
Ivory Coast	27.3	64.3	0.0	53.8	0.0	20.0	50.0	40.0	30.4	158	55	58
Liberia	29.1	46.9	0.0	35.7	0.0	33.3	**	17.6	29.0	210	21	40
Zaire	25.4	59.3	0.0	0.0	25.0	33.3	0.0	33.3	28.3	184	57	30
Gabon	25.2	46.7	0.0	41.7	25.0	100.0	0.0	0.0	28.1	199	27	45
Kampuchea	23.1	100.0	**	60.0	100.0	100.0	0.0	0.0	28.0	125	12	134
Pakistan	26.4	47.1	0.0	22.2	50.0	27.3	0.0	18.7	26.8	246	12	13
Nepal	23.3	48.4	0.0	42.9	**	33.3	20.0	16.7	26.5	226	39	6
Egypt	25.0	45.5	0.0	40.0	25.0	21.4	20.0	15.8	26.2	240	19	12
Sudan	25.2	48.5	0.0	38.5	25.0	18.2	0.0	12.5	26.0	231	20	20
Malaysia	25.0	47.1	0.0	23.1	25.0	27.3	20.0	15.8	25.8	244	23	4
Senegal	24.3	51.7	0.0	30.0	25.0	27.3	0.0	16.7	25.8	244	16	11
Chad	20.9	42.9	0.0	66.7	100.0	0.0	0.0	18.2	25.7	206	17	48
Eq. Guinea	23.6	**	0.0	0.0	100.0	100.0	33.3	**	25.4	63	8	200
Cameroon	24.8	44.1	0.0	23.1	0.0	28.6	20.0	13.3	25.1	231	33	7
Cent. Afr. Rep.	21.9	45.7	0.0	33.3	0.0	27.3	0.0	21.1	25.0	220	22	29
Ecuador	23.5	41.2	0.0	40.0	0.0	33.3	0.0	16.7	24.9	233	34	4
Trin./Tob.	23.5	42.4	0.0	41.7	0.0	30.0	0.0	0.0	24.8	218	25	28
Malta	22.4	51.9	0.0	0.0	**	50.0	**	**	24.7	182	0	89

Indonesia	24.5	40.6	0.0	28.6	25.0	26.7	0.0	15.8	24.5	249	18	4
Oman	24.5	47.1	0.0	9.1	0.0	26.7	0.0	15.8	24.3	243	20	8
Togo	23.0	47.2	0.0	26.7	0.0	15.4	0.0	15.8	24.1	249	14	8
Tunisia	22.9	45.5	0.0	30.8	25.0	21.4	0.0	15.8	24.0	246	20	5
Jamaica	22.3	46.7	0.0	46.7	0.0	11.1	0.0	16.7	24.0	225	37	9
Saudi Arabia	20.9	56.0	0.0	30.8	25.0	0.0	**	17.6	24.0	204	36	31
Peru	22.6	42.9	0.0	47.1	0.0	16.7	0.0	15.8	23.8	231	33	7
Djibouti	19.0	48.1	0.0	46.2	0.0	25.0	**	20.0	23.7	190	14	67
Surinam	20.9	45.5	0.0	35.7	33.3	11.1	0.0	0.0	23.5	213	23	35
Lesotho	25.0	**	0.0	18.2	**	50.0	**	**	23.4	124	17	130
Mauritania	20.3	51.6	0.0	21.4	0.0	25.0	**	18.2	23.1	234	13	24
Bangladesh	22.2	43.7	0.0	12.5	25.0	14.3	**	15.8	22.8	219	34	18
Kenya	20.1	44.4	0.0	33.3	0.0	18.2	0.0	15.8	22.4	255	10	6
Upper Volta	22.7	**	0.0	42.9	50.0	18.2	**	17.6	22.3	184	25	62
Argentina	22.6	33.3	0.0	25.0	20.0	28.6	0.0	15.8	22.1	240	23	8
Sri Lanka	21.2	43.3	0.0	9.1	0.0	27.3	**	17.6	22.0	223	33	15
Niger	20.0	46.4	0.0	25.0	0.0	16.7	0.0	**	22.0	186	33	52
Maldives	20.2	52.6	0.0	0.0	50.0	100.0	**	17.6	21.8	188	14	69
Rwanda	19.0	46.9	0.0	29.4	0.0	21.4	0.0	14.3	21.6	227	11	33
Burundi	19.9	41.2	0.0	25.0	0.0	21.4	0.0	16.7	21.1	247	16	8
Jordan	20.6	41.2	0.0	16.7	25.0	8.3	0.0	15.8	20.8	240	15	16
Qatar	19.3	41.2	0.0	6.7	25.0	30.8	0.0	15.4	20.7	242	15	14
Zambia	19.3	43.7	0.0	22.2	0.0	18.2	0.0	15.8	20.6	252	13	6
Bahrain	19.0	41.2	0.0	6.7	25.0	40.0	0.0	15.8	20.6	248	15	8
Mali	19.3	39.4	0.0	23.5	0.0	25.0	0.0	0.0	20.6	223	16	32
Nigeria	19.4	48.5	0.0	5.9	0.0	14.3	0.0	18.7	20.5	234	18	19
Tanzania	18.9	37.9	0.0	33.3	0.0	16.7	0.0	15.8	20.3	237	24	10

Member	Plen.	1st	2nd	3rd	4th	5th	6th	Spec.	Over.	Votes	Abstn.	Absnt.
Sierra Leone	18.0	40.6	0.0	27.8	0.0	23.1	0.0	0.0	20.3	227	15	29
Gambia	22.4	**	0.0	0.0	40.0	**	**	**	20.3	148	9	114
Kuwait	19.9	42.4	0.0	6.7	25.0	23.1	0.0	11.1	20.2	248	8	15
U. Arab Emirates	19.3	41.2	0.0	0.0	25.0	20.0	0.0	23.5	20.2	248	14	9
Ghana	19.3	37.5	0.0	0.0	0.0	30.8	0.0	17.6	20.1	234	15	22
Panama	18.8	41.4	0.0	8.3	0.0	28.6	0.0	0.0	20.0	200	32	39
Botswana	21.8	**	0.0	25.0	0.0	30.0	**	16.7	20.0	180	17	74
Comoros	21.7	**	0.0	0.0	100.0	50.0	**	**	20.0	135	10	126
Cyprus	17.9	35.7	0.0	30.8	0.0	16.7	0.0	15.4	19.9	211	14	46
Bhutan	18.7	41.9	0.0	0.0	0.0	23.1	**	15.8	19.5	226	32	13
Guinea	17.1	40.6	0.0	0.0	100.0	33.3	0.0	**	19.2	193	17	61
Yugoslavia	19.0	40.6	0.0	0.0	0.0	28.6	0.0	15.8	19.0	253	17	1
Bolivia	16.7	44.4	0.0	12.5	0.0	**	**	11.1	18.5	184	16	71
Yemen, No.	17.1	41.2	0.0	0.0	25.0	12.5	0.0	15.8	18.4	223	19	29
Uganda	15.7	42.4	0.0	9.1	0.0	16.7	0.0	18.7	17.9	229	22	20
Belize	18.2	**	**	0.0	**	**	**	**	17.9	56	6	209
Guyana	17.5	38.7	0.0	0.0	0.0	22.2	0.0	13.3	17.5	234	21	16
Mauritius	17.6	100.0	0.0	0.0	0.0	0.0	**	**	17.3	133	10	128
India	16.3	34.5	0.0	0.0	20.0	33.3	0.0	15.8	17.2	238	31	2
Swaziland	21.7	**	0.0	0.0	0.0	0.0	0.0	**	16.9	118	12	141
Iraq	15.5	41.2	0.0	0.0	25.0	0.0	0.0	15.8	16.3	252	9	10
Congo	16.0	37.1	0.0	0.0	0.0	16.7	0.0	0.0	16.0	244	9	18
São Tomé	12.8	34.5	0.0	0.0	0.0	0.0	**	**	15.1	185	9	77
Madagascar	14.0	38.7	0.0	5.6	0.0	0.0	0.0	15.8	14.9	241	16	14

Iran	11.6	42.4	0.0	8.3	0.0	0.0	0.0	16.7	14.8	223	4	44
Syria	13.7	32.3	0.0	6.2	20.0	0.0	0.0	15.8	14.4	236	3	32
Nicaragua	12.9	34.5	0.0	5.9	0.0	0.0	0.0	0.0	14.3	203	15	53
Benin	12.7	37.5	0.0	0.0	0.0	0.0	0.0	18.7	14.2	233	8	30
Angola	13.6	36.7	0.0	0.0	0.0	0.0	**	**	14.2	211	12	48
Guinea-Bissau	16.4	**	0.0	0.0	0.0	0.0	**	**	13.9	144	17	110
Libya	12.4	36.7	0.0	5.3	0.0	12.5	0.0	11.1	13.6	243	4	24
Algeria	12.1	36.7	0.0	0.0	0.0	0.0	0.0	15.8	12.8	243	18	10
Zimbabwe	13.7	0.0	0.0	25.0	0.0	0.0	**	0.0	12.8	125	5	141
Seychelles	13.5	**	**	**	0.0	**	**	**	12.8	39	0	232
Yemen, So.	11.7	33.3	0.0	0.0	0.0	0.0	0.0	15.8	12.4	251	3	17
Ethiopia	11.9	26.7	0.0	0.0	0.0	14.3	0.0	15.8	12.2	237	12	22
Afghanistan	10.6	25.9	0.0	0.0	0.0	0.0	66.7	12.5	11.5	218	15	38
Laos	7.9	26.7	0.0	0.0	0.0	0.0	75.0	21.4	11.4	210	21	40
Mozambique	11.1	30.0	0.0	0.0	0.0	0.0	0.0	11.8	11.2	240	12	19
Cuba	9.9	24.1	0.0	0.0	0.0	0.0	33.3	15.8	10.5	237	25	9
Cape Verde	12.8	**	0.0	6.2	0.0	0.0	**	8.3	10.4	164	9	98
Vietnam	9.0	24.1	0.0	0.0	0.0	0.0	50.0	16.7	10.3	223	20	28
Grenada	9.4	**	**	16.7	0.0	0.0	**	**	9.3	140	9	122

Note: The data, expressed in percentages, are taken from a computerized vote monitoring system of the Department of State and are broken down by the plenary and seven main committees of the General Assembly. The last four columns provide percentages for overall agreement with the United States and the number of yes/no votes, abstentions, and absences for each country. The 94 non-aligned countries belonging to the United Nations in 1982 are listed in descending order of overall vote coincidence with the United States.

Appendix E
Coincidence of Non-Aligned Voting with the USSR on 302 General Assembly Roll-Call Votes on Which the USSR Voted "Yes" or "No": 1982

Member	Plen.	1st	2nd	3rd	4th	5th	6th	Spec.	Over.	Votes	Abstn.	Absnt.
Seychelles	100.0	**	**	**	100.0	**	**	**	100.0	50	0	252
Vietnam	98.8	100.0	83.3	100.0	100.0	85.7	100.0	100.0	98.2	271	6	25
Laos	97.5	100.0	81.8	100.0	100.0	100.0	100.0	100.0	97.7	263	4	35
Afghanistan	94.8	100.0	77.8	95.0	100.0	85.7	100.0	100.0	95.3	253	10	39
Cuba	94.6	100.0	71.4	90.0	100.0	85.7	66.7	95.7	93.5	278	14	10
São Tomé	90.8	97.1	100.0	100.0	100.0	100.0	**	**	92.6	215	4	83
Belize	92.4	**	**	100.0	**	**	**	**	92.5	67	5	230
Grenada	91.8	**	**	100.0	100.0	100.0	**	**	92.4	158	6	138
Nicaragua	91.6	94.7	71.4	88.2	100.0	100.0	100.0	66.7	91.2	240	11	51
Ethiopia	92.3	100.0	64.3	88.2	100.0	100.0	20.0	93.7	90.8	273	6	23
Cape Verde	91.1	**	66.7	87.5	100.0	**	**	100.0	89.9	188	9	105
Angola	89.9	97.3	60.0	90.0	100.0	100.0	**	**	89.6	241	7	54
Yemen, So.	92.3	100.0	62.5	90.0	100.0	60.0	20.0	95.7	89.5	286	2	14
Mauritius	89.4	0.0	100.0	100.0	100.0	100.0	**	**	89.5	153	10	139
Mozambique	92.4	100.0	62.5	86.7	100.0	54.5	25.0	95.2	89.3	280	6	16
Syria	92.0	94.9	62.5	87.5	83.3	80.0	20.0	95.7	89.0	273	3	26
Guinea-Bissau	87.8	**	100.0	83.3	100.0	100.0	**	**	88.3	163	14	125
Benin	90.4	92.3	66.7	86.7	100.0	50.0	20.0	100.0	88.2	271	3	28
Eq. Guinea	93.0	**	100.0	100.0	0.0	0.0	33.3	**	87.9	66	8	228
Algeria	90.9	94.4	62.5	90.0	100.0	44.4	20.0	95.7	87.5	279	13	10
Uganda	89.4	92.3	62.5	83.3	100.0	60.0	25.0	95.2	87.1	264	18	20
Libya	90.5	94.3	62.5	83.3	100.0	42.9	20.0	95.5	87.0	277	3	22
Madagascar	89.3	92.3	62.5	84.2	100.0	71.4	20.0	95.7	86.9	283	8	11
Bolivia	85.3	90.9	66.7	100.0	100.0	**	**	95.5	86.8	227	12	63
Cyprus	88.5	93.9	100.0	61.5	100.0	40.0	25.0	93.7	86.5	237	14	51

Iran	89.2	91.9	60.0	91.7	100.0	50.0	20.0	95.5	86.2	261	4	37
Congo	89.5	92.5	62.5	90.0	100.0	50.0	20.0	100.0	86.0	272	6	24
Panama	87.3	90.9	71.4	90.9	100.0	80.0	25.0	100.0	86.0	228	28	46
Iraq	89.4	92.3	62.5	85.7	80.0	54.5	20.0	95.7	85.9	283	9	10
Guyana	86.7	91.4	62.5	91.7	100.0	57.1	20.0	100.0	85.2	264	19	19
Ghana	86.9	94.6	62.5	100.0	100.0	36.4	25.0	100.0	85.1	268	14	20
India	87.2	94.3	62.5	86.7	83.3	50.0	25.0	95.7	85.0	273	27	2
Yemen, No.	88.7	91.7	62.5	80.0	80.0	42.9	20.0	95.7	85.0	253	17	32
Maldives	85.7	85.0	62.5	100.0	66.7	0.0	**	95.5	84.8	223	14	65
Guinea	86.1	94.6	60.0	87.5	0.0	50.0	25.0	**	84.6	221	16	65
Nigeria	87.0	87.2	62.5	82.4	100.0	50.0	20.0	100.0	84.4	270	15	17
Yugoslavia	87.0	92.1	62.5	94.7	100.0	33.3	20.0	95.7	84.3	287	14	1
Bhutan	85.7	90.9	62.5	83.3	100.0	45.5	**	95.7	84.3	254	30	18
Bahrain	86.4	92.3	62.5	78.6	80.0	62.5	20.0	95.7	84.2	279	15	8
U. Arab Emirates	86.8	92.1	62.5	84.6	80.0	46.2	20.0	100.0	83.9	279	14	9
Tanzania	86.7	91.4	62.5	57.9	100.0	75.0	0.0	95.7	83.8	272	18	12
Sri Lanka	84.2	91.2	66.7	75.0	100.0	33.3	**	100.0	83.5	254	32	16
Djibouti	85.8	86.2	62.5	53.8	100.0	50.0	**	100.0	83.1	225	14	63
Mauritania	85.4	86.1	62.5	71.4	100.0	50.0	**	100.0	82.9	263	13	26
Burundi	86.3	92.3	62.5	66.7	100.0	41.7	20.0	95.5	82.8	279	16	7
Bangladesh	83.5	89.2	62.5	66.7	80.0	57.1	**	95.7	82.7	255	32	15
Zambia	86.0	89.5	60.0	68.4	100.0	40.0	25.0	95.7	82.6	287	10	5
Togo	84.1	85.0	62.5	80.0	100.0	50.0	100.0	95.7	82.6	281	14	7
Mali	87.0	92.1	62.5	66.7	100.0	42.9	20.0	100.0	82.6	253	15	34
Jordan	85.1	91.9	62.5	66.7	80.0	60.0	0.0	95.7	82.5	268	15	19
Qatar	86.2	92.3	62.5	78.6	80.0	36.4	0.0	93.3	82.3	271	15	16

Member	*Plen.*	*1st*	*2nd*	*3rd*	*4th*	*5th*	*6th*	*Spec.*	*Over.*	*Votes*	*Abstn.*	*Absnt.*
Kuwait	85.6	92.1	62.5	78.6	80.0	33.3	20.0	95.5	82.1	279	8	15
Saudi Arabia	84.1	82.1	62.5	50.0	80.0	100.0	**	100.0	82.1	235	37	30
Kenya	85.4	87.5	62.5	66.7	100.0	40.0	25.0	95.7	81.9	287	10	5
Sierra Leone	86.4	91.7	62.5	61.1	100.0	45.5	25.0	100.0	81.5	254	13	35
Malta	84.0	86.7	62.5	60.0	**	0.0	**	**	81.3	209	0	93
Argentina	82.6	94.1	62.5	70.0	83.3	53.8	25.0	95.7	80.9	277	18	7
Cent. Afr. Rep.	83.9	87.2	63.6	61.5	100.0	33.3	20.0	100.0	80.9	251	21	30
Gabon	82.6	90.6	57.1	63.6	80.0	50.0	100.0	66.7	80.7	223	28	51
Tunisia	84.2	89.5	62.5	61.5	80.0	41.7	20.0	95.7	80.5	277	20	5
Botswana	82.5	**	66.7	70.6	100.0	33.3	**	95.5	80.1	211	16	75
Comoros	81.9	**	64.3	100.0	50.0	0.0	**	**	80.1	161	9	132
Peru	83.9	91.4	62.5	47.1	100.0	40.0	25.0	95.7	80.0	265	29	8
Cameroon	82.5	89.7	62.5	64.3	100.0	50.0	40.0	93.7	80.0	260	32	10
Liberia	79.2	89.2	66.7	53.3	100.0	33.3	**	100.0	80.0	245	20	37
Chad	83.2	86.8	58.3	37.5	33.3	0.0	0.0	100.0	80.0	240	17	45
Ecuador	83.1	87.5	62.5	53.3	100.0	45.5	25.0	95.5	79.8	267	31	4
Nepal	82.7	88.6	66.7	50.0	**	50.0	40.0	95.5	79.8	257	38	7
Senegal	81.8	88.2	60.0	61.9	80.0	55.6	25.0	100.0	79.6	275	16	11
Rwanda	84.8	86.5	62.5	61.1	100.0	41.7	20.0	92.3	79.5	258	9	35
Surinam	84.0	86.5	66.7	57.1	75.0	50.0	25.0	100.0	79.5	234	23	45
Sudan	82.8	86.8	62.5	61.5	80.0	44.4	20.0	94.7	79.4	262	21	19
Lebanon	79.1	82.1	100.0	54.5	100.0	33.3	**	90.9	79.4	199	27	76
Jamaica	82.4	88.2	62.5	56.2	100.0	37.5	20.0	95.5	79.2	259	35	8
Gambia	80.8	**	69.0	100.0	66.7	**	**	**	79.1	172	9	121

Oman	81.1	87.2	62.5	72.7	100.0	38.5	0.0	95.7	78.8	274	20	8
Niger	83.0	84.4	62.5	58.3	100.0	60.0	25.0	**	78.7	207	32	63
Indonesia	81.8	89.7	62.5	53.3	80.0	38.5	25.0	95.7	78.6	285	15	2
Malaysia	81.3	87.2	62.5	53.8	80.0	33.3	40.0	95.7	78.6	276	23	3
Trin./Tob.	83.3	89.5	62.5	50.0	100.0	25.0	25.0	66.7	78.6	243	25	34
Zaire	79.6	84.4	53.8	83.3	80.0	42.9	33.3	100.0	78.3	217	58	27
Egypt	81.8	87.2	62.5	50.0	80.0	41.7	40.0	95.7	78.2	275	16	11
Pakistan	80.5	86.8	60.0	63.2	66.7	44.4	25.0	95.2	78.1	278	10	14
Up. Volta	81.7	**	57.1	50.0	66.7	44.4	**	100.0	78.0	214	25	63
Zimbabwe	81.0	100.0	50.0	58.3	100.0	100.0	**	100.0	77.4	137	5	160
Somalia	80.6	82.8	63.6	46.7	100.0	25.0	25.0	100.0	77.1	245	29	28
Malawi	76.0	81.5	66.7	83.3	100.0	33.3	100.0	90.9	76.3	173	105	24
Kampuchea	82.1	0.0	**	40.0	50.0	0.0	0.0	100.0	76.3	152	12	138
Morocco	78.7	87.5	60.0	38.9	80.0	50.0	25.0	100.0	76.2	265	17	20
Swaziland	77.2	**	62.5	100.0	100.0	0.0	0.0	**	74.2	132	12	158
Ivory Coast	77.7	78.6	57.1	53.8	100.0	37.5	100.0	100.0	73.7	171	57	74
Singapore	76.8	84.8	60.0	53.8	80.0	10.0	40.0	94.7	73.5	238	34	30
Lesotho	75.9	**	61.5	75.0	**	50.0	**	**	73.4	139	16	147
St. Lucia	72.1	100.0	100.0	33.3	66.7	0.0	**	**	71.6	102	11	189

Note: The data, expressed in percentages, are taken from a computerized vote monitoring system of the Department of State and are broken down by the plenary, seven main committees of the General Assembly. The last four columns provide percentages for overall agreement with the USSR and the number of yes/no votes, abstentions, and absences for each country. The 94 non-aligned countries belonging to the United Nations in 1982 are listed in descending order of overall vote coincidence with the USSR.

Appendix F
February 16, 1983, Letter from President Ronald Reagan to Prime Minister Indira Gandhi

February 16, 1983

Dear Madame Prime Minister:

As India assumes the chairmanship of the Non-Aligned Movement for the next three years, permit me to offer you my sincere congratulations and to express best wishes for the success of the meeting of the Non-Aligned Heads of State and Government in New Delhi. The choice of India for this most important responsibility is testimony to the position and prestige it occupies within the Movement as one of its founding members and driving forces. More than 20 years after the late Prime Minister Jawaharlal Nehru contributed so much to the founding of the Non-Aligned Movement, it is particularly fitting that India be its Chairman and that you, his daughter, should assume its leadership.

The United States follows with keen interest the activities of the Non-Aligned Movement, whose original principles calling for greater equality and justice among nations reflect the hopes and aspirations of a significant portion of the world's population and also find expression in the Charter of the United Nations. The United States shares these ideals as fundamental guidelines for relations among states.

President John Kennedy's message to the 25 non-aligned members assembled at Belgrade in September, 1961, said that the United States shared their commitment to "a world of peace in which nations have the freedom to choose their own political and economic systems and to live their own way of life." The United States remains as committed today, as in 1961, to the principles upon which non-alignment is based. They continue to offer hope of peace, stability and full sovereignty among nations toward which we must all work if solutions are to be found to the many problems confronting the world.

I am confident that during India's tenure as Chairman the ideals upon which the Movement was founded will be its guiding principles in its approach to the issues which will confront all of us over the next three years.

Sincerely,

Ronald Reagan

Her Excellency
Indira Gandhi
Prime Minister of India
New Delhi

Appendix G

Letter of October 6, 1981, from Ambassador Jeane Kirkpatrick to Permanent Representatives of 64 Non-Aligned Countries

Argentina
Bahrain
Bangladesh
Bhutan
Bolivia
Botswana
Burundi
Cameroon
Central African Republic
Cyprus
Djibouti
Ecuador
Egypt
Gabon
Gambia
Ghana
India
Indonesia
Ivory Coast
Jamaica
Jordan
Kenya
Kuwait
Lebanon
Lesotho
Liberia
Malaysia
Maldives
Mali
Malta
Mauritania
Mauritius
Morocco
Nepal
Niger
Nigeria
Oman
Pakistan
Panama
Peru
Qatar
Rwanda
St. Lucia
Saudi Arabia
Senegal
Sierra Leone
Singapore
Somalia
Sri Lanka
Sudan
Surinam
Swaziland
Tanzania
Togo
Trinidad and Tobago
Tunisia
Uganda
United Arab Emirates
Upper Volta
Yemen
Yugoslavia
Zaire
Zambia
Zimbabwe

October 6, 1981

Your Excellency:

Since coming to New York as the United States Permanent Representative to the United Nations some ten months ago, I have come to appreciate more warmly the positive role of the United Nations, and to greatly value relations between the United States Mission and that of many other Missions here at Turtle Bay.

Because I sincerely value the good relations between our Missions and the strong bilateral ties between our nations, I wish to share with you now my thoughts on a matter of some importance.

Quite frankly, I was startled to find your government associated with the Communique of the Ministers of Foreign Affairs and Heads of Delegation of the Non-Aligned Countries which was issued on September 28, 1981 in New York.

I well realize, Your Excellency, that your country is but one of some one hundred members of the Non-Aligned Movement, and that the Movement itself is a body of divergent nations. Nonetheless, I am startled that you or your government would or could associate yourselves with a document composed of such base lies and malicious attacks upon the good name of the United States.

I can assure you, Your Excellency, that I would never allow the United States to be associated with any document from any group—no matter how large or diverse—that contained such vicious and erroneous language against your country.

The communique has no more claims to being truly non-aligned than does the Permanent Mission of Cuba which issued it. In a year which sees a continuing military occupation of Afghanistan, Kampuchea and Chad—all with the support of the USSR, the non-aligned communique contains *no* mention of the Soviet Union. Yet it negatively mentions my country—which invades and occupies no one, and undermines no one's independence—nine times by name and dozens of times by implication, making the most absurd and erroneous charges such as:

—that the U.S. perpetrated "aggression" against Libya last August, an "aggression" which "constitutes a threat as well as flagrant violence against the sovereignty, independence and territorial integrity on non-aligned countries" and "a threat to international peace and security" (page 13); and

—that the U.S. participates in "attempts at destabilizing the Government of Grenada, the exertion of economic and other pressures, destabilizing maneuvers against Nicaragua" (page 17).

These, Your Excellency, are only two of the fabrications and vile attacks against the United States, which fill this 21-page document.

I need not elaborate all the falsehoods, nor need I explain to you the truth on these and other issues. For I believe, Your Excellency, that you know the truth about these matters and that, by and large, our countries share values and principles of basic human decency, national independence, self-determination, and non-aggression.

In fact, Your Excellency, I think that you no more believe these vicious lies than do I and I do not believe they are an accurate reflection of your government's outlook. And yet, what are we to think when your government joins in such charges, for that is what you have done in failing to disassociate yourself from them.

I think you will understand how disturbed I feel about this communique and your government's association with it, if only you imagine how you would react to having friendly nations level such charges against your government.

The fact that the United States is a large and powerful nation does not make us less concerned about our good name or the reliability of our friends.

Convinced that this communique does not represent your views, I would very much appreciate hearing from you about it.

With all good wishes, I am

Sincerely yours,

Jeane J. Kirkpatrick

Appendix H
Summary of Day-to-Day Non-Aligned Activities: Oct. 1, 1982– Feb. 24, 1983

October 1 — Request by the chairman of the NACB to the president of the General Assembly to adopt without a vote a draft resolution regarding the death sentence passed on three members of the ANC on August 6, 1982

October 2 — Meeting of the Ministerial Committee of the Non-Aligned Countries on the Iran-Iraq Armed Conflict, New York

Meeting of the Ministerial Committee of the Non-Aligned Countries on Palestine, New York

October 4–9 — Meeting of ministers of foreign affairs and heads of delegation of non-aligned countries at the General Assembly, New York

October 5 — Reception by the president of Cyprus for the representatives of the member countries of the Non-Aligned Contact Group on Cyprus, New York

October 11 — Speech by the permanent representative of Cuba to the United Nations, on behalf of the chairman of the movement, at the solemn session organized by the U.N. Committee Against Apartheid for the Day of Solidarity with South African Political Prisoners

October 21 — Meeting of the permanent representative of Cyprus to the United Nations with the permanent representatives of the member countries of the Non-Aligned Contact Group on Cyprus

Statement by the permanent representative of Cuba to the United Nations in the plenary of the General Assembly, on behalf of the countries forming the Ministerial Committee of the Non-Aligned Countries on the Iran-Iraq Armed Conflict

October 22	Meeting of the Ministerial Committee of the Non-Aligned Countries on Palestine, Nicosia
October 23	Meeting of the Ministerial Committee of the Non-Aligned Countries on Palestine with the chairman of the Executive Committee of the Palestine Liberation Organization, Yasser Arafat, Tunis
November 9	Ninth meeting of the Committee on Co-operation of Broadcasting Organizations of Non-Aligned Countries, Havana
November 11	Third conference of the Non-Aligned News Agencies Pool, Tunis
November 26	Circulation of a message from the minister for foreign affairs of Iran, proposing the establishment of a fund of the non-aligned countries to cover the U.S. contribution to the United Nations should that country discontinue paying its contribution
	Issue by the Group of 77 and the non-aligned countries of a special general statement at UNESCO headquarters, expressing deep concern over the tense situation in Central America and over the possibility of an invasion of Nicaragua
November 28	Circulation of a message from the chairman of the movement to all heads of state or government of non-aligned countries on the threat of an imminent act of aggression against Mozambique by South Africa
	Statement on behalf of the chairman of the movement at the Evening of Solidarity with the Palestinian People, organized by the November 29 Coalition
November 29	Statement by the permanent representative of Cuba to the United Nations at the solemn meeting organized by the United Nations for the International Day of Solidarity with the Palestinian People
December 8	Meeting of the Non-Aligned Working Group on Palestine and the Middle East to consider draft resolutions on the item "Situation in the Middle East"
December 9	Circulation of a message from the secretary-general of the Arab League, addressed to the chairman of the movement on Israeli acts of aggression against the Palestinian and Lebanese peoples

December 14	Meeting of the NACB to examine the preparations for the ministerial meeting at Managua and for the Seventh Summit; the latest South African acts of aggression against Lesotho and Mozambique were also considered
	Meeting of the Non-Aligned Working Group on Southern Africa to consider a draft communiqué relating to South Africa's acts of aggression against Lesotho and Mozambique
December 15	Circulation of a communiqué of the NACB on South Africa's acts of aggression against Lesotho and Mozambique
	Circulation of a note from the Mission of Mozambique to the chairman of the movement, on South Africa's acts of aggression against that country
	Circulation of a note from the Libyan Arab Jamahiriya, in its capacity as chairman of the African Group, enclosing a message from the king of Lesotho with regard to South Africa's acts of aggression against Lesotho
January 4	Circulation of a message from the chairman of the movement in response to a message received from Sam Nujoma, president of SWAPO
January 10–14	Extraordinary ministerial meeting of the NACB, Managua, Nicaragua
January 24	Circulation of a message from the chairman of the movement, addressed to the heads of state or government of non-aligned countries, enclosing a letter from the former president of Mexico, Luis Echeverria, and the president of the council of the Yugoslav project "New International Economic Order," and documents of the Mexican-Yugoslav Symposium on Non-Alignment and the New International Economic Order
	Circulation of a letter convening the meeting on the peaceful use of nuclear energy, to be held in Havana on April 18–21, 1983
January 31	Plenary meeting of the non-aligned countries in New York to consider the draft statutes of the Centre for Science and Technology
February 1	Meeting of the Non-Aligned Contact Group on Cyprus
	Meeting of the Board of Directors of the Non-Aligned Solidarity Funds for Namibia and Southern Africa, at which

it was decided to transfer U.S. $1,170,000 to the London account of SWAPO in accordance with the message from Sam Nujoma, president of SWAPO, to the chairman of the movement; it was also agreed that the chairman of the NACB would inform the movement of the current status of the Non-Aligned Support and Solidarity Fund for the Liberation of Southern Africa

February 8 — Plenary meeting of the non-aligned countries in New York to hear a statement by the permanent observer of the Democratic People's Republic of Korea to the United Nations on intensified imperialist threats against his country and to consider the draft statutes of the Centre for Science and Technology

Circulation of the (revised) final communiqué of the extraordinary ministerial meeting of the NACB at Managua

February 8–10 — Meeting of the Group of Consultants on Small-Scale Fishing and Associated Naval Construction, Havana

February 10 — Meeting of the NACB, acting as preparatory committee for the Seventh Summit, New York

February 15 — Meeting of the NACB, acting as preparatory committee for the Seventh Summit, New York

February 24 — Plenary meeting of non-aligned countries in New York to consider the draft statutes of the Centre for Science and Technology

Circulation of a note convening the meeting of the Group of Experts of Non-Aligned Countries on Island Developing Countries, and Especially the Smaller Ones, to be held August 29–September 2, 1983, in Grenada

Index

North-South issues, 200, 204, 216, 242

About the Author

A career Foreign Service officer, Richard Jackson has been associated with the Department of State since 1965. The present book resulted from a sabbatical project in 1982–83 made possible by Mrs. Una Chapman Cox of Corpus Christi, Texas.

Born in New York City in 1939, Jackson attended St. Mark's School and Princeton University, graduating magna cum laude in 1962. He then studied at the Sorbonne and received a master's degree from The Fletcher School in 1964. Entering the Foreign Service the following year, Jackson was assigned to Somalia (1965–66), Libya (1966–68), Greece (1972–77) and Morocco (1983–). Jackson has also worked on African affairs at the Department of State and served as special assistant to the Undersecretary for Political Affairs (1978–80). He was a political advisor to Ambassadors Donald McHenry and Jeane Kirkpatrick at the UN from 1980–83.

Jackson has published numerous newspaper and magazine articles on international affairs. He received the State Department's Meritorious Honor Award in 1968 and the Superior Honor Award in 1975. Jackson speaks Greek, French, Italian, and Somali.